Crime History and Histories of Crime

Recent Titles in
Contributions in Criminology and Penology

Personality and Peer Influence in Juvenile Corrections
Martin Gold and D. Wayne Osgood

Bad Guys and Good Guys: Moral Polarization and Crime
Daniel S. Claster

Innovative Approaches in the Treatment of Drug Abuse: Program Models and Strategies
James A. Inciardi, Frank M. Tims, and Bennett W. Fletcher, editors

Coca and Cocaine: An Andean Perspective
Felipe E. Mac Gregor, editor

Police Under Pressure: Resolving Disputes
Robert Coulson

Punishing Criminals: Developing Community-Based Intermediate Sanctions
Malcolm Davies

Crack and the Evolution of Anti-Drug Policy
Steven R. Belenko

In Defense of Prisons
Richard A. Wright

Police in Contradiction: The Evolution of the Police Function in Society
Cyril D. Robinson, Richard Scaglion, with J. Michael Olivero

Drug Abuse Treatment: The Implementation of Innovative Approaches
Bennett W. Fletcher, James A. Inciardi, and Arthur M. Horton

State Police in the United States: A Socio-Historical Analysis
H. Kenneth Bechtel

Academic Politics and the History of Criminal Justice Education
Frank Morn

CRIME HISTORY AND HISTORIES OF CRIME

Studies in the Historiography of Crime and Criminal Justice in Modern History

Edited by
Clive Emsley and Louis A. Knafla

Contributions in Criminology and Penology, Number 48

GREENWOOD PRESS
Westport, Connecticut • London

Library of Congress Cataloging-in-Publication Data

Crime history and histories of crime : studies in the historiography of crime and criminal justice in modern history / edited by Clive Emsley and Louis A. Knafla.
p. cm.—(Contributions in criminology and penology, ISSN 0732-4464 ; no. 48)
Includes bibliographical references and index.
ISBN 0-313-28722-8 (alk. paper)
1. Crime—History. 2. Punishment—History. 3. Crime—Historiography. I. Emsley, Clive. II. Knafla, Louis A., 1935–. III. Series.
HV6233.C68 1996
364'.09—dc20 95-6654

British Library Cataloguing in Publication Data is available.

Library of Congress Catalog Card Number: 95-6654
ISBN: 0-313-28722-8
ISSN: 0732-4464

First published in 1996

Greenwood Press, 88 Post Road West, Westport, CT 06881
An imprint of Greenwood Publishing Group, Inc.

Printed in the United States of America

The paper used in this book complies with the Permanent Paper Standard issued by the National Information Standards Organization (Z39.48-1984).

P

In order to keep this title in print and available to the academic community, this edition was produced using digital reprint technology in a relatively short print run. This would not have been attainable using traditional methods. Although the cover has been changed from its original appearance, the text remains the same and all materials and methods used still conform to the highest book-making standards.

Copyright Acknowledgment

Grateful acknowledgment is given for permission to print an updated version of Eric H. Monkkonen's "History of Urban Police" from *Modern Policing*, ed. Michael Tonry and Norval Morris (Chicago: University of Chicago Press, 1992), © 1992 by the University of Chicago.

Contents

Acknowledgments

The editors wish to thank Janice Erion, Olga Liesku, and Mandy Topham for their editorial assistance with the preparation of the book for publication, and several conferences where the volume was planned and worked out with a number of the eventual contributors: namely the Social Science History Association of the United States and the Social History Society of Britain, the European Centre for Policing in Milton Keynes, the Maison des Sciences de l'Homme in Paris, and the umbrella organizations of the Groupe Européen de Recherche sur les Normativités and the International Association for the History of Crime and Criminal Justice. The editors also wish to thank the conference organizers and participants, at which several of the chapters were presented and critiqued; Liz Murphy; Simone Brosig for her assistance with the index; and Arlene Belzer at Greenwood for guiding the manuscript through production. The book was planned from the beginning to cover the countries and the subjects that it contains while allowing complete and final discretion to the authors in their individual contributions, and each chapter was written expressly for the volume. Therefore, the editors wish to thank the authors for their careful attention to detail and for several drafts that many of them composed to meet the general guidelines and the parameters that were devised for this work.

PART I

INTRODUCTION

1

From Medieval Cities to National States, 1350–1850: The Historiography of Crime and Criminal Justice in Europe

Xavier Rousseaux

Even as the number of historical studies in the area grows,[1] the concept of crime is being called into question by the field in which it originated: criminology.[2] The contemporary manifestations of the phenomenon are not the only aspect to come under fire; so, too, is the use of the term in medieval, modern, and contemporary history in that speciality known as the history of crime.[3] Contemporary criminologists have focused primarily on the discrepancy between "real" and "recorded" crime, the famous "dark figure" of impunity. Others have pointed to the discrepancy between legal definitions of crime and local practices. Some Marxists see crime simply as a superstructure determined by class conflicts (conflictual theories of crime),[4] while others highlight the consensus of the authorities and public opinion on the definition of behavior harmful or unacceptable to society (consensual theories of crime). Yet a third current has used crime figures to show that the description in terms of crime was primarily a production of the police or the courts.[5] It is still the case today in many countries that these bodies (*gendarmeries* [national police forces], local police, the courts, the public prosecutor) sometimes, willy nilly, produce perfectly incompatible sets of statistics.

In view of such vigorous criticism of crime figures, echoed by a number of historians,[6] some even deny the existence of crime in the absence of a controlling institution.[7] Without going that far, I feel that most historians should be aware of the many often hard-to-measure biases and discrepancies between a phenomenon described in terms of crime by an authority responsible for control or repression and the reality of the behaviors thus condemned. But do such remarks hold for the historian of prestatistical periods as well? Even more, for he must construct his own figures using material from strikingly diverse institutions. However solid his critical training, there is always the risk that the historian will reproduce in his own documentary work the filtering processes of the repressive institutions. I was led to reflect on this time and again in the course of my doctoral dissertation on urban justice from the late Middle Ages to the beginning of the modern period.[8] I further developed this line of thinking in my research on crime in the southern Netherlands during the Middle Ages and the modern era.[9] At present, I would like to extend this reflection to a critical survey of research in Europe, or at least in the western portion of Europe.

THE HISTORY OF CRIME: AN INVENTORY

Why attempt to embrace four centuries, roughly from 1400 to 1800? First, the history of crime developed for the most part within this span of time. With the exception of Great Britain and the United States, the contemporary period has inspired few if any works of importance, even though there is an abundance of standardized material.[10] The number of seminal theses in the history of crime in contemporary Europe can be counted on the fingers of one hand. This is due in part to the difficulty of consulting judicial and police archives (there is a 100-year waiting period in many countries) and in part to the fact that the history of law and institutions, and even social history, has not paid much attention to periods after the great revolutions of the eighteenth century. While French medievalists have, as of late, produced several far-reaching works,[11] and a sprinkling of approaches to the sixteenth and seventeenth centuries have been published, it is the eighteenth century, with its bailliage accounts and presidial or parliamentary records, that has become the century of the history of crime *par excellence.* The popularity of the Enlightenment can probably be explained by the application of the well-tried methods of the *Annales* school to a manageable corpus of homogenous data, by the ease with which the documents can be read, and by the solid knowledge of eighteenth-century institutions and courts. But if, in the wake of the French historical school of the *Annales,* as it is called, the modern period has become the primary laboratory for quantitative studies of the history of crime, it is to Pierre Chaunu and a handful of research groups that we are indebted.[12] Subsequently, medieval and contemporary crime studies have begun to come into their own in France and are closing the gap with other countries.

French historiography is now well known. But other parts of Europe have also produced valuable research in part patterned on the French historical model and in part inspired by regional genius.[13] A necessarily selective survey of this work allows us nevertheless to trace a few major sources of information, some of the methods used, and the results obtained. It thus appears increasingly useful to look beyond local studies and narrow time periods to a general analysis over the long term. This is why we have chosen to examine crime and criminal justice from the earliest period for which we have enough documents recording actual practice (depending on the region, from the thirteenth to the fifteenth century) until the end of what historians universally call the *ancien régime,* which, in Central Europe, can last into the middle of the nineteenth century.

When attempting to cover such a vast area, it is important not to drown in the documentation. Geographically, my laboratory is confined to Western Europe. In the largely unexplored ocean of judicial archives, a few islands have been reconoitered: the towns of Northern Italy, Flanders, and Occitania, for the thirteenth and fourteenth centuries; the "Lotharingian" regions (Burgundian, Helvetic, Flemish, and Dutch towns) and the English and Nordic countryside, for the fifteenth and sixteenth centuries; and for the eighteenth century, the French provinces, the county of Surrey, and the towns of Neuchâtel, Geneva, Ghent, and Amsterdam. A map of these publications reveals the specificities of this historiography. Germanic and Iberian scholars have, until recently, lagged behind; English studies deal essentially with the Middle Ages, the modern period, and the nineteenth century; Italy emphasizes the Middle Ages; France is a length ahead for the eighteenth century; while the production of the Benelux countries is divided between the Middle Ages and the eighteenth century.

As far as documentation stands, because it is a relatively new field, work in the history of crime is highly dispersed. It is impossible to list the countless articles on criminal records published in local historical journals. The approaches are just as varied: history of criminal law and of legal institutions, studies on deviancy, fringe groups, and popular mentalities. I have therefore based my survey on works strictly defined as history of crime—in other words, systematic, quantitative studies of the archives of repressive institutions that relate these to normative sources. My review therefore does not include punctual qualitative analyses of documents used (e.g., studies of judicial archives that make no reference to the criminal aspect of the material) and historical studies on criminal law based exclusively on normative sources. I have also eliminated work on specific types of delinquency (vagrancy, theft, witchcraft, heresy) except for those studies systematically based on the practice of a specialized institution. My restrictions induced yet another difficulty. Much of the work is unpublished. For instance, regional monographs on the history of crime in medieval France do not number into the hundreds.[14] My sources in this area are therefore comprised of a series of monographic articles taken, in most cases, from university theses.

A broad geographical framework, a vast time span, and primarily monographs combine to create a difficult undertaking; but the difficulty should not obscure the interest of an inventory of crime research in Europe. I intend to take stock of an area which, despite a promising start, has unfortunately become bogged down in the last decade. It seems paradoxical that the abundance of quantitative data has not produced a single solid comparative study and that the exceptional quality of certain documents has tempted very few historians or legal scholars.

The history of medieval crime concentrates, for the most part, on a few regions marked by particularly early urban development: northern Italy,[15] the principalities of northern France and the Netherlands,[16] southern France,[17] the Germanic towns, and England.[18] For the early modern period (1450–1650), the bulk of the studies deal with Italy,[19] the Netherlands,[20] the towns of Switzerland and Germany,[21] the British Isles, and the Nordic countries.[22] The Iberian peninsula is known primarily from work on the Inquisition.

In the eighteenth century, the transition from political power to specialized forms of state power (absolute, parliamentary or enlightened monarchies, oligarchical republics or city-states) affected the organization of justice. The archives grew and became complex. Pioneering historiographic studies have made this period a favorite of scholars. The research has looked into local and high courts in France,[23] England,[24] northwestern Europe,[25] and the Nordic, Germanic, and Helvetic territories.[26] Aside from work on the Inquisition, southern Europe has received less attention.[27] In addition, there are the studies devoted to the new penal structures created by the nineteenth-century nation-states.[28] In the following sections, I will assess the available monographs as sources and as methodological approaches before going on to outline a few thoughts on the main conclusions of the history of crime. In so doing, I will attempt to indicate a few paths of investigation or trail markers for a future history of crime in the West, which remains to be written.

SOURCES AND METHODS

Most results have been obtained by individual researchers exploiting specific original documents. It is therefore all the more important to take a closer look, as most of these authors gloss over the biases and limits introduced by the nature of their material and their choice of method.

Sources

The sources are extremely varied. Nevertheless, the period of urban powers (thirteenth to fifteenth century), that of royal powers (fifteenth to seventeenth century), and that of national powers (eighteenth to nineteenth century), created institutions and thus original sources.

Urban Powers and Judicial Archives (1250–1450)

The bulk of the research on the Middle Ages is based on urban sources, which fall into three classes: normative sources, narrative texts, and administrative and judicial sources. The normative sources were generally written down in the twelfth through thirteenth centuries. These include urban *statuti,* drafted by the Italian communes; charters of freedom wrested from the local landlord; and ordinances or customs written down in the late Middle Ages. From the standpoint of traditional legal history, these documents generally made it possible to define the local norm of repression. Few scholars have viewed them as the result of negotiations among the various powers competing for social control, as so many snapshots camouflaging the diversity of authorities behind an appearance of uniformity.[29]

The narrative texts are generally used to flesh out the facts and figures found in official records or the standards formulated in normative texts. Sometimes, caught up in the romantic historical tradition or the classical positivist tradition of the nineteenth century, scholars have depicted criminal activity exclusively from these sources. Chronicles such as the *Journaux d'un bourgeois de Paris*[30] have served primarily to develop a political, social, or cultural history of violence. One marked example of this tendency is the book *Violence and Civil Disorder in Italian Cities, 1200–1500.*[31] Certain literary works with juridical overtones, such as *Boec der Rabauwen* or the *Roman de Renart* and its European variants, have also attracted specialists of medieval criminal procedure.[32]

The types of administrative and judicial records are highly diverse. In the case of the seigneurial courts, here and there a record has been conserved, usually in a monastery library (the Rolls of Saint-Martin-des-Champs for 1332–1357 or the Abbey of Ramsey).[33] But the majority have been preserved in urban archives.[34] Three traits characterize this documentation. First is the number of authorities exercising social control in any one territory. The example of Brescia under the Malatestas speaks volumes; one register contains sentences handed down by, among others, Pandolfe Malatesta's deputy, the *podestà,* the *jiudice dei malefici,* the official in charge of fortress munitions and the *consul des marchandises,* and so on.[35] In Florence, one analysis of criminal records for 1400–1401 is based on documents from the *podestà,* the *Capitano del Popolo,* and the *Esecutore degli Ordinamenti di Giustizia.* For 1433–1435, we must add those convicted by the *Conservatori delle legge* and, in 1477–1478, the archives of the *Otto di Guardia.*[36] In Brabant, in the town of Nivelles, the account books of the seigneurial officer list together fines meted out by aldermen, urban authorities, peacemakers, boards of trade, as well as settlements with the local landlord for crimes committed.[37] In Ghent, competence to try for crimes is shared between the aldermen of the *keure* and those of the *gedeele.*[38] In fourteenth-century Zurich, not only the council court (*Ratsgericht)* but also the *engere Vogtgericht* could try cases of violence, and the *Schultheissengericht* pronounced specifically on trade matters; nor can we forget the ecclesiastical courts and a court for Jews. It is never clear which of these different jurisdictions was competent to judge a given matter.[39] In Basel, in addition to the council's civil courts, the corporations developed their own judicial system (*Zunftgericht*), which judged members of their trade.[40] In Paris, nearly thirty authorities were competent to hear cases within the city. Given the institutional rivalry, the interest of the archives depends on how each institution prospered in the struggle for political power.

Second, within any agency of social control, it was not always easy to distinguish between administrative and legal archives, and their differentiation came about only gradually. The earliest urban registers usually record both decisions taken by the town oligarchy on administrative or normative matters and repressive measures. For instance, in Nuremberg, the records for 1285 and 1400 are *Acht-, Verbots-, und Fehdebücher* (books of decisions, prohibitions, and settlements of peace).[41] In Utrecht, at the beginning of the fifteenth century, the City Council Book (*Raads Dagelyks Boek*, literally "City Council Day Book") recorded council decisions, private settlements, and punishments.[42] Later, separate books were kept for verdicts usually pronounced by the city council—that is, the Flemish *correctieboeken* or the Italian "books of banishments"—and for their political decisions. Still later, we see veritable criminal records being kept that contain the punishments inflicted on those condemned by the ordinary courts.

Third, a single court may keep a remarkable variety of records. Each institution created its own archival structure according to the characteristics of its system of law (written law or oral procedure) and the balance of force between the legal actors.[43] Nor is it easy to tell if a collection of legal documents reflects systematic administrative activity or some political intent.[44]

Royal Powers and Judicial Archives (1450–1650)

The early modern period (1450–1650) is marked by technical advances in judicial institutions. On the one hand, records became more specialized and thus more diversified. On the other hand, they were standardized and rationalized during the sixteenth century under the twofold influence of the normative organization of criminal procedure and the influx of legal scholars into many jurisdictions.[45] Gradually, these bulky systematic archives supplanted the documents of the Middle Ages. In some regions, like the Netherlands, the medieval series of court records persisted into the seventeenth century, providing particularly rich data on executions and prison costs.[46]

Local Regular Court Records. On the local level, the data in town or seigneurial court archives is better preserved. Around 1500 in most parts of Europe, written records became common, were rationalized, and produced a few series of generic documents common to most western European local courts: preliminary hearings or judicial inquiries, minutes of audiences, verdicts, and written criminal records. These series concentrated on civil and criminal cases heard by the lower and appeals courts. Amsterdam is a good illustration of this evolution. From the fifteenth century to 1568, we have Burgomasters' books listing a mixture of regulations and sentences. The first court records appeared in 1524: *Justicieboeken* (records of corporal punishment) and *Confessieboeken* (records of confessions), obviously the result of the new written procedure.[47] Simultaneously, the use of written procedure in Bohemia was instrumental in creating collections of *pechbücher* for the urban or regional, royal, or seigneurial *Halsgerichte.*[48] Furthermore, as we have seen, some jurisdictions kept records of corporal punishments, such as Amsterdam's *Justicieboeken* or the *Strafenbücher* of Frankfurt and Nuremberg. Even a few executioners' diaries have been preserved.[49]

Infrajudicial and Ecclesiastical Court Records. Other local authorities intervened in the case of minor conflicts. Notaries, whose numbers began to climb in the sixteenth century in countries governed by common law,[50] recorded settlements in cases of misdemeanors. The trades and corporations had their own courts that heard professional conflicts. Other actors have left little trace, notably local worthies or parish priests. Protestant countries had consistory courts. These have been studied for Geneva and Amsterdam.[51] In the Nordic countries, these consistories were the primary courts in the countryside. In England and Scotland, the archdeacon's court remained very active until the sixteenth century.[52]

High Court Records. On the level of vaster political units—principalities—we must add to these classic series the archives produced by princes as they increased the scope of their judicial power and their political administration. The large series are the result of the extension of sovereigns' rights of justice. The development of sovereign's pardon produced large series of letters of pardon from the kings of France, the dukes of Burgundy, the Habsburgs of Spain, the kings of Portugal, and sometimes from important lords (the viscount of Turenne).[53] These series persisted until the mid-seventeenth century, at which time they seem to have been converted to classic royal pardons.

The growth of appeals led to an increase in high court activity (sovereign's councils of justice, *parlements,* imperial courts, audiences, high courts). These jurisdictions grew up in the Nordic countries (Jutland High Court), the Netherlands, France (*Parlements*), England (King's Bench), Spain (*Audiencias*), and Bohemia (the High Court of Prague).[54] They produced the same types of documents in the civil, criminal, lower, and appeals courts: series of claims, judicial inquiries, pleadings, court reporter's minutes, records of arrests or sentences, records of evidence or exhibits, accounts of remands, confiscated objects, and fines, as well as "tools of the trade" produced by the legal personnel (inventories, collections of jurisprudence, legal forms). The mass of material defies any individual attempt at systematic exploitation. Fortunately, however, a few teams of researchers are going through the immense archives of the *Parlement de Paris,* the Grand Council of Mechelin, and the *Reichskammergericht.*

Specific Court Records. A cluster of other jurisdictions emerged with the expansion of principalities. Special jurisdictions were established to control vagrancy (*prévôtés, maréchaussées*).[55] Courts martial were organized more rationally. Ecclesiastical courts played a role that varied with the region and the religious denomination. Some, like the Catholic officialities, dealt exclusively with clergy and violations of religious practice and marriage law. Others, like the Nordic parish courts, acted as courts of ordinary justice. The Mediterranean Inquisition provided documents of an exceptional scope and specificity. From 1540, the *relaciones das causas* set down by the Spanish Inquisition comprise an immense synthesis of the documents sent to Madrid by inquisitorial courts throughout the Habsburg empire (Castille, Aragon, Sicily, Mexico, Peru).[56] Regional court records have been conserved from the Inquisition in Spain, Portugal, Venice, and Frioul.

Yet other courts heard nobles, merchants, and ethnic minorities, while political upheavals gave rise to short-lived political or emergency courts (the Council of Troubles in the Spanish-ruled Netherlands, 1566–1573; the Grands Jours in France; and England's Star Chamber, 1540–1640).[57] The era of monarchs was marked throughout Europe by the growing complexity of administering justice. The spread of written procedure, the multiplication of sovereign edicts, and the influx of legal scholars to the high courts led to the expansion of sovereign courts. These gradually supplanted the local courts by evocation or appeal or by monopolizing certain types of cases.

State Powers and Criminal Archives (1650–1850)

From a documentary standpoint, most series are a continuation of the "modern" series begun in the sixteenth century. Nevertheless, it was in the eighteenth century that the legal machinery became more complex: increasing internal complexity stemming from an extension of the grounds for appeal and the administrative courts, and growing complexity at either end of the court system due to the emergence of two parajudicial institutions, the police and prisons.

Police and Prison Archives. The development of police archives leads to growing numbers of studies on the pretrial phase: the arrest. The records of the special jurisdictions responsible for controlling vagrancy (*prévôtés, maréchaussées, drossarderies*) have been a favorite hunting ground.[58] The exploitation of *registres d'écrous* (prison rolls) is more systematic in crime studies. Studies of banditry, such as the Orgères band,[59] but also studies on social unrest or delinquency in Occitania make more use of the rolls of the *maréchaussées* or urban prisons.[60] Nevertheless, these studies do not always make a clear distinction between arrests and actual convictions.

Penal Archives: Galleys and Houses of Correction. Alongside the traditional records of punishments and convictions, there are archives produced by a more systematic administrative organization of punishment. New penal institutions, such as galleys[61] and houses of correction,[62] produced rolls of galley slaves and admittances to houses of correction. These throw a new light on crime as defined by confinement.

Trial Archives: Various Courts and Appeals. Both improved conservation of data and the growing complexity of appeals procedures imply the combined use of data from ordinary tribunals and appeals courts, usually *parlements* or sovereign courts. Many authors point out that local court decisions were increasingly reviewed by higher courts. The analysis can therefore be done from above, either by looking directly at the total activity of a single high court[63] or at a given judicial area,[64] or from below, by following judgments from a local court, *bailliage,* or *sénéchaussée* up through the higher court,[65] or again by studying all competent courts in a given judicial area. S. Guilleminot's work on the courts in Caen, N. Castan's study on the courts of Languedoc, or Beattie's work on those of Sussex and Surrey use the multi-institutional approach.[66] As B. Garnot shows so well, when thoroughly filtered and decanted, the final criminal broth looks very different from the initial ingredients.[67] The analysis of these documents points to two critical conclusions. First, sources of information on crime are the result of a process of recording by judicial agents (judges) or by parajudicial agents (police officers or jail keepers), or they fall outside the scope of repressive institutions (chronicles, literature, administrative correspondence). Second, each type of document creates an image of crime built up from a specific stage in the recording process: complaint, arrest, inquiry, verdict, punishment.

When a distinction is made between the principal sources on crime, one is forced to recognize the diversity of the documents available to researchers and to detail the specificity of the information contained in each source. Crime, from medieval to modern times (thirteenth through eighteenth centuries), is thus known from a set of extremely different sources whose qualitative or quantitative value varies. It is often regrettable that medievalists do not specify whether the crimes they study are found in minutes of urban court hearings, letters of pardon, or bailiffs' accounts or brotherhood death registers. It is regrettable, too, that modernists do not indicate whether crime is analyzed from the lawsuits, verdicts, lower court records, or courts of appeal, or that contemporary crime historians do not make a distinction between the use of police reports, verdicts, administrative figures, or prison archives. The picture that results largely depends on the type of source used, on how the behavior is regarded by the institution producing the document as well the moment of the regulatory process at which the behavior is captured.[68]

The Methods

Research methods are extremely varied. In fact, it is impossible to regard this body of research as a single, cumulative corpus. An initial survey nevertheless allows us to pin down a few problems induced by the methods used to construct a typology of crime, to choose the data or to calculate the figures.[69]

Defining Crime

The classification of offenses raises two crucial problems: defining the crimes and choosing a counting unit. Most historians have given no critical attention to the definition of crimes. The bulk of studies take for granted the categories used in their sources: learned categories, categories of the times, or legal categories defined by contemporary codes of law. In the main, the difficulty in clearly defining crimes—and legal scholars and classic criminologists are of little help here[70]—is due to the lack of awareness of the successive filtering processes applied to human behaviors by judicial institutions. The same is true of the counting units. Their variety is astounding and rarely justified: cases or suits, offenses, persons accused, or persons indicted. Many authors do not specify whether the crimes they are studying were witnessed, prosecuted, judged in the lower courts or in appeals courts, repressed, or pardoned.

It is therefore imperative to stop compiling data that cannot be compared. I believe that one useful method would be to draw up a comprehensive table using the categories generated by the sources themselves, even if these must be grouped into the broad classic categories: offenses against property, offenses against persons, offending public authority or order, religion and decency, and various other offenses. Ideally a form would be provided in an annex summarizing the definitions arising from practice and grouping them by type.[71] This method would have the advantage of allowing the researcher to locate the original categories. On the one hand, these data could be used to compare information from different studies. On the other hand, the researcher would have a typology modeled on the sources and therefore indicative of the exact way a given authority regarded "delinquency." Such a table should be constructed from the activity of each controlling institution and should list the statistics by cases (inquiries, prosecutions, lower court decisions, appeals), by individuals (suspects, accused, acquitted, convicts, appellants), and by stages in the judicial process (offenses, lower court verdicts, appeals, execution, or pardon).[72]

Calculating Crime

Above and beyond the problem of definition, there are many ways of processing archives. The options reflect the difficulty of extracting data from the mountains of mind-numbing records that are nearly untouched. There are exhaustive studies of a limited period or over the long term, but more often there are samples taken at regular intervals or irregular periods. The basic problem raised by sampling is that it assumes a good knowledge of the overall population or, failing that, a random sample. But the historian is not usually familiar with the population under study—in this case the number of cases, offenses, or delinquents. As for random sampling, the method is hardly applicable in the case of archives, as it assumes a good knowledge of the distribution of the data in the population as a whole. But even the historian experienced in archive work does not always know exactly how well the documents are conserved. In other words, it is possible to sample Inventory 450 of the *Parlement de Paris,* but in the case of the records of the institutions themselves, which are not indexed, the task seems more daunting.

Quantifying Crime

Most statistical methods used by historians of crime in fact often amount simply to counting the number of crimes, listed by typological or chronological order. The first step is to draw up a general table that measures the distribution of offenses and the overall evolution of crime. I have restricted my reflections to the production of only data found in most studies on crime: raw figures in their chronological order (excluding typological classification), analyses of processes, and comparisons between figures dealing with crime and those dealing with the economy. Not all authors provide numerical tables. When they do, these are not always contingency tables.[73] When the figures are exhaustive, the lines and columns have not always been totaled. Many authors use, and rightly so, percentages in their typological and chronological analyses. Unfortunately, they do not always give the absolute number in the table.[74]

Interpreting the Data: Crime Rates and Curves. The earliest historical studies concentrated on constructing global crime rates. But the idea of calculating the rate of crime with respect to the population did not turn out to be productive. The use of a global rate assumed knowledge of all (if not "real," at least visible) offenses committed in a given society. It was not enough to have the number of inhabitants for the period under study for the comparison to be of use. It was also necessary to know the broad characteristics of this population (distribution by sex, age, social group), which is not a simple matter for any time before the second half of the seventeenth century. The crime-rate method had a perverse effect on research. Historians were tempted to fuse data from various sources into a single curve of so-called criminality. This method combined data not only from different trial stages but also from different judicial institutions or material from judicial institutions with administrative data.[75]

The next step was to compare the various rates obtained. One could compare crime rates of different medieval societies, or compare earlier rates of crime with those of today.[76] Such comparisons raise several problems, which come up in other essays.[77] In particular, How valid is it to compare a rate established over a twenty-year period with one calculated over a year? How representative is a rate calculated on the basis of a judicial activity (punishment) compared with one calculated from a police activity (detecting)? How valid is it to compare rates calculated for institutions covering very different territories?

Toward More Sophisticated Statistical Methods. Some sources, however, lend themselves to more refined methods. With certain types of sources (letters of pardon, lists of fines), it should be possible to use some of the methods developed by sociologists, in particular descriptive approaches (factorial analysis, principal components analysis, discriminant analysis, multiple regression analysis) with a view to bringing out the more subtle threads of a given corpus, or again, chronological methods of analysis (time series) or the longitudinal methods of econometrics.[78] But there are few studies of this type.[79]

EXPLAINING CRIME

Like the problematics addressed and the sources or the methods used, the results are heterogeneous in the extreme. However, a historiographic reading reveals two phases in historians' contribution to the study of crime. In the first phase, researchers focused on criminal behaviors, thus painting a picture of criminal activity in preindustrial societies. In the second phase, they turned to the components of social control. In the interests of simplicity, we will synthesize thirty years of crime history using the terms of the debate launched by

J.C.V. Johansen and H. Stevnsborg in their thought-provoking *Annales* article; they suggest that the interpretation of criminality oscillates between two explanatory poles: the "from violence to theft" theory and the "reluctant litigators" theory.[80]

"From Violence to Theft": A History of Crime

The results of most criminal history studies read like a litany of descriptive terms articulated around three elements: criminality, the criminals, and criminogenic factors. The evolution of criminality can be seen, on the one hand, in the interpretations of the fluctuations in the rate of delinquency and, on the other, in the evolution of the internal distribution of types of crime. Little can be said for sure about the first, as the correlations are highly erratic, even for such a theoretically unequivocal offense as murder. While J.C. Chesnais sees a slow and steady decline in these statistics from the nineteenth century to the present, he stresses the difficulty of interpreting statistics that assimilate attempted murder to the real thing.[81] Others, Anglo-Saxon researchers primarily, remark that a curve of judicial activity can be interpreted in terms of crime trends only when conditions make it possible to observe a maximum number of factors.[82] Under the general heading of "criminality," it is the evolution of the respective seriousness of the offenses brought to trial that gave rise to the famous hypothesis of a shift from a criminality comprised of violence to one of theft.[83] I will recall the terms: Based on samplings of *bailliage* rolls,[84] Chaunu's students noticed that violence in eighteenth-century Normandy declined while theft rose. The interpretation consists in the first place of linking the two phenomena: The decline in violence is accompanied by a rise in theft; then in linking the criminal phenomenon to the overall socioeconomic evolution. Eighteenth-century society had grown wealthier, more literate, and more moral. It follows that aggressiveness underwent a shift from the persons of the victims to their property. Economic takeoff, urbanization, industrialization, and refinement of manners can be used to explain the great passage from the rural, poor, and therefore violent *ancien régime* to the rich, urban, and therefore fraudulous contemporary period.[85]

Recent studies[86] have attacked this interpretation. First, they question the link between violence and theft. The decline in violence is not concomitant with the rise in theft. Then, a look at institutions of control (e.g., the police or the notaries) reveals the physical violence absent from the *bailliage* courts and suggests rather a displacement of the responsibility for violence and the specialization of the judicial apparatus toward the end of the eighteenth century.[87] The police or the notary handled the minor aggressions, the judge or the *prévôt* handled the thefts. Moreover, there is no clear link between fraud and urbanization. Some industrialized, urbanized, or desocialized regions continued to show high levels of aggression, while other agricultural regions experienced a rise in theft. Close examination of the sources shows the need for a rectification of this interpretation. Some note that the hypothesis of a shift from violence to theft is based on small samples of trial records and minutes from the hearings of a few royal courts. The results of recent research and studies of other courts—for example, seigneurial courts—relativizes the weight of the documentation on which the hypothesis is based.[88]

Analysis of other sources, such as records of verdicts, shows that the most frequently listed crime (violence) is not necessarily the most severely punished.[89] Judging from the sentences handed down, even the rural *ancien régime,* well before 1750, seems to have lived more in fear of theft than of violence. Research on the late Middle Ages and the beginning of the modern period shows contrasts. Some studies highlight the high rate of offenses against property, and others stress the omnipresence of violence. Once again, the recording institution seems to determine the data retained.[90] The value of the "from violence to theft" theory is that it obliged critics to compare information on Normandy with that from other regions, other institutions, and other sources.

The geographical distribution of crime (town and country), like its seasonal distribution (year, season, time of day), shows few significant correlations. Country judges sometimes lived in town.[91] The seasonality of crime may in fact be the seasonality of crime control. Times of political, economic, and social crisis may be marked by a rise in criminal activity or by its decline. In the Spanish Netherlands, the crisis years 1637–1650 were marked by a rise in indictments. Those of 1663–1682 saw crime decline. In the first period, the crisis induced an increase in prosecution; the second period was characterized by a weakening of the courts.[92]

Most studies feature a chapter on the characteristics of offenders. Crime under the *ancien régime* seems to have been mainly a man's affair. Alongside the ordinary council courts, Basel had a system of trades courts (*Zunftgericht*) with full competence to judge members of the trades.[93] Aside from typically female offenses like prostitution, abortion, witchcraft, and child abandonment, there is an attempt to explain spikes of female offending by women's greater vulnerability in times of economic crisis. Here, too, the results are found wanting. Prior to the eighteenth century, in the case of a female offender, courts often hesitated between prosecuting the woman directly or serving the summons on the husband or father. The youth of the accused is also a dubious concept. In eighteenth-century Bruges, we are told, 75 percent of the offenses were committed by persons between the ages of sixteen and forty-five. In a society that can prosecute the parents for the offenses of their minor children and in which the average age of the population was around thirty-five, can these figures be used to affirm that criminals are characterized by their youth?[94]

Nor is it much easier to ascertain the offenders' profession. The records rarely mention the profession of the accused.[95] Moreover, what are the socioprofessional indications worth? What does the attribution of a profession mean in a society in which many practice several trades and any comparison with trade registers is difficult? Alongside the ordinary council courts, Basel had a system of trades courts (*Zunftgericht*) with full competence to judge members of the trades.[96] The same is true for the *état civil* (information on births, marriages, deaths, etc.).

Geographical origins are just as hard to pin down. Under the *ancien régime,* the only distinction clearly made was between local inhabitants and outsiders. The former were protected by their privileges, and the latter were prime targets for hasty justice. But the sources are not clear on this before the eighteenth century. How then can the impact of outsiders on local crime rates be measured? In the absence of accurate information on classes or socioeconomic strata, is it possible to establish the existence of criminal or criminalized classes under the *ancien régime,*[97] and even as late as the nineteenth century?[98]

Interest in criminogenic factors also stems directly from a criminology focused exclusively on the criminal. But is it actually pertinent to identify on the basis of the vague information in judicial files such internal factors as psychological structures, passion, physical debility, illness, and alcoholism; or external factors like economic, social, and mental situation; crises in agriculture; stagnating employment; waves of insecurity; rents in the social fabric; and breaches in the mental universe?[99] Some authors find these factors in studies on other sources. The rising price of bread is pounced on to explain the rise in food theft. Other analyses find more complex correlations between price curves and indictments. For instance, for the county of Sattfordshire in the eighteenth century, D. Hay shows that the price of commodities and the repression of theft both depend on a third variable, the burden of war on local life.[100] Most descriptions of the structuring and evolution of criminality, criminals, and criminogenic circumstances are thrown into question when variables once evacuated from the observations are reintroduced. That is why it is necessary to return to the beginning and attempt a better description of the problem: What is crime?

"Reluctant Litigators": A History of Judicial Activity

According to Johansen and Stevnsborg, the second theory was advanced in a remarkable article on methodology by Lenman and Parker.[101] Based on their broad knowledge of the pre–eighteenth-century judicial system, they remark that the courts were far from being the only means of litigation in western Europe. Besides going to court, there were a number of forms of compromise, arbitration, and conciliation: medieval arbitration, peacemakers in the towns of the north, and settlement before a notary until the eighteenth century. Given this situation, the number of cases brought before the courts in any jurisdiction in no way accounted for all crime—far from it. Although they stress the contributions of this line of investigation, Johansen and Stevnsborg nevertheless point out that this theory has encountered only moderate resistance.[102]

The aforementioned Danish authors (Johansen and Stevnsborg) do not seem to see the full implications of their hunch. Lenman and Parker's true contribution is to have opened the way to a fundamental criticism of the status of the data found in lower court records. This is an open invitation to resituate the study of crime in the global context of dispute settlement, of which the *ancien régime* courts were only one of the cogs in the wheel. Today studies are broadening the discussion: They extend to the pretrial stage, taking into account all obstacles or filters that intervene before the trial (research into civil courts, infrajustice or settlements out of court, and various conciliators); to the court system itself by the careful study of the relations between the web of tribunals; to the procedure proper by scrutinizing the relation between civil and criminal cases; and to the posttrial stage by following the cases through the appeal and eventual punishment.

This type of research has shifted the main focus from crime itself to the regulation of offenses in three domains. First, there is a trend away from crime rates toward indexes of institutional activity. Analysis of criminality has given way to analysis of repressive activity. Yet our Danish critics do not give the source of their data drawn from "processing the minutes of 16,809 cases heard between the 17th and 18th centuries by the courts of the market town of Elseneur, and those of Falster Island."[103] How did they go about calculating these cases or trials from the complaints or from the sentences? Another result of the "reluctant litigators" theory is the shift of interest from a typology of crime to a typology of agents of control. Several recent monographs highlight the institutional rivalry within local communities and its impact on the social construction of crime.[104]

Second, the shift affects people, too. From criminals, attention turns to the ordinary man. The analyses become more subtle, distinguishing between those suspected, accused, imprisoned, acquitted, or sentenced.[105] Some focus on the ways different periods qualify the offender: factor, criminal, delinquent. Attention also focuses on others involved in penal activity: the judiciary,[106] but also the victims.[107]

Finally, the shift affects the search for explanations. The search for the motives behind criminal behavior is supplanted by research into the factors determining social control. Rather than pursuing the individual into the secret recesses of his unconscious using a biopsychological paradigm, researchers are now investigating the components of institutional practice: production of documents, sociopolitical organization, means of detection (police), processing (procedure), and outcome (dismissal, acquittal, sentencing, punishment) using methods derived from the social sciences or business administration. One may respond to the Danish critics that they do not seem very concerned to evaluate the work of certain agencies as they compile their data: the official statistics from the end of the eighteenth century.

"The Building of the Criminal Justice System": Toward a History of Public Order

Johansen and Stevnsborg have effectively chosen between the two theories: "violence and theft" and "reluctant litigators." They feel that B. Boutelet "hit the jackpot" on the prevailing evolution of crime under the *ancien régime* when he happened upon a small sample of eighty-eight criminal cases in Normandy, whereas they regard the learned demonstrations of the Scottish scholars as an example of "historiographic nearsightedness." But the Danish researchers are just as nearsighted, for, besides their silence on the paths opened up by Lenman and Parker, they also bypassed a key concept in the Scottish article: "The Modern State."

In recent studies on the history of crime, certain titles mention the "return" of the political to the penal or criminal domain.[108] These stress, in particular, the need to take into account, above and beyond social behaviors and judicial activity, a third level: the aims of those who wield political power. Will the next step be a rereading of yet a fourth level, an anthropology of the attitudes and behaviors of the common man with respect to the courts?

Development of the State and the Emergence of Criminal Justice. The importance of the political sphere can be seen first in the intervention of political authorities in judicial practices toward the end of the Middle Ages and in the modern era. Their presence is apparent first in the way crimes were defined and in the blacklisting of criminals. Criminalists described the behaviors that could be tolerated and those that must be punished. This was especially the case of the elastic definition of *lèse majesté.* Sovereign edicts divulged these definitions to the justice officers. Representatives of the crown also stipulated the methods of repression to be used. The growing monopoly of ex-officio prosecution by representatives of the prince and the increasing prevalence of inquisitory written procedure over traditional means of regulating violence are both the expression and the means of the symbolic and practical strengthening of state powers.

Finally, the sovereigns relied essentially on the dialectics of pardon and repression by increasing, on the one hand, the application of the death penalty for *lèse majesté* (with an eye mainly to their potential rivals, the nobles) and, on the other hand, the power to pardon crimes by the use of letters of pardon. Robert Muchembled's work discusses this dialectic between mercy and repression as it is revealed by the joint of the corpus of Artesian documents dealing with violence (letters of pardon and *bailliage* or *gouvernance* accounts).[109] He reviews and confirms the shift, between the fifteenth and seventeenth centuries, in the Netherlands from justice by taxation (fines) to punitive justice.[110]

Modernization of the State, Control of Criminal Justice. This transition seems to have become determinant between the fifteenth and sixteenth centuries. Many studies focus on describing dispute settlement as it was practiced in free towns subjected to growing pressure from territorial states. This is the case in recent studies on sixteenth-century Dutch and German towns: Amsterdam, Utrecht, Antwerp, Brussels, Cologne, Augsburg, Regensburg, and Nuremberg. Even in regions characterized by the fragmentation of power, such as the Holy Empire, we see a veritable "theater of horrors" growing up in the judicial systems of the towns of Germany, the Netherlands, and the Nordic countries.[111] "The advancement of the movement to prohibit feuds, forbidding all forms of revenge, including the feud and the consolidation of territorial states assuming sole power over life and death, determined this development.''[112] The sixteenth century saw the simultaneous development of repressive legislation, increasingly sensitive authorities, and perhaps an acculturation on the part of the people to religious and moral deviancy (religious dissidents, witches, and members of fringe groups were hunted) as well as the birth of a punitive model based on corporal punishment and public disgrace. For a long time this model, developed by historians of crime, confirmed by modernists, and popularized by certain penal philosophers,[113] countenanced the idea of the bloody and barbarous nature of the old system of justice. However, recent research into medieval practices in the same regions shows that the use of torture and corporal punishment was much more moderate than once thought.[114] It is not easy to follow this evolution at the end of the seventeenth and during the eighteenth century. The studies are few and do not deal with the same settings. We have seen that, in France, there is a discrepancy between research on the local courts (*bailliages, sénéchaussées*) and work based on records of appeals courts (*parlements*). Moreover, the omission of the seigneurial courts, regarded as a minor part of the system of criminal management, can at times distort the perspective. Likewise, many authors give too much weight to the role of judicial institutions, whereas new institutions of detection were emerging in both the town and the countryside: the police and the *maréchaussée.* Outside France, research on several large and medium-sized towns (including Amsterdam, Neuchâtel, and Ghent) and a few regional monographs (such as Sussex) have divulged new information about eighteenth-century penal practices. A certain crisis in criminal justice is evident. The records show criticism of the procedure and of corporal punishment, inflation in the number of cases, a growing wariness on the part of citizens vis-à-vis the courts (decline in prosecution for theft in England, increase of dismissals in France), and multiplication of trial reforms, indicating that, in late eighteenth-century Europe, the reform of criminal justice and the reaction against crime fed the political debate.[115] The case of Bohemia confirms what we already know about the major European monarchies: They were bent on rationalizing justice. There were only twenty-nine high courts in the first half of the eighteenth century. In the second half of the century, they had become part of the judicial reform, comprising the cores of Joseph II's nineteen administrative circles.[116] Finally, the influence of the Judicial Revolution, introduced by the French revolutionaries, reshuffled the cards for a large portion of continental Europe. The nationalization of the system of justice and the restructuring of the courts was a revolution in research. A few recent studies concern themselves with criminal courts and, to a lesser extent, correctional courts and *juges de police*[117] in France and Napoleonic Europe.

State Intervention and Monopoly on the Settlement of Violence. This analysis of *ancien régime* crime encourages us to proceed to the nineteenth century. I do not intend to make a detailed inventory but rather to indicate to those interested in the *ancien régime* that the process begun at that time persisted throughout the nineteenth century. Recent surveys of work in France and England indicate a number of paths of investigation and propose a critical reading of the objects most discussed in the analyses of crime and its explanatory factors.[118]

For France, a first group of studies is comprised of statistical analyses, primarily of the *Comptes Généraux de l'Administration de la Justice Criminelle.* On the national, regional, and local levels, general studies on criminality, analyses of a particular sector (female criminality, juvenile delinquency), or quantitative analysis "almost inevitably leads to adopting the criteria used for evaluating criminality": typology of offenses and classification of delinquents.[119] The geographical and socioprofessional distribution of the offenders enter into the problematics of the "dangerous classes."[120] For the countryside, theses in regional history "sometimes call upon criminal statistics to elucidate certain cases of community resistance."[121]

Yet another research trend stresses criticism of statistical sources (the way they are constructed) and the repeated selections introduced by criminal administration.[122] Statistical sources measure repression (acquittals, dismissals by examining magistrates, convictions), selection (dismissals by public prosecutors), and prosecution (cases brought by private parties, associations, state organs, and public prosecutors). This reversal of perspective means that "the reality analyzed is palpably different."[123] Giving preeminence to the criminal justice system and the repression of deviancy "leads to abandoning the aspect of transgression of the norm that underlies criminal behavior," for most of these studies focus on "the criminal apparatus" (litigation, judicial institutions, police, and punishing agencies).[124]

Other approaches study deviancy as an indicator of the tensions present in a given society. Court records shed light on the relations between persons and between social classes, and between local groups and the state. These approaches favor "strange cases" or certain categories of deviancy (crimes of passion, vice, infanticide, and political crimes). They also dwell on the factors that lead to "transgressing social norms,"[125] the economic situation, urbanization, and migrations. Some deal with the problematics of the integration of distinctive regions into the French nation, the periodization of which has been reworked by Eugen Weber.[126]

Modernization of crime, state intervention, civilization of society:[127] The three movements appear to be concomitant, but it is still difficult to assess the role of each in the complex process through which a state system of justice is formed. From this standpoint, one thing is clear in Europe: There is a link between the process of forming political units founded on national sentiment (national states) and that of organizing the regulation of internal conflicts by the state.[128] State police forces (*gendarmeries*), public prosecutors, courts, prisons, statistics, and judges all collaborate in the state's increasing hold on the course of justice. This is true of a number of continental states (France, Italy Belgium, Prussia),[129] and even in England, where private initiative traditionally predominated in the judicial process.[130] Clive Emsley's conclusions on English criminality can be extended to Europe from 1750 to 1850: "The reorganisation and rationalisation of the criminal law, the changes in punishment and the creation of new organs of containment and control all linked with the changing economic and social order. These developments also needed, and benefited from, a state which was increasingly prepared to be interventionist."[131]

Over the long term, a certain view of history comes to link the manifestations of crime to those of power. The perspective shifts from criminality to criminal policy, from the criminals themselves to the princes who govern them, from the causes of crime to the motives for political intervention in the field of repression. In the West, the incursion into criminal concerns of politics, which is largely absent from historical studies of criminality, encounters the problematics of the construction of the modern state, an area of investigation largely ignorant of the judicial and penal spheres.[132] But are not forms of power, so variable between the thirteenth and nineteenth centuries, just as instrumental as agencies of social control and human behaviors in constructing criminality?

My last task is to interpret the direction of these thirty years of historiography. From crime to the state, by way of penal institutions, the movement is not a series of stages, each one rejecting the accomplishments of the former. A close reading of the history of crime publications has led me to stress the extreme diversity of methods and results. The "records of offenses" or, more exactly, "records of control" are in fact sources much coveted and exploited by specialists in various areas motivated by different intentions.[133] Some hunt through them on the trail of crime as a reality in itself, independent of judicial intervention, borrowing their approach from social history or historical anthropology. Others, skeptical about the possibility of "capturing" crime, prefer an approach that ponders the specificities of judicial formulation: They see their research as a part of either a new legal history[134] or traditional sociology of penal institutions.[135] Others are more interested in the impact of criminal policies on the definition, prosecution, and repression of crime.

Being aware of the bearing of judicial institutions and, through them, of political debates on the formulation of crime, specialists may be divided between two tendencies. Some, consciously or unconsciously, will favor one approach to the detriment of the other. Others will attempt a synthesis of the various views of crime. A number of researchers are still not aware of the choices they make in their research and hence propagate a naïve image of crime. Others choose their camp and favor one or another approach: crime and criminals, criminal justice, or criminal policy.

Others attempt a more complex approach to the phenomenon, trying to gather up the various strands of politics, institutions, and behaviors that affect the constructed object that some call crime.[136] This is a difficult approach that excludes any simplistic causal explanations. But it is also an exciting one, which attempts to sort out the various logics present in a trial: from the power that defines to the judge who interprets and the accused who reacts. For all involved, everything is eloquent: legal doctrine and institutional flow chart, procedure and sentence, indicted behavior, and accused's word, providing that no single element is regarded as absolute and each is assigned its place within a coherent and complex scheme of the mechanisms of social order and disorder. I believe that only such an approach can account for the complexity of the object and is capable of providing a synthesis of the place of crime in the history of humanity.

CONCLUSION

Is there any such thing as a type of criminality characteristic of the *ancien régime?* I asked myself this as I was reading the visible tip of the secondary literature on criminality in Europe. I have approached the question by looking at a few aspects of the documentation, methods, and research results. Although I am aware that I have only grazed the surface of the subject, the answer must, for the time being, be no.

If, by criminality, we mean what researchers frequently refer to in their article titles, there is no such thing as *ancien régime* criminality in Europe. There are as many kinds of criminality as there are studies. Each regional expression, each historical period has its own criminality. The criminality of the eighteenth century is no longer that of the thirteenth. British crime is not Italian *criminalità.* A history of the word and its variations remains to be undertaken. Within every anthropologically coherent society, each agent of control refracts a personal image of criminality. The criminality of the Florentine *podestà* is not that of the *Tribunal del l'Arte della Lana.* The criminalities of bailiffs, aldermen, or peacemakers in the northern cities are not the same. The criminality of the *Parlement* is not that of the *Châtelet;* that of the *assizes* is not that of the Star Chamber. It is therefore important to be able to refer to a typology that shows the institutional and political structure of each jurisdiction.

At the core of any institution of social control, the series of documents produced at each stage of the process act as prisms, diffracting a fragmentary, changing picture of criminal reality and multiplying the points of view according to the source: complaint, inquiry, record of imprisonments, indictments, trials, confession under torture, sentences, or *libro dei Giustiziati.* One longs for a systematic typology of the sources dealing with the regulation of conflict in Europe. If we accept that criminality always comes to us as translated by some document, the choices of research methods, counting units, methods of calculation, and ways of presenting results produce an ever-shifting picture of crime. Exhaustive research or sampling studies of a given moment or over the long term do not give the same picture of criminality. There is still room for a detailed study of the methodology of research reports.

There are as many readings of criminality as there are researchers. The historian of societies, mentalities, or cultures, the legal scholar, the sociologist, or the anthropologist will favor the criminality that interests and, in certain cases, fascinates him or her. The fact that the observer is necessarily implicated in the construction of the object of observation has been sufficiently discussed of late in the social sciences; I do not dwell on it here.

NOTES

1. This chapter is a revised, shortened, and rewritten version of a paper published in French under the title "Existe-t-il une criminalité d'ancien régime (13e–18e s.)? Réflexions sur l'histoire de la criminalité en Europe," in *Histoire et Criminalité de l'Antiquité au XXe siècle. Nouvelles approches. Actes du colloque de Dijon, 2–5 Octobre 1991,* ed. Benoît Garnot (Dijon, 1992), 123–66. For an extended bibliography covering the period of this essay, see Xavier Rousseaux, "Criminality and Criminal Justice History in Europe (1250–1850): Bibliographical Essay," *Criminal Justice History* 14 (1993): 159–81.

2. Philippe Robert, "Au théâtre pénal, quelques hypothèses pour une lecture sociologique du crime," *Déviance et société* 9:2 (1985): 89–105.

3. Philippe Robert and René Lévy, "Histoire et question pénale," *Revue d'histoire moderne et contemporaine* 27 (1985): 481–526.

4. This, aside from the case of England, influenced by the trio of Eric Hobsbawm, E.P. Thompson, and George Rudé, may explain most Marxist historians' lack of interest for crime history and, more paradoxically, their relative neglect of judicial archives as sources of social history.

5. J.I. Kitsuse and A.V. Cicourel, "A Note on the Use of Official Statistics," *Social Problems* 12 (1963): 131–39; Philippe Robert, "Les statistiques criminelles et la recherche," *Déviance et société* 5:2 (1981): 187–203.

6. V.A.C. Gatrell, "The Decline of Theft and Violence in Victorian and Edwardian England," in *Crime and the Law: The Social History of Crime in Western Europe since 1500,* ed. V.A.C. Gatrell, Bruce Lenman, and Geoffrey Parker (London, 1980), 238–370; V.A.C. Gatrell and T.B. Hadden, "Criminal Statistics and Their Interpretation," in *Nineteenth-Century Society: Essays in the Use of Quantitative Methods for the Study of Social Data,* ed. E.A. Wrigley (Cambridge, 1972), 336–96.

7. Jason Ditton, *Contrololgy: Beyond the New Criminology* (London, 1979).

8. Xavier Rousseaux, "Taxer ou châtier? L'émergence du pénal. Enquête sur la justice nivelloise (1400–1650)," 2 vols. (Doctoral Dissertation, Université catholique de Louvain, 1990).

9. Xavier Rousseaux, "Entre crime et pouvoir, l'histoire de la criminalité dans les Pays-Bas d'Ancien Régime," in M.S. Dupont-Bouchat and Xavier Rousseaux, eds., *Crime, justices et pouvoirs, La Criminalité en Wallonie sous l'Ancien Régime* (forthcoming).

10. René Lévy and Xavier Rousseaux, "Etats, justice pénale et histoire: bilans et perspectives," *Droit et société* 20–21 (1992): 249–74.

11. Among others, B. Geremek for Parisian fringe groups, N. Gonthier for Lyon, R. Muchembled for the north, C. Gauvard for letters of pardon, and R. Lavoie and J. Chiffoleau for the archives of Provence and the territories of the Avignon papacy.

12. Besides the quantitative school of Caen, there is P. Deyon's group in Lille, the Castans group in Toulouse, and the work on Acquitania, Brittany, Provence, and Paris of Y.M. Bercé, Y.M. Vovelle, André Zysberg, and Arlette Farge.

13. See Zorzi's comments on the influence of traditional North American and Italian

research on the historiography of Renaissance Italy: A. Zorzi, "Guistizia e società a Firenze in età comunale: spunti per una prima riflessione," *Ricerche storiche* 18 (1988): 449–95.

14. J. Chiffoleau, *Les justices du Pape Délinquence et criminalité dans la region d'Avignon* (Paris, 1984); C. Gauvard, *De grace especial: Crime, Etat et Société en France à la fin du Moyen-Age,* 2 vols. (Paris, 1991).

15. See the essays of G.A. Bruckner, S. Chojnacki, W.H. Gundesheimer, and J. Larner in *Violence and Civil Disorder in Italian Cities,* ed. Leo Martines (Los Angeles, 1972); and A. Zorzi, "Aspects de la justice crimenelle dans les villes italiennes du bas moyen âge," *Déviance et société* 15:4 (1991): 439–54.

16. For the Netherlands, see F. Vanhemelryck, *De criminaliteit in de ammanie van Brussel van de late middeleeuwen tot het einde van het Ancien Régime (1404–1789)* (Brussels, 1981); Rousseaux, "Taxer ou châtier?"; D.A. Berents, *Misdaad in de Middeleeuwen* (Utrecht, 1976); *Misdaad, zoen en straf,* ed. H.A. Diederiks and H.W. Roodenburg (Hilversum, 1991).

17. For southern France, see Chiffoleau, *Les justices du Pape;* R. Lavoie, "Les statistiques criminelles et le visage du justicier," *Provence historique* 48 (1979): 3–20; N. Gonthier, "Délinquance, justice et société en Lyonnais (fin XIIIe siècle-début XVIe siècle)," 4 vols. (Doctoral Dissertation, Université de Lyon III, 1988).

18. For Nuremberg and Zurich, see Martin Schüssler, "German Crime in the Middle Ages: A Statistical Analysis of the Nuremberg Outlawry Books, 1285–1400," *Criminal Justice History* 13 (1992): 1–60; and S. Burghartz, "Disziplinierung oder Konfliktreglung?" *Zeitschrift für Historische Forschung* 16 (1989): 385–407. For England, see Barbara Hanawalt, *Crime and Conflict in English Communities, 1300–1348* (Cambridge, Mass., 1979).

19. Judith A. Hook, "Justice, Authority and the Creation of the Ancien Régime in Italy," *Transactions of the Royal Historical Society* 34 (1984): 71–89; *Stato, società e giustizia nella Repubblica Veneta (XV–XVIII),* ed. G. Cozzi, 2 vols. (Rome, 1980 and 1985).

20. There is considerable work now on different areas of the Low Countries. See, for Artois, Robert Muchembled, "Crime et société urbain. Arras au temps de Charles-Quint (1528–1549)," in *La France d'Ancien Régime. Etudes réunies en l'honour de Pierre Goubert,* 2 vols. (Toulouse, 1984), 2: 481–90; for Flanders, C. Fouret, "Douai au XVIe siècle: une socialilité de l'agression," *Revue d'histoire moderne et contemporaine* 34 (1987): 3–30; for Brabant, Vanhemelryck, *De criminaliteit;* for Nivelles, Rousseaux, "Taxer ou châtier?"; for Luxemburg, M.S. Dupont-Bouchat, "La violence et la peur. Des mentalités et des moeurs à Saint-Hubert au XVIIe siècle," *Saint-Hubert d'Ardenne, Cahiers d'histoire* 2 (1978): 55–92.

21. See E.W. Monter, "Crime and Punishment in Calvin's Geneva, 1562," *Archiv für Reformationsgeschichte* 64 (1973): 281–87; Richard Van Dülmen, *Theatre of Horror: Crime and Punishment in Early Modern Germany* (Cambridge, 1990); G. Schwerhoff, *Kriminalität, Herrschaft und Gesellschaft in einer frühneuzeitlichen Stadt* (Bonn, 1991).

22. For England, see J.A. Sharpe, *Crime in 17th Century England: A County Study* (Cambridge, 1983); Joe Samaha, *Law and Order: The Rule of Law in Elizabethan Essex; Hanging for Felony* (New York, 1974); Keith Wrightson and David Levine, *Poverty and Piety in an English Village: Terling* (London, 1979); K.M. Brown, *Bloodfeud in Scotland 1573–1625* (Edinburgh, 1986). For the Nordic countries, see Eva Österberg and D. Lindström, *Crime and Social Control in Medieval and Early Modern Swedish Towns* (Upp-

sala, 1988); Jan Sundin, "Control, Punishment and Reconciliation," in *Tradition and Transition* (Umea, 1981).

23. See Arlette Farge, *Le vol d'aliments à Paris au XVIIIe siècle* (Paris, 1974); Nicole Castan, *Justice et répression en Languedoc à l'epoque des Lumières* (Paris, 1980); idem, *Les criminels en Languedoc* (Toulouse, 1977).

24. For England, see J.M. Beattie, *Crime and the Courts in England 1660–1800* (Oxford, 1986); J.A. Sharpe, *Crime in Early Modern England* (London, 1984); Clive Emsley, *Crime and Society in England 1750–1900* (London, 1987).

25. On local courts, see, for the Austrian Netherlands and Ghent, A.M. Roets, "Rudessen, dieften ende andere crimen." Misdadigheid te Ghent in de 17de en de 18de eeuw" (Doctoral Dissertation, Rijksuniversiteit Ghent, 1987); for the United Provinces, see S. Faber, *Strafrechtspleging en criminaliteit te Amsterdam (1680–1811). De nieuwe menslievenheid* (Arnhem, 1983).

26. For the Nordic countries, see J.C.V. Johansen, "Falster and Elsinore, 1680–1705: A Comparative Study of Rural and Urban Crime," *Social History* 15:1 (1990): 97–109; J.C.V. Johansen and H. Stevnsborg, "Hasard ou myopie?" *Annales ESC* 41:3 (1986): 601–24; for the Austrian territories, see F. Hartl, *Das Wiener Kriminalgericht* (Graz, 1973); for the Germanic regions, see Herbert Reinke, "Criminal Justice in the North-Western Territories of 18th Century Germany," in *Le politiche criminali nel XVIII secolo,* ed. L. Berlinguer and F. Colao (Milan, 1990); for the Helvetic zone, see Philippe Henry, *Crime, Justice et Société dans la principauté de Neuchâtel au XVIIIe siècle (1707–1806)* (Neuchâtel, 1984).

27. For Italy, see O. di Simplicio, "La criminalità a Siena (1561–1808). Problemi di ricerca," *Quaderni Storici* 49 (1982): 242–64; for the Iberian Peninsula, see Ruth Pike, *Penal Servitude in Early Modern Spain* (Madison, 1983).

28. See the surveys by René Lévy and Philippe Robert, "Histoire et question pénale . . . ," and J.C. Farcy, "L'historiographie de la criminalité en histoire contemporaine," in *Histoire et criminalité,* ed. Garnot; Clive Emsley, *Crime and Society.*

29. A more political reading of medieval normative texts can be found in recent work on, for instance, the French, Italian, or Low Countries towns: C. Gauvard, *De grace especial;* A. Zorzi, "Aspetti e problemi dell'amminstrazione della giustizia penale nelle Repubblica Fiorentina," *Archivio storico italiano* 533 (1987): 391–453, and 534 (1987): 527–78; J. Hook, "Justice, Authority and the Creation of the Ancien Régime"; Xavier Rousseaux, "Taxer ou châtier?"

30. B. Geremek, *Les marginaux parisiens aux XIVe–XVe siècles* (Paris, 1976); C. Gauvard, *De grace especial.*

31. *Violence and Civil Disorder in Italian Cities, 1200–1500,* ed. L. Martines (Los Angeles, 1972), a work characterized by a largely psychologizing outlook.

32. D.A. Berents, *Het werk van de vos. Samenleving en criminaliteit in de late middeleeuwen* (Zutphen, 1988).

33. *Registre criminel de la justice de Saint-Martin-des-Champs à Paris au XIVe siècle,* ed. L. Tanon (Paris, 1877); *Court Rolls of the Abbey of Ramsey and the Honor of Clare,* ed. W.O. Ault (New Haven, 1928).

34. "Registre de l'Echevinage de Saint-Jean-d'Angély," ed. D. D'Aussy, *Archives historiques de la Saintonge et de l'Aunis,* 24 (1895), 26 (1897), and 32 (1902). These records cover the period 1332–1426.

35. G. Bonfiglio Dosio, "Crimanlità ed emarginazione a Brescia nel primo Quattrocento," *Archivio storico Italiano* 495–96 (1978): 113–64.

36. Zorzi, "Aspetti e problemi," 428–29.

37. Rousseaux, "Taxer ou châtier?"

38. D.M. Nicholas, "Crime and Punishment in 14th-Century Ghent," *Revue belge de Philologie et d'Histoire* 48:2 (1970): 289–334, and 48:4 (1970): 1141–76.

39. Burghartz, "Disziplinierung oder konfiktregelung?," 188.

40. K. Simon-Muscheid, "Gewalt und Ehre in spätmittelalterlichen Handwerk am Leispiel Basels," *Zeitschrift für Historische Forschung* 18:4 (1991): 1–31.

41. Schüssler, "A Statistical Analysis."

42. Berents, *Misdaad in de middeleeuwen,* 7.

43. This holds as well for high court records, and the best studied medieval example is the *Parlement de Paris.*

44. A few extraordinary court records, like that of the Châtelet, have obviously been written by a legal clerk preoccupied with reform and security: Gauvard, *De grace especial,* 1: 33–45. The official files of most seigneurial courts contain, for the most part, cases bearing on the landlord's rights: ibid., 45–48.

45. John Langbein, *Prosecuting Crime in the Renaissance: England, Germany, France* (Cambridge, Mass., 1974). H.J. Berman, *Law and Revolution. The Formation of the Western Legal Tradition* (Cambridge, Mass., 1983); R. Van Caenegem, *Judges, Legislators and Professors. Chapters in European Legal History* (Cambridge, 1985).

46. See Robert Muchembled, *Le temps des supplices. De l'obeissance sous les Rois absolus. XVe–XVIIIe siècles* (Paris, 1992): 88ff.

47. J. Boomgaard, "Het amsterdaamse criminaliteitspatroon, in de late middeleeuwn," in *Misdaad, zoen en straf,* ed. H.A. Diederiks and H.W. Roodenburg (Hilversum, 1991), 103.

48. J. Panek, "Die Halsgerichtsbarkeit der böhmischen Städte und Märkte vom 16. bis zum 18. Jahrhundert," *Mitteilungen des Instituts für Österreiches Geschichtsforschung* 96 (1988): 96, 99.

49. For instance, the diary of Master Franz de Nuremberger, cited by Van Dülmen, *Theatre of Horror,* 156–57.

50. See Alfred Soman, "L'infra-justice à Paris d'après les archives notoriales," *Histoire, economie, société* 3 (1982): 369–76.

51. E.W. Monter, "The Consistory of Geneva, 1559–1569," *Bibliothèque d'Humanisme et Renaissance, Travaux et documents* 38 (1976): 467–84; A.H. Huussen, "The Archives of Infra-Judicial Institutions: The Examples of the Calvinist Consistories in the Dutch Republic. Some Preliminary Observations" (paper presented at the Edinburgh Economic History Congress, 1978); H.W. Roodenburg, *Onder Censuur. De kerkelijke tuchte in de Gereformeerde Gemeente van Amsterdam 1578–1700* (Hilversum, 1990).

52. Sharpe, *Crime in Early Modern England;* M.J. Ingram, *Church Courts, Sex and Marriage in England 1570–1640* (Cambridge, 1987); Ralph Houlbrooke, *Church Courts and the People during the English Reformation 1520–1570* (Oxford, 1979).

53. The bibliography on letters of pardon is growing. Of the work on sources, see, for the letters of the kings of France, C. Gauvard, *De grace especial;* P. Charbonnier, "Les lettres de rémission relatives à l'Auvergne entre 1350 et 1390," in *35e Congrès de la Fédération des sociétés savantes du Centre, Bulletin hist. sc. Auvergne* 86:64 (1975): 475–84. For the Burgundy and Habsburgs series, see Robert Muchembled, *La violence au village: Sociabilité et comportments populaires en Artois du XVe au XVIIe siècle* (Turnhout, 1989). For those of the king of Portugal, see L.M. Duarte, "Justice et criminalité au Moyen Age et au debut de l'Epoque Moderne: les traces, les silences, les

problèmes," in *Le politiche criminali,* ed. Berlinguer and Colao. For nonsovereigns' pardons, see P. Flandin-Bléty, "Lettres de rémission des vicomtes de Turenne aux XIVe et XVe siècles," *Mémoires de la société pour l'histoire du droit... bourguignons* 45 (1988): 125–42.

54. Bernard Schnapper, "La justice criminelle rendue par le parlement de Paris sous le règue de François Ier," *Revue d'Histoire du Droit français et étranger* 42 (1974): 252–84; C. Plessix-Buisset, *Le crimininel devant ses juges en Bretagne aux 16e et 17e siècles* (Paris, 1988); Sharpe, *Crime in Early Modern England;* Panek, "Die Halsgerichtbarkeit."

55. Muchembled, *Le temps des supplices,* 105ff.; Xavier Rousseaux, "L'incrimination du vagabondage en Brabant (14e–18e siècles). Langages du droit et réalités de la pratique," in *Langage et Droit à travers l'histoire, Réalités et fictions* (Louvain-Paris, 1989), 147–83.

56. *The Inquisition in Early Modern Europe: Studies on Sources and Methods,* ed. J. Tedeschi, G. Henningsen, and C. Amiel (Dekalb, 1986).

57. On the Council of Troubles, see L. Gachard, "Notice sur le Conseil des Troubles institué par le duc d'Albe," *Bulletin de l'Académie royale des sciences, des lettres et des beaux-arts de Belgique* 46:2 (1849): 50–78; A.L.E. Verheyden, *Le Conseil des Troubles. Liste des condamnés (1567–1573)* (Brussels, 1961); Arlette Lebigre, *Les Grands Jours d'Auvergne, desordres et répression au XVIIe siècle* (Paris, 1976); Sharpe, *Crime in Early Modern England,* 22–23.

58. For the kingdom of France, see Nicole Castan, "La justice expéditive," *Annales ESC* 31 (1976): 331–61; for the Germanic regions, see Carsten Küther, *Räuber und Gaunder in Deutschland. Das organisierte Bandenwesen im 18. und frühen 19. Jahrhundert* (Göttingen, 1976).

59. For a recent collection on the problem in Europe, see *Bande armate, Banditi, Banditismo e repressione di giustizia negli stati europei di antico regime,* ed. Gherardo Ortalli (Rome, 1986).

60. Iain A. Cameron, *Crime and Repression in the Auvergne and the Guyenne 1720–1790* (Cambridge, 1981); Julius R. Ruff, *Crime, Justice and Public Order in Old Regime France. The Sénéchaussées of Libourne and Bazas 1696–1789* (London, 1984).

61. André Zysberg, *Les galériens. Vie et destins de 60.000 forçats sur les galères de France, 1680–1748* (Paris, 1987).

62. *The Emergence of Carceral Institutions: Prisons, Galleys and Lunatic Asylums 1550–1900,* ed. Pieter Spierenburg (Rotterdam, 1984); Georg Rusche and Otto Kirkheimer, *Punishment and Social Structure* (New York, 1939); Michel Foucault, *Discipline and Punish: The Birth of the Prison* (Harmondsworth, 1979), English translation of *Surveiller et punir. Naissance de la Prison* (Paris, 1975).

63. P. Dautricourt, "La criminalité, et la répression au Parlement de Flandres au XVIIIe siècle (1721–1790)" (Doctoral Dissertation, Université de Lille, 1912).

64. Benoît Garnot, "La criminalité en Anjou au XVIIIe siècle," *Revue historique* 54 (1985): 305–16.

65. M.M. Murraciole, "Quelques aperçus sur la criminalité en Haute-Bretagne dans la deuxième moitié du XVIIIe siècle," *Annales de Bretagne et des Pays de l'Ouest* 88 (1981): 305–26.

66. Guilleminot, "La justice d'ancien régime"; Castan, *Justice et répression;* Beattie, *Crime and the Courts.*

67. Benoît Garnot, "Une illusion historiographique: justice et criminalité au XVIIIe siècle," *Revue historique* 570 (1989): 362–79.

68. For a remarkable typology of sources, see Gauvard, *De grace especial,* 1: 17–57.

69. Ibid.

70. See observations on methodology in René Lévy and Philippe Robert, "Le sociologue et l'histoire pénale," *Annales ESC* 39 (1984), 2: 400–422; Robert and Lévy, "Histoire et question pénale"; A. Davidovitch, "Criminalité et répression en France depuis un siècle (1851–1952)," *Revue Française de Sociologie* (1961): 30–49.

71. Johansen and Stevnsborg, "Hasard ou myopie?" suggests one such form.

72. Schnapper's work on the *Parlements* of Bordeaux and Paris in the sixteenth century is one example of rigorous treatment of criminal statistics.

73. J.A. Goris, "Zeden en criminaliteit te Antwerpen in de tweede helft der XIVe euw, naar de rekeningen der schouten van 1358 tot 1387," *Revue Belge de Philologie et d'Histoire* 5 (1926): 871–86.

74. Hanawalt, *Crime and Conflict;* D.A. Berents, *Het werk van de vos. Samenleving en criminaliteit in de late middeleeuwen* (Zutphen, 1988). The same holds for the eighteenth century: See the work of Nicole Castan and N.W. Morgensen, "Crime and Punishment in 18th-century France. The example of the Pays d'Auge," *Histoire Sociale/Social History* 10 (1977): 337–53.

75. This method is illustrated in certain important theses: C. Fouret, "L'amour, la violence et le pouvoir: la criminalité à Douai de 1496 à 1520" (Doctoral Dissertation, Lille, 1984); Roets, "Rudessen dieften ende andere crimen"; Vanhemelryck, *De criminaliteit in de ammanie van Brussel.*

76. D.A. Berents compares information taken from records of sentences pronounced by aldermen in Utrecht between 1550 and 1570 with offenses recorded in the Dutch monthly police and court statistics in 1974, with the exception of traffic violations (Berents, *Misdaad,* 10–11): They were "omitted because they are of an entirely different nature from medieval criminal cases" (p. 151 n. 23).

77. Muchembled, "Crime et société urbaine"; idem, *La violence au village,* 21.

78. See the special number of *Histoire et Mesure* 6:1/2 (1991): 5–189 (Séries temporelles et Histoire); Soumyo D. Moitra, *Crime and Punishments. A Comparative Study of Temporal Variations* (Freiburg, 1987)—Criminological Research Reports by the Max Planck Institute for Foreign and International Penal Law, vol. 28; Larry W. Isaac and Larry J. Griffin, "Ahistoricism in Time-Series Analyses of Historical Process: Critique, Redirection, and Illustrations from U.S. Labor History," *American Sociological Review* 54:6 (1989): 873–90; Stephen E. Grossbart, "Quantitative and Social Science Methods for Historians. An Annotated Bibliography of Selected Books and Articles," *Historical Methods* 25 (1992): 100–120; David de la Croix, Xavier Rousseaux, and Jean-Pierre Urbain, *To Fine or to Punish in the Late Middle Ages: Some Insights from Time Series Analysis. The Nivelles Court Budget, 1424–1536* (Maastricht, Limburg University, 1993), Research Memorandum, RM 93-008.

79. C. Gauvard, "L'image du roi justicier en France à la Fin du Moyen Age, d'après les lettres de rémission," in *La faute, la répression et le pardon. Actes du 107e Congrès National des Sociétés savantes, Brest 1982. Section de Philolgie et d'histoire jusqu'à 1610* (Paris: Ministère de l'Education Nationale. Comitédes Travaux Historiques et Scientifiques, 1984), 165–92.

80. Johansen and Stevnsborg, "Hasard ou myopie?"

81. J.C. Chesnais, *Les morts violentes en France depuis 1826, comparisons internationles* (Paris, 1976); P.E.H. Hair, "Deaths from Violence in Britain: A Tentative Secular Survey," in *Population Studies* 25 (1971), 5–24; Lawrence Stone, "Interpersonal Violence in English Society 1300–1980," *Past and Present* 101 (1983): 22–33; J.A. Sharpe, "The History of Violence in England: Some Observations," *Past and Present* 108 (1985): 206–15, and Stone, "A Rejoinder," ibid., 216–24; J.C. Chesnais, *Histoire de la violence en Occident de 1800 à nos jours* (Paris, 1981); Muchembled, *La violence au village.*

82. V.A.C. Gatrell, "The Decline of Theft and Violence in Victorian and Edwardian England," in Gatrell, Lenman, and Parker, *Crime and the Law,* 238–337.

83. Pieter Spierenburg, "Criminele geschiedenis Een literatuuroverzicht," *Tijdschrift voor Sociale Geschiedenis* 23 (1981): 251–64 at p. 253.

84. In particular, B. Boutelet, but also Gégot, Champin, Margot Mogensen, Crépillon, and Boucheron.

85. Emanuel Le Roy-Ladurie, "La décroissance du crime au XVIIIe siècle; bilan d'historiens," *Contrepoint* 9 (1973): 227–33; Pierre Chaunu, preface to *Marginalité Déviance et Pauvreté en France, XIVe–XIXe siècles* (Caen, 1981), in *Cahiers des Annales de Normandie,* 13. In *Surveiller et punir,* Foucault develops his theory of the differential management of illegalities, using the work of Chaunu's group and Mogensen in particular.

86. Nicole Castan sees no decline in the prosecution of violence in Languedoc during the last thirty years of the *ancien régime.* But she does point out the contrast between urban preoccupations centering on petty thefts and the countryside preoccupied with assault: "Délinquance traditionnelle et répression critique à la fin de l'Ancien Régime dans les pays de langue d'oc," *Annales Historiques de la Révolution Française* 228 (1977): 182–203.

87. Olwen H. Hufton, *The Poor of Eighteenth Century France* (Oxford, 1974); Richard Cobb, *The Police and the People* (Oxford, 1969); Castan, *Les criminels de Languedoc;* M.S. Dupont-Bouchat and Xavier Rousseaux, "La prix du sang. Sang et justice à l'époque moderne (1400–1800)," in *Mentalités* 1 (1988): 43–72, at pp. 65–67.

88. Olwen H. Hufton, "Crime in Pre-Industrial Europe," *IAHCCJ Newsletter* 4 (1981): 11–12; Lenman and Parker, "The State, the Community and the Criminal Law," in *Crime and the Law,* ed. Gatrell, Lenman, and Parker, 46–47. The latter harshly—and perhaps a bit unjustly—criticize Soman's ambitious projects on the *Parlement de Paris* and P. Chaunu's on crime in Normandy and the illusion that quantitative analysis is a universal panacea. See also Johansen and Stevnsborg, "Hasard ou myopie?" and Garnot, "Une illusion."

89. Xavier Rousseaux, "Ordre et violence. Criminalité et repression dans une ville brabançonne: Nivelles (1646–1695)," *Révue de droit pénale et de criminologie* 66:7 (1986): 649–92.

90. A discussion of these problems can be found in Österberg and Lindström, *Crime and Social Control.*

91. Xavier Rousseaux, "Criminalité et répression en milieu rural et urbain au XVIIe siècle: la région nivelloise (1646–1695)," in *Crime, justices et pouvoir,* ed. Dupont-Bouchat and Rousseaux; idem, "L'activité judiciaire dans la société rurale en Brabant wallon (XVIIe–XVIIIe siècle): Indice de tensions sociales ou instrument de pouvoir?" in *Les structures du pouvoir dans les communautes rurales en Belgique et dans les pays limitrophes (XIIe–XIXe siècle)* (Brussels, 1988), 311–44. The arm of the urban judicial

apparatus can be long indeed in societies lacking a sufficient number of professional judges.

92. Rousseaux, "Ordre et violence." Everything hinges on local structures of "criminal" repression.

93. For Europe, see the analyses by R. Jütte, "Geschlechtsspezifische Kriminalität im Späten Mittelalter und in der Frühen Neuzeit," *Zeitschrift der Savigny-Stiftung für Rechtsgeschichte, Germ. Abt.*, 108 (1991): 86–116; C.Z. Wiener, "Sex Roles and Crime in Late Elizabethan Hertfordshire," *Journal of Social History* 8 (1975): 38–60; J.M. Beattie, "The Criminality of Women in Eighteenth-Century England," *Journal of Social History* 8 (1975): 80–116; A.M. Roets, "Vrouwen en criminaliteit: Gent in de achttiende eeuw," *Tijdschrift voor Geschiedenis* 95 (1982): 363–78; E. Kloek, "Criminality and Gender in Leiden's Confessieboeken, 1678–1794," *Criminal Justice History* 11 (1990): 1–29.

94. F. Vanhemelryck, "Misdaad en straf in de meierij van Rode in de XVe en XVIe eeuw," *Eigen Schoon en de Brabander* 57 (1975): 233–54, 399–422.

95. Vanhemelryck, *De criminaliteit,* 66.

96. Simon-Muscheid, "Gewalt und Ehre."

97. J.A. Sharpe, "Was er een 'criminal class' in vroeg-moderne Europa? Enig Engels materiaal," *Tijdschrift voor Criminologie* (1978): 211–23; Castan, "La justice expéditive," 331–61; Spierenburg, *Criminele geschiedenis,* 257.

98. Louis Chevalier, *Classes laborieuses, classes dangereuses à Paris, pendant la première moitié du XIXe siècle* (Paris, 2d ed., 1978); E.P. Thompson, *Whigs and Hunters: The Origin of the Black Act* (London, 1975).

99. Vanhemelryck, *De criminaliteit,* 345–410. See also the comments by R. Roth, "Evaluation of the Contribution of Historical Research to Crime Policy," in *Historical Research on Crime and Criminal Research. Reports Presented to the Sixth Criminological Colloquim* (Strasbourg, 1985), 79–80.

100. Douglas Hay, "War, Dearth and Theft in the Eighteenth Century," *Past and Present* 95 (1982): 117–60.

101. Lenman and Parker, "Crime and the State."

102. Johansen and Stevnsborg, "Hasard ou myopie?" 604.

103. Ibid.

104. For the Middle Ages, see the work on Brescia, Florence, Nivelles (Bonfiglio Dosio, Zorzi, Rousseaux); for the seventeenth century, the courts of Caen (Guilleminot); for the eighteenth century, Languedoc (the Castans), Brittany (Mer), Amsterdam (Faber), Surrey (Beattie).

105. See the preceding analysis of most of the studies on high courts (*parlements* and provincial councils).

106. See B. Guenée, *Tribunaux, et gens de justice dans le bailliage de Senlis à la fin du Moyen Age (vers 1380–vers 1550)* (Paris, 1963); F. Autrand, *Naissance d'un grand corps de l'Etat. Les gens du Parlement de Paris 1345–1454* (Paris, 1981); M. Gresset and J.P. Royer, *La société judiciaire depuis le XVIIIe siècle* (Paris, 1979); J.P. Royer, R. Martinage, and P. Lecocq, *Juges et notables au XIXe siècle* (Paris, 1982).

107. Yves Castan was the first to point out the deeply "sociable" character of the social relations induced by trials: *Honnêtetê et relations sociales en Languedoc, 1715–1780* (Paris, 1974).

108. Gauvard, *De grace especial;* Muchembled, *Le temps des supplices;* Lévy and Rousseaux, "Etat justice pénale et histoire."

109. Muchembled, *La violence au village;* idem, *Le temps des supplices.*

110. Rousseaux, "Taxer ou châtier?."

111. Schwerhoff, *Köln Im Kreuzverhör;* Pieter Spierenburg, *The Spectacle of Suffering Executions and the Evolution of Repression* (Cambridge, 1984); Österberg and Lindström, *Crime and Social Control;* van Dülmen, *Theatre of Horror.*

112. van Dülmen, *Theatre of Horror,* 133.

113. Foucault, *Discipline and Punish.*

114. For examples for Nuremberg, see Büchholz and Schüssler; for Zürich, see Burghartz; for Basel, see Simon-Muscheid.

115. *Le politiche criminali nel XVIII secolo,* ed. L. Berlinguer and F. Colao (Milan, 1990).

116. Panek, *Die Halsgerichtbarkeit,* 105ff.

117. For an attempt at a synthesis based entirely on the archives of the criminal court of the department Nord, see R. Martinage, *Punir le crime. La répression judiciare depuis la code pénal* (Lille, 1989).

118. René Lévy, "Crime, the Judicial System, and Punishment in Modern France," in this volume; Farcy, "L'historiographie de la criminalité en histoire contemporaine," in *Histoire et criminalité,* ed. Garnot; for England, see Emsley, *Crime and Society.*

119. Farcy, "L'historiographie," 34.

120. Chevalier, *Classes laborieuses.*

121. Farcy, "L'historiographie," 34.

122. B. Aubusson de Cavarlay, M.S. Huré, and M.L. Pottier, *Les statistiques criminelles de 1831 à 1981. La base Davido, séries générales* (Paris, 1989).

123. Farcy, "L'historiographie," 39.

124. Lévy, "Crime."

125. Farcy, "L'historiographie," 43.

126. Eugen Weber, *Peasants into Frenchmen. The Modernization of Rural France, 1870–1914* (Stanford, 1976).

127. Eva Österberg, "Social Arena or Theater of Power? The Courts, Crime and the Early Modern State in Sweden," in *Theatres of Power: Social Control and Criminality in Historical Perspective,* ed. H. Pihlajamäki (Helsinki, 1992), 8–24; Muchembled, *Le temps des supplices.*

128. Lévy and Rousseaux, "Etat et justice pénale."

129. Lévy, "Crime"; Farcy, "L'historiographie."

130. Emsley, *Crime and Society.*

131. Ibid., 247.

132. See, in particular, main publications resulting from the research program "Genèse de l'Etat moderne," summarized in *L'Etat moderne: genèse. Bilans et perspectives,* ed. J.P. Genet (Paris, 1990). Curiously, there is no research on the role of criminal justice in the genesis of the state.

133. On this point, see reports presented by Mario Sbriccoli, Pieter Spierenburg, James Sharpe, René Lévy, Xavier Rousseaux, and comments made by Ditlev Tamm, Nicole Castan, Robert Muchembled, and Clive Emsley at the meeting organized in January 1991 at the Maison des Sciences de l'Homme in honor of Yves Castan, "Twelve Years of Research on the History of Crime and Criminal Justice (1978/1990)," *IAHCCJ Bulletin* 14 (1991).

134. Bernard Schnapper, *Voies nouvelles en histoire du Droit. La justice, la famille, la répression pénale (XVIe–XXe siècles)* (Paris, 1991); Mario Sbriccoli, "Histoire de la

criminalité et histoire du droit. Le rôle des sources juridiques dans l'histoire du crime et de la justice criminelle,'' in *IAHCCJ Bulletin* 14 (1991): 86–105.

135. Robert and Lévy, ''La sociologue et l'histoire pénale.''

136. See the recent comments by Farcy, ''L'historiographie.''

2

Structure, Conjuncture, and Event in the Historiography of Modern Criminal Justice History

Louis A. Knafla

The historiography of crime and criminal justice in European history is, with the exception of modern England and France, relatively underwritten.[1] The labyrinth of jurisdictions of so many different communes and states—civil and ecclesiastical, local, national, and imperial—precludes easy conceptualization. The heterodox systems of recordkeeping, the archival losses occasioned by war and revolution, and the numerous languages and dialects preclude effective research. These problems, however, are being overcome gradually and in part by the assistance generated by a number of research-oriented groups and organizations. They include the Social Science History associations in Britain and the United States, the Maison des Sciences de L'Homme in France, the International Association for the History of Crime and Criminal Justice, the Council of Europe, various legal history societies in the European countries, and the growing number of national Law and Society associations which are developing currently in Australia, Canada, and the United States. The problems are also being overcome in part by the increasing number of conferences and congresses addressed to specific subjects in the field and by the efforts of social and legal historians, historical criminologists, and law and society scholars who have turned increasingly to the history of crime and criminal justice for their individual research projects.

The modern history of crime and criminal justice is perceived in this book to date from the eighteenth century. With regard to Europe, it is placed in that century which witnessed—especially from the late eighteenth and early nineteenth centuries—the disintegration of monarchial governments and the rise of secular nation-states. The term *modern* also applies to those institutions that emerged from the transformation of European societies in the seventeenth and the eighteenth centuries and in response to war and industrialization on a Continental as well as a North Atlantic scale. Thus, the creation of national legal systems, police, political parties, bureaucracies, national legal systems, and foreign colonies contributed to a reshaping of elites, a redefinition of public order, and new forms of social control. Industrialization, urbanization, and the central state also contributed to new forms of deviance and criminality, which, in turn, were met with new attitudes and forms of punishment that are still with us today.

The notion of modern history, however, is somewhat different for the continents beyond Europe. For North America, the term *modern* represents the overthrow of imperial rule in the American colonies in the late eighteenth century and the institution of representative government in the Canadian colonies from then and over the next half century. For Central and South America, it represents the development of their independence from European conquest in the nineteenth century, and for Australia and New Zealand it represents their growing autonomy following the end of Britain's dumping ground of convicts in the mid-nineteenth century. But modern history in the Americas and Pacifica is also related to the process of industrialization, urbanization, the growth of the central state, bureaucratic government, and war from the mid-nineteenth century onward. Thus, the institutions, issues, and problems which came to dominate Europe in the nineteenth century spread, like the colonization that preceded them, to the Americas and Pacifica with the massive immigration and commerce that followed. In this perspective, the history of crime and criminal justice in modern Europe can be used as a context for its examination in Canada, the United States, Mexico, Brazil, Australia, and New Zealand.[2]

CRIME AND RECORDED CRIME: THE DARK FIGURE?

Historians still have not come to grips with the problem of incorporating literary and records evidence for the study of crime. As a number of the chapters in this book illustrate, scholars are still debating how to come to terms in dealing with the problem. The subject comes up in virtually every conference on crime and especially in papers with quantitative analysis based on modern records.

Many states generate their own national statistics on crime and have a vested interest in the propogation of these statistics to the exclusion of most other sources of information. This can be seen, for example, in the career of Lambert Adolphe Quetelet, the earliest criminal statistician (1796–1874), who was also one of the earliest social scientists.[3] It can also be seen in the rise and use of modern statistics in western Europe, the United States, and Canada.

The recovery and accessibility of court and legal records have increased dramatically since the late nineteenth century and have aided the study of recorded crime. The records of the central state now pose a formidable resource in all of the OECD countries. The organization of these records, however, and the problem of finding aids, indexes, and accessibility still remain formidable deterrents to all but the most committed researchers.[4] The records of the police are just now being opened to students as their value is at last being recognized.[5] So too are the records of prisons, which still are subject to draconian disposition schedules with restricted access.[6]

Another problem with regard to records concerns local courts and jurisdictions. Too often, researchers restrict themselves to the records of the central courts and the central state, ignoring the rich archives of local courts and authorities, which range from the police and jails to municipal courts and magistrates. While in the past the context of the records of the central criminal courts was often literary evidence, perhaps the central jurisdiction can be placed within the context of the communal and municipal so a wider records structure can be created for eventual comparison with literary and other qualitative sources.

There have been a number of major shifts in the study of crime in recent years. One of them is a movement away from the sensational crimes (such as bandits and witches) to crimes in the home and the workplace. Thus, there is a new trilogy of criminality that could be described as white- and blue-collar crime in the workplace, domestic violence in the family, and regulatory offenses in the community. What is also needed, however, is a methodology to study these crimes and offenses at the level of the community, both within a region and without, and across the national divides in terms of the structure (the long *durée*), the conjuncture (midterm development), and the event (the particular moment). René Lévy devotes some attention to this problem in both the civil and common law traditions.

A further problem in the study of crime concerns definition. Historians have traditionally examined crime from the criminal records. Recent work, however, has shown that in some societies and communities, contemporaries used civil actions and the civil courts to control criminal activities by the threat of monetary payment, loss of job, withdrawal of services, or exclusion from the community. The evidence suggests that the social control mechanism could involve far more than just the criminal prosecution. Thus, we also need to look at civil actions in civil jurisdictions for the study of crime. Even today, for example, civil injunctions can be used to withdraw licenses from offenders.[7]

A further problem is the ever-changing definition of what constitutes crime or criminal activity. For example, in modern times we have lost much of petty theft as authorities—on whom the burden of prosecution now rests—become increasingly loath to prosecute low-valued monetary crimes because of the increasing cost of the public prosecutorial system. But we have also seen a tremendous increase in sexual crimes as society's sensitivity has changed from toleration to degrees of nonacceptance in the area of customary gender relations. With regard to individual crimes of violence, for example, we have lost the crime of infanticide since at least the mid-nineteenth century, and in some countries we have gained the crime of abortion.[8] Moreover, child abuse and wife beating, activities which were once permitted and at times extolled, are now among the most prominent crimes in society. Indeed, these ever-changing definitions of what constitutes crime have also affected what is regarded as both serious and violent crime.

CRIME AND THE STATE

The role of the central state in the history of crime and criminal justice has been a prominent one in Europe since the sixteenth century. Its historiography in modern times was spurred by the work of the Tillys in the 1960s and 1970s, which was funded by numerous programs of the Ford Foundation and the Social Science Research Council, featured in sessions of the Social Science History Association, and followed up by scholars and institutes in France and the Netherlands in particular.

The totality of this work proposed that Europe was in cultural, religious, and social disarray from the sixteenth to the eighteenth centuries and that its older authoritarian structures were in various stages of disintegration. The rise of the nation-state was seen as a response to war and threats to order, and the creation of national taxation, armies, police, foreign colonies, and industrialization enabled an alliance to be forged between landed and commercial elites to form strong central states.[9] The alleged result of these developments was that communities lost control of public space and the distribution of goods and services and that workers lost control of the means of production.[10] Thus, the rise of the nation-state was equated with the rise of social control.[11] More recent research, however, has shown that crime as an expression of rural or civic unrest, or of deviance, is not so easily identified.[12] It has also demonstrated that patterns of policing have reflected variant and often conflicting interests[13] and that forms of punishment—the ultimate weapon of the central state to enforce its hegemony upon society—reflected social, economic, and psychological concerns which developed independent of the interests of the state.[14]

State control may indeed be a heavily nuanced subject. On the one hand, it may be exercised by the elite, but it often requires tacit approval by large sections of society. On the other hand, most violence is actually at the expense of the lower orders, both in terms of physical and injury and of property damage. Since these people are in the least favorable position of recouping their losses, we must also see that they fear the dangerous elements among themselves as much as, if not more than, the elites above them, who have at their disposal the machinery for defense of life and property (namely, arms, money, and government).

Thus, it is interesting to note that there is little contemporary work that looks at crimes of the well-to-do as the white-collar crime that is being studied in contemporary society. These crimes have been given great opportunities with the development of the nation-state through its bureaucracies, contracts, commerce, and promotion of industrialization. The source of these crimes, moreover, is seldom found in the records of the state; it is found more often in the records of private and public companies and in the interstices of fraudulent and legitimate business practices.[15]

One of the major changes in modern times has been the impact of the public prosecutor and the shift in prosecutorial energy from the victim to the community or the state. This coincides with the origins of the modern police. Prosecutions often become motivated by public policy and financial considerations, which force the jurisdiction to set priorities among the crimes and offenses which comprise the criminal law. While personal interests are sacrificed for public ones, the element of vindication (as well as vexatious prosecutions) is weeded out of the criminal justice system. It is also interesting to note, however, that in some countries—especially the United States and Canada—the victim is returning to prominence in victim confrontation with the accused and the creation of victim aid societies.

Finally, perhaps more work is needed on the roles played by nonstate organizations in the informal criminal justice system, which also influences definitions and prosecutions of crime. For example, the mafia in Italy can be seen not only as organized groups of criminals committing crimes but also as (1) mediators in disputes who maintain the older, traditional forms of honor and socioeconomic status; and (2) a collective force to keep the peace on the streets and in the workplace. Brigandage in Italy and Spain could be seen in the same roles, in addition to the Robin Hood tradition in England, the gunslinger in the United States, and the bandit in Mexico and South America. At times, these people are not brigands, gunslingers, and bandits at all but groups of people who are labeled as such by the state for the purpose of extinguishing them.

Moreover, the authorities of the state have shown themselves capable of using nonstate violence to maintain the exercise of fear over a segment of the population, thereby legitimizing violent crime. Examples include the Ku Klux Klan in the United States and Hitler's youth gangs in Germany. Citizens have likewise accepted the fact of state officials using violence on their behalf. Examples of this phenomenon include the *gendarmes* in France and the police in England, both of whom were so situated in the violent dockland culture of nineteenth- and early twentieth-century Marseilles and Liverpool.[16]

CRIMINALITY

The long-term trends in the history of criminality have been established relatively recently in the historical literature.[17] Serious recorded crime swept upward from the fifteenth century to the early seventeenth and then went into a long decline to the mid- or late nineteenth century, from which it has begun a gradual increase that is today approaching the early seventeenth-century peak.[18] In more modern times, it has flattened out in the mid- and later nineteenth centuries,[19] and the real increase has been since World War II.[20]

There are, however, several problems with this paradigm. First, homicide may not be the best index of criminality for the long *durée.* One author has questioned the official statistics for homicides and suggests that the real trend may be somewhat different.[21] Another author, moreover, has shown that the great decrease in capital crimes from 1600 to 1800 was accompanied by an equally significant increase in petty crime.[22] There are also other indicators which may be even more important than homicides. Domestic violence, for example, was not a crime at all before the late nineteenth century, and in some countries—such as Great Britain and the United States—the police were told not to become involved in family disputes as recently as the early 1990s.

Another element of criminality involves class. The old paradigm of crime as an activity of the poor or unemployed against the propertied, and the resulting theory of the criminal law as a tool of the state to maintain class control and the supremacy of the elite, has been allowed to go too far in the historiography. Crime as an innate element of the human condition (in Christian terms the Ten Commandments) involves a large proportion of the unpropertied committing crimes against themselves (as in property crimes, the theft of wood from forests) or of the elite doing the same (as in personal crimes, assaults and duels).

What is needed, perhaps, are some new theories of criminality to explain upon better reflection the records' evidence for the role of class, occupation, and gender in recorded criminality.[23] Some recent studies have begun to emerge on both occupational and gender crime, and there is considerable room for development of the larger view in both Europe and the Americas.[24] A current debate concerns the question of female versus male criminality in the long *durée.*[25] One major difference may be a shift in prosecution from that of the overmighty subject to the criminalization of the poor.[26] Another may be the problem of defining class in an increasingly pluralistic society.[27]

Criminality has been linked increasingly to poverty as well as to place: to pockets of society, groups of people, districts of cities, and the rural countryside. In other words, criminality is being found to be situationally determined.[28] As Clive Emsley has demonstrated, work on collective action, protest, and social crime in national contexts in the past two decades has necessitated the creation of alternative definitions.[29] The cunning woman in England, the *muchachos* and *caballeristas* in Spain, the *strollica* in Italy, the *znakhar* in Russia, the *caudillo* in Mexico, and the role of *charivari* and *samosud* as cultural artifacts reflect the complex structure of social relations and order on the rural landscape. Moreover, the emphasis on the impact of industrialization and urbanization in the study of criminal justice history has perhaps been overdone. A peasant, or working-class, *mentalité* incorporates recourse to, and participation in, the law as well as serving the grist of much of its operation.

INTERNAL-EXTERNAL FACTORS

The relationship of war to crime and criminality has been a major subject from the eighteenth century to the present. What happens to the level of criminality in times of war fought on other lands, what happens to criminality in occupied territories and in active war zones, and what happens when armed forces are disbanded and return to their communities are questions which are engaging the current generation of historians. The Hay-Beattie paradigm holds that recorded crime drops significantly at the beginning of war and increases dramatically at the end.[30] But an equally important element concerns the nature of such societies themselves. The paradigm may or may not hold for countries which have high levels of, or occasions for, engaging in war and arms making; and the suggestion can be offered that countries such as these become more violent and crime oriented than others.[31]

There must also be an effort to see the state in non-Whiggish terms, appreciating the tensions which exist in all societies—ancient, medieval, and modern. For example, in Europe and North America in the nineteenth and twentieth centuries, one could invite single, rowdy males into a community where either male workers were needed or more workers were needed to keep wage rates low. In other economic conditions, the elite would request the state to arrest, prosecute, and jail such people as a dangerous or criminous class. State control, therefore, is not always something to be decided on by the state solely to control its society. The exercise of the criminal law may well hinge on external as well as internal factors, depending on the mixture of political and economic conditions.

The state itself, moreover, is a subject that is often misunderstood. Keith Wrightson has proposed that there are in fact two levels, and concepts, of order—the nation-state and the local community—and that too much criminal justice history has been written from the level of the state.[32] This is even more significant for the nineteenth and twentieth centuries than it is for the early modern era, and its significance has been documented in research, especially for England, France, and the United States.[33]

Considerations such as these lie at the heart of the historiography of crime and criminal justice in Europe and the Americas as well as in Asia and the Pacific. What is needed is not only specialized research into the localities and the national states but also the ideas which will eventually form the bridges that link the experiences of peoples and societies both laterally[34] and in structure, conjuncture, and event.

Lateral experiences cry out for analysis, and the first chapter in this volume provides the reader with a sophisticated overview of the main currents in the history of crime and criminal justice in Europe from late medieval times into the early nineteenth century; from the emergence of the state out of the communal worlds of a rural environment, to the age of the Enlightenment, revolution, and the urban, industrial, and bureaucratic nation state.[35] Rousseaux's views on the introduction of criminality, the rise of professional court systems, and the transformation of punishment assist us in coming to a better understanding of the national studies that follow in this book.

The chapters that follow are national and regional rather than thematic. They cover ten countries, the European section comprising England, France, Germany,

Italy, and the Scandinavia countries, and the section on the Americas and the Pacific comprising Canada, the United States, Mexico, Brazil, Australia, and New Zealand. Written by scholars from nine different countries who are recognized experts in their fields, the chapters represent the most forward-thinking writing in the profession. The rationale for the national and thematic approach is that most of the scholarship has been, and is being done, at the national, regional, and local levels. The historiography of the major themes is still in its early stages, and tracing a theme through a variety of legal cultures that are still relatively underwritten, not to mention coping with many languages, is a formidable task. Nonetheless, virtually all of the authors have addressed what we consider here to be some of the major themes in the historiography of crime and criminal justice history—namely, notions of criminality, the criminal courts, police, gender, bandits, and punishment.

Concepts of criminality are discussed throughout the chapters, more usually in their individual circumstances than in any theoretical construct. The roles of class, gender, ethnicity, and socioeconomic conditions are often prevalent depending on time and place. The chapters also point to the increasing amount of work that has been done on the machinery of the criminal justice system, particularly with reference to magistrates, juries, and policemen. As a result, the system is seen as much more highly textured than it has been portrayed in the traditional literature.[36]

The rise of the modern police form an additional theme that has become central to the history of crime since the Industrial Revolution. While work on the police has been prominent in countries such as England and the United States, there are major gaps in the history of the French *gendarmerie* and the Italian *carabinieri*, while some areas of policing such as Nazi-occupied Europe during World War II remain quite sensitive. As scholars dig into the archives of the individual police forces themselves, as opposed to relying on official reports and newspaper accounts, the police become not only a more integral part of the criminal justice system, but also an important occupational group of society with their own aims and aspirations.

Most authors point to the relative lack of females prosecuted for crime, except for prostitution. This may be in part because offenses involving women have had a relatively low priority in developing criminal justice systems, although women have commonly figured as victims of particular forms of assault. Much of the initial work was undertaken by researchers interested specifically in women's history, though the impact is now clearly filtering through to those whose primary focus is crime and the criminal justice system. While particular instances of female criminality are examined throughout this book, their impact on the long-term *durée* is one that will bear increasing attention in both gender and criminal justice studies.[37]

Bandits (brigands, bushrangers, and gunslingers) represent a major group of people who have emerged in this work. They recur throughout the later chapters, and the group emerges as one of great variety with many different roles. Perhaps the time has come to study them laterally, across countries and continents,[38] as well as in their localities, and as impediments to the establishment of the central state and national commercial and industrial enterprise. Lacking theoretical discussion, the label has been applied at times indiscriminately to a variety of groups as individual officials, not to mention historians, have thought fit in order to make comprehensive symbols out of the rich cultural diversity of the social order.

Finally, the subject of punishment has been dominated by philosophical works that have examined its history. The writings of Norbert Elias, Michel Foucault, David Garland, Otto Kirchheimer, and Georg Rusche are prominent but not exclusive of that work. They have provided broad, interpretive sweeps, but are not research oriented. Current studies, however, reveal a shift to the history of punishment based on archival work, and especially on the records of prisons.[39] The authors in this book provide considerable insight into the circumstances and considerations that go into sentences of punishment in numerous countries. On a general level they owe a debt to the theoretical writing in their national contexts, although the authors do not subscribe necessarily to all the views in those works.

While the historiography of crime and criminal justice in modern history is relatively underwritten, the research and writing, both old and new, is considerable. The bibliographical essay at the end of this volume provides some guidelines to the major works from Europe to the Americas and the Pacific. And while the labyrinth of jurisdictions of so many different communes and states—civil and ecclesiastical, local, national, and imperial—precludes easy conceptualization, the chapters in this book are rich in suggestions for writing, and rewriting, the history of the major themes not only across the long *durée* (the structure), but also in the eras that predominate historical study (the conjunctures), and the individual episodes (events), which continue to drive the popular study of crime in our society as well as of its history in the past.

NOTES

1. The major French works are limited to specific localities, and little has been done for the twentieth century. For Great Britain, there is a distinct lack of such scholarship for Wales, Scotland, and Ireland.

2. It would also be interesting to examine the subject from an Islamic, rather than from a Christian, perspective and to study the interaction of Islamic and Christian criminal justice systems.

3. Lambert A.J. Quetelet, *Recherches sur la population, les naissances, les deces, les prisons, les depots de medicite, etc.* (New York, 1827).

4. For example, see the recent collection of essays entitled *Legal Records in the Commonwealth,* ed. William Twining and Emma Varnden Quick (Aldershot, 1994).

5. Ian Bridgeman and Clive Emsley, *A Guide to the Archives of the Police Forces of England and Wales* (London, 1989).

6. For this and all areas of criminal justice history in Europe, see the splendid com-

pilation of Xavier Rousseaux, "Criminality and Criminal Justice History in Europe, 1250–1850: A Select Bibliography," *Criminal Justice History* 14 (1993): 159–81. For punishment in general, see Pieter Spierenburg, *The Spectacle of Suffering. Executions and the Evolution of Repression: From a Preindustrial Metropolis to the European Experience* (Cambridge, 1984); and David Garland, *Punishment and Modern Society* (Oxford, 1990).

7. *The Sunday Times,* 20 June 1994.

8. Lionel Rose, *Massacre of the Innocents: Infanticide in Great Britain 1800–1939* (London, 1986).

9. Charles Tilly, "Reflections on the History of European State-Making," in his *The Formation of National States in Western Europe* (Princeton, 1975), 3–83; and Charles Tilly, Louise Tilly, and Richard Tilly, *The Rebellious Century 1830–1930* (London, 1975).

10. *Class Conflict and Collective Action,* ed. Charles and Louise Tilly (Beverly Hills, 1981).

11. For example, see Howard Zehr, *Crime and the Development of Modern Society: Patterns of Criminality in Nineteenth-Century Germany and France* (London, 1976); B. Ingham, *Political Crime in Europe: A Comparative Study of France, Germany and England* (Los Angeles, 1979); and *Social Control and the State: Historical and Comparative Essays,* ed. A. Scull and S. Cohen (Oxford, 1983).

12. See, in general, *The Poor in Western Europe in the 18th and 19th Centuries,* ed. S.J. Wolfe (London, 1986); and *Power and Protest in the Countryside: Studies of Rural Protest in Asia, Europe, and Latin America,* ed. Robert P. Weller and Scott Evan Guggenheim (Durham, 1982).

13. *Past and Present Colloquium on Police and Policing* (Oxford, 1984); *Maintien de l'ordre et polices en France et en Europe au XIXe siècle,* ed. Alain Faure (Paris, 1987); and *Policing Western Europe: Politics, Professionalization and Public Order 1850–1940,* ed. Clive Emsley and Barbara Weinberger (Westport, 1991).

14. Pierre Deyon, *Le temps des prisons: essai sur l'histoire de la deliquance et les origins du systèm pénetentaire* (Lille, 1975); Michael Ignatieff, *A Just Measure of Pain: The Penitentiary in the Industrial Revolution* (New York, 1978); Michel Foucault, *Discipline and Punish* (New York, 1977) and the original French edition, *Surveiller et punir* (Paris, 1975); *The Emergence of Carceral Institutions: Prisons, Galleys and Lunatic Asylums 1550–1900,* ed. Pieter Spierenburg (Rotterdam, 1984); and Phillipe Robert and René Lévy, "Histoire et Question Pénale," *Revue d'histoire moderne et contemporaine* 32 (1985): 481–526.

15. For example, the classic study of George Robb, *White-Collar Crime in Modern England: Financial Fraud and Business Morality 1845–1929* (Cambridge, 1992).

16. Mike Brogden, *On The Mersey Beat. Policing Liverpool Between The Wars* (Oxford and New York, 1991); and Marie Thérèse Vogel, "Les Polices des villes entre local et national: l'administration des polices urbaines sous la III republique" (Doctoral dissertation, Grenoble, 1993).

17. The original debate hinged on the work of P.E.H. Hair, "Deaths from Violence in Britain: A Tentative Secular Survey," *Population Studies* 25 (1971): 5–24; Ted Robert Gurr, "Historical Trends in Violent Crime: A Critical Review of the Evidence," *Crime and Justice* 3 (1981): 295–353; Lawrence Stone, "Interpersonal Violence in English Society, 1300–1980," *Past and Present* 101 (1983): 22–33; and J.A. Sharpe and

Lawrence Stone, "Debate: The History of Violence in England," *Past and Present* 108 (1985): 206–24.

18. *Crime, Police and the Courts in British History,* ed. Louis A. Knafla (Westport, 1990), ix–xiv.

19. V.A.C. Gatrell, "The Decline of Theft and Violence in Victorian and Edwardian England," in *Crime and the Law: The Social History of Crime in Western Europe Since 1500,* ed. V.A.C. Gatrell, Bruce Lenman, and Geoffrey Parker (London, 1980).

20. Terence Morris, *Crime and Criminal Justice Since 1945* (Oxford, 1989).

21. J.S. Cockburn, "Patterns of Violence in English Society: Homicide in Kent 1560–1985," *Past and Present* 130 (1991): 70–106.

22. J.M. Beattie, *Crime and the Courts in England 1660–1800* (Oxford, 1986).

23. For example, see the recent research essays in *Law, Society, and the State: Essays in Modern Legal History,* ed. Louis A. Knafla and Susan W.S. Binnie (Toronto, 1995).

24. For example, see Nancy Leys Stepan, *'The Hour of Eugenics': Race, Gender, and Nation in Latin America* (Ithaca and London, 1991).

25. Malcolm Feeley, "The Decline of Women in the Criminal Process: A Comparative Study," *Criminal Justice History* 15 (1994).

26. A theme of J.A. Sharpe, *Crime in Early Modern England 1550–1750* (London and New York, 1986).

27. The subject of legal pluralism is one that has yet to catch the imagination of writers on this subject.

28. For one example in the early modern period, see Louis A. Knafla, *Kent at Law 1602. The County Jurisdiction: Assizes and Sessions of the Peace* (London, 1994), vii–xxxiii.

29. Clive Emsley, "Crime and Criminal Justice in the European Countryside: Some Questions for Comparison," *Criminal Justice History* 14 (1993): 1–16.

30. Douglas Hay, "War, Dearth and Theft in the Eighteenth Century: The Record of the English Courts," *Past and Present* 95 (1982): 117–60; Beattie, *Crime and the Courts;* and the critique of Joanna Innes and John Styles, "The Crime Wave: Recent Writing on Crime and Criminal Justice in Eighteenth-Century England," *Journal of British Studies* 25 (1986): 380–435.

31. See also *The Civilian in War,* ed. Jeremy Noakes (Exeter, 1992).

32. Keith Wrightson, "Two Concepts of Order: Justices, Constables and Jurymen in Seventeenth-Century England," in *An Ungovernable People: The English and Their Law in the Seventeenth and Eighteenth Centuries,* ed. John Brewer and John Styles (London, 1980).

33. See the discussions in the chapters by Clive Emsley, René Lévy, Eric Monkkonen, and Jim Phillips, especially.

34. For recent attempts to establish such links, see *Policing the Empire: Government, Authority, and Control,* ed. David M. Anderson and David Killingray (Manchester and New York, 1991); Sir Thomas Skyrme, *History of the Justices of the Peace* (Chichester, 1991), 3 vols.; and Knafla and Binnie, *Law, Society, and the State.*

35. This was the object, for example, of the famous Warwick conference on the history of crime in 1984, out of which emerged two edited books: Francis G. Snyder and Douglas Hay, *Labour, Law and Crime* (London, 1987); and Douglas Hay and Francis G. Snyder, *Policing and Prosecution in Britain 1750–1850* (Oxford, 1989).

36. See, for example, the superficial but still often used survey by Michael Weisser, *Crime and Punishment in Early Modern Europe* (Hassocks, 1979). At the na-

tional level, the most useful example is the twin set for England: Sharpe, *Crime in Early Modern England 1550–1750*, and Clive Emsley, *Crime and Society in England 1750–1900* (London: 1987, 2nd ed. 1996 forthcoming).

37. See, for example, the provocative analysis and assessment by Malcolm Feeley, "The Decline of Women in the Criminal Process: A Comparative History."

38. There have been several recent studies of bandits, or gunslingers, in the North American borderlands; see, for example, Richard W. Slatta, *Cowboys of the Americas* (New Haven, 1990). There have also been studies of individual borderlands from a sociolegal perspective, one of the most recent being the essays edited by John McLaren, Hamar Foster, and Chet Orloff, in *Law for the Elephant, Law for the Beaver—Essays in the Legal History of the North American West* (Regina, 1992). For differences between the British and American views of criminal intent, see Richard Maxwell Brown, *No Duty to Retreat: Violence and Values in American History and Society* (New York, 1992). For crime and violence at the apex of the western North American frontier, see Louis A. Knafla, "Violence on the Western Canadian Frontier: A Historical Perspective," in *Violence in Canada*, ed. Jeffrey Ian Ross (Toronto, 1995).

39. This has been the case especially for England, France, the Netherlands, the United States, Canada, and New Zealand. For recent major studies, see V.A.C. Gatrell, *The Hanging Tree: Executions and the English People 1770–1868* (Oxford, 1994); Alexander W. Pisciotta, *Benevolent Repression: Social Control and the American Reformatory-Prison Movement* (London and New York, 1994); and John Pratt, *Punishment in a Perfect Society: The New Zealand Penal System, 1840–1939* (Wellington, 1992).

PART II

WESTERN EUROPE

3

Gender, Class, and the Courts: Scandinavia

Eva Österberg

MAIN TRENDS IN RECENT SCANDINAVIAN HISTORIOGRAPHY

In the 1960s and 1970s, Scandinavian historical research saw the triumph of social history and theories based on the social sciences. The welfare state gave priority to sociopolitical discourse and turned to geographers, sociologists, and political scientists for solutions to its problems. The historical muse took up a stance in the very center of reality, concentrating on social conflicts and previously invisible groups. Neopositivism, Marxism, or critical theory provided the tools.[1]

The main furrow in Scandinavian social history was the analysis of the working classes that typified different periods or places: peasants, craftsmen, and industrial workers—male majority cultures, even though the emphasis was not on the ruling political elites. It was only gradually that other groups, such as women or prisoners in jail, began to come into focus.

With this turn of the tide, criminality occasionally appeared on the agenda of historical research. This began with the spectacular witch trials. In 1971, the Swedish witch trials were examined by Bengt Ankarloo from the point of view of social and legal history. The focus of this penetrating study was on the great persecutions of the 1660s and 1670s.[2] A comparable analysis was published in Norway in the early 1980s by Hans Eyvind Næss.[3] Both Næss and Ankarloo returned to this problem of witchcraft in a comparative anthology from 1987, in which anthropological approaches and new international research were given more scope in the interpretations. The other Nordic countries were represented in this volume by contributions from Kirsten Hastrup (Iceland), Antero Heikkinen and Timo Kervinen (Finland), and Jens Christian V. Johansen (Denmark).[4] Johansen has also recently published his doctoral dissertation on witchcraft in Jutland in the seventeenth century.[5]

Taken together, all these studies show that witch trials in the Scandinavian countries were both similar to and different from corresponding phenomena in other countries. At the same time, there were also significant differences within Scandinavia. As in most European countries, the persecutions in Sweden, Denmark, and Norway chiefly afflicted old women; men accused of witchcraft, for example, account for only about 20 percent of the cases in Norway and 15 percent in Sweden. In Finland and Iceland, on the other hand, it was men who practiced witchcraft.

The perspectives which the Scandinavian historians have applied in their efforts to explain the witch trials also show some variation. Ankarloo and Næss believe that the phenomenon belongs, roughly speaking, to the early modern period, especially the latter part of the seventeenth century, the time when the witch trials culminated in Sweden and Norway. They see the cause in a combination of church and state activity, popular conceptions, and social tensions in the communities as a result of population growth (Næss), a surplus of women (Ankarloo), and socioeconomic problems of various kinds (Ankarloo and Næss). In contrast, Johansen emphasizes the years 1617–1625, when 60 percent of the total charges of witchcraft in Jutland were made during that century. He sees this chiefly as an enforcement wave occasioned by a new ordinance enacted in Denmark in 1617. The rather sudden end to the wave of trials, in his view, was due to conflicts within the church: Some of the clergy developed a distaste for accusations of witchcraft.[6] As regards witchcraft, then, Scandinavian research can be described as having been rather early, thanks to the important work of Ankarloo and Næss in particular. Moreover, Næss presents interesting findings about other crimes in the sixteenth and seventeenth centuries.[7]

In more general terms, however, it was only a few years into the 1980s that the history of crime and criminal justice became a vigorous research field in Scandinavia. It was only then that Scandinavian historians began to show the distinct influence of British and French research into criminality; and it was only then that historians and legal historians from the Scandinavian countries began to make their contribution to the international debate. As in other countries, there were discussions of theories and fragments of theories taken from, for instance, Norbert Elias, Michel Foucault, Michael Weisser, or E. P. Thompson.[8]

It was no coincidence that scholars from the 1980s became fascinated with norms and breaches of norms. In recent decades, society in general has seen a growing interest in problems of value systems, mentalities, civilization processes, and culture. In many places in Europe, the 1980s have brought crises for the social engineers of the welfare state. It has become obvious that modern society has not been able to solve tomorrow's fateful questions about the environment and the quality of life. People show a growing distrust for politicians and administrators who, as prisoners of the modern concept of rationality, are trying to draw the map of the future. People have instead become aware of how the long lines of development and cultural comparisons can give us fresh insight into societal value systems; this sometimes opens the way to criticism of our own civilization.[9]

To put it somewhat crudely, it can be said that historiographical trends in Scandinavia in the period 1960–1990 first concentrated on conflicts and socioeconomic structures and then broadened the scope to consider what forces lay behind integration in society, including mental and legal structures. Today's debate about Europe, for example, covers issues such as regional, national, and transnational identities, in which not only religion and ethnicity but also legal traditions play a significant role. Against this background, one might expect an extensive amount of research into criminality and criminal justice in Scandinavia, and this is indeed what we find. It is perhaps in Sweden and Norway that most progress has been made, with a large number of scholars from many universities publishing important works in recent years.

As in international research,[10] the starting point in Sweden has generally been a pragmatic definition of criminality as "behaviour which is classified as criminal by the law, which is thereby registered in judicial sources, and which can lead to punishment."[11] Historians have been fully aware of the problems inherent in this definition. The young Norwegian historian Erling Sandmo, for example, makes several astute reservations in his analysis of eighteenth-century criminality in one area of Norway. In early society, he says, it was more difficult to equate "lawbreaker" with "criminal" than it is today. The authorities still did not fully control the judicial apparatus. It was not just representatives of the state who decided what behavior should be censured and perhaps punished. The main basis of the legal system was that the involved parties brought the matter to court themselves. Criminality in this period is thus a rough umbrella term for all actions which were defined as breaches of norms on different social and discursive levels.[12] Nevertheless, historians have no option but to begin by analyzing the court records, but they must then carry on a ceaseless, qualified discussion of what the crime statistics actually tell us.

Let us look at the periods examined in Scandinavian research. We find that the sources make it difficult to go back farther than the fifteenth century. Yet it has been possible to establish with a fair degree of certainty the long-term trends in the pattern of criminality from the sixteenth century to the present, at least in Sweden. In Norway, the emphasis in today's research appears to have been on the period from the sixteenth to the eighteenth centuries, while the Finnish studies have primarily focused on one type of criminality—violence. Danish historians have laid the basis for systematic analyses by compiling a large computer database of archival material, but only a fraction of their findings has been published.

This chapter cannot hope to cover all the research. I have chosen instead to highlight three themes which appear to me to be of particular interest in an international context:

1. The long-term trends as regards different types of crime and any relation they might have to concepts such as civilization and modernization.
2. Criminality from the point of view of gender and class. Are any crimes gender specific, what was female criminality like, and how should it be interpreted? Who commits the crimes: ordinary decent people or the underprivileged from the lower social strata?
3. The overall work and function of the courts in society.

Finally, I discuss the need for comparative Scandinavian research into judicial practice and criminality.

CRIME IN TIME: MAIN PATTERNS

At the start of the 1980s, we still had a deficient knowledge of the panorama of crime in the Scandinavian countries in different centuries. Legal historians had concentrated on the study of the official norms; local historians had used isolated cases to illustrate unusual squabbles or colorful tragedies in the community. No one had systematically analyzed judicial practice and criminality in early times.

A striking exception, however, was a bold hypothetical synthesis in an article by Knut Sveri from 1974, based on some material from Stockholm.[13] Sveri sketched some of the changes in criminality, which later research has been able to establish by more comprehensive empirical analysis. He envisaged, for example, that violence declined between the Middle Ages and the present. Yet his chronology was coarse. By and large, he let early society, with a high frequency of violence, extend all the way to the nineteenth century. The years 1850–1940 are seen as a transitional period with a general decline in the amount of crime. Modern society since then has been permeated by economic criminality. It is particularly unsatisfying that Sveri devotes so little discussion to the dynamics within preindustrial society.

Another early attempt to draw conclusions about changes in criminality was made in 1976 by Heikki Ylikangas. He studied violent crime in Finland, a subject to which he later returned in an inspiring book.[14] Ylikangas showed that violence tended in general to decline in Finland from the middle of the sixteenth century. At the same time, he drew attention to a remarkable wave of violence in Österbotten in the nineteenth century. In his explanations of these two phenomena, Ylikangas discusses both the economic factors that lead to increased criminality and the collective value systems and social structures that create—or dissolve—social control.

A few years into the 1980s, two historical research projects on criminality and judicial practice were started in Sweden. They were conducted in parallel, with some collaboration. One was led by Eva Österberg at Lund University, the other by Jan Sundin at Linköping University. Another project led by the economic historians Arne Jarrick and Johan Söderberg at Stockholm University is also working with legal cases in an attempt to capture the emergence of modern humankind and individualism. Research into crime and punishment at Umeå University is being conducted by, among others, Johan Liljequist and Marja Taussi Sjöberg. A large network of young researchers, spread over all the Swedish universities, with more or less formal links to these projects, has been established and has also resulted in a Scandinavian research community in the field. The research that has been produced within or alongside these projects has certain features in common. It shows the inspiration of international research. Theories which have had an impact on other countries have been deliberately tested on Scandinavian material. Most studies combine quantitative and qualitative analysis.

As a result of these efforts, we now have a clear picture of fluctuations in criminality in Sweden from the Middle Ages to the present. Obviously, the sources do not allow a complete analysis of many regions. For the Middle Ages and the sixteenth century, for example, court records are preserved from only some towns and rural judicial districts (the hundreds). Some fiscal records from the sixteenth century, however, also provide details of the crimes that led to fines. From the seventeenth century on, the Swedish material is fairly ample, and in fortunate cases it is possible to combine several kinds of sources from different levels of the judicial process: local court records, fine payment rolls, lists of summonses, and material from the courts of appeal.[15]

Future research will qualify the results that have been obtained. But more and more areas have been studied, both rural and urban, in the south of Sweden as well as in the central and northern parts. It is worth emphasizing that alongside the British and perhaps the French studies, Swedish research already gives the clearest picture in Europe of changes in criminality in the period 1400–1960. What does this picture look like? In a lengthy article from 1990, based on my own analyses and the findings of other historians, I have attempted a synthesis that covers several centuries.[16] This was the first effort of its kind in Scandinavia. The following are the major results.

Everything indicates that crimes of violence, when seen in relation to the size of the population, underwent a considerable reduction sometime during the early modern period. This applies especially to lethal violence. Historians are not in agreement about the exact chronology.[17] In any event, however, the number of recorded crimes of violence was clearly much lower in most of the eighteenth century than it had been in the fifteenth and sixteenth centuries. The conclusions about the medieval period are based on research into the towns of Stockholm and Arboga by myself and Dag Lindström.[18]

Another finding is that violence increased again at the start of the nineteenth century, a phenomenon with parallels in other European countries. This, however, should be seen as a ripple on the surface after the great wave had subsided—that is, after crimes of violence had stabilized at a lower level than in the Middle Ages. This impression is reinforced by the subsequent period, the latter part of the nineteenth century and the beginning of the twentieth century, when the figures are once again lower. In qualitative terms, however, the signs of unrest in the first half of the nineteenth century are extremely interesting. Birgitta Odén's analyses of physical and verbal violence against parents confirm the picture of the first half of the nineteenth century as a period of radical social change.[19] It was also in this period that the sociopolitical debate in Sweden reflected the anxious concerns about "the dangerous lower classes."[20]

The early modern period, then, stands out as a time when the patterns of criminality changed. The decline in violence has given us reason to discuss whether the thesis of a transition *de la violence au vol* is applicable to Scandinavia as well—that is, whether a preponderance of violent crime gave way to a predominance of theft. There is nothing to suggest, however, that the thesis as a whole is corroborated by the Swedish material for the sixteenth to the nineteenth centuries. Violence declined, it is true, but there was no general tendency toward an increase in thefts during these centuries. On the contrary, theft remained a rather small category of crime in the Swedish courts from the Middle Ages until relatively recently, unlike the picture in many countries in southern Europe.[21] As I have maintained, it was neither in the era of mercantile capitalism of the seventeenth and eighteenth centuries nor in the incipient industrialism of the nineteenth century that theft increased significantly. It was only in the welfare state of the postwar period.[22]

To the extent that modernization is seen as synonymous with industrialization and urbanization, it has nothing to do with the transition from violence to theft. If the change in the pattern of crime is to be discussed in such terms at all, then modernization must be seen as a process that extends from the early modern period up to the present. The process, moreover, consists of several subsidiary processes with different effects for different social groups, and it is not irreversible in all its elements.[23]

Another significant finding concerns changes which make the overall structure of criminality more complex. One example of this is the occasional increase in the number of cases concerning commerce and production after the mid-sixteenth century. This reflects the increased intervention of the state in trade in a kingdom which was on the verge of an expansive foreign policy.[24] Another example is the way the church and the state together acted to control sexuality. This is seen with particular clarity in directives from the 1560s and 1570s and an appendix to the law of 1608. Harsher punishments—the death penalty in several cases—in the spirit of Mosaic law were prescribed for extramarital sex.[25] Finally, several researchers also emphasize a change in the overall work of the courts, which gives a similar indication of a general change in society. Criminal cases, especially crimes of violence, still dominated in the courts in the sixteenth century. A little into the seventeenth century, however, and even more so in the eighteenth century, the proportions shifted so that the court instead became a forum for judging and resolving debts and disputes about land.[26]

The most comprehensive study of the total criminality and its variations in Scandinavia is now Jan Sundin's book *För Gud, Staten och Folket.* The main basis of this work is a set of case studies of one rural court (Gullberg Hundred in Östergötland in central Sweden) and one urban court (Linköping in Östergötland). Sundin supplements this with material from northern and southern Sweden. Throughout his study, he compares his findings with previous Swedish analyses and the results of British, German, and French research. Sundin largely confirms the long-term trends from the start of the seventeenth century to the middle of the nineteenth century which I found in my preliminary synthesis. It is important that this confirmation has come from a study that covers such a large body of material and systematically compares town with countryside. The findings vary to some extent between the two areas, it is true, but Sundin likewise observes a decline in violent crime when comparing the eighteenth century with the seventeenth, and he too finds a renewed rise in violence at the start of the nineteenth century. From the seventeenth century onward there is an increase in crimes against state regulations in the sphere of commerce, and the courts gradually become more occupied with economic disputes and cases of debt. In addition, Sundin concludes that thefts in general were on a lower level in preindustrial Scandinavia than in many countries in continental Europe. Yet Sundin's study also discerns nuances in the pattern. He finds, for example, that criminality in society was already on the increase from the end of the eighteenth century, and minor crimes of violence vary in keeping with the ups and downs of the socioeconomic cycle to a greater extent than was previously asserted.[27]

It is valuable that we have obtained a more complete picture of eighteenth-century criminality through Sundin's study than earlier research provided. Among other things, he provides interesting examples of the illegal use of natural resources, such as felling trees and stealing wood. Above all, he presents new findings that shed light on gender and class aspects of criminality. (I shall return to some of these findings later.) According to both my own and Sundin's conclusions, the quantitative fluctuations in crime were due not just to the fact that people chose to behave in a different way because, for example, the economy impelled them to do so or the social networks had become more diversified. Nor are they solely dependent on state initiatives to criminalize and control. They also depend on what alternative forums for social control existed during different periods.[28] The theory of a civilizing process has thus come to be discussed in Swedish historiography less as a matter of pure disciplining from above, as a symbiosis of Elias and Foucault is sometimes perceived. Instead a more complex process is implied in which the efforts of the authorities were sometimes combined with and sometimes counteracted by shifts in social relations and mentalities within the communities themselves—an interpretation which is in fact not incompatible with Elias.

It is hard to ignore the joint aspirations of the Swedish state and church to control and educate the population in the seventeenth and eighteenth centuries. This is part of the traditional historical view of the period. The Lutheran clergy played a significant role in the everyday drama. This probably contributed to a reduction in the tendency toward violence and, above all, to the criminalization of extramarital sex. At the same time, demographic realities may have played a role. One characteristic of the seventeenth century in Sweden is that young men, who are most disposed to violence in all cultures, were conscripted for war. It was the old men and the women who had to look after the farms at home.[29]

Yet modern research also looks for interpretations which start from the common people as actors rather than as objects of disciplining. People may have felt that it was in the interests of the community to curb brutality.[30] The change in the work of the courts from a predomination of violence to an increasing number of civil cases, such as debts and property disputes, may have come about because the peasant population itself changed its behavior and values. This in turn, in the opinion of Johan Söderberg and others, was due to the growth of the economic sphere and the fact that social relations were increasingly bound by contracts. Conflicts came to be about land and debts more than about persons and honor.[31]

The reduction in violence in the early modern period has thus been explained in different ways. In contrast, it has often been assumed automatically that the Middle Ages and the sixteenth century were characterized by unrestrained aggression. The reason for this is probably the stereotype of the Middle Ages as a dark period, which modern theorists of civilization and modernization have unreflectingly assumed from the negative way the medieval period was portrayed in the Renaissance. In modern research, however, this view too has been challenged. I have asked, for example, whether we can really say that we have identified a violent society when we find so many examples of fights being brought to court. Does this not rather show us that people wanted to restrict spontaneous aggression and that they used the courts as popular instruments for handling conflicts? Did the courts try charges of violent crime in order to compensate men for their wounded honor in forms that were socially acceptable at least as much as to discipline "primitive" aggressive people?[32]

The concept of honor has in fact assumed major importance in the interpretation of crimes of violence in early times. The fact that even cases of trivial violence were brought before the Swedish courts can be seen as a sign that brawls were often fought over matters of honor. The man who dealt the blow had asserted his honor in doing so. On the other hand, the victim of the blow obtained redress through the court.[33] Honor as a decisive element in the popular mentality of early times is also found in recent Norwegian research into criminality. Jørn Sandnes has published the first study of criminality, including sociopolitical unrest, in Norway during the sixteenth and seventeenth centuries. Corresponding to the Swedish results, his findings show that violence was a frequent category of crime in Norwegian society, whereas thefts were fairly unusual. He seeks an explanation in a "traditional mentality." A man who stole lost all honor in the sight of the community, whereas a man who fought was instead protecting his honor.[34]

Original views of violence and honor have been put forward by Erling Sandmo in his analysis of a relatively closed Norwegian community in the latter part of the eighteenth century. A significant finding is that not all fights ended up in court. What decided whether a case would be brought to court was not the degree of violence in itself but the disposition of the brawling parties; if the man who started the fight bore a grudge or was truly angry, the honor of the victim was threatened. Sandmo relates crimes of violence to charges of defamation in his interpretation. Cases of defamation were in fact more common than violent crimes in Rendalen in the eighteenth century. Sandmo's qualitative analysis of criminal cases is sophisticated, problematizing the concepts of "society" and "person." What was at stake in cases of defamation and violence was not an individual, isolated sovereignty but an individual's position and status as a member of a community. Defamation was, in Sandmo's opinion, dangerous on two levels. Not only did it threaten the individual, who defined himself as a member of a community, but it also threatened society as a whole, since honor was one of its most powerful integrative forces.[35]

Regarding changes in the level of violence in the early modern period in Norway, Næss has maintained that the sixteenth century saw an increase in violence as a result of population pressure and social tensions. Sandnes's findings, however, are closer to those obtained for Sweden. Violence was probably very common in the Middle Ages and tended to decline gradually in the sixteenth and seventeenth centuries.[36] Sandmo also shows that violence took up less of the courts' time in the latter part of the eighteenth century. A more prominent category of crime was extramarital sex. By far the largest category, however, consisted of debt cases, which made up about 61 percent of the total number of cases in the years 1763–1797.[37] The Norwegian findings, like the Swedish, thus reveal a transition in the cases handled by courts from the sixteenth to the eighteenth century. If this is to be summed up in a simple formula, it would not be "from violence to theft" but "from violence to dispute/debt." Or why not "from honor to economy"?

CRIMINALITY FROM THE PERSPECTIVE OF GENDER AND CLASS

The major international theses that have been used to categorize phases of criminality have been concerned mostly with male criminality.[38] In all periods and in all cultures, women have been a minority among criminals, whereas young men have normally been an overrepresented group. As Lindström and I have shown, it was exceptional, for example, that women were found guilty of manslaughter in the medieval towns of Sweden, and women as a rule accounted for no more than 10 to 20 percent of the thefts. This proportion could rise in times of economic difficulty, as in the opening phase of Sweden's Age of Greatness; in 1620–1624, for instance, over 40 percent of the people convicted of theft in Stockholm were women.[39] The pattern is the same later on. Only one in ten cases of murder and manslaughter was perpetrated by a women in Sweden during the period 1870–1980, and the proportion of women accused of assault never exceeded 5 percent in the nineteenth or twentieth centuries. Only 10 to 20 percent of the thefts were normally committed by women in the same centuries.[40]

Witchcraft, on the other hand, was a specifically female crime in Sweden, Norway, and Denmark. This suggests that the seventeenth century was a dramatic period from the point of view of women. It should also make us realize that women were unevenly distributed among the various categories of crime. Jan Sundin shows that women figure above all in crimes associated with their social roles: They are brought to court, for example, when they have given birth to children outside wedlock, when they have broken a regulation about serving beer, when they have pilfered something to do with maintaining the home, or when they have tittle-tattled about the morals of other women.[41]

The category of crime which interests Sundin above all is sexual offenses. In the Middle Ages, more men than women were brought to court for illicit sex.[42] After the Reformation, on the other hand, more women than men were made to answer for their actions, and the control of extramarital sex was tightened. As Sundin puts it, the church's concept of sin in the seventeenth century created a formally more "gender-neutral" judicial system. Women as well as men appeared in court accused of sex outside marriage. From the start of the seventeenth century until 1810, when illicit sex as a first and second offense was decriminalized for women, a steady stream of women appeared in court on sexual charges. In the seventeenth century and at the beginning of the eighteenth century, men also had to answer for these deeds to a large extent, or else they voluntarily accepted responsibility as a consequence of pressure from the community. Toward the end of the eighteenth century, however, the laws were liberalized, and control of the circumstances surrounding illegitimate births became more lax. More and more men were able to avoid conviction. It was only some years into the nineteenth century that the decriminalization of sexuality reached so far that women also escaped having to appear in court for illicit sex.[43]

That it was not just the church but also the state which was actively committed to curbing extramarital sex is, in Sundin's opinion, virtually unique to Sweden: "A comparison shows that the Swedish model with a greater engagement in sexual issues on the part of the secular courts, and with an increasing criminalization of the women, was an extreme case. Not even the puritan colonies in North America were able to show such a consistent commitment to religious questions of morality as orthodox Sweden."[44] Sundin's comparison with other European countries is striking. Whether the phenomenon is unique to Sweden or to all the Scandinavian countries, however, is perhaps still not settled. Næss has calculated that the proportion of women in the total criminal statistics for Rogaland in Norway was about 11 percent in 1623–1629 versus 29 percent in

1691–1697. The change, in his opinion, was due to an increase in sexual offenses.[45]

The seventeenth century is interesting in other ways from the female point of view. As Hilde Sandvik has shown for Norway, women were often actors in economic cases at the local courts. Women could enter into binding contracts; they could take advantage of the court as a public sphere; they could bring charges and be charged. In short, they had legal capacity.[46] Sundin's material likewise shows women as active in numerous civil cases: for example, they were plaintiffs in 15 percent of the civil cases in Linköping in the 1640s.[47]

We see before us something which may appear to be a puzzling combination. On the one hand, women in the seventeenth century were persecuted as witches and their extramarital sex was vigorously criminalized. On the other hand, they could act with full authority as plaintiffs in civil cases and as witnesses in criminal cases. A key to this apparent contradiction may lie in the demographic and economic realities of the time. In Sweden, for example, there was a surplus of women due to the conscription of men. This gave women more responsible tasks in production. It is possible that this in turn led to a male reaction. Patriarchalism as an ideological system may be seen not only as a principle of social organization in general but also hypothetically as an expression of male resistance.[48] Jan Sundin also comes close to an explanation of this kind when he writes that "witch trials and the control of extramarital sex helped to define the limits of the woman's role."[49]

Witchcraft, sexual offenses, and infanticide are in many ways the "typical" women's crimes of the seventeenth and eighteenth centuries. Johan Liljequist's doctoral dissertation is about another crime that is strikingly specific for one gender but this time committed by men: He analyzes bestiality. Those accused of sexual intercourse with animals were generally men aged between fifteen and nineteen. The charge was often brought by women in the community, but it sometimes happened that men accused each other, and some men even gave themselves up. In the period 1635–1778, no less than six hundred or seven hundred people were executed in Sweden for bestiality, with a culmination in the first half of the eighteenth century. This exceeds the number of victims of the witch trials. According to Liljequist, there is scarcely any comparable phenomenon in any other European country. Nor did all countries have any special term for this type of forbidden sexuality outside Sweden. People spoke in more general terms about unnatural sex or sodomy.[50]

Liljequist's thesis is a successful example of history with an anthropological inspiration. The bestiality trials as Liljequist describes them are not primarily an example of a process controlled by the authorities to reform peasant culture, although this is undoubtedly one aspect. What he shows is that it was more common, from the beginning, for the local population to take the initiative for the trials. The charges must therefore be understood on the basis of a popular problematization of the deed. Important elements in the interpretation are a "traditional division of labor between the genders and between children and adults, which led to different roles in relation to animals,'' along with strong popular conceptions about the physical impurity that was a consequence for both man and beast if the two were intimate in an improper way.[51] Thus, although the judicial system in Scandinavia tried in principle to be neutral regarding gender and to give both men and women legal capacity with responsibility for their actions, men and women were by no means equally distributed over the categories of crime. Something similar can be said about criminality from the point of view of class.

The violent criminals of the Middle Ages, the sixteenth century, and the seventeenth century, as Dag Lindström and I have shown, included goldsmiths, shoemakers, peasants, and farmhands alike. They were generally one-time offenders. Being brought to court on account of a fight evidently involved no social stigma. It could happen to anyone. The only group that appears to be overrepresented, at least in certain periods, consists of foot soldiers, horse soldiers, and sailors.[52] Sundin also observes that ordinary people were charged for physical and verbal conflicts. With his large body of evidence, however, he is able to differentiate the categories of crime more consistently with regard to social groups. His findings show that military men, for example, are overrepresented in some areas but not in all.

By and large, the dividing line between people with and without property reveals itself in the following way in court records. Propertied groups may appear in court in conjunction with assault, offenses against official regulations, cases concerning property, and sometimes premarital sex and adultery. The unpropertied groups may appear in court primarily accused of assault, sexual offenses, and theft. In short, anyone could be charged for assault in early society. In contrast, it was mostly men with property who found themselves in conflict with state regulations, while it was servant men and maids who stole or whose sexuality was under strict control.[53]

But what happened when they appeared in court, the servant man and the goldsmith, the landless laborer and the peasant? Did the court close its eyes when it pleased, to become an instrument for social injustice? It is difficult to provide a simple and unambiguous answer to this question. The answer is particularly complicated in a judicial system like that in Sweden-Finland or Norway, where laymen long had a considerable influence in the courts. Jan Sundin arrives at the following cautious, and not unreasonable, conclusion: ''The courts were often repressive instruments . . . , but this does not mean that they always took the part of the strong when the law clearly spoke another language. Even a seventeenth-century crofter who had stolen a turnip could receive the protection of the local court when he had been too harshly dealt with by a nobleman.''[54] This area in particular requires much more research looking in greater depth at the individual cases. We must try to interpret not only the judgments but also the subtle nuances and cultural symbolism of the social situation.[55]

THE OVERALL WORK OF THE COURTS AND THEIR FUNCTION IN SOCIETY

Taking their inspiration partly from Durkheim, British historians have maintained that judicial development underwent a fundamental change from the Middle Ages to the nineteenth century: from restitutive justice and community law to punitive justice and state law. In the first case, the exercise of justice was close to the community and predicated on its participation. The purpose of punishment was generally to give compensation and redress to the offended party and to reintegrate the offender in the social community. Punitive law and state law, on the other hand, meant increased control on the part of the state. It aimed to protect society, to deter people from crime, and to adjust the punishment to suit clearly defined criminal acts. In parallel to this, the state adopted a new way of using Roman law in the field of civil law. Naturally, the positions were not absolutely clear cut in reality. It cannot be said that one form of judicial practice was succeeded by another at an exact point in time. But, as Lenman and Parker emphasize, a gradual transition is obvious in the early modern period. This was "one of the central (yet most neglected) developments of European history, constituting a revolutionary change in legal methods and in the techniques of social control."[56]

According to Douglas Hay, the courts in England in the eighteenth century increasingly became an instrument for the state (which introduced one new regulation after another to protect trade and property) and also for the ruling classes.[57] The courts thus tended to become a selective tool for class justice. At the same time, the law had become the ideological cement of society to a greater extent than before, maintaining the picture of justice by being just on occasions and not letting itself be too crudely manipulated by the interests of one class.[58]

This development has parallels in Scandinavia, as several historians have shown. In Sweden-Finland and Denmark-Norway, too, the early modern period saw a change in the relation of the court to the growing power of the state and in the focus of the state's activities. I commented on this earlier in this chapter. In Sweden, for instance, the state increased its control over judicial procedure and the courts from the end of the sixteenth century, toughening the penalties for sexual offenses and introducing a number of new rules and statutes affecting commerce and other fields. People who refused to pay their dues or fulfill their communal obligations were brought to court. The courts in a sense assumed the role of a theater of power.[59] As I mentioned earlier, the criminal cases were gradually outnumbered by cases concerning debts and disputes about economic issues.[60] New trades developed in the eighteenth and nineteenth centuries, and conflicts arose about, for instance, forest resources. At the same time, there were wider gaps between propertied and unpropertied, between town and country, between early capitalists and peasants.

In a recently published doctoral dissertation, Maria Ågren analyzes in particular the role of the law and the courts in the so-called proletarianization process of the latter half of the eighteenth century and the early nineteenth century. More and more crofters and smallholders were then transformed into landless wage laborers or vagrants. Ågren shows that the process was in some cases hastened—or completed—by the intervention of the courts against encumbered crofters. It is striking that harsh legislation against debtors, which had been introduced as early as the end of the seventeenth century and confirmed in a law of 1734, could be used with such dire consequences in a later socioeconomic situation. The legislation at the end of the seventeenth century strengthened the position of creditors against the kind of debtors that were relevant then: noblemen and owners of large estates. Toward the end of the eighteenth century, it was completely different groups who were in debt: smallholders and crofters. Ågren's analysis is an interesting example of the way the law affects people not just by occasionally introducing new rules or repealing old ones but also by the way old norms take on a new function in a society undergoing change.[61]

At the same time, the Scandinavian results suggest that the courts always retained their function as a social arena for a large part of the population. Through the jury of peasants in the rural courts and of burghers in the town courts, the administration of justice was clearly anchored among the people, especially in Sweden-Finland and Norway. Until the end of the seventeenth century, judicial procedure allowed men and women accused of a crime to clear themselves of the charge by denying their guilt on oath, with the denial confirmed on oath by twelve respectable men (and sometimes even women). This priority of character witnesses over eyewitnesses and concrete evidence shows that the professionalization of justice still had its limitations in the seventeenth century. The local courts in the countryside were not just the instrument of the state. They also represented the community against the state, and they articulated grievances and demands to superior authorities. Knowledge of the law was widespread, and legal arguments were used not only by those schooled in the law but also by peasants in conflict with each other or with their superiors. The courts, although they represented power and authority, were also forums where individuals and groups could resolve their conflicts through reconciliations and financial compensation. As Erling Sandmo has put it, the courts had a social discursive function.[62]

CONCLUDING REMARKS

Research in the Scandinavian countries has thus come a long way toward establishing the major trends in criminality from the Middle Ages to the present day. What we still lack is a Scandinavian synthesis. The findings that have been obtained in the individual countries indicate similarities within Scandinavia as well as similarities with other European countries such as England. There is thus reason to ask whether we are dealing with a specifically Scandinavian pattern. Or does a closer analysis show that criminality and criminal justice in

Scandinavia fall into several different regional patterns? We need more regional comparisons. Much also remains to be clarified before we arrive at models for female criminality or women as actors in the courts. It is also urgent to conduct deeper analyses of the courts as an arena for normative and social interaction, especially in the transition from early "justice by negotiation" to a more professional state justice. What consequences did this transition have for the popular sense of justice? We may hope that much of this will be studied as part of a newly conceived Nordic research project under the joint leadership of Eva Österberg in Lund (Nordic coordinator), Ditlev Tamm in Copenhagen, Sølvi Sogner in Oslo, and Heikki Ylikangas in Helsinki. Already today, however, we can begin to reflect on the existing results in a Scandinavian and an international perspective.

Ever since the Middle Ages, the Scandinavian countries had codified laws written in the vernacular languages. With the exception of Denmark, national legal uniformity was achieved in the Middle Ages, while in Denmark this came about in the 1680s.[63] In Scandinavia, then, there was no counterpart to the English system of unwritten customary law or the French system, in which national judicial homogeneity was not achieved until the nineteenth century. In Sweden-Finland and Norway in particular, peasant representatives played an important role in local courts for a long time. The social structure and its impact on the institutions of the community, along with the relatively large cultural uniformity, provide a likely explanation for two observations that have been made from the Scandinavian evidence: (1) that thefts in general long remained much less common in Scandinavia than in many regions of Europe with a more "feudal" and commercial character; and (2) that local justice never came to be dominated by the nobility and prosperous industrialists, as historians have claimed was sometimes the case in England.

A third comparative finding is that the control of extramarital sex was efficient in seventeenth- and eighteenth-century Sweden (and perhaps also in other Scandinavian countries). This was probably due to several interacting factors. Few countries saw the state and the church in such willing and efficient cooperation to safeguard family life with the help of the law. Yet peasants and their wives in the communities also had an interest in monitoring the norm. No one wanted to see the district being flooded with illegitimate children; the traditional peasant mentality was anxious to preserve family life and property.

Lawrence Stone has claimed that a study of legal cases mostly gives us an insight into marginal and atypical human destinies. Other scholars, such as E. P. Thompson, argue instead that those who appear in court are often perfectly ordinary people who have become involved in incidents that are typical of a particular historical period.[64] In this case, the analysis of crime and judicial practice reveals the large characteristic societal processes, whether civilization, commercialization, modernization, or proletarianization. The Scandinavian findings appear to a large extent to support Thompson. Yet they do not legitimate any abstract, linear model dividing development into neat phases. Civilization has often proved to be a process with obstacles; the modernization paradigm, in its conventional form, does not work well for explaining criminality; and all crime statistics rise and fall within the bounds of the major phases. Criminality thus illustrates that historians must work with more than one concept of change at the same time. There are tenacious structures and major long-term processes, but there are also swift changes and temporary turbulence.

NOTES

1. See also Birgitta Odén, *Forskarutbildningens förändringar 1890–1975: Historia, statskunskap, kulturgeografi, ekonomisk historia* (Lund, 1991).
2. Bengt Ankarloo, *Trolldomsprocesserna i Sverige* (Lund, 1971).
3. Hans Eyvind Næss, *Trolldomsprosessene i Norge på 1500–1600-talet: En retts- og sosialhistorisk undersøkelse* (Oslo, 1982); *Med bål og brann: Trolldomsprosesser i Norge* (Oslo, 1984).
4. Bengt Ankarloo and Gustav Henningsen, eds., *Häxornas Europa* (Lund, 1987); English translation, *Early Modern European Witchcraft* (Oxford, 1990).
5. Jens Christian V. Johansen, *Da Djævelen var ude . . . : Trolddom i det 17. århundredes Danmark* (Odense, 1991).
6. Johansen, *Da Djævelen var ude,* 159ff.
7. Næss, *Med bål og brann,* 14–20.
8. For a discussion of Elias, see, for example, Eva Österberg, "Violence among Peasants: Comparative Perspectives on Sixteenth- and Seventeenth-century Sweden," in *Europe and Scandinavia: Aspects of the Process of Integration in the 17th Century,* ed. Göran Rystad (Lund, 1983); also in a slightly extended version in Österberg, *Mentalities and Other Realities: Essays in Medieval and Early Modern Scandinavian History* (Lund, 1991); Österberg, "Kontroll och kriminalitet i Sverige från medeltid till nutid: Tendenser och tolkningar," *Scandia* 57:1 (1991): 65–87, also forthcoming in a version in English: "Criminality, Social Control, and the Early Modern State: Evidence and Interpretations in Scandinavian Historiography," *Social Science History* (1992). Elias is also discussed by Johan Söderberg, "En fråga om civilisering: Brottmål och tvister i svenska häradsrätter 1540–1660," *Historisk Tjidskrift* (1990): 2; and by Jan Sundin, *För Gud, Staten och Folket: Brott och rättskipning i Sverige 1600–1840* (Lund, 1992), 418-21, 456–59. Foucault is critically discussed by Jonas Liljequist, *Brott, Synd och Straff: Tidelagsbrottet i Sverige under 1600–och 1700-talet* (Umeå, 1992).
9. See also Eva Österberg, "Gräset och historien," in *Kulturrådet* (1992): 1–2, *Den svenska historien m m.*
10. See, for example, J.A. Sharpe, "The History of Crime in Late Medieval and Early Modern England: A Review of the Field," *Social History* 7 (1982): 188; idem, *Crime in Early Modern England 1550–1750* (London, 1984), 4.
11. See, for example, Eva Österberg and Dag Lindström, *Crime and Social Control in Medieval and Early Modern Swedish Towns* (Uppsala, 1988), 71; Österberg, "Kontroll och kriminalitet i Sverige," 67.
12. Erling Sandmo, *Tingets tenkemåter: Kriminalitet og rettssaker i Rendalen, 1763–97* (Oslo, 1992), 12–15.
13. Knut Sveri, "Brottslighetens volym och struktur," in *Samhällsförändringar och brottslighet,* ed. Åke Daun et al. (Stockholm, 1974).

14. Heikki Ylikangas, "Major Fluctuations in Crimes of Violence in Finland: A Historical Analysis," *Scandinavian Journal of History* (1976); *Knivjunkrarna: Våldskriminalitet i Sydösterbotten 1790–1825* (Borgå, 1985).

15. For a discussion of the material see, for example, Österberg and Lindström, *Crime and Social Control,* 37–38, 68–77; Sundin, *För Gud, Staten och Folket,* 15–22.

16. Österberg, "Kontroll och kriminalitet i Sverige." Findings for the Middle Ages are based on Österberg and Lindström, *Crime and Social Control;* see also Österberg, "Social Arena or Theatre of Power? The Courts, Crime and the Early Modern State in Sweden," in *Theatres of Power: Social Control and Criminality in Historical Perspective,* ed. Heikki Pihlajamäki (Helsinki, 1992), 8–24.

17. See Österberg, "Kontroll och kriminalitet i Sverige," and Söderberg, "En fråga om civilisering." I date the great reduction in violence to the period 1650–1750, whereas Söderberg argues for the possibility that violence began to decline as early as the sixteenth century.

18. Eva Österberg, "Brott och straff i svenska småstäder under medeltid och vasatid: Svensk kriminalitet i europeiskt perspektiv," in *Över gränser: Festskrift till Birgitta Odén* (Lund, 1987), 473–504; Österberg and Lindström, *Crime and Social Control;* Dag Lindström, "Våld, förtal och förlikningar i Stockholm 1475–1625," *Rättshistoriska studier* 14 (Lund, 1988).

19. Birgitta Odén, "Relationer mellan generationerna: Rättsläget 1300–1900," in *Maktpolitik och husfrid: Studier i internationell och svensk historia tillägnade Göran Rystad* (Lund, 1991).

20. See Birgit Petersson, *Den farliga underklassen: Studier i fattigdom och brottslighet i 1800-talets Sverige* (Umeå, 1983).

21. Sveri, "Brottslighetens volym och struktur."

22. Österberg, "Kontroll och kriminalitet i Sverige," 75–76.

23. For a critical discussion of the modernization paradigm and the relation between criminality and modernization, see Eva Österberg, "Crime and Modernization: The Swedish Evidence," paper presented at the Sixteenth Annual Meeting of the Social Science History Association, 1991, New Orleans. For the concept of modernization, see also L. Thornstam, B. Odén, and A. Svanberg, *Äldre i samhället förr, nu och i framtiden,* part 1, *Teorier och forskningsansatser* (Lund, 1982).

24. Österberg, "Kontroll och kriminalitet i Sverige."

25. On sexual crimes, see also Eva Österberg, "Den gamla goda tiden: Bilder och motbilder i ett modernt forskningsläge om det äldre agrarsamhället," *Scandia* 48:1 (1982): 31–60; an English version, "The Good Old Times: Contrasting Pictures of Swedish Peasant Society," can be found in my *Mentalities and Other Realities: Essays in Medieval and Early Modern Scandinavian History* (Lund, 1991), 61–88.

26. Österberg, "Kontroll och kriminalitet i Sverige"; see also "Bönder och centralmakt i det tidigmoderna Sverige: Konflikt—kompromiss—politisk kultur," *Scandia* 55: 1 (1989): 73–95, or the English version, "Local Political Culture versus the State: Patterns of Interaction in Pre-industrial Sweden," in my *Mentalities and Other Realities: Essays in Medieval and Early Modern Scandinavian History* (Lund, 1991), 176–91; Maria Ågren, "Att lösa ekonomiska tvister—Domstolarnas främsta sysselsättning på 1700-talet?" *Historisk Tidskrift* 67:1 (1988): 481–511; Söderberg, "En fråga om civilisering"; Marja Taussi Sjöberg, "Tinget som social arena," in *Historia nu—18 Umeåforskare om det förflutna* (Umeå, 1988).

27. Sundin, *För Gud, Staten och Folket* (Lund, 1992), 109ff., 219, 228–51, 285–98, 413–21, 439–47, 456–59.

28. Österberg, "Kontroll och kriminalitet i Sverige"; "Bönder och centralmakt i det tidigmoderna Sverige"; Sundin, *För Gud, Staten och Folket;* Söderberg, "En fråga om civilisering"; Liljequist, *Brott, Synd och Straff;* see also Kenneth Johansson, "Brott och straff i Albo härad ca 1600–1850," (1993) dissertation, Lund University, Department of History.

29. See, for example, Österberg, "Kontroll och kriminalitet i Sverige," 80; Sundin, *För Gud, Staten och Folket,* 458ff.

30. See, for example, Österberg and Lindström, *Crime and Social Control,* 55.

31. Söderberg, "En fråga om civilisering"; Sundin, *För Gud, Staten och Folket,* 458.

32. See, for example, Österberg, "Violence among Peasants," and "Brott och straff i svenska småstäder"; Sundin, *För Gud, Staten och Folket.*

33. Österberg and Lindström, *Crime and Social Control,* 55.

34. Jørn Sandnes, *Kniven, ølet og æren* (Oslo, 1990), 48ff., 117.

35. Sandmo, *Tingets tenkemåter,* 69, 85, 92, 125.

36. Sandnes, *Kniven, ølet og æren,* 60ff., 80ff.

37. Sandmo, *Tingets tenkemåter,* 43–53.

38. This was pointed out, for example, by Sølvi Sogner in an oral comment on the theme of criminality and control at the Nordic Historians' Meeting in Umeå in 1991. The idea has also been developed in Österberg, "Crime and Modernization."

39. Österberg and Lindström, *Crime and Social Control,* 115.

40. See Hanns von Hofer, *Brott och straff i Sverige: Historisk kriminalstatistik 1750–1984: Diagram, tabeller och kommentarer* (Stockholm, 1984), 1:1, 2, 2:3, 3:4, 5:5; also Österberg, "Crime and Modernization."

41. Sundin, *För Gud, Staten och Folket,* 466.

42. Österberg and Lindström, *Crime and Social Control,* 130.

43. Sundin, *För Gud, Staten och Folket,* 318ff. This topic is the subject of Marie Lindstedt's doctoral dissertation, currently in progress at the Department of History, Lund University.

44. Sundin, *För Gud, Staten och Folket,* 135–36.

45. Næss, *Med bål og brann,* 70.

46. Hilde Sandvik, "Kvinners rettslige handleevne: Tingbøker som kilde til forholdet mellom kjønnene," *Historisk Tjidskrift* 70:2 (1991): 282–92.

47. Sundin, *För Gud, Staten och Folket,* 103ff.

48. For a discussion of this hypothesis see, for example, Eva Österberg, "Folklig mentalitet och statlig makt: Perspektiv på 1500- och 1600-talens Sverige," *Scandia* 58: 1 (1992): 93.

49. Sundin, *För Gud, Staten och Folket,* 467.

50. Liljequist, *Brott, Synd och Straff,* 1–23.

51. Ibid., 159–71.

52. Österberg, "Violence among Peasants"; Österberg and Lindström, *Crime and Social Control,* 50, 99.

53. Sundin, *För Gud, Staten och Folket,* 98–101, 187.

54. Ibid., 471.

55. For a fruitful attempt at this kind of profound qualitative analysis, see Kenneth Johansson, "Herrar och bönder: Om jurisdiktionen i några småländska friherrskap på 1600-talet," *Scandia* 56:2 (1990): 161–91.

56. See, for example, B. Lenman and G. Parker, "The State, the Community and the Criminal Law in Early Modern Europe," in *Crime and the Law: The Social History of Crime in Western Europe,* ed. V.A.C. Gatrell, B. Lenman, and G. Parker (London, 1980), 11–48, quotation at p. 23.

57. Douglas Hay, "Property, Authority, and the Criminal Law," in *Albion's Fatal Tree: Crime and Society in Eighteenth-Century England,* ed. Douglas Hay et al. (London, 1975), 17–63.

58. E.P. Thompson, *Whigs and Hunters: The Origin of the Black Act* (London, 1975), 263.

59. See, for example, Eva Österberg, "Social Arena or Theatre of Power?"; Marja Taussi Sjöberg, "Civil and Criminal Cases in Seventeenth Century Judicial Proceedings in Sweden," in *Theatres of Power: Social Control and Criminality in Historical Perspective,* ed. Heikki Pihlajamäki (Helsinki, 1992), 25–40; Sundin, *För Gud, Staten och Folket,* 1ff., 121–36.

60. Ågren, "Att lösa ekonomiska tvister"; Österberg, "Bönder och centralmakt"; Sandmo, *Tingets tenkemåter;* Sundin, *För Gud, Staten och Folket,* 1ff., 121–36.

61. Maria Ågren, *Jord och gäld: Social skiktning och rättslig konflikt i södra Dalarna ca 1650–1850* (Uppsala, 1992).

62. Sandmo, *Tingets tenkemåter,* 32; cf. Österberg, "Kontroll och kriminalitet"; Sundin, *För Gud, Staten och Folket;* and Johansson, "Brott och straff i Albo härad."

63. See, for example, Ditlev Tamm, *Lærebog i dansk retshistorie* (Copenhagen, 1989).

64. Lawrence Stone, "The Revival of Narrative," *Past and Present* 85 (1979): 22; Thompson, *Whigs and Hunters,* 194.

4

Albion's Felonious Attractions: Reflections upon the History of Crime in England

Clive Emsley

It may be possible to conceive of a society without crime; it is probably impossible to find such a society in history. Yet it is only in the last two decades that academic social historians—indeed, any academic historians—have seriously considered crime as an area worthy of study.[1] The move among historians of English social history[2] into the area of crime and criminal justice was signaled by a conference of the Labour History Society in 1972.[3] Several issues which were given a first public airing there were presented in detail three years later in two significant, pioneering volumes: *Albion's Fatal Tree* and *Whigs and Hunters*.[4] The essays in the former, especially Douglas Hay's challenging analysis of the role of the law in maintaining the Hanoverian elite, set the agenda for much subsequent research.

The new interest in crime and criminality was, perhaps, a natural extension from the study of riots and rioters generated by the work of historians such as George Rudé a decade earlier. If rioters were not the dregs of society acting out of animalistic motives and prompted by drink and the promise of loot, then perhaps criminals were also ordinary people rather than a distinct, identifiable group outside society—"the criminal class"—as much of the popular literature, and indeed as positivist criminology, tended to portray them.[5] It was also expected that the evidence of the criminal records would give social historians new angles for understanding the lives and attitudes of the lower orders—the unemployed, the indigent, and, above all, the working classes.

CRIME RATES AND OFFENDERS

While it is comforting to think of crime as an objective concept existing ''out there,'' it takes very little thought to see that this will not do. Most of the new generation of historians of crime have accepted the view that crime can only be defined by the law, and as such it is an action which can be suppressed by a court or an accredited agent of law enforcement and can be punished. A crime is thus specific to a particular time and place. However, within this definition some have sought to develop the notion of social crime; that is, offenses which, while subject to legal sanction, can nevertheless receive a wide measure of legitimation within a specific community.[6] Poaching, smuggling, and wrecking are obvious examples, but they have only comprised a tiny percentage of the crimes brought before the courts. Social crime also poses other problems of definition. Some of these ''social'' offenders, while not mad, were certainly bad and dangerous to know; and some of the large gangs involved in poaching and smuggling were as much involved in capitalist enterprise as persons involved with new factories during the Industrial Revolution.[7] But if the concept is ultimately nebulous, social crime does serve to highlight different attitudes toward the law and certain offenses and the continuing opportunity for the jurist's view of social order to clash with that of local communities.

Closely linked with the notion of social crime, and the subject of much early research, was the appropriation of goods from the workplace. It was no coincidence that much of the early work was focused on periods like the eighteenth century, when there were significant moves toward a capitalist, industrial economy. Stated baldly, the initial hypothesis was that the increasing development of a capitalist economy and the shift to wage labor meant that employers began using the law to end ''usages of the trade'': thus when carpenters took their ''chips,'' tailors their ''cabbage,'' or weavers their ''thrums,'' they were increasingly likely to find themselves prosecuted for theft. The hypothesis also appeared to have applicability in the countryside, where harvesters and their wives gleaned in the fields and where other poor country folk took wood and nuts from what had been common land.

Thus the law of theft in particular, it was asserted, became central to developing class relationships. The formulation appears persuasive and has been forcefully restated by Peter Linebaugh in *The London Hanged,* where the central thesis is ''first, that the forms of exploitation pertaining to capitalist relations caused or modified the forms of criminal activity, and, second, that the converse was true, namely that the forms of crime caused major changes in capitalism. In short, people became so poor that they stole to live, and their misappropriating led to manifold innovations in civil society.''[8] But much of the research between the publication of *Albion's Fatal Tree* and *The London Hanged* has suggested that the situation was far more complex. First, the number of these prosecutions was never particularly great. It is also probable that the workers themselves preferred a regular wage to reliance on the traditional usages. Finally, to date, the evidence does not appear to show any overall increase in the prosecution of employees for this kind of embezzlement during the shift to, and consolidation of, the new economy.

David Philips has demonstrated a marked increase in prosecutions for industrial theft in the Black Country from 1836 to 1860. This, he suggests, was the result of increasing numbers of coal and iron masters, determined to stamp out traditional rights and perks, who gradually became the dominant group on the county bench. In addition, the Criminal Justice Act of 1855 made prosecutions easier, cheaper, and quicker.[9] But Philips is concentrating on only one, specific industrial area. John Styles has questioned the extent to which the eighteenth century saw any deliberate criminalization of customary work practices backed up by better policing of the trades and tougher sentences of offenders;[10] while Peter King has shown that farmers found it impossible always to mobilize the law to their advantage against gleaners and that, in spite of the apparent legal attack on gleaning in the late eighteenth century, from 1750 to 1850 the poor's level of access to the gleaning fields seems to have remained constant.[11]

Historians keen to explore links between crime and the growth of capitalism might do better to start with G. R. Rubin's and David Sugarman's suggestions on how to set about a new history of law and material society using the civil law to explore the development of absolute private property and of credit and contract.[12] Alternatively, they can follow the example of George Robb and focus on white-collar crime. The scale of financial fraud in Victorian and Edwardian Britain was enormous. Perhaps as many as one-sixth of company promotions in the Victorian period were fraudulent, while men like Harry Lawson, Ernest Hooley, Whitaker Wright, and Horatio Bottomley gleefully collected millions of pounds from hundreds of thousands of investors sublimely ignorant of stocks, shares, and the mysteries of the financial markets. The evidence of such fraud is less common in police and court records than in reports to shareholders, bankruptcy reports, and in the evidence collected by parliamentary inquiries into financial crises and company law. In some instances, directors and clerks caught with their fingers in the till were not prosecuted for fear that such a proceeding would be bad publicity and undermine confidence in a business.[13]

At least since Victorian times, students of crime have been aware of the "dark figure"—that is, the number of offenses never reported—which makes it impossible to know actual levels of crime. For the early modern period and well into the nineteenth century, historians have counted assize and quarter sessions indictment membranes in an attempt to get some idea of the problem of scale, the kinds of crime committed, and whether or not crime might be said to have been rising or falling. National statistics, collected by the government, exist from 1805 but are not especially detailed until after 1856, when the County and Borough Police Act required information on crimes reported to the police as well as on arrests and prosecutions in the different courts. The work on the statistics has suggested two periods of rising prosecutions (possibly indicative of rising crime) from about 1560 to 1630 and from about 1780 to 1850.[14] Particularly interesting is the way that both of these periods also witnessed, first, demographic growth contributing to serious problems for the poorer sections of society and, second, fears for the social order among many of the better off. More localized fluctuations in the statistics have suggested some link between property crime and both war and the trade cycle, at least in the eighteenth and nineteenth centuries. Eighteenth-century historians have noted an increase in indictments for theft in times of dearth and especially in the immediate aftermath of wars. The marked upswing in prosecutions, and allegedly also in crime, at the beginning of the nineteenth century began as the Napoleonic wars drew toward their conclusion; while the peak in the statistics for property crime in the nineteenth century coincided with the depression of 1842, possibly the worst year for unemployment in the century.[15] The problem, of course, is to explain whether the statistics represent an actual increase in crime or greater concerns about it prompting a greater inclination to prosecute on the part of those private individuals who were the victims of, especially, property theft. The twentieth-century statistics, by which time the decision to prosecute was largely in the hands of the police, have not yet been subjected to any serious historical analysis; however, those for the periods immediately following the First and Second World Wars do not appear to show any similar upswing.

The statistical evidence of those brought before the courts, at least since the eighteenth century, reveals that most offenders were young males accused of property crime. The number of female offenders appears to have been largest in cities and towns, where single women were isolated from the communities of their birth and prey to an uncertain job market. A recent study of criminal cases at the Old Bailey between 1687 and 1912, however, suggests a significant decline in the prosecution of women on charges of felony beginning in the eighteenth century and argues that this decline was less the result of women being less criminous and more the result of a shift to more private forms of social control.[16] Turning back to offenders both male and female, periods of dearth often saw an increase in the number of older offenders, suggesting that desperation pushed some breadwinners to theft; though in the 1840s it appears that the same problem encouraged older men to find work, and a steady wage, in the ranks of the new police.[17] Violent crime was by no means as common as theft, and theft rarely involved violence; though this was not how people perceived the problem of crime during the nineteenth century: When Dickens portrayed the professional thief Bill Sikes as a heartless killer, he both drew on, and fed, the fears of his readers. There has been heated debate about the level of both violence and homicide in the early modern period, whether a decline in the latter is a measure of a decline in the former, and whether society was generally becoming less brutalized and violent. The comfortable notion that crime within a feudal society was characterized by violence, and that the shift to a capitalist society witnessed a corresponding shift to property-based crime, is not borne out by the evidence. Homicide does seem to have declined steadily from the beginning of the nineteenth century and was often, perhaps increasingly, a crime committed within the family or among acquaintances. But arguments about the scale of violence within English society during different periods, and why, if at all, it declined, are far from resolved.[18]

Statistical work remains an important starting point for any local study, but, in terms of analysis, it has probably been taken about as far as it can go, particularly with V. A. C. Gatrell's exhaustive study of the nineteenth-century criminal statistics;[19] and there are problems. Most of the work which has been done to date has concentrated on indicted crime—that is, the more serious kinds of offense, notably felonies. A felony was a crime committed with the deliberate, evil intent to harm another. Such offenses, following indictment, were tried before a jury either at quarter sessions presided over by county or borough magistrates, or at assizes presided over by royal judges. However, more and more offenders, at least from the late seventeenth century, were tried summarily by magistrates sitting in petty sessions without juries. Until these sessions were given greater formality in the mid-nineteenth century, the proceedings could take place in a magistrate's parlor or in a tavern, and the records of the proceedings were rarely registered in the formal quarter sessions books.

Robert Shoemaker has suggested that in London and Middlesex at the end of the seventeenth and beginning of the eighteenth centuries, there were perhaps nine times as many defendants prosecuted for misdemeanors as felonies. The word *misdemeanor* covered a wide variety of offenses, ranging from petty property crime (fraud, petty theft, trespass) to offenses against the peace (assault, defamation, riot), against the poor law, and against morality. There are few indictment membranes to count in these instances; some misdemeanors were settled by the mediation of a justice, some by summary conviction, some by use of a recognizance ("perhaps the most popular legal procedure in urban Middlesex during this period"), and a very small percentage by indictment at quarter sessions. But the overall levels of misdemeanor prosecutions, particularly those concerning victimless crimes like prostitution or adultery, are less easy, and often impossible, to relate to economic factors in the way that felonies have been linked with both the trade cycle and the disruption of war. Active justices, zealous moral reformers like the Societies for the Reformation of Manners, and informers were much more significant for the level of misdemeanor than felony prosecutions; and much depended on the particular community and the moral attitudes of its leaders at particular moments. Nevertheless, Shoemaker's work raises problems about the validity of counting indictment membranes from quarter sessions and assizes to estimate felony patterns since he shows that some justices were prepared to settle felonies informally and since he is forced to conclude that "cases of petty theft were increasingly prosecuted by commitment to houses of correction [by justices acting summarily] in lieu of prosecution by recognizance or indictment."[20] The evidence of what went on in the justice's parlor and in petty sessions during the seventeenth and eighteenth centuries is scattered and fragmentary, yet further, detailed analysis is now essential.

While Shoemaker's challenge is indirect about the validity of much statistical work on felony crime, others have been more specific; they emphasize the weaknesses of crime figures, however constructed. Can we, for example, be sure that people reported crime and prosecuted it in the same way year after year? Might not dearth have encouraged some victims to be more generous to offenders? Or might dearth also have encouraged victims, and magistrates, to lash out with a prosecution to deter other potential offenders? Why were some crimes reported and prosecuted and not others? How can the historian make allowance for changes in the law leading to changes in the categorization of crime? Recent research has drawn attention to the problem of malicious prosecutions during the eighteenth and nineteenth centuries.[21] These were probably a minority, but again, what allowance should be made for these? Indeed, how can allowance be made in assessing statistical patterns? What percentage of the lost property recorded by the police was actually stolen and listed as "lost" for police purposes? When the crime statistics are put alongside some of the moral panics wherein an episode, person, or group of persons becomes defined as a threat to the values and interests of society,[22] then the criticisms of the skeptics gain weight. The "garotting" scares of the mid-ninteenth century are the obvious, or at least the best researched example. While the statistics of street robbery show little marked change, the press and parliament temporarily became obsessed with the menace, and ferocious legislation was enacted specifically to punish the perpetrators and to deter others.[23] Work on the less high-profile offenses of bookmaking and dangerous driving also suggest the use of bogeyman figures like the garotter to justify the content of new laws and the reasons for passing them.[24] Of course, it may be inevitable that attempts to establish thresholds of criminal intent result in the demonizing of archetypes, but there is clearly scope for more detailed and more varied analyses of how penal and police reformers used incidents to boost their campaigns and how, as well as reporting crime, newspapers manufactured news to boost their sales.[25]

Garotters were perceived to be members of the "dangerous" or "criminal classes," labels which became popular in Victorian Britain. Such labels were, and indeed remain, convenient for categorizing offenders as persons outside society and making war upon it; the idea of a "war" against crime itself goes back at least to the late eighteenth century. Yet if such terms are little more than a century or two old, the work of Paul Slack and A. L. Beier shows that the concepts were embryonic in the early modern perceptions of the vagrant, when even to be a vagrant was to commit an offense.[26] However, vagrants, almost by definition, can rarely have made much from the thefts they were accused of committing, and they remained very different from what was probably a relatively small number of individuals who did make the bulk of their livelihood from criminal activities and who appear to have been predominantly city dwellers.

Vagrants were not organized; some urban offenders, and particularly receivers, were. One or two notorious individuals have been studied, notably Jonathan Wild and Ikey Solomons (supposedly the original for Dickens's Fagin);[27] but while the popular historians have commonly drawn on Mayhew's and similar commentators' references to the "Swell Mob," we still lack detailed investigations into the history of organized crime. Philip Jenkins and Gary W. Porter have published a short pointer as to what might be done with their examination of vice rings in mid–twentieth-century London;[28] but it would also be valuable to look beyond the Messina brothers and the Kray brothers, whose notoriety seems now to be acquiring a mantle of romanticism, and to focus on the more workaday professional offender. In June 1992, for example, as this chapter went through yet another draft, several men were convicted in London for a sophisticated operation involving the theft, respraying, renumbering (engine block as well as registration), and resale of Peugeot 205 cars. If mass production and modern garage facilities have offered opportunities for the consumer, how far have they also offered opportunities to the professional offender? Many professional criminals—that is, individuals who sought to make the bulk of their living from criminal activity—were, by their nature, probably identifiable as recidivists, and the recidivist greatly concerned Victorian prison reformers. But the scale of recidivism and who the recidivists were—issues which might be investigated by a study of both court and jail records—remain unexplored.

Organized crime, like most other crime, seems to have been male dominated. The Victorian criminal class was perceived as essentially male and adult. Several useful essays have described a growing awareness of juvenile offenders from the late eighteenth century. These offenders were not labeled as part of the criminal class, and while legislation scarcely recognized them as a distinct type, there was an increasing desire to protect any such from immoral parents and from exposure to recidivists in the prisons. Industrial schools and reformatories were established to educate juvenile offenders into the accepted norms of behavior and their place in the social hierarchy. But these were insufficient in numbers and often, it seems, ignored by magistrates when passing sentence. Toward the end of the Victorian period, voluntary youth workers sought to prevent deliquency by establishing clubs and organizations to socialize the vulnerable and substitute for the bad parent and bad environment.[29]

The female equivalent of the criminal was the prostitute. Whatever their offense, policemen commonly labeled female offenders as prostitutes. Moreover, the Contagious Diseases Acts of the 1860s and the periodic instructions to the police to sweep prostitution from the streets brought large numbers of ordinary, young, working-class women under an oppressive and sometimes arbitrary police scrutiny.[30] Such examples reveal the way in which the law and perceptions of criminality interacted with and reinforced cultural norms like the subordinate position of women. While the English legal system liked to boast that all were equal before it, a study of the courts in nineteenth-century Kent suggests that such equality was tempered by the extent to which the accused conformed to cultural and gender stereotypes. In particular, women who inflicted physical violence, whatever the provocation, were looked at askance for behaving in a manner alien to the accepted perception of feminity, while alleged rape victims were suspect for being, at least temporarily, outside male supervision and for publicly declaring their loss of sexual innocence.[31] The extent to which the role of gender shaped Victorian attitudes and responses to criminality is a theme which has been perceptively and thoroughly explored by Lucia Zedner;[32] while several authors have addressed the issue of domestic violence, charting the shifts in the general acceptance of a man's right to discipline his wife and how this was dealt with by communities, courts, and the law.[33] As in many other areas of social history, gender issues are just beginning to be opened up, and they probably constitute one of the most fruitful areas for future research.

POLICE, COURTS, AND PENAL POLICY

The history of the police has come under scrutiny as part and parcel of the study of the history of crime and criminal justice. Until the mid-1970s, English police history tended to be the preserve of retired policemen or of civil servants formerly linked with the police. They shared the perceptions voiced by the nineteenth-century police reformers that the system of parish constables had been getting progressively worse since the portrayal of Dogberry, Verges, and Elbow by that eminent Elizabethan social commentator William Shakespeare. They argued, at least by implication, that the police system of England and Wales, internationally recognized as second to none, had sprung almost fully formed from the far-sighted ideas of Henry and Sir John Fielding in Bow Street, later to be developed by the stipendiary magistrate Patrick Colquhoun and the Benthamite Edwin Chadwick. These ideas were recognized by similarly far-sighted politicians, like Sir Robert Peel, as the way to check the real increase in crime and mob violence, and Peel chose equally far-sighted administrators to organize the Metropolitan Police when it was established in London in 1829. The success of the Metropolitan Police model was rapidly perceived by honest, law-abiding citizens and was consequently adopted elsewhere across the country, except where a few myopic or foolish magistrates had to be pushed into action by the obligatory requirements of the County and Borough Police Act in 1856.[34]

The first serious challenge to this orthodoxy came with the seminal essays of Robert Storch, who argued that a crucial element behind the creation of the new police was a desire to control the new working class and to impose a new level of discipline. At the same time, Storch demonstrated a depth and longevity of working-class hostility to the "blue locusts" which others had missed or ignored.[35] The danger of this revisionism is that it can become as tautological as the Whig view inasmuch as the police, rather than being the successful solution to society's problems of rising crime and mob violence, become instead the successful solution to the bourgeoisie's need for a compliant work force. More recent studies have shown that policing before the police was not as inadequate and ineffectual as the reformers and the Whig histories argued. The Tudor and early Stuart constable studied by Joan Kent was not simply Shakespeare's Dogberry and was probably much more in sympathy with his community's perceptions of justice and order than the abstract notions of the jurist.[36] Serious, detailed research on the constables and the watchmen of late Stuart and Hanoverian England is still lacking, though some of the evidence deployed in more general studies is suggestive.[37]

The Irish experience of coping with insurrection and major disorder, which led to the creation of the Peace Preservation Force in the second decade of the nineteenth century, fed significantly into the English police reforms and especially the creation of the Metropolitan Police. The latter force was by no means the natural outcome of the moves begun by the Fieldings and the proposals of Colquhoun.[38] The evidence collected by the Royal Commission on the Rural Constabulary between 1836 and 1839 was only used to the extent that it suited the case which Chadwick argued in the Commission's Report. It is now being examined critically by David Philips and Robert Storch; the implication of their work so far is that a whole variety of expedients and different law-enforcement models were being experimented with by rural elites before the Royal Commission began its deliberations, and that there was both sense and rationality behind the alternatives to the adoption of the Metropolitan Police model.[39]

The early period of professional, bureaucratic policing has now been worked over thoroughly.[40] However, with the exception of their role in industrial disorders,[41] the history of the police in the twentieth century awaits a thorough critical investigation. A recent wide-ranging text, which attempts to look at the policeman as a worker as well as surveying the development of the police as an institution, has described a history very different from the traditional and comfortable Whig view. Moreover, it argues that in the twentieth century, changes in Home Office attitudes, linked with the impact of total war and the fear of mass industrial protest and of political subversion, gradually brought centralization to the English police and contributed to an increasing remoteness from the public.[42]

Studies of the police would constitute part of what Peter Linebaugh condemns as a growing "conceptual timidity" in the history of crime as it has been "increasingly transformed into the history of administration or 'the machinery of justice.' "[43] While there has been much work on different aspects of the administration of justice, there remain some significant gaps. Linebaugh's most ferocious academic critic, John Langbein, has described in detail the way that the rules of trial and the adversarial system developed in the courts during the eighteenth century; and John Beattie has traced the increasing presence of defense counsel at the Old Bailey until, by the 1830s, it was confidently being argued by law reformers that the system should be regularized since counsel representing both the defense and the prosecution would ensure a more effective, impartial form of justice rather than the old, discretionary system. Others have located the jury socially, stressed its significance, and described the interplay between judge, jurors, victim/prosecutor, and witnesses in eighteenth-century criminal courts, where the number of barristers was increasing but still remained relatively few, especially for the defense.[44] Yet little has been done on assessing the moment at which lawyers became involved in the judicial process. In what amounts almost to an aside in his massive study of crime and the courts in the eighteenth century, John Beattie notes that Lancashire magistrates were concerned at the very beginning of the nineteenth century about the increasing appearance of lawyers advising suspects during magistrates' preliminary examinations "not only . . . at the public places appointed for doing the business, but even at the dwelling house of the magistrates."[45]

Similarly, little has been done on the nineteenth century as a whole, when professional lawyers succeeded in getting a strong grip on the assize courts and, to a slightly lesser extent, on the courts of quarter sessions. The police increasingly took over prosecutions in a process recognized by historians but scarcely analyzed;[46] and new legislation gave a different shape to the trial as jurors became the audience for an adversarial contest between professional lawyers. From 1836, all those accused of felonies were allowed to have a defense counsel trained in the law, and from 1898 a defendant could be a competent witness in his or her own defense. However, while professionals and trained experts were taking over in the courts of assize and quarter sessions, more and more defendants were appearing before petty sessions, sometimes known also as police courts; and while there was a growth in the number of stipendiary magistrates recruited from men with a legal training, the overwhelming majority of the magistracy remained lay. Jennifer Davis's study of the London police courts illuminates the attitudes and behavior of the metropolitan stipendiaries and their aspirations to providing justice for the poor person.[47] But the interaction between stipendiaries and lay magistrates in the provinces, their developing attitudes to the police, to offenders, and to punishments remains largely unexplored.

The Whig interpretation of changes in punishment, notably the reduction of capital statutes and the development of the penitentiary system, has also been challenged. The Whig view, like the late eighteenth- and early nineteenth-century reformers, stressed the "Bloody Code" of the Hanoverians, with its steady increase in capital statutes imposing the death penalty for relatively minor thefts; prison, in contrast, was seen as humane and civilized, combining reformation with punishment. However, in *The Hanging Tree* V.A.C. Gatrell has presented a powerful challenge to the idea that Sir Robert Peel's reorganization of the criminal law during the 1820s had much to do with humanitarianism. The problem, according to Gatrell, was that from the last two decades of the eighteenth century, and then particularly after the end of the Napoleonic wars, there was an increasing number of successful prosecutions under capital statutes. The government was faced with a dilemma: It could continue executing the usual percentages of convicted felons and face an ever-increasing number of executions, something which might not be tolerated by the populace; or it could keep increasing the number of pardons, something which might make the law resemble even more of a lottery. None of this is to deny the possibility of new sensibilities, and the fervor and dedication of penal reformers. But it makes it possible to see Peel's reforms as more in keeping with his ideas of conservatism;

he was reforming the penal law to ensure the fundamental preservation of the system.[48]

Much of the recent work on prisons (as well as police) owes a debt to the stimulating arguments of Michel Foucault and his perception of new forms of knowledge, which, from the eighteenth century, embodied a new, enclosing, and restricting orientation to the body.[49] But the frontal assault on the traditional view of changes in punishment in England came from Michael Ignatieff's analysis of the motivations of great prison reformers and their links with the new factory entrepreneurs. Ignatieff's work implied that there was precious little which could be called humane and civilized about the model penitentiary, Pentonville, which opened in 1842.[50] But with the prisons too, revisionism has been qualified; the link between prison and factory and the demands for a disciplined work force might seem natural and logical, yet in Lancashire, a center of the new industry and capitalism, the ratepayers showed little inclination to provide the money necessary for any new penitentiary, and across the country as a whole the prison reformers never presented a unified group with a unified set of aims.[51]

In a series of important essays, Randall McGowan has teased out the philosophy which underpinned the movement for penal reform. Humanitarianism is a great deal more complex in McGowan's reading than in the traditional Whig view. He stresses the significance of changing images of God, from the sixteenth- and seventeenth-century God of Wrath to the God of Love of the eighteenth century, who possessed much milder feelings toward His creation and who was much keener to reform than to damn and punish. McGowan suggests that the penal reformers were seeking to present a more pleasing image of the criminal justice system. They had aspirations toward creating a society based on "sympathy"—"a connection with other people based on feeling and concern"—and within which social harmony and understanding were supreme. The new prison, in this analysis, was not an end in itself; it was "a special application of the benevolent influences felt to be at work in society" and which would restore the hardened offender to being an individual in tune with the more humane society.[52]

Victorian prison administration swung between a focus on the reform of the offender to make him, and less commonly her, a useful member of society, and a focus on punishment and retribution. Progressively the prison system was centralized culminating in the legislation of 1877 which brought all local prisons under central direction and the martinet supervision of Sir Edmund Du Cane. The developments of the second half of the nineteenth century have been chronicled exhaustively, but rather differently, in two massive volumes. Seán McConville focuses significantly on the personalities of those involved in prison administration—initially the Earl of Carnarvon, who provided the blueprint for penal reform locally, by his work as a county magistrate in Hampshire, and nationally, as chairman of a House of Lords Committee in the early 1860s, and then Du Cane.[53] But he also stresses the importance of the expansion of the Victorian bureaucracy and the generational difference between Du Cane and young Home Office clerks of the closing decades of the century; many of these disliked Du Cane's autocratic manner and were, at the same time, resented by Du Cane because of their increasing power and influence. The fifth volume of Sir Leon Radzinowicz's monumental *History of English Criminal Law and Its Administration,* co-authored with Roger Hood, has rather less focus on individuals and administrative rivalries, and includes the big convict prisons as well as local prisons in its survey of penal policies and the attitudes that underpinned them from the mid-nineteenth century until the First World War.[54] This volume is critical of the revisionists and stresses that, as the Victorian period progressed, there were increasing moves away from strict incarceration and toward the emergence of a liberal, optimistic approach to penal policy which characterized the years between the two world wars. In many ways Radzinowicz and Hood may be seen as reshaping the Whig tradition, portraying a legal system becoming more humane and civilized. Further, as Martin J. Wiener has noted, "the focus remains on pragmatic grapplings with particular problems that are evaluated by their approach to modern solutions."[55] Much of the difficulty is, of course, that the extent to which punishment can be considered more humane is relative. Gentlemen who allowed their sons to be thrashed at Eton, Harrow, or Rugby can have had little compunction about legislating for the flogging of a garotter in Pentonville; while electric shock treatment to galvanize a malingering convict must have seemed a very progressive use of one of the miracles of modern science. Philip Priestley's use of convict autobiographies has given us some interesting insights into the organization and administration of the nineteenth- and twentieth-century prison,[56] though both of his books might have benefited from more consideration of the authors and their motives in writing as they did. Other than this, the administration of the prisons after their nationalization in 1877 remains largely unexplored. So too (with the notable exceptions of William James Forsythe's broad survey of the techniques of reform employed under the Prison Commission and of Victor Bailey's study of legislation concerning the juvenile offender[57]) is the whole field of penal policy in the twentieth century, especially the perennial debates between those inclining toward reform and rehabilitation and those seeking first and foremost to punish.

The "Bloody Code" of the eighteenth century is where much of the current research started. Douglas Hay argued that the increase in capital statutes was central to the aim of the Hanoverian elite to uphold a social system based on the grossly unequal distribution of property. In the theater of the court, judges meted out justice tempered with mercy and alleged impartiality, insisting that all were equal before the law. To the extent that peers of the realm, like Lord Ferrers in 1760, could be executed publicly for murder, there was equality. Furthermore, the idea of equality before the law was more than just rhetoric; the ruling elite believed in it and, at times, found itself seriously constrained by it. The point was that the law was overwhelmingly concerned with the defense of property.[58] Hay's thesis has been the subject of a ferocious attack by John Langbein, whose vehement insistence that the Marxist historical method throws as little light on the "Bloody Code" as it does on the development of the flush toilet tends to distract from some of the more reasoned criticism. In particular, Langbein makes the significant point that the increase in the number of capital statutes during the eighteenth century was more apparent than real since the English law lacked general definitions, especially for embezzlement and larceny, and parliament was therefore continually legislating to compensate for generality with particularity.[59] Peter King's work on Essex reveals that the use of the law, and the use of discretion within the law, was not confined to a ruling elite but was well understood and employed by the "middling sort." He, and others, have highlighted the important role played by the jury in the seventeenth- and eighteenth-century criminal trial and noted that such juries appear generally to have been drawn from the "middling sort." Socially, this clearly set jurors above the majority of those brought before the courts on indictments for felony, but it remains a matter of dispute the extent to which the verdicts of these jurors can be said, with any confidence, to have been upholding the rule of the Hanoverian elite.[60]

To take up Langbein's point about the increase in capital statutes being more apparant than real, this also needs to be asked: What did members of the late Stuart and Hanoverian parliaments think they were doing as they passed the new capital statutes? John Beattie, in his magisterial study of crime and the courts, has shown that there was considerable debate during the late seventeenth and eighteenth centuries about the death penalty and the need for alternatives.[61] The preliminary conclusions of Joanna Innes's and John Styles's investigation into legislation between 1688 and 1800 reveal that parliament was never merely a rubber stamp for capital statutes, that there could be heated debates about the inclusion of the death penalty, that some bills were thrown out, and that others lost through lack of time.[62]

There has been nothing for the Victorian period and after which has generated controversy and stimulated research quite like Hay's analysis of the Hanoverian legal code. George Robb's work on white-collar crime suggests close links between businessmen and the landed elite in parliament, which, underpinned by the ideology of laissez faire, kept legislative regulation of the city of London to a minimum. At the same time, the courts appear to have been more lenient with major fraudsters than with members of the criminal class. The Victorians believed in individual responsibility but also considered shame and a loss of social status to be a punishment. To the extent that bankruptcy and the exposure of fraud frequently prompted suicide, such notions clearly had meaning.[63]

Martin J. Wiener has produced a convincing and thought-provoking account of how the Hanoverian code was reconstructed during the Victorian period by an intellectual revolution involving the new notions of rationality and individual self-responsibility. Thus, Wiener maintains that in the first half of the century, the law was deployed increasingly "as an instrument for developing self-discipline and gratification-deferring personalities in the population at large." Toward the end of the century, in contrast, as social scientists and medical men came under the influence of Darwinism, criminality was seen less as a problem of moral character and more the result of weakness and degeneracy, and penal policy was refocused accordingly.[64] Wiener's work is valuably supplemented, and in some ways qualified, by Lucia Zedner's analysis of Victorian attitudes to female criminality and the problems which these posed for the developing penal system.[65]

Drawing on much of the recent work on crime, V. A. C. Gatrell has described a significant shift in the way that crime and the criminal were understood from the early nineteenth century. It is probably orthodoxy now that Benthamite reform was much harsher and regimenting than the traditional Whig view would allow; following this, Gatrell has developed a challenging theory of the rise of the ''policeman state.'' Attention moved from the iniquity of individual offenses, he suggests, with the offenses acquiring new meanings invariably overlaid with metaphors of disease; criminals became identified as individuals with special afflictions threatening society as a whole rather than just their victims. To meet these problems, a law-and-order bureaucracy was developed, and order became identified as an organizing principle of the state. Eschewing ideas of a ruling-class conspiracy or of disciplinary discourses, Gatrell nevertheless believes that increasingly ''liberty'' became less a natural right guaranteed by the state and more something defined by the state and left over once ''order'' had been established.[66]

LOOKING AHEAD

Twenty years of research has undermined the traditional Whig views of crime, police, and punishment; it has also forced qualifications of many of the initial hypotheses with which the work began. There is now a new agenda, part of which (notably gender issues) has developed separately but part of which is the result of the recent research. In particular, investigation is required of the summary courts, of constables and watchmen, of recidivists and professional criminals. More work on the twentieth century would be valuable. There is also another angle which might be explored to shed light on some of the initial questions that social historians set out to answer with their foray into criminal justice.

Most of the research to date has concentrated on the criminal law; there is every justification for believing that the civil law could prove equally informative and, as noted earlier, Rubin and Sugarman have pointed the way in this respect.[67] Cases in which the law of tort was used against certain forms of appropriation in business matters would probably yield interesting insights about the development of capitalism. It is not necessary to read far into the Dickens canon to note the occurrence of debt, debtors' courts, and prisons. An exploration of such issues in the records of the quarter sessions for the sixteenth and seventeenth centuries and the courts of requests for the eighteenth and nineteenth centuries would add significantly to the historian's perception of developing economic and social relations, but the debtor has been generally ignored.[68] Conflicts in the civil courts between landlord and tenant also contain much of relevance to our understanding of social relations,[69] and other cases from the largely unexplored papers of the Victorian and Edwardian county courts probably contain much of value on domestic issues, indebtedness, wage arrestment, and so forth. The analysis of such cases would, moreover, help to develop our own conceptions of crime and criminality as well as our understanding of how people in the past viewed them and the law itself.

NOTES

1. An earlier, much shorter version of this chapter first appeared in the *Social History Society Newsletter* 16:1 (Spring 1991): 3–7. My thanks to the editor and the society for permission to develop the paper for republication here. My thanks also to Peter King and Louis Knafla for helpful comments on earlier drafts.

2. My failure to say anything about Scotland or Ireland is not deliberate English myopia; there has been very little work done on Scotland, while disorder and the "troubles" have been the focus for much of the research on Ireland; Wales, in contrast, is well served by the work of David Jones, which, working out from the statistical evidence, broadens into a model of what this kind of research can be. See David J.V. Jones, *Crime in Nineteenth-Century Wales* (Cardiff, 1992); idem, "'Where Did It All Go Wrong?' Crime in Swansea 1938–1968," *Welsh History Review* 15 (1990): 240–74.

3. "Conference Report," *Bulletin of the Society for the Study of Labour History* 25 (1972): 5–12.

4. Douglas Hay, Peter Linebaugh, E.P. Thompson et al., *Albion's Fatal Tree: Crime and Society in Eighteenth-Century England* (London, 1975); E.P. Thompson, *Whigs and Hunters: The Origin of the Black Act* (London, 1975).

5. Kellow Chesney, *The Victorian Underworld* (London, 1970) draws heavily on the investigative journalism of Victorian lowlife. J.J. Tobias, *Crime and Industrial Society in the Nineteenth Century* (London, 1967) is based on a broader range of sources; it is unfair to label this book as "popular" history (it was, after all, a Ph.D. thesis), but it is infused with positivist criminology and remains generally uncritical of the prejudices of Victorian penal reformers.

6. Among the best arguments for the concept of social crime is John G. Rule, "Social Crime in the Rural South in the Eighteenth and Early Nineteenth Centuries," *Southern History* 1 (1979): 135–53.

7. For poaching, P.B. Munsche, *Gentlemen and Poachers: The English Game Laws 1671–1831* (Cambridge, 1981). For smuggling, I rely on Paul Muskett's research for a doctoral thesis at the Open University.

8. Peter Linebaugh, *The London Hanged: Crime and Civil Society in the Eighteenth Century* (London, 1991), xxi.

9. David Philips, *Crime and Authority in Victorian England* (London, 1977), 180–91.

10. For the debate on eighteenth-century workplace crime see, John Rule, *The Experience of Labour in Eighteenth-Century Industry* (London, 1981), 124–46; John Styles, "Embezzlement, Industry and the Law in England, 1500–1800," in *Manufacture in Town and Country before the Factory,* ed. Maxime Berg, Pat Howard, and Michael Sonenscher

(Cambridge, 1983, 173–210); Adrian J. Randall, "Peculiar Perquisites and Pernicious Practices: Embezzlement in the West of England Woollen Industry c. 1750–1840," *International Review of Social History* 35 (1990): 193–219.

11. Peter King, "Gleaners, Farmers and the Failure of Legal Sanctions in England 1750–1850," *Past and Present* 125 (1989): 116–50, and idem, "Customary Rights and Women's Earnings: The Importance of Gleaning to the Rural Labouring Poor, 1750–1850," *Economic History Review* 44 (1991): 461–76.

12. David Sugarman and G.R. Rubin, "Towards a New History of Law and Material Society in England, 1750–1914," in *Law, Economy and Society: Essays in the History of English Law 1750–1914,* ed. G.R. Rubin and David Sugarman (Abingdon, 1984), 1–123.

13. George Robb, *White-Collar Crime in Modern England: Financial Fraud and Business Morality 1845–1929* (Cambridge, 1992).

14. Sarah Mercer, "Crime in Late Seventeenth-Century Yorkshire; An Exception to a National Pattern," *Northern History* 27 (1991): 106–19, warns against accepting the national pattern for the earlier period and finds a different peak for prosecutions in Yorkshire coming in the 1660s and 1670s.

15. For surveys of the statistical work see J.A. Sharpe, *Crime in Early Modern England 1550–1750* (London, 1984), chap. 3, and Clive Emsley, *Crime and Society in England 1750–1900* (London, 1987), chap. 2. For detail on the interrelationship between property crime, war, and dearth, see Douglas Hay, "War, Dearth and Theft in the Eighteenth Century: The Record of the English Courts," *Past and Present* 95 (1982): 117–60, and J.M. Beattie, *Crime and the Courts in England 1660–1800* (Oxford, 1986), 202–35.

16. Malcolm M. Feeley and Deborah L. Little, "The Vanishing Female: The Decline of Women in the Criminal Process, 1687–1912," *Law and Society Review* 25 (1991): 720–57.

17. W.J. Lowe, "The Lancashire Constabulary, 1845–1870: The Social and Occupational Function of a Victorian Police Force," *Criminal Justice History* 4 (1983): 41–62, at 46.

18. Lawrence Stone, "Interpersonal Violence in English Society, 1300–1980," *Past and Present* 101 (1983): 22–33; J.A. Sharpe, "The History of Violence in England: Some Observations," *Past and Present* 108 (1985): 206–15; Lawrence Stone, "A Rejoinder," in ibid., 21–24; J.S. Cockburn, "Patterns of Violence in English Society: Homicide in Kent 1560–1985," *Past and Present* 130 (1991): 70–106.

19. V.A.C. Gatrell, "The Decline of Theft and Violence in Victorian and Edwardian England," in *Crime and the Law: The Social History of Crime in Western Europe since 1500,* ed. V.A.C. Gatrell, Bruce Lenman, and Geoffrey Parker (London, 1980), 238–370.

20. Robert B. Shoemaker, *Prosecution and Punishment: Petty Crime and the Law in London and Rural Middlesex, c. 1660–1725* (Cambridge, 1991); quotations at 111, 177. This stress on misdemeanors as opposed to felonies is also to be found in Mercer, "Crime in Late Seventeenth-Century Yorkshire."

21. Douglas Hay, "Prosecution and Power: Malicious Prosecution in the English Courts, 1750–1850," in *Policing and Prosecution in Britain 1750–1850,* ed. Douglas Hay and Francis Synder (Oxford, 1989), 343–95; see also Ruth Paley, "Thief-takers in London in the Age of the McDaniel Gang, c. 1745–1754," in ibid., 338–39.

22. The term *moral panic* was coined by Stanley Cohen in his study of the activities

of the "mods" and "rockers" during the 1960s: Cohen, *Folk Devils and Moral Panics: The Creation of the Mods and Rockers* (London, 1972).

23. Rob Sindall, *Street Violence in the Nineteenth Century: Media Panic or Real Danger* (Leicester, 1990).

24. David Dixon, *From Prohibition to Regulation: Bookmaking, Anti-Gambling, and the Law* (Oxford, 1991), 34–37; Clive Emsley "'Mother, What *Did* Policemen Do When There Weren't Any Motors?' The Law, the Police and the Regulation of Motor Traffic in England 1900–1939," *Historical Journal* 36 (1993): 357–81.

25. Peter King, "Newspaper Reporting, Prosecution Practice and Perceptions of Urban Crime; the Colchester Crime Wave of 1765," *Continuity and Change* 2 (1987): 423–54.

26. Paul Slack, "Vagrants and Vagrancy in England 1598–1664," *Economic History Review,* 2d ser., 27 (1974): 360–79; A.L. Beier, *Masterless Men: The Vagrancy Problem in Britain 1560–1640* (London, 1985). For the Victorian vagrant and crime, see David Jones, *Crime, Protest, Community and Police in Nineteenth-Century Britain* (London, 1982), chap. 7.

27. Gerald Howson, *Thief-Taker General: The Rise and Fall of Jonathan Wild* (London, 1970); J.J. Tobias, *Prince of Fences: The Life and Crimes of Ikey Solomons* (London, 1974).

28. Philip Jenkins and Gary W. Porter, "Before the Krays: Organized Crime in London, 1920–1960," *Criminal Justice History* 9 (1988): 209–30.

29. See Susan Margery, "The Invention of Juvenile Delinquency in Early Nineteenth-Century England," *Labour History* 34 (1978): 11–27; Margaret May, "Innocence and Experience: The Evolution of Juvenile Delinquency in the Mid-Nineteenth Century," *Victorian Studies* 17 (1973): 7–29; John R. Gillis, "The Evolution of Juvenile Delinquency in England, 1890–1914," *Past and Present* 67 (1975): 96–126.

30. See Paul McHugh, *Prostitution and Social Reform* (London, 1980), and Judith R. Walkowitz, *Prostitution and Victorian Society: Women, Class and the State* (Cambridge, 1980).

31. Carolyn A. Conley, *The Unwritten Law: Criminal Justice in Victorian Kent* (New York, 1991), chap. 3.

32. Lucia Zedner, *Women, Crime and Custody in Victorian England* (Oxford, 1991).

33. Nancy Tomes, "A 'Torrent of Abuse': Crimes of Violence between Working-Class Men and Women in Victorian London 1840–1875," *Journal of Social History* 11 (1978): 328–45; Margaret Hunt, "Wife Beating, Domesticity and Women's Independence in Eighteenth-Century London," *Gender and History* 4 (1992): 10–33; Maeve Doggett, *Marriage, Wife-Beating and the Law in Victorian England* (London, 1992).

34. Such ideas are to be found in the works of Charles Reith, *The Police Idea* (Oxford, 1938), *British Police and the Democratic Ideal* (Oxford, 1943), *The Blind Eye of History* (London, 1952); in T.A. Critchley, *A History of Police in England and Wales* (London, 1967); in David Ascoli, *The Queen's Peace: The Origins and Development of the Metropolitan Police 1829–1979* (London, 1979); and in a large number of force histories written at the time of the police amalgamations during the 1960s.

35. Robert D. Storch, "'The Plague of Blue Locusts': Police Reform and Popular Resistance in Northern England 1840–1857," *International Review of Social History* 20 (1975): 61–90; idem, "The Policeman as Domestic Missionary: Urban Discipline and Popular Culture in Northern England 1850–1880," *Journal of Social History* 9 (1976): 481–509.

36. Joan R. Kent, *The English Village Constable 1580–1642: A Social and Administrative Study* (Oxford, 1986).

37. Emsley, *Crime and Society,* 174; Ruth Paley, "'An Imperfect, Inadequate and Wretched System'? Policing London before Peel," *Criminal Justice History* 10 (1989): 95–130.

38. Stanley H. Palmer, *Police and Protest in England and Ireland 1780–1850* (Cambridge, 1988); Paley, "'An Imperfect, Inadequate and Wretched System'?"

39. Robert D. Storch, "Policing Rural Southern England before the Police: Opinion and Practice, 1830–1856," in *Policing and Prosecution,* ed. Hay and Snyder, 211–66; David Philips and Robert D. Storch, "Whigs and Coppers: The Grey Ministry's National Police Scheme, 1832," *Historical Research* 67 (1994): 75–90.

40. In addition to the work of Paley and Palmer and the forthcoming work of Philips and Storch, see Carolyn Steedman, *Policing the Victorian Community: The Formation of English Provincial Police Forces 1856–1880* (London, 1984).

41. Roger Geary, *Policing Industrial Disputes 1893 to 1985* (Cambridge, 1985); Jane Morgan, *Conflict and Order: The Police and Labour Disputes in England and Wales 1900–1939* (Oxford, 1987); Barbara Weinberger, *Keeping the Peace? Policing Strikes in Britain 1906–1926* (Oxford, 1991).

42. Clive Emsley, *The English Police: A Political and Social History* (Hemel Hempstead, 1991).

43. Linebaugh, *The London Hanged,* xviii.

44. John H. Langbein, "The Criminal Trial before the Lawyers," *University of Chicago Law Review* 45 (1978): 263–316; idem, "Shaping the Eighteenth-Century Criminal Trial: A View from the Ryder Sources," *University of Chicago Law Review* 50 (1983): 1–136; Beattie, *Crime and the Courts,* Part II, passim; idem, "Scales of Justice: Defense Counsel and the English Criminal Trial in the Eighteenth and Nineteenth Centuries," *Law and History Review* 9 (1991): 221–67; P.J.R. King, "Decision-Makers and Decision-Making in the English Criminal Law," *Historical Journal* 27 (1984): 25–58; Thomas A. Green, *Verdict According to Conscience: Perspectives on the English Criminal Trial Jury, 1200–1800* (Chicago, 1985); *Twelve Good Men and True: The Criminal Trial Jury in England 1200–1800,* ed. J.S. Cockburn and Thomas A. Green (Princeton, 1988).

45. Beattie, *Crime and the Courts,* 276–77.

46. Emsley, *Crime and Society,* 149, 167 n. 50.

47. Jennifer Davis, "'A Poor Man's System of Justice.' The London Police Courts in the Second Half of the Nineteenth Century," *Historical Journal* 27 (1984): 309–35.

48. V.A.C. Gatrell, *The Hanging Tree: Execution and the English People 1770–1868* (Oxford, 1994).

49. Michel Foucault, *Discipline and Punish: The Birth of the Modern Prison* (London, 1977).

50. Michael Ignatieff, *A Just Measure of Pain: The Penitentiary in the Industrial Revolution 1750–1850* (London, 1978).

51. Margaret De Lacy, *Prison Reform in Lancashire, 1700–1850: A Study in Local Administration* (Manchester, 1986); W.J. Forsythe, *The Reform of Prisons, 1830–1900* (London, 1987). Ignatieff himself has modified his position; see his "State, Civil Society, and Total Institutions: A Critique of Recent Social Histories of Punishment," in *Social Control and the State,* ed. Stanley Cohen and Andrew Scull (Oxford, 1984).

52. Randall McGowan, "The Image of Justice and Reform of the Criminal Law in Early Nineteenth-Century England," *Buffalo Law Review* 32 (1983): 89–125; idem, "A

Powerful Sympathy: Terror, the Prison, and Humanitarian Reform in Early Nineteenth-Century Britain,'' *Journal of British Studies* 25 (1986): 312–34; quotations at 314, 329; idem, ''The Changing Face of God's Justice: The Debates over Divine and Human Punishment in Eighteenth-Century England,'' *Criminal Justice History* 9 (1988): 63–98.

53. Seán McConville, *English Local Prisons. Next Only to Death* (London, 1994).

54. Leon Radzinowicz and Roger Hood, *The Emergence of Penal Policy in Victorian and Edwardian England* (London, 1986). This volume has been reissued separately (Oxford, 1990), but without the massive bibliography.

55. Martin J. Wiener, ''The March of Penal Progress,'' *Journal of British Studies* 26 (1987): 83–96, quotation at 95.

56. Philip Priestley, *Victorian Prison Lives: English Prison Biography 1830–1914* (London, 1985); idem, *Jail Journies: The English Prison Experience 1918–1990* (London, 1989).

57. William James Forsythe, *Penal Discipline, Reformatory Projects and the English Prison Commission, 1895–1939* (Exeter, 1991); Victor Bailey, *Delinquency and Citizenship: Reclaiming the Young Offender 1914–1948* (Oxford, 1987).

58. Douglas Hay, ''Property, Authority and the Criminal Law,'' in *Albion's Fatal Tree.* For the way in which the rhetoric of the law also acted as a constraint on the elite, see Thompson, *Whigs and Hunters,* especially 258–69, and Clive Emsley, ''Repression, 'Terror' and the Rule of Law in England during the Decade of the French Revolution,'' *English Historical Review* 100 (1985): 801–25.

59. John Langbein, ''Albion's Fatal Flaws,'' *Past and Present* 98 (1983): 96–120.

60. King, ''Decision-Makers and Decision-Making''; Green, *Verdict According to Conscience;* the debates about the jury are rehearsed fully in *Twelve Good Men and True,* ed. Cockburn and Green; see, with reference to the seventeenth and eighteenth centuries, the essays by Cockburn, Stephen K. Roberts, J.M. Beattie, King, and Douglas Hay, and Green's own retrospective essay, which concludes the volume.

61. Beattie, *Crime and the Courts,* 455–46, 469–70, 513–39, 530–38, and 582–92.

62. Joanna Innes and John Styles, ''The Crime Wave: Recent Writing on Crime and Criminal Justice in Eighteenth-Century England,'' *Journal of British Studies* 25 (1986): 380–435.

63. Robb, *White-Collar Crime,* chap. 7.

64. Martin J. Wiener, *Reconstructing the Criminal: Culture, Law and Policy in England, 1830–1914* (Cambridge, 1990), quotation at 91.

65. Zedner, *Women, Crime and Custody.*

66. V.A.C. Gatrell, ''Crime, Authority and the Policeman State,'' in *The Cambridge Social History of Britain 1750–1950,* 3 vols., ed. F.M.L. Thompson (Cambridge, 1990), 3: 243–310.

67. *Law, Economy and Society,* ed. Rubin and Sugarman.

68. The notable exception is Joanna Innes, ''The King's Bench Prison in the Later Eighteenth Century: Law, Authority and Order in a London Debtors' Prison,'' in *An Ungovernable People: The English and Their Law in the Seventeenth and Eighteenth Centuries,* ed. John Brewer and John Styles (London, 1980), 250–98.

69. David Englander, *Landlord and Tenant in Urban Britain, 1838–1918* (Oxford, 1983).

5

Crime, the Judicial System, and Punishment in Modern France

René Lévy

In this chapter, I will attempt to review work published since the mid-1980s on the history of crime and criminal justice in nineteenth- and twentieth-century France, along the same lines as a previous piece written in collaboration with Philippe Robert, dealing with earlier publications.[1] For the sake of continuity, the same outline will be used, so trends in the field will be clearly underlined. Therefore, cases, the judicial institution, the police, and punishment will be discussed in that order.

In 1985, a great discrepancy was evidenced between the wealth of data available for the nineteenth century and the little research actually done. This is no longer true: Historiography has progressed considerably in several directions, but unevenly depending on the period and the subject. The most obvious advance, and the most encouraging one for future research in this field, resides in the constitution of several tools, which will be indispensable for researchers from now on. These are the *Guide des archives judiciaires et pénitentiaires (1800–1958) (Guide to Judicial and Correctional Archives [1800–1958])* and the publication of both the sets of criminal statistics for 1831 to 1981 and correctional statistics.

The *Guide to Judicial and Correctional Archives,* established by Jean-Claude Farcy[2] under the auspices of the Ministry of Justice,[3] first briefly discusses the present state of historical research, gives some idea of the varied nature of the archives (most of which are unexploited), and sketches some of the prospects for research. It then goes on to provide a description of judicial institutions and of their evolution during the reference period; a subject nomenclature for archived documents; an inventory of national resources; and various appendices useful for the comprehension of the archives. The largest part is devoted to the inventory of "départemental" archives and includes a detailed description of existing material along with the references of the corresponding research tools.

Another tool, devised by a team headed by Bruno Aubusson de Cavarlay,[4] gives researchers unprecedented access to an enormous database constituted by the *Compte Général de la Justice Criminelle (CGJC),* published almost uninterruptedly although with some modifications, from 1825 to 1981. Now entered in a computerized database, this information henceforth offers the considerable advantage of being stripped of most of its hidden traps, which resided in the successive changes over the years in the nomenclatures used by the authors of these statistics. The volume published in 1990 contains a critical presentation of 200 series of raw data from the *CGJC* (numbers and activity of auxiliaries to the Public Prosecutor's office and activity of the latter, of examining magistrates, and of courts). A forthcoming volume will contain a set of calculations on these series and some graphs; another will cover the series offense by offense. At the end of this project, researchers will have access to the contents of the 150 volumes of the *CGJC* in a concentrated, "cleaned," and commented form. That will probably be the right time to reexamine attentively all of the studies based on these statistics in light of this reordering. A note on judicial statistics would not be complete without reference to the major, critical reedition of the 1880 *CGJC* volume, which contained an annotated recapitulation of statistics for the 1826–1880 period.[5]

Correctional statistics have benefited from the "Séries Pénitentiaires Temporelles" database ("Base SEPT") produced under the direction of Pierre Tournier,[6] which contains no less than 310 chronological series relative to the 1968–1990 period. Data pertain to the prison population in general (demographic structure, criminal categories, input and output, length of detention, rates of occupancy of prisons, suicides) as well as to specific groups of inmates (pretrial prisoners, sentenced prisoners, women, young people, foreigners).[7] Last, there is the reconstitution of correctional statistics from 1852 to the present, published by Marie-Danièle Barré.[8]

All in all, these tools should give new impetus to research in the history of crime and criminal justice. However, even without the availability of these tools, much work has been done in recent years both in France and elsewhere. I will now move on to this, in the order set out earlier in this chapter.

CASES

French law distinguishes between three categories of offenses of increasing seriousness: (1) *contraventions* (minor offenses), which are judged by *tribunaux de police;* (2) *délits* (moderately serious offenses), which are judged by *tribunaux correctionnels;* and (3) *crimes* (major offenses), which are judged by *cours d'assises,* in which a jury sits.[9] Research on the different types of cases treated by the criminal justice system in the nineteenth century is both sparse and disparate in nature. Some authors have concentrated on one type of jurisdiction, others on one type of offense, and still others on a territory of varying size or on a period, long or short. Furthermore, these four "variables" may be variously combined.

Local monographs form the majority; they usually take the *département* (the basic administrative district in France) as their framework. Phillipe Homéril and Bernard Schnapper described the activity of a *départemental* criminal court between 1791 and 1800; Renée Martinage dealt with *crimes* in the Nord *département* between 1810 and 1950, while Marie-Renée Santucci was concerned with *délits* in the Hérault *département* between 1825 and 1885. Frédéric Chauvaud, on the other hand, made a detailed examination of a small town, Rambouillet, and its rural surroundings between 1811 and 1871. Benjamin Martin presented an overview of all of France, but only for felonies committed under the Third Republic, from 1870 to 1940.[10]

Other studies confine themselves to a specific type of offense or offenders: a particular gang of highway robbers during the revolutionary period in Ile-de-France,[11] in Normandie,[12] or in twentieth-century Cévennes;[13] desertion during the Revolution or the Empire,[14] or in the Pyrénées between 1800 and 1848;[15] crime among Corsicans in Marseille between 1825 and 1880 or sex-related affairs between 1825 and 1885 in the same city, or abortion from 1825 to 1923;[16] or crimes of passion in the last decades of the nineteenth century.[17] Chauvaud's attempt to describe changes in violence and in images of it in nineteenth-century France is more ambitious.[18]

Several of these investigations are of a more or less quantitative nature and are based either on the *Compte Général* or on a quantified examination of judicial records. Unfortunately, use of these data is often less than satisfactory. The most frequent defect remains the authors' uncertainty regarding the status of the data they use. The idea that, more than anything else, criminal statistics reflect the functioning of the criminal justice system that produces them is not yet generally accepted. No longer can anyone omit the statement that these data are biased and cannot be viewed as a direct reflection of crime, but this is often mere lip service. Martin gives a good example of this when, after relevantly mentioning the defects in criminal justice statistics, he writes that "for all their deficiencies, the statistics of the *Compte Général* are the best statistics available. Used with circumspection, they provide at least good approximations for the situation of crime and criminals during the Third Republic."[19] As a result, most of these authors use statistics alternatively as an image of crime and as a reflection on repression, without realizing that the two positions are usually mutually exclusive.[20]

Further, some surprising methodological biases prevail. Martin, for instance deals indiscriminately with the entire Third Republic; he totals up crimes of the same sort recorded over this seventy-year period and then crosses these totals with a number of variables, the result being that he rules out any analysis of variations in the structure of these cases. The postulate is that French criminal justice was the same in 1870 and in 1940. A much more rigorous assessment of the data can be found in a study of the French criminal courts from 1934 to 1954.[21]

There is also the question of how important it is to study assize court cases only.[22] Martinage clearly shows that the history of this jurisdiction is one of steady decline, indicated by a decreasing number of cases handled. She also shows that this trend, along with the changes she detects in the types of cases judged, is mainly the outcome of practical and/or legal modifications in the competency of the assize court (de facto and de jure "correctionalization"—that is referral to *tribunaux correctionnels* for moderately serious offenses, with no jury). The assizes and *tribunaux correctionnels* are communicating vessels, with the latter defying the laws of physics, gradually emptying the former of its contents. There is therefore reason to believe that it would be more relevant to study *correctionnel* cases, if a choice must be made, since these are a better indicator of the social role of criminal justice in the nineteenth and twentieth centuries. This in fact is what makes Santucci's regional study valuable: It makes probes at twenty-year intervals (1825, 1845, 1865, 1885), which record the main changes in the course of the period.[23] In this respect, the trend in cases is inseparably linked with the transformation in the role of the public prosecutor's office, itself tied to the development of policing institutions.[24]

As for the substance, all of these studies develop previous findings without revolutionizing our knowledge. The theme is always "the twofold obsession with property and sex," as Michelle Perrot put it.[25] However, where sex is concerned, the nuances advanced by Donovan's study are worth mentioning. In an analysis of the sex-related cases at the *correctionnel* court of Marseille (1825–1885), Donovan finds that the frequency of this type of suit increased during the nineteenth century. The sentences meted out tended to grow lighter, with major differences depending on the offense, nonetheless. Generally speaking, the criminal justice system was mostly concerned with moralizing public places and protecting juveniles, but was lax when sexual practices did not involve public exposure.[26]

In another field, there is the interesting analysis of lumbering disputes by Santucci, showing that the conflict between the peasants' traditional users' rights and the new forms of industrial exploitation of the forest not only affected the increasingly powerful forestry department and the inhabitants but also the communes, who owned the woods, and businessmen, who had no scruples about buying illegally cut lumber. The rural exodus, as much if not more than legislative reforms, was responsible for the rapid disappearance of this type of criminal case at the midcentury.[27]

THE JUDICIAL INSTITUTION

The bicentennial of the French Revolution undeniably stimulated historical research, as shown by the publication of several collective works,[28] the object of which is in fact broader than criminal justice per se. As for the law-making activity of the Revolution, the reading of the criminal codes between 1791 and 1810, by Lascoumes, Poncela, and Lenoël, is noteworthy.[29] These authors analyze the contents of the criminal codes or projects of codes of the time, in an attempt to identify those social interests and values which were thus transformed into legally protected objects. By ascertaining whether the revolutionary texts broke with the past and, if so, how with respect to actual criminalization on the books and not simply in debates over abstract ideals, their purpose was to grasp criminalization as a whole as an expression of the main lines structuring the social order. The authors, explicitly inspired by Michel Foucault, are mostly interested in the texts and the discourse surrounding them, but hardly at all in the actors in the law-making process or in political events. Other authors, such as M. Dorigny and Roberto Martucci,[30] pay more attention to the latter. Revolutionary law making is also dealt with, but from the angle of judicial organization, in a thorough study by Halpérin on the Court of Cassation.[31]

It is probably juries that have been most studied from this standpoint in recent years. Considering the extremely limited role it plays in the functioning of modern criminal justice, it is difficult to imagine the passions unleashed by the issue of the jury throughout the nineteenth century and how significant it was in political argument. Research on the subject may be divided into two broad types: work centered on the institutional aspect (organization, competencies, composition, trends), and studies concerned essentially with the actual functioning of juries.

The first category includes studies devoted to the inception of the institution. The French jury was borrowed from the English model and was intended to symbolize democracy and to limit the power of judges. The debates at the Constituent Assembly have been studied in detail, especially by Antonio Padoa Schioppa and Bernard Schnapper, as well as in the first part of the collective work headed by Martinage and Royer.[32] The evolution of the institution and the controversies over it, fluctuating with French politics, have been remarkably described by Schnapper and in greater detail by Françoise Lombard.[33] At the crossroads of institutional history and of the history of court practices, we find a number of recent studies on the social composition of juries, based on the examination of lists of jurors: Schnapper studies western France between 1840 and 1860; Santucci the Hérault *département* from 1811 to 1872; and Lombard the jurors in the Nord *département* in the nineteenth and twentieth centuries. Each political regime changed the rules of access to the function of juror, in an attempt to favor its own sociological base. These studies show that the actual composition of juries depended greatly on how the laws were applied by the local authorities in charge of drawing up the lists, but also on the lucky candidates' great propensity to seek dispensation from this unpaid, burdensome duty.[34]

This leads us to the few studies devoted to the functioning of juries. Among other things, they show that the selection of jurors on the basis of social class does not in itself guarantee the jury's docility: At least during the first half of the century, and even later in some regions, not only did jurors apply local values—that is, their own assessment of the seriousness of crimes—to the trial, but they partook in the complex interplay of local systems of social control and accommodation as well.[35] Research on periods during which this type of social relations no longer prevailed also tends to show that jurors continued to assert distinctly different values from those of professional judges and authorities in general, thus generating constant criticism of their alleged incompetence.[36] In the last analysis, the conflict was emptied of its stakes by increasing use of *correctionnel* courts, as Donovan clearly shows for the case of abortion.[37]

In comparison to research on jurors, who might be considered sometime judges, work on professionals, particularly magistrates, remains exceptional. Previous studies had emphasized the impact of politics on the careers of judges in particularly unstable nineteenth-century France. A few authors have pursued this vein.[38] Marie-José Couailhac does not overlook this aspect but mostly concentrates on the professional life of judges of the Grenoble Court of Appeals between 1815 and 1870, while J.-P. Jourdan is more concerned with judges as a social group. Christophe Charle takes a similar approach in his study on the shaping and reproduction of *élites* at the beginning of the Third Republic (1880–1900); he includes judges from the Court of Cassation, whose social trajectory is compared with that of other high-ranking officials, university professors, and businessmen.[39] Last, there is the work supervised by Philippe Robert, which traces the legislative history of one of the themes that most obsesses the contemporary criminal justice system: pretrial detention, with particular emphasis on the actors involved.[40]

THE POLICE

Until recently, historical research into police institutions was probably the field with the most yawning gaps, especially for the nineteenth and twentieth centuries.[41] The situation has definitely improved, although unevenly so for the different aspects of this vast area, which the public finds so fascinating that editors are encouraged to publish numerous mediocre or anecdotal books. Be this as it may, most research has concentrated on the 1848–1914 period. Clive Emsley is the only researcher to have described the functioning and everyday practices of the Paris police during the early nineteenth century. Bollenot looked into the difficulties of the political police corps in the agitated city of Lyons under the July Monarchy.[42]

The outstanding event in research on the second half of the century is Berlière's work on the police institution under the Third Republic, from 1875 to

1914.[43] He studied the republican police doctrine and the organization of police forces and police practices, one after the other, with no concessions to the picturesque or the gratuitous anecdote, in an area where this is particularly tempting. *Affairs* are only mentioned when they illustrate some facet of legal or political debate, an aspect of the organization or the functioning of the institution, or the conceptions, representations, or practices of actors.

First, Berlière shows that the distinctive features of the present police were developed during the 1875–1914 period, with specialized departments, definition of tasks, professionalization, incipient technical unification, and the use of criminalistics. He also shows that the grand ideals defended by the republicans in the opposition under the Second Empire hardly resisted the test of power, at a time when the latter was terribly fragile; if there was such a thing as a "republican police force," it does not show in its structures or in its methods.[44] The Third Republic did not put an end to divisions between police forces, although it did reinforce the tendancy toward governmentalization and centralization by empirical, circumstantial decision making. The great innovation in this field was the creation of a truly national judicial police department (the famous Tiger Brigades, created by Clémenceau in 1907, which did not receive its first automobile for twelve brigades until 1911). It gradually incorporated scientific policing methods, without sacrificing more traditional means, and thus radically modified the popular image of the police, with the help of the press and novels. The trend, in comparison with earlier regimes, is perhaps most spectacular in the field of crowd control: From July 1893 to May 1919, no one was killed in demonstrations in Paris, the merit for which goes mostly to the Prefect Lépine.[45] It is impossible to go into greater detail here on a work which deals with all aspects of the institution and takes special interest in its actors, be they officials or personnel (with the birth of police unionism, for instance); this institution may be credited with the fact that the police are less faceless than in the past[46] thanks to Berlière's numerous publications.[47]

Other works, such as those by Vigier et al., deal with more limited aspects of the policing institution. They are the outcome of colloquia held in 1983 and 1986 under the auspices of the *Société d'Histoire de la Révolution de 1848 et des Révolutions du XIXe siècle* and are mostly devoted to political repression, with the first volume concentrating on the agents of repression and the second volume on its victims.[48] However, the first volume does make a few incursions into the policing of everyday life, including the surveillance of street vendors and of theaters, public order in rural contexts, and local conflicts between mayors and police superintendants.[49] The relationship between state and local police authorities during the Third Republic is now being researched within the perspective of administrative history.

Along with political policing, policing of morals was no doubt the most controversial facet of police work during the nineteenth century. Recent research does not contradict Alain Corbin's classic on the subject. Jill Harsin differs mostly by some nuances in the assessment of the replacement of the *maison close* (brothel) by the *maison de rendez-vous* (meeting house) and by a lesser interest in the change in the male clientele's taste. Berlière is mostly interested in the way in which the police viewed and handled prostitution, their concern with morality problems when engaged in other policing tasks (political or judicial police work), and the effects of this system on the functioning of the police as a whole. Last, where the other authors mostly deal with Paris and big cities, Jo Termeaux describes daily life and the control of brothels in the small towns of western France.[50]

Almost nothing has been done on the period between the two world wars.[51] The role of the police during World War II is mentioned in investigations on collaboration and deportation, but there apparently have been only two comprehensive studies, which do not exhaust the subject.[52] Kasten insists on the fact that the Germans needed the French police's cooperation. In his view, the latter were neither traitors nor inclined toward the Resistance; they were merely "good Frenchmen," driven by an extreme nationalism, who collaborated insofar as it served what they considered French interests. Longuechaud, on the other hand, corroborates the thesis according to which the Vichy government tended to be more radical than was demanded by the Germans, in an attempt to maintain the illusion that it still had a degree of independence. Furthermore, the author feels that the continued existence of a French government, however weakened (especially following the occupation of the "free zone" in late 1942), maintained the fiction among police officers that they were doing their duty. He does nevertheless see the *gendarmerie* as more reticent to collaborate than the police department. This view is corroborated by J.F. Sweets on the basis of a regional study.[53]

Be this as it may, the French police did play an active role in fighting the Resistance, as is shown in Couderc's work, based on the archives of the *Renseignements Généraux,* the political branch of the Paris police department. In spite of an overly journalistic style, this book has the merit of discussing the reality of the purge at the Liberation and of showing how the cold war caused the same police workers to be "whitewashed" and enrolled in the fight against communism, a specialty they had developed under the Germans during the Occupation.[54] Generally speaking, there has been a tendancy in recent years to reevaluate the responsibility of the French police authorities in the application of Nazi policies; one sign of this is the indictment, for crimes against humanity, of René Bousquet, head of the Vichy police until 1943 and therefore in close contact with the German authorities.[55]

The behavior of the police during the Algerian War has not been studied as a whole. Only the police's murderous repression of the October 13, 1961, demonstration by Algerians in Paris, allegedly causing several hundreds of deaths among demonstrators and about which the blackout was total (the official count was six deaths), has been the object of several recent investigations.[56]

Historiography of the police has essentially neglected the *gendarmerie,* despite its importance in this mainly rural country, in which it was the only state police for an extensive period. It is true that works on nineteenth-century rural resistance to the growing power of the state, of desertion or failure to report to the army,[57] and of local modes of conflict handling[58] necessarily discuss it; but it has not yet been the object of any far-reaching study comparable to those dealing with the *Maréchaussée* under the *ancien régime.*[59]

This review of research devoted to the police would not be complete without some mention of the major mutation represented by the development of technical and scientific policing at the turn of the twentieth century and which is inseparable from the science-minded climate of the time and the emerging of criminology, at the crossroads of medicine and the social sciences.[60] Not long ago, David Garland deplored the lack of any thorough history of criminology, its evolution, and its impact on society, which is devoid both of idealization and of denunciation: "What is missing is any detailed account of the formation of the criminological programme, its internal characteristics and conflicts and, most importantly, of the processes whereby this programme entered into the strategies and institutions of government."[61]

A recent outburst of research has tended to fill this gap, particularly for France. The ideological background, pervaded with catastrophism (with the idea of degeneracy, or national decline), had already been remarkably depicted by Nye and more recently by Pick (who compares the destiny of the idea of degeneracy in France, Italy, and England) as well as by Harris.[62] Criminology itself as an enterprise was studied in detail by Martine Kaluszynski through the French School organized around the *Archives d'anthropologie criminelle* (1886–1914). She points out its leaders and participants, their conceptions (radically opposed to those of the Lombroso School), their internal debates, and how the group became structured through controversy with the other currents in criminology, particularly during international conferences. She also describes the relations of this group, dominated by doctors and entertained with sociologists and jurists. *Histoire de la criminologie française,* edited by Laurent Mucchielli, is more encompassing. It provides an overview of the various intellectual currents which merged into criminology in the nineteenth century in the context of a broad sweep of the history of science.[63]

Alphonse Bertillon, who was a member of the group from its inception, is the central figure in the modernization of the judicial police, thanks to his invention of a means of identification consistent with the then virulent obsession with recidivism described by Schnapper.[64] The circumstances surrounding Bertillon's rise to success and his particularly good luck are now well known.[65] Berlière goes even further, with his description of how scientific policing developed, how it became institutionalized, the illusions it fostered, with the subsequent disappointment, and how it finally contributed to a revalorization of the image of the police.[66]

PUNISHMENT

In this field, most researchers have concerned themselves with sentences involving personal restraint, such as prison and hard labor. Recent historiography on imprisonment is essentially indebted to the work of Jacques Petit, which somewhat eclipsed Patricia O'Brien's book, whose notoriety in France suffered from its belated translation.[67] The former covers a century of history (1780–1875) and begins by drawing a thorough picture of the beginnings of criminal prison, from the many forms of confinement used at the end of the *ancien régime,*[68] its ratification by the *Assemblée Constituante* and the difficulties in its implementation up to the Napoleonic reforms, followed by the evolution of the criminal prison until the end of the Second Empire. Rather than confining itself to the history of the controversies over criminal imprisonment during the course of the nineteenth century,[69] Petit's book completes that aspect with a particularly valuable emphasis on the social environment, including the weight of political contingencies, economic and financial constraints, and the social actors involved (including lawmakers, theoreticians, philanthropists, administrative officials, and entrepreneurs). One outstanding aspect is Petit's detailed study of the system known as the *entreprise générale,* in application until the very last years of the nineteenth century, whereby prisons were transformed into semiprivate enterprises in which inmates were exploited by an entrepreneur who was in charge of their upkeep. He describes everyday life in prisons, both for inmates and for guards, along with the growth of the increasingly powerful correctional administration, which finally took control of these custodial establishments.

The nineteenth-century *prison pénale* is something of an "obscure guillotine" (by analogy to the Guyane hard labor camp, known as the "dry guillotine"), which not only killed far more people than the actual guillotine but eliminated the most underprivileged inmates (those with the least aptitude for survival) rather than the hardened criminals. In addition to this decisive work, which may be seen as the culminating point in the great project launched by M. Foucault, there have been several limited studies on the same period, dealing with children in prison[70] and political prisoners.[71] Jean-Claude Vimont's thesis on the evolution of imprisonment for political reasons between 1810 and 1848 will be a reference work on the latter aspect.[72]

Much less is known about the later periods, on the other hand. Exploratory and partial studies are still the rule. For the beginning of the Third Republic, Robert Badinter has attempted an overview of the studies presented at a seminar on prisons between 1871 and 1914, in which he mostly emphasizes the contradictions between the Republicans' judicial humanism and their refusal to reform prisons. In one short, synthetic chapter, Michel Pierre takes the topic up to 1938, but there is a terrible lack of detailed studies on the between-war period. Carlier's work on prison staffs is the only piece available.[73]

The history of punishment, and of internment in particular, takes on a special character with World War II, and it belongs to a specific area of historiography.

Many books, in recent years, have reminded readers of the non-negligable role played by France in the *univers concentrationnaire* (concentration-camp world).[74] However, it is the growing awareness of France's specific participation in it, especially through the opening of internment camps before the war and the Occupation, that is particularly interesting and promising. Hence the concern with reintegrating these "black years" in the long term, ranging from the latter years of the Third Republic to the end of the post–World War II purge, to gain a better perspective on their specificity and thus strengthen ties with specialists on criminal justice topics.[75]

The postwar period and the Fourth Republic have received little attention so far. There is one study of social services in prisons from 1945 to 1958, by Faugeron and Le Boulaire, and an analysis of correctional policies from 1945 to the present, by Faugeron.[76] Last, in another line of thought, Bernard Laffargue and Thierry Godefroy have been working at establishing links between the evolution of prison populations and changes on the labor market between 1870 and 1985, in continuation of Georg Rusche and Otto Kirchheimer's famous work.[77]

Aside from prison, hard labor colonies were the other form of personal restraint—or should one say death penalty?—in the nineteenth century. Following the same line as in his great book on galley slaves, André Zysberg shows the continuity between the galleys and the hard labor colonies set up by the *Constituante;* in this respect, the *ancien régime* only ends with the *Restauration* (1815–1830). He also shows that in the mainland hard labor colonies, personal restraint did not imply incarceration, making hard labor radically different from criminal imprisonment. Convicts sent to penal servitude worked on the Navy's large construction projects and mingled freely with free workers within the world of the ports.[78] The desire for more severe punishment, the determination to eliminate these people, and the interests of the Navy, which was in charge of the colonies and also gradually introducing new ship-building techniques (thus reducing the need for convicts in its dockyards), sent hard labor colonies overseas to Algeria, Guyana, and New Caledonia. M. Pierre summarizes the history of penal servitude, whereas Odile Krakovitch investigates women convicts, who might easily have been completely overlooked, given their small numbers (from 1859 to 1914, approximately 2,000 women were sent to penal servitude, as compared to nearly 100,000 men between 1852 and 1938). Krakovitch has also devoted an article to the preliminary findings of an investigation of another ignored minority among convicts in Guyana: criminals from the nearby French Caribbean islands. The latter took the habit of sending their offenders, including petty delinquents, to Guyana as early as 1852, for lack of correctional facilities of their own, while their counterparts from the mainland were only sent there after 1885, through relegation.[79] Several recent books have also dealt with the New Caledonia colony, with emphasis on the Communards, who were sent there after 1870.[80]

Other research on punishment includes several publications on executioners, stimulated by the Bicentennial of the French Revolution, symbolized by the guillotine. The most recommendable of these was written by Jacques Delarue, who uses extensive documentation and is serious in his handling of sources; the same cannot be said of Barbara Lévy or B. Lecherbonnier.[81] In these pages, emphasis has been placed on the various aspects of the criminal justice institutions. There is another possible formulation, which would tend to stress the place of the latter in social relations, and a good many of the aforementioned studies would fit into that framework.

The history of the state in France is generally represented as the gradual rise of royalty, which finally succeeded in establishing its hegemony—that is, its criminal justice—over a territory which grew to its present size over the centuries through conquest or annexation. This process, clearly established under Louis XIV, was completed with the rationalization of the administrative and judicial structures achieved by the Revolution and made permanent by the First Empire. Eugen Weber has succeeded in upsetting this mollifying picture, and although he does not question the existence of the integration process itself, he does raise some major questions regarding its periodization. He feels that this effort was only completed during the Third Republic, particularly through the linguistic unification of the country by compulsory schooling and military service for all.[82] This thesis, which Weber restricts to rural France and which cannot be extensively discussed here, is echoed by several of the aforementioned works.

The resistance of the rural population ranges from traditional forms such as insubordination and desertion, lumbering offenses, illicit hunting, and jacqueries to some forms that are more subtly appropriate to the new institutions, such as the subversion of the institution of the jury, or other aspects of the functioning of the criminal justice system.[83] Even in the interwar period, the mediocre adventure of a bandit in the Cévénol region is cloaked in the local imagery of banditry, which partakes in this tradition of resistance to the central government.[84] The Corsican case so accurately described by Wilson is of course the most striking example of strong, long-standing particularism persisting well into the twentieth century in the form of private vengeance.[85] A much more systematic rereading of historical studies would of course be necessary to sound the validity of Weber's thesis. We will confine ourselves to noting that the aforementioned studies concentrate on economically declining mountainous areas or islands, relatively cut off from the rest of the country.[86] Further, they indicate a definite decline in the virulence of resistance, even in those regions, toward midcentury.[87]

Last, as the exaggerated case of Corsica would suggest, the instrumentalization of state law and criminal justice in the framework of traditional social relations is profoundly ambiguous: first, because the very presence of the state makes it an actor to be reckoned with, even if in terms of transforming it into an asset in a conflict; next, because the authorities may consent to this instrumentalization to some extent, either because they deem themselves too weak to act directly as yet or because they view it as an indirect way of getting a foothold in the vendetta scene and of gaining a degree of legitimacy. The key role played in this process by government officials and judges who are natives of the area deserves a study in itself.

CONCLUSION

In a recent essay, Xavier Rousseaux and myself have discussed what we view as the three consecutive periods in historical thought, in light of research on criminal justice published since the late 1970s: the study of crime, the study of the functioning of the criminal justice system, and the inclusion of the political sphere.[88] All sorts of factors are involved in the transition from one conceptual framework to another. These may include the number of research workers, the weight of different intellectual traditions, concern with criminal justice issues, and so forth. On the whole, however, we did feel that the change from "history from below," in which judicial archives were viewed as a way of approaching the "historically voiceless," to an analysis of the functioning of criminal justice institutions, took place when the problematic nature of the information available became apparent. As the complexity of repression became increasingly obvious, interest in the political dimension developed, with questions on the role of norms, processes, and criminal justice institutions in political and social domination, with special emphasis on the actors and the stakes involved for them. As James Sharpe has put it,

> The history of crime was initially regarded as an excellent medium through which "history from below," the reconstruction of the lives and mentalities of groups who are often excluded from mainstream history, might be explored. Paradoxically, despite its contribution in this respect, it now seems that some of the most important insights to be gained from studying crime and law enforcement in the past are those bearing on the ways in which authority was maintained and controlling groups maintained their rule.[89]

How can the state of research on crime and criminal justice in France be characterized from this perspective? It seems to me that it is somewhat heterogeneous: In some fields, such as the study of cases, many authors are still fascinated by the study of crime and are unable to draw all of the logical consequences of the challenging of the status of data. In other areas, we find analyses of the internal functioning of institutions alongside studies emphasizing the political, but rarely a satisfactory combination of the two. This, in my opinion, is the result of the scattered interests and the small number of researchers involved, who cannot really be termed a "scientific community."

In my opinion, the heterogeneity of conceptual frameworks derives from the presence of scholars belonging to very different, noncommunicating intellectual traditions—that is, historians of law and historians of social history. The former tend to take more interest in the history of crime or of criminal justice–related ideas and institutions but often remain fettered in obsolete criminological conceptions and are relatively insensitive to the social and political context. The latter are much more aware of all forms of domination, of historical contingency, and of the stakes involved for actors but are less familiar with the legal aspects and with the functioning of institutions. Further, the fact that the two groups often look down on each other is not conducive to intellectual exchanges.

In addition, few historians specialize in these areas. Many of those mentioned here are not deeply involved but have done work in the field because they encountered some facet of the "criminal justice question" in the course of research on regional history or on political or social history. At this point, one may wonder about the value or prestige attached by historians to different objects of research, and there is every reason to fear that criminal justice questions would not be very high on the list. This means that the increased interest in this area in recent years is fragile. The reader will have noticed the emphasis on a number of doctoral theses, which make important contributions in different fields or will constitute references but which are only known to a small circle of specialists, for lack of a publisher. Nor is there any guarantee that the authors will be materially able to pursue their research efforts in the same direction.

The present overview would not be complete without a word about the difficulties of publication. It is a well-known fact that history is the area of the social sciences in which French publishers have the greatest commercial success. In our field, however, the price paid for this is the practically complete rejection of any collective works (whose readership is too small) and a great reticence about scholarly works, allegedly too austere for their "educated nonspecialist readership" (in the words of publishers). This means that since neither the conception of new projects, arising from the confrontation of different views, nor their culmination with the publication of scientifically rigorous works has any place on the book market, research too often goes unrecognized.

NOTES

A slightly different version of this chapter was delivered at the round table on *Historiography of Crime and Criminal Justice in Civil Law Regimes* of the Social Science History Association's sixteenth Annual Meeting (New Orleans, 31 October–3 November 1991).

1. Philippe Robert and René Lévy, "Histoire et question pénale," *Revue d'Histoire Moderne et Contemporaine* 27 (1985): 481–526; Philippe Robert and René Lévy, "A Changing Penal Economy in French Society: In Search of a Historical View," *Historical Social Research* 37 (1986): 17–38. The various bibliographic tools available, and especially the *Bibliographie annuelle de l'histoire de France,* furnished the material for this analysis. The present chapter does not pretend to be exhaustive; however, I have attempted to include the most significant research, inasmuch as I had access to it.

2. Jean-Claude Farcy, *Guide des archives judiciaires et pénitentiaires, 1800–1958* (Paris, 1992).

3. The same author has also published an enormous bibliography (30,616 references)

also financed by the ministry of Justice and which completes the range of available tools: *Deux siècles d'histoire de la justice (1789–1989). Eléments de bibliographie* (Paris, 1990). See Jean-Claude Farcy, "Le casier judiciaire au XIX° siècle," *Bulletin du centre d'histoire de la France contemporaine* 11 (1990): 31–48, on the individual criminal record as well.

4. Bruno Aubusson De Cavarlay, Marie-Sylvie Huré, and Marie-Lys Pottier, *Les statistiques criminelles de 1831 à 1981. La base de données Davido, séries générales* (Paris, 1989).

5. *Compte général de l'administration de la justice criminelle en France pendant l'année 1880 et rapport relatif aux années 1826 à 1880,* ed. M. Perrot and Ph. Robert (Genève/Paris, 1989).

6. Pierre Tournier and Bessie Leconte, *Séries pénitentiaires temporelles 1968–1990* (Paris, 1990); Jean Macioszek and Pierre Tournier, *Base de données "SEPT" (séries pénitentiaires temporelles), représentations graphiques* (Paris, 1991).

7. These data may be obtained by simple request to P. Tournier, CESDIP, 4, Rue de Mondovi, 75001–Paris, France.

8. Marie-Danièle Barré, "130 années de statistique pénitentiaire en France," *Déviance et société,* 10:2 (1986): 107–28.

9. For a survey of the historiography of crime, see J.-C. Farcy, "L'historiographie de la criminalité en histoire contemporaine," in *Histoire et criminalité de l'Antiquité au XXè siècle, nouvelles approches,* ed. Benoît Garnot (Dijon, 1992), 31–44.

10. Philippe Hommeril, "La criminalité dans le département du Calvados pendant la Révolution, d'après les jugements du tribunal révolutionnaire," *Annales de Normandie* 39:3 (1989): 285–311; Bernard Schnapper, "L'activité du tribunal criminel de la Vienne (1792–1800)," in *La Révolution et l'ordre juridique privé: rationalité ou scandale?* (Paris, 1988), 2: 623–38 (*). Schnapper's papers hereafter signaled by (*) have been republished recently in Bernard Schnapper, *Voies nouvelles en histoire du droit. La justice, la famille, la répression pénale (XVI°–XX° siècles)* (Paris, 1991); Renée Martinage, *Punir le crime: la répression judiciaire depuis le Code pénal* (Villeneuve d'Ascq, 1989); Marie-Renée Santucci, *Délinquance et répression au XIXè siècle. L'exemple de l'Hérault* (Paris, 1986); Frédéric Chauvaud, "Tensions et conflits. Aspects de la vie rurale au XIXè siècle d'après les archives judiciaires. L'exemple de l'arrondissement de Rambouillet *(1811–1871)*" (Université de Paris X-Nanterre, thesis 1988); Benjamin F. Martin, *Crime and Criminal Justice under the Third Republic* (Baton Rouge, 1990); see also Annie Gay, "La délinquance dans le vignoble jurassien au temps du Premier Empire," in *Histoire et criminalité,* 211–22; Michelle Ros, "La criminalité dans les Pyrénées-Orientales au XIXè siècle," in *Histoire et criminalité,* 231–40.

11. André Zysberg, "L'affaire d'Orgères: justice pénale et défense sociale, 1790–1800," in *La Révolution et l'ordre juridique privé,* 2: 639–52.

12. F. Renault, "Autour de Robillard, pour une microsociologie du banditisme directorial dans l'Eure," *Ann. Normandie* 39:3 (1989): 313–28.

13. Régine Pénisson et al., *Téjédor: un homme, un pays, une époque* (Montpellier, 1985).

14. Allan Forrest, *Déserteurs et insoumis sous la Révolution et l'Empire* (Paris, 1988). (English version, *Conscripts and Deserters: The Army and French Society during the Revolution and Empire* [New York, 1979]).

15. Jean-François Soulet, *Les Pyrénées au XIX° siècle* (Toulouse, 1987), 471ff.

16. Respectively, J.M. Donovan, "The Uprooting Theory of Crime and the Corsicans

of Marseille (1825–1880)," *French Historical Studies* 13:4 (1984): 500–528; "Justice and Sexuality in Victorian Marseille, 1825–1885," *Journal of Social History* 21:2 (1987): 229–62; "Abortion, the Law, and Juries in France, 1825–1923," *Criminal Justice History* 9 (1988): 157–88; "Infanticide and Juries in France, 1825–1913," *Journal of Family History* 2 (1991): 157–76. See also Stephen Wilson, "Infanticide, Child Abandonment, and Female Honour in Nineteenth-Century Corsica," *Comparative Studies in Society and History* 4 (1988): 762–83; Annick Tillier, "L'infanticide devant les Cours d'assises en Bretagne, 1825–1865," *Histoire de la justice* 7 (1994): 89–116.

17. Joëlle Guillais, *La chair de l'autre. Le crime passionnel au XIX° siècle* (Paris, 1986); Ruth Harris, *Murders and Madness: Medicine, Law, and Society in the Fin de Siècle* (Oxford, 1989).

18. Frédéric Chauvaud, *De Pierre Rivière à Landru, la violence apprivoisée au XIXè siècle* (Turnhout, 1991).

19. Martin, *Crime and Criminal Justice under the Third Republic,* 4–5.

20. This is, for instance, the case for Hommeril, "La criminalité dans le département du Calvados," 285–311; for Santucci, *Délinquance et répression au XIXè siècle;* Martinage, *Punir le crime;* and for A.R. Gillis, "Crime and State Surveillance in Nineteenth-Century France," *American Journal of Sociology* 95:2 (1989): 307–41. But Donovan, "Justice and Sexuality" and "Abortion," avoids this trap.

21. Martin, *Crime and Criminal Justice under the Third Republic.* Bruno Aubusson de Cavarlay, Marie-Sylvie Huré, and Marie-Lys Pottier, *La justice pénale en France, Résultats statistiques (1934–1954), Les Cahiers de l'IHTP* 23 (Paris, 1993).

22. See note 10.

23. Martinage, *Punir le crime;* Santucci, *Délinquance et répression au XIXè siècle.* For a more detailed analysis of the latter, see my review in the *Revue historique,* CCLXXIX:2 (1989): 418–20.

24. Réné Lévy, "Un aspect de la mutation de l'économie répressive au XIX° siècle: la loi de 1863 sur le flagrant délit," *Revue historique* CCLXXIV:1 (1986): 43–77; Bernard Schnapper, "L'action pénale, le ministère public et les associations: naissance et contestation d'un quasi-monopole (XIX°–XX° siècles)," *Archives de politique criminelle* 10 (1988): 19–34 (*). Gillis, "Crime and State Surveillance," like Tilly, attempts to establish a connection between the growth of crime and that of police forces, but his statistical sophistication does not balance out a rather superficial approach to the functioning of criminal justice and suffers from an erroneous conception of the status of statistics.

25. Michelle Perrot, "Délinquance et système pénitentiaire en France au XIX° siècle," *Annales ESC* 1 (1975): 75.

26. Donovan, "Justice and Sexuality."

27. Santucci, *Délinquance et répression au XIXè siècle,* 168–82; see also Soulet, *Les Pyrénées au XIX° siècle,* 502ff.

28. *La Révolution et l'ordre juridique privé; Une autre justice, 1789–1989,* ed. Robert Badinter (Paris, 1989); *La Révolution de la justice,* ed. Philippe Boucher (Paris, 1989).

29. Pierre Lascoumes, Pierrette Poncela, and Pierre Lenoel, *Au nom de l'ordre: une histoire politique du Code pénal* (Paris, 1989); see also Lascoumes and Poncela, "La République . . . en réprimant. Les processus d'incrimination sous la Constituanteé," in *La Révolution et l'ordre juridique privé,* 2: 593–607.

30. M. Dorigny, "Les Girondins dans les comités de législation: luttes politiques et débats juridiques," in *La Révolution et l'ordre juridique privé,* 1: 241–248; Roberto

Martucci, "Le 'parti de la réforme criminelle' à la Constituante," in *La Révolution et l'ordre juridique privé,* 1:229–39; Roberto Martucci, "Qu'est-ce que la lèse-nation? A propos du problème de l'infraction politique sous la Constituante: 1789–1791," *Déviance et société* 14:4 (1990): 377–93. Martucci is also the author of a reference work on law making by the Constituent Assembly: *La Costituente ed il problema penale in Francia (1789–1791). Alle origini del processio accusatorio: i decreti Beaumetz* (Milan, 1984).

31. Jean-Louis Halperin, *Le tribunal de cassation et les pouvoirs sous la Révolution, 1790–1799* (Paris, 1987).

32. Antonio Padoa Schioppa, "La giuria all'Assembla Costituente francese," in *The Trial Jury in England, France, Germany, 1700–1900,* ed. A. Padoa Schioppa (Berlin, 1987), 75–163; A. Padoa Schioppa, "Le jury d'Adrien Duport," in *La Révolution et l'ordre juridique privé,* 2: 609–22; Bernard Schnapper, "Le jury criminel, un mythe démocratique (1791–1800)," *Histoire de la justice* 1 (1988): 9–17; B. Schnapper, "Le jury criminel," in *Une autre justice, 1789–1989,* ed. R. Badinter, 149–70; *Les destinées du jury criminel,* ed. Renée Martinage and Jean-Pierre Royer (Hellemmes, 1990). See also Jean-Jacques Clère, "Les constituants et l'organisation de la procédure pénale," in *La Révolution et l'ordre juridique privé,* 2: 441–56.

33. B. Schnapper, "Le jury français aux XIX° et XX° siècles," in *The Trial Jury in England, France, Germany, 1700–1900,* 165–239 (*); Françoise Lombard, *Les jurés, justice représentative et représentations de la justice* (Paris, 1993).

34. B. Schnapper, "De l'origine sociale des jurés entre 1840 et 1860," in *Les destinées du jury criminel,* ed. Renée Martinage and Jean-Pierre Royer (Hellemmes, 1990), 115–38; M.-R. Santucci, "Être ou ne pas être juré au XIXè siècle," in *Les destinées du jury criminel,* 139–73; Lombard, *Les jurés.*

35. Elisabeth Claverie, "De la difficulté de faire un citoyen: les 'acquittements scandaleux' du jury dans la France provinciale du début du XIX° siècle," *Etudes rurales* 95–96 (1984): 143–66; Yves Pourcher, "Des assises de grâce? Le jury de la cour d'assises de la Lozère au XIX° siècle," *Etudes rurales* 95–96 (1984): 167–80; Y. Pourcher, *Les maîtres du granit. Les notables de Lozère du XVIII° siècle à nos jours* (Paris, 1987): chap. 2; Stephen Wilson, *Feuding Conflict and Banditry in XIXth Century Corsica* (Cambridge, 1988).

36. Guillais, *La chair de l'autre; Le crime passionnel au XIX° siècle* (Paris, 1986). Ruth Harris, *Murders and Madness: Medicine, Law, and Society in the Fin de Siècle* (Oxford, 1989); Lombard, *Les jurés;* L. Gruel, *Pardons et châtiments. Les jurés français face aux violences criminelles* (Paris, 1991).

37. Donovan, "Abortion."

38. Christophe Charle, "Justice et politique au début de la III° République: la carrière du Procureur V. Delise," *Revue administrative* 38:224 (1985): 132–37; R. Martinage, "L'épuration des magistrats du Nord en 1883," *Revue du Nord* 68:270 (1986): 663–76; Martin, *Crime and Criminal Justice under the Third Republic,* 191–233; Jean-François Tanguy, "La plus grande épuration judiciaire de la France contemporaine: 1879–1883. Application au cas de quelques magistrats de l'Ouest," in Philippe Vigier et al., *Répression et prison politique en France et en Europe au XIXè siècle* (Paris, 1990), 126–44.

39. Marie-José Couailhac, *Les magistrats dauphinois, 1815–1870* (Grenoble, 1987); J.-P. Jourdan, "Les juges de paix de l'Aquitaine méridionale (Landes, Basses-Pyrénées, Hautes-Pyrénées) de 1870 à 1914," *Annales du Midi* 100:183 (1988): 287–306; J.-P. Jourdan, "Les magistrats de la Cour d'appel de Pau au XIX° siècle (1811–1914): élé-

ments de sociologie," *Revue de Pau et du Béarn* 15 (1988): 233–60; Christophe Charle, *Les élites de la République, 1880–1900* (Paris, 1987).

40. *Entre l'ordre et la liberté, les lois sur la détention provisoire depuis la fin du XVIII° siècle*, ed. Philippe Robert (Paris, 1992).

41. This gap was in fact evidenced throughout the French social sciences. For possible explanations of this situation, see Dominique Monjardet, "Police et sociologie: questions croisées," *Déviance et société*, 9:4 (1985): 297–312; Claude Journès, "Pour une science politique de la police," in *Police et politique*, ed. C. Journès (Lyon, 1988), 9–26; Jean-Marc Berlière, "L'institution policière en France sous la Troisième République" (Dijon, University de Bourgogne, doctoral diss. 1991), 3: 93–106.

42. Clive Emsley, "Policing the Streets of Early Nineteenth-Century Paris," *French History* 1:2 (1987): 257–82; G. Bollenot, "Le modèle français de police secrète au début du XIX° siècle," in *Police et politique*, 51–68.

43. Berlière, "L'institution policière en France."

44. Jean-Pierre Machelon, in a study of legal and judicial documentation, had already shown that the Third Republic was not the "golden age" of liberties it has often been depicted to be (*La République contre les libertés? Les restrictions aux libertés publiques, 1879–1914* (Paris, 1976).

45. On Lépine, see especially Jean-Marc Berlière, *Le préfet Lépine: vers la naissance de la police moderne* (Paris, 1993). Georges Carrot provides an abundant documentation on crowd control during the nineteenth and twentieth centuries, particularly with respect to regulations and organization: *Le maintien de l'ordre en France depuis la fin de l'Ancien régime jusqu'en 1968* (Toulouse, 1984); *Le maintien de l'ordre en France au XX° siècle* (Paris, 1991); J.-Ch. Jauffret ("Armée et pouvoir politique. La question des troupes spéciales chargées du maintien de l'ordre en france de 1871 à 1914," *Revue historique*, CCLXX:1, 547 [1983]: 97–144) is the authority on the specific point of the creation of a specialized police corps. On an attempt to resort to special recruits during a strike, see Michel Bergès, "Police, milice et société. Un épisode de la III° République (1920)," in *Police et société*, ed. Jean-Louis Loubet del Bayle (Toulouse, 1988), 203–29. On the broader issue of the demonstration as a political and social fact, see *La manifestation*, ed. Pierre Favre (Paris, 1990).

46. As Clive Emsley put it, "The French Police Ubiquitous and Faceless," *French History* 3:2 (1989): 222–27.

47. Different aspects of this research have already been published, besides *Le préfet Lépine*, see J.-M. Berlière: "Contribution à l'étude de la praxis policière sous la III° République. Une leçon de police administrative: préfet et commissaires spéciaux face au syndicat PLM en janvier 1919," *Annales de Bourgogne* 58:231 (1986): 137–43; "La professionalisation de la police en France: un phénomène nouveau au début du XX° siècle," *Déviance et société*, 11:1 (1987): 100–41; "La guerre des polices à la Belle époque," *L'Histoire* 117 (1988): 38–46; "Alexandre Jacob, gentleman cambrioleur," *L'Histoire* 127 (1989): 18–24; "La professionalisation: revendication des policiers et objectif des pouvoirs au début de la III° République," *Revue d'Histoire Mod. et Contemp.* 3 (1990): 398–428; "Policiers et prostituées à la Belle Epoque," *L'Histoire* 138 (1990): 56–63; "Police et libertés sous la III° République: le problème de la police des moeurs," *Revue historique*, CCLXXXIII:2 (1990): 235–75; *L'institution policière en France sous la Troisième République*; "Les nouveaux corps de police créés par la III° République: processus sociétal ou politique?" in *Urban Violence, Public Order and Social Control* (Sao Paulo, 1991); "The Professionalization of the Police under the Third

Republic in France, 1875–1914," in *Policing Western Europe, 1850–1940. Politics, Professionalization and Public Order,* ed. C. Emsley and Barbara Weinberger (Westport, 1991), 36–54; "L'article X du Code d'Instruction Criminelle sous la III° République: un danger permanent pour la liberté de chacun?" *Bulletin du Centre d'Histoire de la France Contemporaine* 12 (1991): 5–28; *La police des moeurs sous la IIIe République* (Paris, 1992). "Quand un métayer veut être bien gardé, il nourrit ses chiens: La difficile naissance du syndicalisme policier: problèmes et ambiguités," *Le Mouvement Social* 164 (1993), 25–61.

48. Philippe Vigier et al., *Maintien de l'ordre et polices en France et en Europe au XIX siècle* (Paris, 1987); Vigier et al., *Répression et prison politique en France.* On political policing, see Jean-Paul Brunet, whose work on police provocation during the contemporary period analyzes a number of famous affairs without seeing police conspiracies everywhere, as do so many works on the subject. It is unfortunate, however, that it confines itself to the political sphere and does not attempt to break the phenomenon down into its occurrences at different periods: *La police de l'ombre. Indicateurs et provocateurs dans la France contemporaine* (Paris, 1990).

49. Jean-Claude Thoenig and Michel Bergès, *L'étatisation des police municipales. Bordeaux et le pouvoir central 1884–1941* (Paris, 1993); Marie Vogel, "Les polices des villes entre le local et le national. L'administration des polices urbaines sous la IIIe République", 3 vols. (University de Grenoble, doctoral diss., 1993).

50. Alain Corbin, *Les filles de noce. Misère sexuelle et prostitution aux 19° et 20° siècles* (Paris, 1978); Jill Harsin, *Policing Prostitution in 19th Century Paris* (Princeton, 1985); J.M. Berlière, *La police des moeurs sous la IIIe République* (Paris, 1992); Berlière, "Policiers et prostitutées"; Berlière, "Police et libertés sous la III° République"; J. Termeaux, *Maisons closes de province* (Mayenne, 1986). On Marseille, see Marie-Françoise Attard-Maraninchi, "La prostitution à Marseille au XXè siècle: l'échec du contrôle spatial," in *Histoire et criminalité,* 392–99.

51. Except for Martin's very uneven work, *Crime and Criminal Justice under the Third Republic* and Marie Vogel, "Politiques policières et systèmes locaux: les polices des villes dans l'entre-deux-guerres," *Revue française de sociologie* 3 (1994): 413–34. An ambitious research project on the French police from the 1930s to the 1960s is underway at the Institut d'Histoire du Temps Présent in Paris, directed by Denis Peschanski and Jean-Marc Berlière.

52. Bernd Kasten, "Gute Franzosen," *Die französische Polizei und die deusche Besetzungsmacht in besetzten Frankreich 1940–1944* (Sigmaringen, 1993); Henri Longuechaud, *"Conformément à l'ordre de nos chefs," Le drame des forces de l'ordre sous l'Occupation 1940–1944* (Paris, 1985).

53. J.F. Sweets, "La police et la population dans la France de Vichy: une étude de cas conforme et fidèle," *Guerres mondiales* 39:155 (1989): 63–73.

54. F. Couderc, *Les RG sous l'Occupation. Quand la police française traquait les résistants* (Paris, 1992).

55. Michaël R. Marrus and Robert O. Paxton, *Vichy et les Juifs* (Paris, 1981); Serge Klarsfeld, *Vichy-Auschwitz. Le rôle de Vichy dans la solution finale de la question juive en France, 1942* (Paris, 1983); B. Lambert, *Bousquet, Papon, Touvier, inculpés de crimes contre l'humanité. Dossiers d'accusation* (Paris, n.d.). Bousquet was murdered by a madman shortly before his trial in June 1993.

56. Michel Levine, *Les ratonnades d'octobre. Un meurtre collectif à Paris en 1961*

(Paris, 1985); Anne Tristan, *Le silence du fleuve* (Bezons, 1991); J.-L. Einaudi, *La bataille de Paris, 17 octobre 1961* (Paris, 1991).

57. Forrest, *Déserteurs et insoumis.*

58. Wilson, *Feuding Conflict and Banditry.*

59. At least since Payne's work on the Second Empire: Howard C. Payne, *The Police State of Louis Napoleon Bonaparte, 1851–1860* (Seattle, 1966). Pierre Miquel's anecdotal work is insufficient: *Les gendarmes* (Paris, 1991); Berlière, "L'institution policière en France," 2: 788–812, devotes one short chapter to it, mostly viewed from the police department's vantage point. See however, Terry W. Strieter, "The Faceless Police of the Second Empire: A Social Profile of the Gendarmes of Mid-Nineteenth-century France," *French History* 8:2 (1994): 167–95.

60. For a pleasant introduction to this topic, see Pierre Darmon, *Médecins et assassins à la Belle Epoque* (Paris, 1989). But above all, there is a dazzling article by Ginzburg on "the paradigm of evidence" which pervades the humanities at the end of the nineteenth century: Carlo Ginzburg, "Signes, Traces, Pistes. Racines d'un paradigme de l'indice," *Le Débat* 6 (1980): 3–44.

61. David Garland, *Punishment and Welfare, A History of Penal Strategies* (Hants, 1985), 78.

62. R.A. Nye, *Crime, Madness & Politics in Modern France. The Medical Concept of National Decline* (Princeton, 1984); D. Pick, *Faces of Degeneration: A European Disorder, c. 1848–c. 1918* (Cambridge, 1989); Harris, *Murders and Madness.*

63. Martine Kaluszynski, "La criminologie en mouvement. Naissance et développement d'une science sociale en France à la fin du XIX° siècle. Autour des 'Archives de l'Anthropologie criminelle' d'A. Lacassagne" (Paris, Université Paris VII, thesis, 1988); M. Kaluszynski, "Les Congrès internationaux d'anthropologie criminelle," *Mil Neuf cent; Revue d'histoire intellectuelle* 7 (1989): 59–70. See also Marc Renneville, "L'anthropologie du criminel en France," *Criminologie* 2 (1994): 185–209; *Histoire de la criminologie française,* ed. Laurent Mucchielli (Paris, 1994).

64. B. Schnapper, "La récidive, une obsession créatrice au XIX° siècle," in *Le récidivisme* (Paris, 1985), 24–64(*).

65. M. Kaluszynski, "Alphonse Bértillon et l'anthropométrie," in Vigier et al., *Maintien de l'ordre et polices,* 269–85; Berlière, "L'institution policière en France," 2: 1225–41.

66. Berlière, "L'institution policière en France," 2: 1242–98. On this subject, there is the remarkable but little known work devoted by Christian Phéline to the place of photography in this process: "L'image accusatrice," *Les Cahiers de la photographie* 17 (1985). On the specific question of the control of foreigners, who were the most frequent targets of these new identification techniques, see Gérard Noiriel's books: *Le creuset français: histoire de l'immigration 19°–20° siècles* (Paris, 1988), 70–124; *La tyrannie du national. Le droit d'asile en Europe 1793–1993* (Paris, 1991), 156–245.

67. Jacques G. Petit, *Ces peines obscures, la prison pénale en France, 1780–1875* (Paris, 1990); Patricia O'Brien, *Correction ou châtiment? Histoire des prisons en France au XIX° siècle* (Paris, 1988) (English version, *The Promise of Punishment: Prisons in Nineteenth-Century France* [Princeton, 1982]).

68. See chaps. 1 and 2, written by Nicole Castan in Jacques G. Petit et al., *Histoire des Bagnes, Galères et prisons, XIII°–XX° siècles* (Toulouse, 1991); also, R. Martinage, "Les origines de la pénologie dans le Code pénal de 1791," in *La Révolution et l'ordre juridique privé,* 1: 15–29.

69. See, for instance Gordon Wright, *Between the Guillotine and Liberty: Two Centuries of the Crime Problem in France* (New York, 1983).

70. B. Cavaye-Sabathé, "L'enfant et la prison au XIX° siècle: l'exemple toulousain," *Annales du Midi* 99:178 (1987): 193–208; M. Perrot, "Les enfants de la Petite-Roquette," *L'Histoire* 100 (1987): 30–38.

71. Vigier et al., *Répression et prison politique en France.*

72. Jean-Claude Vimont, *La prison politique en France: genèse d'un mode d'incarcération specifique 19è–20è siècles* (Paris, 1993).

73. Robert Badinter, *La prison républicaine* (Paris, 1992); Michel Pierre, chap. 9 in Petit et al., *Histoire des Bagnes, Galères et prisons;* C. Carlier et al., *L'administration pénitentiaire et son personnel dans la France de l'entre-deux-guerres. Vol. 1: L'impossible réforme* (Paris, 1989); Michel Fize discusses work in prisons at that time: "Le travail dans les prisons, 1873–1914," *Revue de science criminelle et de droit pénal comparé* 2 (1990): 297–309.

74. As David Rousset entitled his book, *L'univers concentrationnaire* (Paris, 1965). Among recent works on this subject, those by Kaspi and Grynberg are noteworthy: André Kaspi, *Les juifs pendant l'Occupation* (Paris, 1991); Anne Grynberg, *Les camps de la honte. Les internés juifs des camps français 1939–1944* (Paris, 1991). The "concentration camps" for enemy aliens and suspects during World War I, were largely forgotten until Jean-Claude Farcy, *Les camps de concentration français de la première guerre mondiale (1914–1920)* (Paris, 1995). The only study of French prisons during World War II is Pierre Pédron, *La prison sous Vichy* (Paris, 1993).

75. This is what makes the research program entitled "Judgements, exclusions and punishment in France from the late 1930s to the early 1950s," run by Henry Rousso and Denis Peschanski at the Institut d'Histoire du Temps Présent so valuable.

76. Claude Faugeron and Jean-Michel Le Boulaire, *La création du service social des prisons et l'évolution de la réforme pénitentiaire en France de 1945 à 1958* (Paris, 1988); C. Faugeron, chaps. 10 and 11 in Petit et al., *Histoire des Bagnes, Galères et prisons.*

77. Bernard Laffargue and Thierry Godefroy, "Economic Cycles and Punishment: Unemployment and Imprisonment. A Time-Series Study: France, 1920–1985," *Contemporary Crises* 13:4 (1989): 371–404; B. Laffargue and Th. Godefroy, "La prison républicaine et son environnement économique. Population en prison et marché du travail (1870–1914)," *Déviance et société* 14:1 (1990): 39–58; see also Th. Godefroy and B. Laffargue, *Changements économiques et répression pénale. Plus de chômage, plus d'emprisonnement?* (Paris, 1991); Georg Rusche and Otto Kirchheimer, *Punishment and Social Structure* (New York, 1939). The latter has just been published in France for the first time with an extended introduction *Peine et structure sociale,* ed. René Lévy and Hartwig Zander (Paris, 1994).

78. André Zysberg, *Les galériens, vie et destin de 60 000 forçats sur les galères de France, 1680–1748* (Paris, 1987); A. Zysberg, chaps. 6 and 7 in Petit et al., *Histoire des Bagnes, Galères et prisons.*

79. M. Pierre summarizes the history of penal servitude in Petit et al., *Histoire des Bagnes, Galères et prisons,* chap. 8; Odile Krakovitch, "Les Antillais et les bagnes de Cayenne, nouvelle approche de la répression dans les Caraïbes," *Revue historique,* CCLXXXIV:1, 575 (1990): 89–100; O. Krakovitch, *Les femmes bagnardes* (Paris, 1990).

80. J. Baronnet and J. Chalon, *Communards en Nouvelle-Calédonie: histoire de la déportation* (Paris, 1987); *Souvenirs amers. Mémoires de François-Camille Cron (1836–1902), déporté de la Commune en Nouvelle-Calédonie,* ed. Ph. Blon (Paris, 1989); L.

Redon, *Les galères de la République. Mémoires d'un communard déporté en Nouvelle-Calédonie* (Paris, 1990). Several books devoted to the galleys or to hard labor colonies should be mentioned for their excellent iconography: A. Zysberg and R. Burlet, *Gloire et misère des galères* (Paris, 1988); M. Pierre, *Le dernier exil, histoire des bagnes et des forçats* (Paris, 1989); P. Lacourrège and P. Alibert, *Nouvelle-Calédonie: Au temps des bagnes* (Paris, 1986).

81. Jacques Delarue, *Le métier de bourreau, du Moyen-Age à aujourd'hui* (Paris, 1989); Barbara Lévy, *Une dynastie de bourreaux, les Sanson* (Paris, 1989); B. Lecherbonnier, *Bourreaux de père en fils, Les Sanson 1688–1847* (Paris, 1989).

82. Eugen Weber, *La fin des terroirs. La modernisation de la France rurale 1870–1914* (Paris, 1983) (English version, *Peasants into Frenchmen: The Modernization of Rural France 1870–1914* [Stanford, 1976]).

83. Santucci, *Délinquance et répression au XIXè siècle . . .*, mentions the collective nature of lumbering offenses or of illegal hunting and fishing in the Hérault *département;* Soulet, *Les Pyrénées au XIX° siècle,* 1: 134) speaks of "the golden age of pyrénéan *communalism*" in the first half of the nineteenth century, when the village community was defending its ancestral collective rights against the state, and he devotes 400 pages to various individual and collective forms of rejection of integration, ranging from "repugnance" for the French language to jacqueries, and including lumbering offenses, refusal to serve in the military, and smuggling (Soulet, *Les Pyrénées au XIX° siècle,* 2: 265–642). Pourcher, writing about the Lozère département, also speaks of the refusal of military service and the subversion of the jury institution ("Des assises de grâce?"; *Les maîtres du granit*). Claverie agrees that this institution was subverted during the first half of the nineteenth century by traditional social relations throughout much of the country, as she had already shown for the Gévaudan region ("De la difficulté de faire un citoyen"; E. Claverie and P. Lamaison, *L'impossible mariage, violence et parenté en Gévaudan, XVII°, XVIII° et XIX° siècles* (Paris, 1982).

84. Pénisson, *Téjédor.*

85. Wilson, *Feuding Conflict and Banditry.*

86. The case of Nice at the time of its annexion (1860) is quite different: The local leaders, and those in the legal professions in particular, demanded that an Appeals Court be maintained for the sake of tradition, in the best interest of the public and for the defense of its interests, although they apparently did not challenge legal and judicial integration; see E. Hildesheimer, "La question de la cour d'appel et de l'organisation judiciaire à Nice en 1860," *Nice Historique* 3 (1986): 65–74.

87. Christian Thibon, studying the Pyrénées area, views the Second Empire as the actual turning point: "L'ordre public villageois: le cas du Pays de Sault (1848–1914)," in Vigier et al., *Maintien de l'ordre et polices en France,* 309–25.

88. René Lévy and Xavier Rousseaux, "Etats, justice pénale et histoire: bilan et perspectives," *Droit et société* 20–21 (1992): 249–78.

89. James Sharpe, "The History of Crime in England, c. 1300–1914. An Overview of Recent Publications," *British Journal of Criminology* 28:2 (1988): 124–37.

6

Crime, Police, and the "Good Order": Germany

Alf Lüdtke and Herbert Reinke

PREHISTORY

In Germany, modern crime and criminal justice history had a late start. A study of the history of crime, published in 1951, was for almost a quarter of a century the only relevant publication in this field. This book, written by Gustav Radbruch and Heinrich Gwinner was—for a number of reasons—a singular publication.[1] It was peculiar, because the authors explicitly understood their book as an attempt to write a social history of crime and not a history of criminal law.[2] In addition, it was noteworthy because of the prominence of one of the authors: Gustav Radbruch was one of the leading jurists of the Weimar Republic, and, as a member of the Social Democratic Party, he served for some years as the *Reichsminister* of justice during this period. Probably due to this fact, the book was reprinted in 1991, although now it is rather outdated. But until the mid-1970s, Radbruch's and Gwinner's book remained the only major text in the field. For some time, German social historians focused their interest on other topics, and German law historians concentrated (and continue to do so) primarily on the history of civil law. There were, of course, some dissertations submitted at law faculties, which dealt with German criminal justice history, but in general the history of law has meant civil law. German universities have attached history of law chairs almost exclusively to the domain of civil law.[3]

In the mid-1970s, Carsten Küther's study of organized banditry from the eighteenth to the early twentieth centuries, and Dirk Blasius's research into bourgeois society and criminality in early nineteenth-century Prussia, marked the beginnings of a modern crime and criminal justice history in Germany.[4] Both authors, above all Dirk Blasius, attempted an "early" synthesis by covering an extensive range of crime and criminal justice aspects, such as criminality, criminal law, the police, the courts, and the prisons. The scope of crime and criminal justice history research, which has emerged in Germany since the mid-1970s, is much narrower; the monographs subsequently published have tended to concentrate on specific aspects of the system. In particular, the topic of the police has gained the major interest of German historians, with a number of studies already published and others currently in preparation.[5] Compared to the history of the police, other topics have attracted little interest among German historians. Some research explores the development of criminality in German society, primarily in the *ancien régime* and during the nineteenth century. Most recent developments of criminality are also under scrutiny.[6] Almost absent are, however, large-scale and sophisticated statistical analyses of German crime and criminal justice history; although the prerequisites for this type of research are good. For the nineteenth and twentieth centuries, German statistical offices have provided a vast amount of statistical information.[7] The results of Canadian and American historians who are engaged in statistical analyses of Germany's criminal past demonstrate the chances that a quantitative approach offers.[8] Other themes, such as a modern social and political history of criminal law,[9] the history of the prison system,[10] or the history of capital punishment,[11] have attracted few historians.

THE SOCIAL HISTORY OF CRIME IN GERMAN HISTORIOGRAPHY

Carsten Küther and Dirk Blasius, the pioneers of modern German crime and criminal justice history, conceptualized their research subject—crime and criminal justice in the eighteenth (Küther) and the first half of the nineteenth century (Blasius)—by using concepts developed and employed by English and American historians. This meant primarily that their research was guided by conflict theories of crime and criminal justice and by the concepts of social criminality and social banditry, developed and elaborated by Eric Hobsbawm, Edward P. Thompson, and others. In addition to these conflict theory notions, theoretical approaches deriving from criminology and sociology, especially those subsumed under the heading "labeling theories," have served (and continue to serve) as a conceptual background for explaining crime and criminal justice patterns in the past. Influenced by labeling theories, German historians stress the making of crime and perceive criminalization patterns as indicators of power and domination instead of seeing criminality as *phenomen sui generis.*[12] However, efforts to focus more thoroughly on the dimensions of the sociocultural and symbolic construction of crime and the "criminal" and to analyze the narratives and visual strategies that are employed are just beginning.[13]

Küther understands banditry as the expression of a direct, primitive, and archaic form of political and social protest, in which members of a rural vagrant lower class showed their opposition to the absolutist state and the ruling elites. Küther's study revolves around the idea of a *Gegengesellschaft,* a countersociety on the roads of eighteenth- and early nineteenth-century Germany.[14] Küther's first book has been widely recognized as an important contribution to the beginning of modern crime and criminal justice history in Germany.

More recent research into banditry and vagrants in *ancien régime* Germany underlines this position but questions Küther's assumptions about social banditry and about a vagrant countersociety. Uwe Dancker, whose research is based on a wide range of source material, is considered by many critics as one of the most comprehensive and elaborated contributors to German historiography on this subject. He has explicitly rejected Küther's views on the political and social aspects of banditry and vagrant criminals.[15] Instead, Dancker perceives banditry as a separate but compliant subculture. Accordingly, bandits, rather than acting as noncommercial and, thus, "alternative" entrepreneurs, were engaged in entrepreneurial activities conforming with the norms of the established society: Both appreciated material values, organizational efficiency, division of labor, and so forth. Other German historians do not share Dancker's interpretations; but in general, his critique of the notion of social criminality—in the sense of a countersociety, including its political implications—is widely accepted by most of those German historians, who have worked in the area subsequently.[16]

Dirk Blasius, whose book on criminality and bourgeois society in early nineteenth-century Prussia is a pioneering study, discusses the social consequences of economic change for the lower strata of Prussian society in the first half of the nineteenth century. During that period, the Prussian economic and social landscape was primarily shaped by agrarian production, though some regions relied on protoindustry, and at a few locations first signs of factory industrialization became visible. Blasius describes how the changes in the agricultural system—especially from *ancien régime* uses of land, such as the use of common fields and forests, to "sharp" private-property landownership—led to the impoverishment of lower social strata in the Prussian countryside. Many other European societies shared this experience. To assess its effects, Blasius uses the scale of woodtheft as the major indicator. He perceives woodtheft as both subsistence criminality and a form of resistance, exercised by the poor to defend the traditional rural economic and social system. Blasius provides another example of these patterns by describing the attempts to enforce control "from above." The example he gives is the attempt of the Rhenish bourgeoisie to enforce the penalization of the specific contemporary forms of delinquency. In a small follow-up study on criminality and everyday life, Blasius has remained within this interpretative framework.[17] He argues that this type of subsistence criminality was accompanied by attitudes of "righteousness" on the side of the lower classes, directed toward those "on top."

In recent years, German historians have tried to elaborate the concept of "social criminality." It has been explored with reference to rural criminality and woodtheft in northwestern regions of Germany at the end of the eighteenth and the beginning of the nineteenth century, and the social organization and extent of theft in the Hamburg harbor in the 1890s and the first quarter of the twentieth century; both studies also have provided more complex explanatory patterns for understanding the history of crime.[18] Thus, woodtheft cannot be understood simply as an indicator of cleavages between those "on top" and those "at the bottom" of rural society but also has to be conceived as a result of conflicts within increasingly differentiated rural communities, with local peasantries stratified along the lines of landownership and land use. The example of the Hamburg docks underlines the growing stratification of the working class and the efforts of social-democratic working-class organizations to enforce orderliness among their members. With these strategies, the unions tried to gain from employers and city authorities an official recognition in labor disputes. Orderliness in this context meant that high levels of union membership correlated with low levels of criminality on the docks.

These two studies indicate a new conceptual approach in the German historiography of crime.[19] German historians still use the social-criminality paradigm as an interpretative category for understanding the history of crime and criminal justice, but it is no longer prevailing because, increasingly, approaches which use, in a broad sense, social-anthropological concepts toward crime and criminal justice have gained ground. Most of these studies focus on specific phenomena occurring in rural communities, such as arson, infanticide, poaching, adultery, and fornication. In particular, local studies show that these phenomena were transformed into deviance or criminality as a result of a complex interactive process, which included, besides the instigator (as the "arsonist," the "infanticidal mother," and the "poacher"), the members of the rural community among whom the malefactor lived as well as authorities from outside the community.[20]

The use value of local studies becomes even more evident when the intricacies of patterns of particular crimes and their shifts are scrutinized. Gerd Schwerhoff, for example, demonstrates that violence against persons and property crimes did occur in Cologne at a surprisingly low rate. Offenses against good order and the authorities add up to almost 35 percent, which is only 2 percent less than those of violence against persons and property crimes.[21] Those proportions differ widely from those which generally seem to have dominated in early modern times in Western and Central Europe. Schwerhoff also explores a dimension of changes that hitherto had not been studied. He observes remarkable changes occurring during short periods of time. For instance, the first decade of the seventeenth century saw an enormous increase in offenses against persons, ranging from violence to injury and manslaughter, and also offenses against authority and religion. Comparable figures of those who were labeled as offenders of morals but also of property laws remained much more stable.

Schwerhoff confirms assumptions on the usage of public space as streets, marketplaces, and inns: They were dominated by males and, hence, the offenders and criminals were overwhelmingly males. However, regarding marriage crimes and sexual delicts, the balance changes. On this turf, women operated on rather equal grounds. But Schwerhoff also makes clear that it was also in these cases that domestic violence remained mostly unreported or unrecognized. While in most studies on criminality the individuals who committed an offense or a crime are presented as anonymous perpetrators, Schwerhoff treats his subjects differently. He calls people by their respective names—for instance, Johann Nollen, who was tortured for attempted murder (p. 113ff.), or the vagrant Matheis Otto, who was severely flogged (p. 147) in order to correct his supposedly immoral behavior.

The aim to relate the production of regulations and the application of norms to the practices of both authorities and subordinate social groups and classes informs three recently published regional studies. Two of them reconstruct significant features of the *longue durée* of criminality in two southern German states—in Bavaria and Baden, respectively. Regarding the Bavarian case, Wolfgang Behringer observes a sharp increase of incidents that were considered either as *crimen maiestatis laesae* or as crimes against state from the late sixteenth to the late eighteenth century. He interprets these variations as the result of increasing emphasis of state officials on controlling and breaking various disobediences. At the same time, the author underlines the enormous amount of crimes against property. Related figures (roughly about 50 percent of the crimes reported) coincide with figures from other European regions and states.[22] Discussing developments in the state of Baden, Peter Wettmann-Jungblut argues that changing figures of criminality do not reflect mental changes but shifting socioeconomic relationships.[23] For example, he refers to bandits and vagrant people who were held suspicious of many crimes, especially crimes against property, according to local sources. However, what the author considers as changes of economic and social contexts include a fundamental shift of the notion of property. While property according to the older notions of the "common law" (*gemeines Recht*) implied obligations of the propertied against the property poor or propertyless members of society, the notion which gained ground throughout the eighteenth century abandoned such bonds.[24] That is, the understanding of the Roman law granting unrestricted usage of individual property increasingly dominated the perceptions of the propertied and local as well as state authorities.[25]

Peter Wettmann-Jungblut tends to neglect the cultural dimension. Renate Blickle, however, fruitfully elaborates on shared claims of self-defense (*defensio*) based on notions of a general right to survive. Thus, she can distinguish between resistance aiming at the overthrow of authority and a behavior which was much more widespread and by which Bavarian peasants "defended" an arena of their own, enabling them to provide for their survival. It was the authorities who exploited the vagueness of law and, in turn, labeled the "defenders" of a subsistence of their own as unruly if not rebellious.

Tax defraudation and smuggling have been neglected so far in studies on social crime and criminality in German states. Norbert Finzsch devotes a chapter to smuggling in the French-administered Rhenish provinces around 1800; only Volker Jarren focuses on this issue at large. He covers the period from 1818 to 1854 in the Prussian industrializing provinces of the Rhineland and Westphalia.[26] The analysis shows that smuggling did not correlate directly with the conjunctures of subsistence, as in cases of woodtheft and other forms of petty criminality. However, Jarren can show seasonal cycles of smuggling. That is, in the dead seasons of agrarian production, as in fall and winter, and during the slumps of protoindustry and of manufacturing, people on a large scale turned to smuggling. Not only the propertyless and property poor ventured into smuggling as one of their legitimate modes of subsistence. Jarren also depicts forms of organized and sustained smuggling by merchants and others who aimed at speculative profits. In fact, the efforts of the state to wipe out smuggling by instigating local merchants' antismuggle cartels ironically seems to have worked the other way. These cartels turned existing networks of exchange between legal and illegal trading into respectable and legal activities. Even more, the uninterrupted and increasingly violent repression of those who smuggled small amounts of salt, tobacco, or coffee on a day-to-day or seasonal basis (or who were employed as carriers of the speculative smugglers) underlined the selective attention of custom officials and of state authorities in general. It was the petty smugglers who were considered part of the "classes dangereuses" of the *Vormärz.* To the officials it was only the combination of intensified passport control, extended police surveillance, and, in particular, less restrictive usage of firearms that would render effective control of smugglers. Thus, in 1834 a new law granted the usage of guns in border areas even against fleeing suspects.

POLICE, CRIMINAL JUSTICE, AND THE EMERGING MODERN STATE

Since the early nineteenth century and the times of Friedrich Carl von Savigny, the eminent professor of law at Berlin University, German historians of law considered the study of civil law as the most rewarding. But even they did not detach themselves from the aura of the power of state, which fundamentally shaped the juridical approach at German learning institutions. Thus, the institutionalization of state power and the elaboration of legal codes in the late eighteenth and the early nineteenth centuries appeared as two sides of the same coin.

The "general" historians colluded because they were primarily interested in the concepts and justifications of state power and its execution. In this perspective, legal titles and institutions of law enforcement figured as the embodiment of state. Accordingly, researchers neglected the impact of vested interests on the complicated process in which princely "sovereigns" emerged from numerous aristocratic contenders for power. Historical accounts deemphasized activities of rulers or dominating elites to enlarge their particular share of society's products and resources.[27] In contrast, rulers' declarations to foster the "common weal" were taken as evidence of their actions and practices. In other words, ideas and programs of advisers to the respective court appeared as representative of the main tendencies of state making. Furthermore, the historians' emphasis of the "common weal" resonated with their strong interest in "good police" and those bureaucracies which branched out from claims of policing. Police, or in its distinctive traditional appellation *Polizey,* as both institution and legitimation to guard the loyal citizens, appeared as the center of the "modern state."[28]

Therefore, it cannot come as a surprise that research turned to concepts of police (*Polizey*) and policing. Here it was the "sciences of police (*Polizey*)" that attracted particular interest. These numerous and mostly lengthy *Traktaten* elaborated on all aspects of "good housekeeping" in the household of each "housefather" as well as in the "whole house" of the public domain. A prominent example of the related research is Hans Maier's book on police or, as he put it, the "older German discourse on government and administration" (originally published in 1966; a revised edition appeared in 1980, and the latter was reprinted as a pocket book in 1986).[29] Maier stressed three aspects of the public reasoning as reflected in hundreds of pamphlets, articles, and books, which circulated in the German states since the late seventeenth century.

First, Maier interpreted police as directly related to those concepts of authority which had been developed in the neo-Aristotelian thinking about the state since the high and later Middle Ages. Accordingly, the ever totalizing police regulations did not substantially differ from previous efforts of princely authorities or of communal and church bodies to support the "good subjects" in their striving for a "good life." Second, Maier emphasized a point which can be taken as an ironic shift. In his view, the amount and intensity of police regulations in the seventeenth and eighteenth centuries created restrictions to claims of absolute power. If princes actually stuck to the line of *sic volo, sic iubeo* (thus I wish it, thus I command it), they could no longer hope to turn their aspiration into practice, because the "forest of orders" made it unavoidable to stick to either the most recent or the most fundamental of these orders. If princes or their ministers neglected that guideline, the officials and servants of the prince or, for that matter, of the state could not perform services and duties in a way which remained calculable for both authorities and their subjects. In other words, Maier perceived the intensification of policing not as a means to expand state power and monarchical domination but to curb it. Policing appears as a one-way road leading toward "rule of law."

Since Maier stuck to the legal rhetoric of orders, he ignored the practice, which was stimulated and justified by claims of "good police." Therefore, the various strands and sectors of disciplinary activities, especially efforts for "social regulation" and "social disciplining," were not taken into account. Maier neither considered the discretionary dimension of police practice nor was interested in the experiences and practices of the subjects of state or, as it were, the masses of the policed.

The effort to scrutinize the legal aspects of the police of the *ancien régime (Polizey)* has stimulated further research. Rainer Schulze studied the relationship between police orders and general laws.[30] First, he shows the enormous variations and differences between academic authors who dealt with the matter of the relationship between laws and orders. Second, Schulze confirms Maier's view: In the long run, intensified policing became a vantage point for constructing relationships of domination in legal terms. Peter Preu pursues a different view. He focuses on the Prussian codifications of the 1780s and 1790s (*Allgemeines Gesetzbuch* and *Allgemeines Landrecht*). Here, he cautions against a view taking any formulation of police competencies and regulations as the seed for its possible restriction. In contrast, in a meticulous analysis of the intricacies of the codification process, he makes clear that a broad notion of police which included security and welfare still prevailed.

The regulation of everyday life was at the center of that activity which revolved around "good police." Accordingly, the "well-ordered police state" (Marc Raeff) was based on a network of detailed prescriptions which painstakingly aimed at "civilizing" those common customs and practices that were despised by the respectable segments of society as "plebeian."[31] For instance, the opulence or scarcity of meals but also the hierarchy of clothing were prescribed in painstaking detail. These ordinances were repeated and refined permanently. However, Wolfgang Kaschuba has argued that the actual meaning of these texts was not totally shaped by the dominant, because ordinances were related to and reflected the social logic of communal settings. That is, these police orders can be read both ways: as agenda of disciplining but also as protocols of people's aspirations and interests of their own.[32]

The repetitiveness of these orders reflected widespread neglect if not determined disobedience by those whom the authorities considered their objects. On another plane, however, policing had an enormous impact. Stefan Breuer has argued that social disciplining substantially differed from previous efforts of "social control." In Breuer's view, social control aims at limited restrictions while social disciplining has as its goal the total erasion of deviant behavior. Thus, policing worked even if many actual prescriptions were never accepted or obeyed. The reiterative declaration of ordinances remolded whole clusters of orientation. One of its results was to redefine the demarcation between the normal and the abnormal.[33] In this perspective, even successful efforts to avoid rules reflected the growing encroachment of state and police and indicated a change of the social field of force. In criticizing this point, Martin Dinges referred to poor women in *ancien régime* Bordeaux who instrumentalized not only relief institutions and police regulations but also the established code of male honor for accumulating economic resources and defending a sphere of their own.[34] However, Dinges's examples of people's active appropriation of seemingly disciplinary settings does not contradict the thesis that policing still had a fundamental impact on their orientations. Behavior in forms of one's own might still be penetrated or "colored" by the disciplining efforts of the authorities.

Of course, Gerd Schwerhoff makes a proper point when he calls for local and regional studies of the practices of policing and, in particular, of criminal justice. His own research on late sixteenth- and seventeenth-century Cologne provides a splendid example. He shows by careful analysis that the *Turmbücher* (i.e., the detailed protocols of the interrogations of detainees who were incarcerated in a particular tower, or prison) depicts a whole spectrum of offenses and crimes. Besides intriguing details on short-term shifts of proportion and scale of various sorts of crime, he shows that large groups of the population readily accepted, if not actively supported, violent and brutal sanctioning crimes. Executions and their theatrical performances appear not as only repressive and manipulative actions from above. Instead, they are shown as opportunities for various social groups and layers of this community to express their notions of justice.

RAPID SOCIOECONOMIC TRANSFORMATION AND CONTINUING EMPHASIS ON "GOOD ORDER," 1789 TO 1815–1871

In the German states, both the French Revolution and Napoleonic imperialism motivated, or at least accelerated, multiple efforts to break with long-standing practices of policing offenders and judging criminals.[35] Most imminent were impacts in the Rhenish territories, which were occupied in 1794 by French troops (and incorporated into the French Empire in 1801), but also in the states of the Rhenish Federation and the Napoleonic vassal states of northwestern Germany. Here, revolutionary French law and rule directly inspired reforms of the systems of internal administration and jurisdiction. The results were manifold. Regarding the agencies of poor relief, Norbert Finzsch shows in a meticulous case study of the city of Cologne and, more generally, the *Département de la Röer* (on the left bank of the Rhine) the swift and rigorous bureaucratization of this branch of policing after 1794.[36] In Prussia, on the other hand, the Revolution had become a nightmare to the factions of the landed elite and the bureaucracy. In their efforts to counter both potential revolution of the people and Napoleonic imperialism, the alliance of landed aristocrats and of leading administrative officials triggered a "revolution from above." In particular, far-ranging reorganizations of the whole texture of administration and jurisdiction were intensified or started anew.[37]

Studies on the actual workings of the criminal courts after 1815 are rare (except for Blasius, as noted above;[38] in the Rhenish provinces of the state of Prussia, the courts until the 1870s applied a system of law fundamentally different from the one that was in effect in the Eastern provinces). This lack of attention pertains also to the level of police courts—that is, the sanctions of petty offenses by police authorities in a summary procedure. In general, the internal and police administrations have been more thoroughly researched. These analyses underline that the claim of intensified state control of society was obstructed from its beginning. At least in the Prussian countryside, estate owners, mostly stemming from the landed aristocracy, clung to their powers of police attached to their status as local lords (*Gutsherren*). However, not only hostile social and political forces intervened. Alf Lüdtke shows in his study on police practices in towns and the countryside the almost uncontested continuity of the traditional encompassing notion of police (*Polizey*) from 1815 well into the later nineteenth century. Accordingly, police officials, whether on the local or the national level, felt entitled to grant themselves legitimacy for whatever conduct they displayed facing the policed. A second feature from the *ancien régime* was pursued after 1815. State and communal officials continuously relied on the military in any case they considered an emergency for public order and safety. At the same time, local police and the newly founded national *gendarmerie* were kept small for fiscal reasons. In addition, these few local police servants remained almost without any professional training (except for training on the job when they patrolled their beat). Hence, whenever and wherever local authorities felt threatened, the military and its blunt force was called in for support. Authorities were not driven to develop alternatives to violently "calming" suspicious individuals or gatherings in public places at "short shrift."[39] One of the effects was that discrimination of the various groups of property poor and propertyless—in particular, vagrant males and females—was imbued with massive state violence.[40]

Traditionally, political crime had been the only topic of police studies dealing with this period. In 1940, Heinrich Obenaus had published his study on the political police of Prussia during the *Vormärz*. But only the recent studies by Wolfram Siemann give a detailed and comprehensive account of the beginnings and further developments of political police. Siemann scrutinized the archival material of the various German states and of the "German Federation (*Bund*)" from 1815 until the founding of the Second Reich in 1870–1871. Siemann painstakingly reconstructs the phases and forms of the making of a modern political police in the German states. Of particular importance were the *Karlsbader Beschlüsse* of 1819—that is, the first formal agreement between the governments of the Federation orchestrated by Austria's Prime Minister Metternich. Its main object was to speed up the flow of information on suspected revolutionaries and political agitators. Siemann reveals a special mode of interaction, if not of intimacy, among those police officials who had become responsible to collect and investigate evidence and to imprison any suspect. In his view, this small circle of men turned into a completely extralegal institution. The dynamics of their task only too easily placed the discretionary powers of police beyond any limits. Interestingly enough, the Prussian authorities explicitly named this network of police officials as their model when they set out to crush the social democratic party and to found anew a political police in 1878.[41]

THE GERMAN POLICE DURING THE IMPERIAL PERIOD (1871–1918)

German research into the police in the period of the *Kaiserreich* focuses on the position of the police in the political system of the Empire and its role in the economic and social struggles. The understanding of the police is considerably influenced by a conceptual framework, whose major arguments have derived from a paradigm developed by the members of the ''Bielefeld School of Social History.'' Basically, it characterizes the *Kaiserreich* as a fragile coalition between traditional elites (the military, the landed nobility, the state bureaucracy) and sectors of the new bourgeois elites, mainly the industrial entrepreneurs. In the economic and political system of the *Kaiserreich,* law-and-order maintenance by the police not only meant the control and suppression of criminality but also political policing in a straightforward sense, including the control of the working class and the suppression of its unions and political organizations.[42]

The first German study aiming at a comprehensive historical analysis of the police within the economic, political, and social structures of this period has been that of Albrecht Funk. In his book about the shaping of the state monopoly of power in Prussia between 1848 and 1914, Funk tries to relate organizational development of the police, including its everyday practices, to the structures of the contemporary Prussian political system. In particular, he attempts to locate police authority (*Polizeigewalt*) within the overall structures of the state's monopoly of power.[43]

Funk describes police development in Prussia as a correlate of the increasing economic, social, and political cleavages of the *Kaiserreich.* The ruling old and the new Prussian elites sought to cope with the threats to the economic and social order, perceived as deriving from the working class, by a number of politics and strategies, among them the quantitative and qualitative increase of the state police. Funk illustrates this development (which included efforts to increase the professionalization and the specialization of the police and attempts to strengthen the police efficiency by gradually abolishing its welfare functions) as well as the gradual transformation of local police forces into state police units. These efforts were primarily directed against contemporary social movements rather than the consequences of increasing ''ordinary'' crime. Thomas Lindenberger's research into the maintenance of law and order on the streets of Berlin, covering the decade before World War I, gives a number of examples of how this specific strategy was operating in the context of everyday policing activities.[44]

The growing bureaucratization of the police force was another central aspect of police development in nineteenth-century Prussia. Funk has been among the first to trace the details of this bureaucratization. He shows that it was not only a function of the institutional and organizational growth of the Prussian police in this period but a strategy to restrict the authority of the police, in principle unlimited, by submitting it to bureaucratic rules of performance. Funk develops his arguments by drawing extensively from source material on the Berlin police force.

Other research has shifted the focus, with studies of the police and policing in other parts of Prussia.[45] This adds new perspectives to the overall picture, showing that the reality was more complex than the Berlin-centered view suggests. A monograph by Ralph Jessen on police development and the exercise of power in parts of the *Ruhrgebiet,* dealing with the period between 1848 and 1914, focuses on a region of booming coal mines and steel industries and extremely fast-growing urban agglomerations, which were seen as the Prussian "Wild West."[46] This region attracted large numbers of transient unskilled young male workers, who were recruited from Eastern parts of Germany for work in the coal mines. Except for few *gendarmerie* personnel, most of the police in this region were communal or municipal. After the turn of the century, in some of the urban centers in this region, the municipal police forces were transformed into state police forces. On the basis of extremely good local archive material, Jessen describes the attempts to modernize and professionalize municipial police forces.[47] He understands this modernization of police forces as a strategy to adapt the police to the growing control requirements, originating from urbanization patterns in the *Ruhrgebiet.* But municipal police development meant not only growing control strategies; a characteristic of "big-city police" during this period was the persistence of large-scale welfare functions as part of police activities.[48] These patterns resulted in an "overpolicing," which was abolished only gradually. In the decades before World War I, welfare activities carried out by the police were increasingly replaced by activities from professional welfare institutions and their personnel.[49] During World War I, welfare activities carried out by the police regained importance both quantitatively and qualitatively. However, from the beginning of the Weimar Republic period, the police concentrated on military-type antiriot policing.[50]

GERMAN POLICE IN THE WEIMAR REPUBLIC PERIOD (1918–1933)

Since the beginnings of German historical research into the period between 1918 and 1933, a number of *Leitmotive* have guided the study of the Weimar Republic. These *Leitmotive* pertain to the structural constraints which impeded the democratic development of the Weimar Republic, leading to its failure and the Nazi seizure of power. In the early 1950s, one of the pioneers of German research into the Weimar Republic, Karl Dietrich Bracher, delineated these structural constraints, which he understands as key factors for the failure.[51] Among these factors, Bracher lists members of the state bureaucracy, their political conservatism, and negative attitudes toward the newly constituted Republic and its parliamentary system. Subsequent research into the state bureaucracy in the Weimar Republic since then has described the attempts to change the social structure of the bureaucracy's personnel, especially the attempts to recruit individuals who would be more loyal to the Republic and its institutions. These strategies were also applied to the Prussian police, which for almost the entire Weimar Republic period was directed by a Prussian Minister of the Interior, who was a member of the Social Democratic Party. In the historical literature concerning the final phase of the Weimar Republic, this social democratically guided police is often mentioned. The interest focuses on the question whether the Prussian police could have prevented the removal of the democratic Prussian government in 1932, a removal which was the pretext for the Nazi seizure of power. Although most historians have denied the possibilities of preventing the Nazi seizure of power by using police force, this theme lingers on in "official" police histories.[52]

Most of the monographs concerning the police of the Weimar Republic, which have tried to analyze comprehensively German police development in this period, relate their arguments more or less to these *Leitmotive,* but often without going deep into analytical detail. The institutional and organizational developments of the Prussian police in the early years of the Republic are traced in a study by Johannes Buder, who describes the growth of the Prussian police in the turbulent years from 1918 to 1923.[53] One of the key elements of police development in the Weimar Republic period was the creation of a paramilitary antiriot police unit, the *Sicherheitspolizei,* or SIPO. The SIPO became the cornerstone of police development in Weimar Germany. It not only reflected the state's organizational response to the revolutionary turbulence in the immediate period after World War I, but it also served as a paradigm for everyday policing in Weimar Germany, as military-type behavior. The tactics became a prevailing policing pattern, to some extent even more prevalent than in the pre-1918 period.[54]

Recently, Peter Lessmann, who traced the development of the Prussian police from 1918 to 1933, and Thomas Kurz, who analyzed the Berlin *Blutmai,* have shown to what extent these patterns turned out to be a dominant police feature in that period.[55] Lessmann dealt with the social characteristics of the Prussian police personnel, its recruitment, training, unions and political attitudes and orientations. The analysis of political attitudes and orientations implicitly includes the question whether the police was one of the structural constraints on democratic development in Weimar Germany. Lessmann not only stresses that the ranks of the police officers were recruited more or less exclusively from the ranks of army officers with World War I experience, but he also describes in detail how military strategies and military behavior patterns were at the center of training practices in the Prussian police. In addition to these details, Thomas Kurz has given a precise and detailed account of how these patterns revealed themselves in practice.[56] He follows the May 1929 incidents in Berlin, when the Berlin police cracked down on a working-class area of Berlin, leaving two dozen inhabitants dead with only few policemen wounded. Lessmann also goes into detail about the years 1929–1933, when the Prussian police had to cope again with acute civil turbulence. He discusses whether and how the Prussian police could have prevented the Nazi seizure of power. He concludes that it was impossible given how the disintegration of the political system of the Weimar Republic also affected the police.

In contrast to the extensive efforts of German historians regarding analysis of the political role of the police in the Weimar Republic,[57] the relations between the police and "ordinary" crime have been of little interest. In a recent article on the continuities of police perceptions of professional criminals, the so-called *Berufsverbrecher,* Patrick Wagner traces the rise of this *Feindbild* from the late years of the Weimar Republic into the Nazi period.[58] He shows that the *Berufsverbrecher* was increasingly related to eugenecist notions of noncorrectibility, leading ultimately to extermination strategies against those who were labeled "professional criminals" in the later years of the Nazi period.

A number of studies emphasize the continuous impact of notions of welfare on the framing police activities during the Weimar Republic. These authors stress that efforts to regulate and control everybody and everything remained strong. Thus, repressive policing and the pursuit of welfare activities emerge as a joint venture. David Crew has underlined that social policies directed toward help for families implied and even relied on rigid control of the behavior of the households of those who had become clients of the welfare agencies.[59] Ursula Nienhaus, in an article on the development of female police, has described how the small forces of female police inaugurated in the 1920s acted as an institution not only to help "endangered" juveniles but also as agents for surveillance and correction of their clientele.[60] Herbert Reinke is among those who stress that this particular continuity had become operative already during and especially in the later *Kaiserreich.*[61]

CRIMINAL JUSTICE AND POLICE UNDER FASCISM: CONTINUITY OR RUPTURE?

For decades in West and East Germany, interpretations of Fascism prevailed which emphasized the actions of dominant figures and/or elites who had cooperated with Nazism; they alternatively stressed the contraints of socioeconomic and political structures. People and institutions below the "heights of commando" of society and polity passed for victims of both manipulation and terror. This view also offered a convenient look at the police and the criminal justice system. If the German society in general and numerous bodies and institutions in particular had been forced to obey orders "from above," police had not made an exception. Accordingly, the Nazi party and Nazi organizations had instrumentalized and "abused" the police as a whole and the individual officials.[62] It was they who had imposed special laws and orders which nobody could dare to reject. It was they who implanted party members into the police apparatus, and it was they who had installed an apparatus that was perceived as an uncontrolled superpower of and within society, the *Geheime Staatspolizei (Gestapo)* or Secret State Police. Accordingly, questions about perpetrators or complaints among the police were ignored. Nobody touched even a limited issue. No attention was paid, for instance, to the reaction of police to the immediate shift from the rule of relatively stable law to the dominance of special government orders and ministerial decrees after the Nazi takeover on 30 January 1993. Why did this widely proclaimed change not stir hesitancy if not disobedience, at least among those officials who had been trained during the Republic?

Nonattentiveness to police contrasts with attention on other professional groups and institutions; their behavior prior to and during Nazism has been put under scrutiny during the past ten years. Thus, acceptance of and compliance with Nazism has become an object of intensive research. How could it happen that highly trained experts who were substantially interested in the contents of their work became keen to support policies of brutal exclusion of "dangerous elements" and, even more, of the extermination of whole peoples?[63] Regarding police and criminal justice, the first and principal question is which modes of perception and which practices of the everyday made it possible that the overwhelming majority of police officials and state prosecutors, of judges and lawyers not only stayed on but actively contributed to the execution of Nazi policies. Obviously, notions of "good order" and its opposite, images of "unruliness" or "immorality," had become mental backbones to the personnel of these institutions for generations. After 1933, these perceptions bridged whatever gap might have separated Weimar from the "national revolution" the Nazi party claimed. Thus, police and the judiciary perceived the changes as the final fulfilment of goals they had long demanded. Most of them felt entitled to intervene with full force against and sentence rigorously all sorts of presumed enemies to the assumed and aspired German *Volksgemeinschaft*.[64]

Lothar Gruchmann has extensively researched the various attitudes and steps of the criminal justice system toward compliance with Nazism. His particular focus is on the perceptions and activities of the *Reichs* Ministry of Justice until the beginning of World War II.[65] In detail he pursues the build-up of the (security) police, including the criminal police, but he centers on the *Gestapo*, which started from late February 1933. The arbitrariness of its repression was based on the "Ordinance on the Protection of People and *Reich*" from 28 February 1933, issued the day after the burning of the *Reichstag* building. On the level of rule making and rule enforcement from above, Gruchmann discusses such decisive processes as the intransigent expansion of the "preventive custody by police."[66] Not the least, this study reveals the struggle between the branches of government, and especially between government and the Nazi party, in many telling details: Officials tried to defend their claims, party or police (and SS) officials created *faits accomplis* and acted on their disapproval of, for instance, any intervention of the courts.[67] A recent collection of essays by Klaus Bästlein et al. turns to the necessary reconstruction of the actual workings of courts. The contributions analyze in poignant detail the wide array of their collusive practices in the district of the Hamburg jurisdiction.[68] Shown are the ruthless judicial repression of homosexuals; described is the persecution of malcontents and critics. Another part of this encroachment on suspects and those sentenced was the tightening of the penal system.

The justice system itself was an active element in establishing Nazi rule. Both Gruchmann and Bästlein meticulously render account of related transitions or continuities from before to after 1933. However, only the volume on Hamburg pursues aspects of personal compliance or support. The involvement of the personnel is also the vantage point of Ingo Müller and, more comprehensively, Ralph Angermund. Angermund is particularly successful in his effort to show in subtle reconstruction the personal, social, and ideological continuities from the pre-1933 judiciary to its practice after 1933.[69] In contrast, Müller concentrates on certain cases and shows the course and impact of respective decisions—that is, how individual judges and courts ruled in various arenas of the justice system and what the consequences for the accused were. Müller includes the "special courts" (*Sondergerichte*), which were newly established in March 1933 and had as their task to sanction behavior of people that the authorities perceived as politically dangerous. More thoroughly, though, this field has been researched by Klaus Bästlein and Anna Blumberg-Ebel.[70] The results are mostly parallel: among judges, affiliation of class and "national" political orientation reinforced each other. Thus, people from lower social strata and presumed or outspoken left political orientation were treated more harshly than, for instance, Catholic priests who were charged with contempt of the *Führer* by the *Gestapo*. The inclination of most judges toward the "strong state" and their emphasis on law and order cushioned whatever potential skepticism they had against Nazi approaches to transform the justice system and its hierarchy. Except for a handful of instances, never divergent norms or values but conflicts with police/*Gestapo* over respective competencies alarmed the judiciary.

Those few studies which focus on the police after 1933 show the overwhelming majority of police officials uninterruptedly performing their respective tasks due to orders and expectations of their superiors.[71] They accepted if not supported the seclusion of those who were marked as "enemies" of the *Reich* and German *Volk*. Policemen did not hesitate to label by themselves suspects as "dangerous" and "alien" to the people's community (*Volksgemeinschaft*). Most policemen readily participated in the persecution of these "internal enemies." For generations, preventive detection and seclusion of presumed aliens had been a central feature of policing. To the police, public order on the local spot blended seamlessly with the security of the *Reich* at large. This longstanding and well-reputed orientation served as a convenient clue to expand the policing of public order on to new terrain.

The emancipation of police from almost any restrictive limits of the law (or, more practically, interventions of judges or courts) was one Nazi road toward "rule by decree" (*Massnahmestaat,* according to Ernst Fraenkel).[72] One of the far-ranging changes pertained to the detention of suspects. Here, the criminal police and, most actively, Secret State Police claimed and acquired unchecked powers; these powers were confirmed by decree only in 1938. Thus, police after 1933 actively subverted the "rule of law." The normality of daily repression of others weakened those scruples which might have hindered participation of the police in executing the Holocaust.[73] Or, to put it more bluntly, police continuously and actively contributed to sustain Fascist domination.

The *Gestapo* figures most prominently in the accounts of Nazi domination in general and Nazi terror in particular. This Secret State Police developed in an arena of its own, created and safeguarded against competing agencies of both the state and the Nazi party. *Gestapo* was a bureaucratic apparatus dwelling on its distance from state and centralized power. In the capacity of Nazi terror, the *Gestapo* homogenized the political polices of the German states in the process of their coordination (*Gleichschaltung*) during the first weeks of Nazi domination (the *Gestapo* law of 1936 confirmed a structure that had been established in 1933).[74] As to the public appeal, *Gestapo* rapidly acquired the fame of being present everywhere and everytime. However, recent research has questioned this image. First, a study by Reinhard Mann has raised doubts. Using the files of the *Stapostelle* Düsseldorf, he showed that at least one-third of the investigations of the *Gestapo* were triggered by information or denunciation from the general public.[75] Second, these data also indicated that denunciations reached a peak from 1939 to 1941–1942, parallel to *Blitzkrieg* and seeming military success.

More recently, two studies have confirmed this research. Robert Gellately has published a broad-ranging, in-depth account of *Gestapo* activities in certain areas drawing on material of both the Düsseldorf (and the Cologne) *Stapostellen* as well as the one at Würzburg.[76] He argues convincingly that even in areas like the Catholic Lower Franconia and the town of Würzburg, the enforcement of anti-Semitic policies was widely supported: "A sufficient number of people [came] forward, for whatever reason, to offer information when they witnessed non-compliant behaviour of any kind."[77] However, in this subtle and balanced account, not only the "flood of denunciations" is analyzed; the author also traces its surprising but enormous drop-back when the observation and control of Poles during the war was required. Gellately finally discusses cases in which the *Gestapo* considered reported behavior of individual Germans who did not comply as "oppositional" or "treasonous." This scrupulous account shows that it was particularly anti-Semitism blended with traditional notions of respectability and orderliness which functioned as a common ground for compliance not only with the *Führer* but with *Gestapo* terror on the spot.

Klays-Michael Mallmann and Gerhard Paul exacerbate this view in their study on the whole spectrum of Nazi domination in the Saar area (the western part of the country, which had been under French control after 1919 and voted for Nazi Germany in 1935). Both authors originally aimed at showing popular resistance against Nazism or, at least, the range of noncompliance with Nazism. Their detailed analysis of people's everyday life, however, compelled them to revise their assumptions. The result is a painstaking reconstruction of personnel, organization, and practices of the local post at Saarbrücken *(Stapostelle)*.[78] The authors show, for instance, that less than 50 percent of the rank-and-file *Gestapo* officials were members of the Nazi party or Nazi organizations. Here, as elsewhere, many of the *Gestapo* officials were recruited from the criminal police. The likeliness that this background strengthened the *Gestapo*'s ability to persecute political and racial adversaries is underrated, however. The authors emphasize the limits of the local *Gestapo*'s professionalization by presenting details on their bureaucratic mismanagement, not the least their inefficient card files of suspects. Mallmann and Paul also point to the inability of the local post to keep track of the "flood" or orders issued from the central ageny, the *Gestapa (Geheimes Staatspolizeiamt)* in Berlin. During the war, deprofessionalization increased because many experienced officials were transferred to the SD *(Sicherheitsdienst)* or the Secret Military Police.[79] Thus, this account of the deficiencies of a local post and its workings underlines the crucial role of support and cooperation of the broad majority of the German citizens. Only people's readiness to render their knowledge can explain the *Gestapo*'s relative success in crushing oppositional circles and in sanctioning a vast array of noncompliances to Nazi policies.

POLICE IN GERMANY AFTER 1945

For the Allied occupying forces, the police of Nazi Germany was one of the institutions which had to be controlled and subjugated for an effective military government of occupied Germany. The Allied forces not only wanted control, they wanted also to reconstruct the German police completely. Although in practice each of the Allies proceeded in its zone in a different way, certain general principles were agreed on, such as the abolition of the *Gestapo,* the dismissal of Nazis among the police personnel, and complete reversal of the centralizing policy pursued by the Nazis with reference to the police. In the British zone, this reversal led more or less to a complete abolition of the traditional German police system. The military government and the German authorities alike aimed at implementing what was perceived as the English model. They replaced state police by local and communal police forces.

These developments have led the official German police historiography to characterize the years after 1945 as a "new start" for the police.[80] Other research tends to stress the continuities. In his book on police development in West Germany after 1945, Falco Werkentin focuses on these continuities.[81] He describes how the gradual return of police authority to German hands in the second half of the 1940s meant, above all, the reintroduction of German police structures. In the case of the British zone, this reintroduction resulted in the abolition of all communal and local police forces and, in the case of the "young" Federal Republic, the reintroduction and remilitarization of riot police units; the latter were shaped according to the riot police model established by the governments of the Weimar Republic. Until now, this first comprehensive study of the police and policing in West Germany has seen few follow-up studies.[82] Similarly, little has been written on the history of the police and policing in the Soviet occupied zone and, after 1949, the German Democratic Republic (GDR),[83] except for a number of official police histories, commissioned by the former Ministry of the Interior of the GDR and published in the 1970s and the early 1980s.[84] Recently, however, the political police and the state security of the GDR, the well-known STASI, have found an increasing interest among historians and political scientists.[85]

THE HISTORIOGRAPHY OF CRIME, POLICE, AND CRIMINAL JUSTICE IN GERMANY IN THE 1990s: A CONCLUSION AND A TENTATIVE FORECAST

Since its late start in the mid-1970s, German historiography has accumulated considerable knowledge about the history of crime and criminal justice in Germany. The history of early modern crime and criminal justice and, in particular, the development of police have stimulated increasing interest among German scholars. Interest in these topics is further enhanced by a number of networks organizing the researchers in this field, notably with regular meetings.[86]

A late start provided advantages, too. This seems to be one reason why research on the history of crime, criminal justice, and police in Germany never fell into the traps of crude versions of the labeling approach. Most studies are well aware of the necessity to relate claims for and conflicts about law, justice, or "good order" to social figurations as a whole. However, Michel Foucault's plea for studying power as a fluid set of relationships and, thus, for considering the ubiquity of domination in modern society beyond institutional settings has mostly been ignored. Foucault's reasoning on power has stirred many skeptical if not hostile reactions. But it seems possible to conceive of power as a relationship and still be aware of social actors and of the inequal distribution of capacities which either enable or hinder people to act "powerfully." In fact, Foucault's notion forcefully calls for studies which relate the changing appeals of norms on normality, crime, and the criminal to the multilayered "field of force" of society.

There also exist a number of *lacunae.* As noted in the introductory remarks, the history of criminal law and the history of penal institutions (particularly the history of prisons) is almost absent in German crime and criminal justice history. In addition, those dynamics which cut across distinctions between actors and victims (or clients) are absent. They are related to life cycles and to the generational connectedness of both those who contribute to define and to enforce (or to obstruct and reverse) norms but also to those who seek fair treatment and, in the end, justice. In other thematic areas, research concentrates on deliberately chosen or narrowly confined time periods. This applies to some extent to police history also, although German police history is gradually expanding into the Nazi period and, most recently, into the period after 1945. The availability of the archive of the state security and the political police of the former GDR means that this specific aspect of post-1945 policing will probably gain much attention in the next few years. Therefore, efforts should begin to raise and sustain interest in other themes and periods.[87]

NOTES

1. Gustav Radbruch and Heinrich Gwinner, *Geschichte des Verbrechens. Versuch einer historischen Kriminologie* (Stuttgart, 1951, repr. Frankfurt am Main, 1991).

2. See, for example, Eberhard Schmidt, *Einführung in die Geschichte der deutschen Strafrechtspflege*, 3d ed. (Gottingen, 1965); the first two editions were published in 1947 and 1951; see also Thomas Krause, *Die Strafrechtspflege im Kurfurstentum und Königreich Hannover vom Ende des 17. bis zum ersten Drittel des 19. Jahrhunderts* (Hildeheim, 1991).

3. The complicated relations between German historiography and the history of law are discussed in Dieter Grimm, *Recht und Staat in der bürgerlichen Gesellschaft* (Frankfurt am Main, 1987), and in a number of contributions to the proceedings of the 1986 meeting of the German law historians, in *Akten des 26. Deutschen Rechtshistorikertages,* ed. D. Simon (Frankfurt am Main, 1987).

4. Carsten Küther, *Räuber und Gauner in Deutschland. Das organisierte Bandenwesen im 18. und frühen 19. Jahrhundert* (Göttingen, 1976); Dirk Blasius, *Bürgerliche Gesellschaft und Kriminalität. Zur Sozialgeschichte Preussens im Vormärz* (Göttingen, 1976). Both books were published in the historiographical series *Kritische Studien zur Geschichtswissenschaft,* which at that time was the frontrunner of a modern social history in Germany. Among the general editors of this series are Jürgen Kocka and Hans-Jürgen Wehler.

5. Information about some essentials (authors, topics, etc.) of current German crime and criminal justice history is available in the following volumes: *"Sicherheit" und "Wohlfahrt." Polizie, Gesellschaft und Herrschaft im 19. und 20. Jahrhundert,* ed. Alf Lüdtke (Frankfurt am Main, 1992); *". . . nur für die Sicherheit da . . ."? Zur Geschichte der Polizei im 19. und 20. Jahrhundert,* ed. Herbert Reinke (Frankfurt am Main, 1993).

6. A research group around Heinz Steinert at the University of Frankfurt has compared criminalization patterns in some European countries in the decades after World War II.

7. The history of criminal statistics is reviewed in Helmut Graff, *Die deutsche Kriminalstatistik. Geschichte und Gegenwart* (Stuttgart, 1975). Graff unfortunately omits the development of police statistics in nineteenth-century Germany. See also Herbert Reinke, "Die 'Liaison' des Strafrechts mit der Statistik. Zu den Anfängen kriminalstatistischer Zählungen im 18. und 19. Jahrhundert," *Zeitschrift für Neuere Rechtsgeschichte* 12 (1990): 169–79; Helmut Thomé, "Gesellschaftliche Modernisierung und Kriminalität. Zum stand der sozialhistorischen Kriminalitätsforschung," *Zeitschrift für Soziologie* 20x (1991): 135–60, argues for more quantitative analysis in this field.

8. Howard Zehr, *Crime and the Development of Modern Society. Patterns of Criminality in Nineteenth Century Germany and France* (London, 1976); Eric A. Johnson, "Patterns of Crime in Imperial Germany" (Ph.D. diss., University of Pennsylvania, 1976). Johnson has elaborated on this topic in a number of articles and essays, recently under the heading: "Cities Don't Cause Crime: Urban Rural Differences in Late Nineteenth and Early Twentieth Century German Criminality," *Social Science History* 16

(1992): 129–76; and now by the same author, *Urbanization and Crime: Germany 1871–1914* (Cambridge, 1995).

9. *Die Carolina: Die Peinliche Gerichtsordnung Kaiser Karls V.* ed. Friedrich-Christian Schroeder (Darmstadt, 1986), has collected a number of older and more recent articles about the major German *ancien régime* penal code.

10. Among the few available studies, see Thomas Berger, *Die konstante Repression. Zur Geschichte des Strafvollzugs in Preussen nach 1850* (Frankfurt am Main, 1974); Paul Sauer, *Im Namen des Königs. Strafgesetzgebung und Strafvollzug im Königreich Württemberg 1806 bis 1871* (Stuttgart, 1984); Bernhard Stier, *Fürsorge und Disziplinierung im Zeitalter des Absolutismus: Das Pforzheimer Zucht- und Waisenhaus und die badische Sozialpolitik im 18. Jahrhundert* (Sigmaringen, 1988); Michael Frank, "Kriminalität Strafrechtspflege und sozialer Wandel. Das Zuchthaus Detmold 1752–1801," *Westfälische Forschungen* 42 (1992): 273–308.

11. Richard van Dülmen, *Theater des Schreckens: Gerichtspraxis und Strafrituale in der frühen Neuzeit* (München 1988; English translation, *Theatre of Horror* [Cambridge, 1990]); see also Richard J. Evans, "Offentlichkeit und Autorität. Zur Geschichte der Hinrichtungen in Deutschland vom Allgemeinen Landrecht bis zum Dritten Reichen," in *Räuber, Volk und Obrigkeit. Studien zur Geschichte der Kriminalität in Deutschland seit dem 18. Jahrhundert,* ed. Heinz Reif (Frankfurt am Main, 1984), 155–258.

12. Blasius, *Bürgerliche Gesellschaft,* 10; for a recent application of labeling theory approaches, see Gerd Schwerhoff, *Köln im Kreuzverhör: Kriminalität, Herrschaft und Gesellschaft in einer frühneuzeitlichen Stadt* (Bonn, 1991).

13. Stimulating are Peter Becker, "Vom 'Haltlosen' zur 'Bestie.' Das polizeiliche Bild des 'Verbrechers' im 19. Jahrhundert," in *"Sicherheit" und "Wohlfahrt,"* ed. Alf Lüdtke (Frankfurt am Main, 1992), 267–94. One dimension that hitherto has been much neglected is the visual and architectural signs of law (and justice), especially in the context of signs of domination, as "mapped" from the Middle Ages until the twentieth century by Gernot Kocher, *Zeichen und Symbole des Rechts: Eine historische Ikonographie* (Munich, 1992).

14. Küther elaborated on this topic in his follow-up study: Carsten Küther, *Menschen auf der Strasse. Vagierende Unterschichten in Bayern, Franken und Schwaben in der zweiten Hälfte des 18. Jahrhunderts* (Göttingen, 1983).

15. Uwe Dancker, *Räuberbanden im Alten Reich. Eim Beitrag zur Geschichte von Herrschaft und Kriminalität in der Frühen Neuzeit,* 2 vols. (Frankfurt am Main, 1988).

16. See, for instance, Eckhard Formella, *Rechtsbruch und Rechtsdurchsetzung im Herzogtum Holstein um die Mitte des 19. Jahrhunderts. Ein Beitrag zum Verhältnis vom Kriminalität, Gesellschaft und Staat* (Neumünster, 1985); Bernd D. Plaum, *Strafrecht, Kriminalpolitik und Kriminalität im Fürstentum Siegen 1750–1810* (St. Katharinen, 1990); Volker Jarren, *Schmuggel und Schmuggelbekämpfung in den preussischen Westprovinzen 1818–1854* (Paderborn, 1992); Wolfgang Behringer, "Mörder, Diebe, Einbrecher. Verbrechen und Strafen in Kurbayern vom 16. bis 18. Jahrhundert," in *Verbrechen, Strafen und sozial Kontrolle,* ed. R. van Dülmen (Frankfurt am Main, 1990), 85–132; Peter Wettmann-Jungblut, "Stelen in rechter hungersnodt'. Diebstahl, Eigentumsschutz und strafrechtliche Kontrolle im vorindustriellen Baden," ibid., 133–78. For a critic of the social-criminality notion from the point of view of early modern history, see G. Schwerhoff, *Köln im Kreuzverhör.* Among early modern historians, the application of the notion of "criminality" is generally questioned. See *Mit den Waffen*

der Justiz. Zur Kriminalgeschichte des späten Mittelalters und der Frühen Neuzeit, ed. Andreas Blauert and Gerd Schwerhoff (Frankfurt am Main, 1993).

17. Dirk Blasius, *Kriminalität und Alltag: Zur Konfliktgeschichte des Alltagslebens im 19. Jahrhundert* (Göttingen, 1978).

18. Josef Mooser, " 'Furcht bewahrt das Holz'. Holzdiebstahl und sozialer Konflikt in der ländlichen Gesellschaft 1800–1850 an westfälischen Beispielen," in *Räuber, Volk und Obrigkeit. Studien zur Geschichte der Kriminalität in Deutschland seit dem 18. Jahrhundert,* ed. Heinz Reif (Frankfurt am Main, 1984), 43–99; Michael Grüttner, "Unterklassenkriminalität in Hamburg. Güterberaubungen im Hamburger Hafen 1888–1923," ibid., 153–84. Both studies have derived from larger research contexts: Josef Mooser, *Ländliche Klassengesellschaft 1770–1848. Bauern und Unterschichten, Landwirtschaft und Gewerbe im östlichen Westfalen* (Göttingen, 1984); Michael Grüttner, *Arbeitswelt an der Waterkante. Sozialgeschichte der Hamburger Hafenarbeiter 1886–1914* (Göttingen, 1984).

19. These two authors are represented, among others, in the following volume: *The German Underworld: Deviants and Outcasts in German History,* ed. Richard J. Evans (London, 1991).

20. See Regina Schulte, *Das Dorf im Verhör. Brandstifter, Kindsmöderinnen und Wilderer vor den Schranken des bürgerlichen Gerichts, Oberbayern 1848–1910* (Reinbek, 1989) (English translation, *The Village in Court* [Cambridge, 1994]), who has given up to now the most comprehensive application of the anthropological approach in German crime and criminal justice history. For research about infanticide, see also Otto Ulbricht, *Kindsmord und Aufklärung in Deutschland* (München, 1990), and Richard van Dülmen, *Frauen vor Gericht. Kindsmord in der Frühen Neuzeit* (Frankfurt am Main, 1991).

21. Schwerhoff, *Köln im Kreuzverhör,* 447.

22. Wolfgang Behringer, "Mörder, Diebe, Ehebrecher. Verbrechen und Strafen in Kurbayern vom 16. bis 18. Jahrhundert," in *Verbrechen, Strafen und soziale Kontrolle. Studien zur historischen Kulturforschung,* ed. Richard van Dülmen (Frankfurt am Main, 1990), 85–132.

23. Peter Wettmann-Jungblut, " 'Stelen inn rechter hungersnodt'. Diebstahl, Eigentumsschutz und strafrechtliche Kontrolle im vorindustriellen Baden 1600–1850," in *Verbrechen, Strafen und soziale Kontrolle. Studien zur historischen Kulturforschung,* ed. Richard van Dülmen (Frankfurt am Main, 1990), 133–77.

24. On the common law notion, see Renate Blickle, "Hausnotdurft. Ein Fundamentalrecht in der altständischen Ordnung Bayerns," in *Grund- und Freiheitsrechte von der ständischen zur spätbürgerlichen Gesellschaft,* ed. Günther Birtsch (Göttingen, 1987), 42–64; Renate Blickle, "Nahrung und Eigentum als Kategorien in der ständischen Gesellschaft," in *Ständische Gesellschafgt und soziale Mobilität,* ed. Winfried Schulze (München, 1988), 73–93. On the shift, cf. Dieter Schwab, "Eigentum," in *Geschichtliche Grundbegriffe* 2 (Stuttgart, 1975): 65–115.

25. For studies on the establishment of administrative forces of police, for example, see Peter Nitschke, *Verbrechensbekämpfung und Verwaltung. Die Entstehung der Polizei in der Grafschaft Lippe 1700–1814* (München and New York, 1990).

26. Volker Jarren, *Schmuggel und Schmuggelbekämpfungen in preussischen Westprovinzen, 1818–1854* (Paderborn, 1992); for Austria, see the brilliant analysis by Edith Saurer, *Strasse, Schmuggel, Lottospiel. Materielle Kultur und Staat in Niederösterreich, Böhmen und Lombardo-Venetien im frühen 19. Jahrhundert* (Göttingen, 1989).

27. For a contrasting perspective, see Charles Tilly, *Coercion, Capital, and European States A.D. 990–1990* (Cambridge, Mass., and Oxford, 1990) and, even more bold, his "War Making and State Making as Organized Crime," in *Bringing the State Back In,* ed. Peter Evans, Dietrich Rueschemeyer, and Theda Skocpol (Cambridge, Mass., 1985), 169–91.

28. On the notion, cf. Gerhard Oestreich, "Policey und Prudentia civilis in der barocken Gesellschaft von Stadt und Staat," in *Strukturprobleme der frühen Neuzeit,* ed. G. Oestreich (Berlin, 1980), 367–79. Still representative of the mainstream of historiography on the modern state is Ernst Rudolf Huber, *Deutsche Verwaltungsgeschichte seit 1789,* vols. 1–8. (Stuttgart, 1957–1990). See also Kurt G.A. Jeserich, Hans Pohl, and Georg-Christoph von Unruh, *Deutsche Verwaltungsgeschichte,* vols. 1–6. (Stuttgart, 1983–1988). Different views have been advanced by Hans Rosenberg, *Bureaucracy, Aristocracy and Autocracy: The Prussian Experience 1660–1815* (Cambridge, Mass., 1968). In their wake, historians leaning on social science approaches pursued "critical" views in state and state bureaucracies. For a comprehensive account, see Hans-Ulrich Wehler, *Deutsche Gesellschaftsgeschichte,* vols, 1 and 2 (München, 1989); on the *Das deutsche Kaiserreich 1871–1918,* 7th ed. (Göttingen, 1987); or, on particular policies, Wolfgang Neugebauer, *Absolutistischer Staat und Schhulwirklichkeit in Brandenburg-Preussen* (Berlin, 1985). Gerhard A. Ritter provides a history of both the concepts and the workings of the institutions in his account of the history of the *Sozialstaat:* See his *Der Sozialstaat: Entstehung und Entwicklung im internationalen Vergleich* (München, 1989).

29. Hans Maier, *Die ältere deutsche Staats und Verwaltungslehre,* 2d ed. (Munich, 1980). For the development of academic disciplines and the whole realm of public law, see Michael Stolleis, *Geschichte des öffentlichen Rechts in Deutschland,* vol. 1: *Reichspublizistik und Policeywissenschaft, 1600–1800* (München, 1988).

30. Rainer Schulze, *Policey und Gesetzgebungslehre im 18. Jahrhundert* (Berlin, 1982).

31. Marc Raeff, *The Well-Ordered Police State. Social and Institutional Change through Law in the Germanies and Russia 1600–1800* (New Haven and London, 1983). In a very one-dimensional view, Raeff only stresses the dynamics and the modernization effects of the "late seventeenth century ordinances," ibid., 171.

32. Wolfgang Kaschuba, "Kommunalismus als sozialer 'common sense': Zur Konzeption von Lebenswelt und Alltagskultur im neuzeitlichen Gemeindegedanken," in *Landgemeinde und Stadtgemeinde in Mitteleuropa,* ed. Peter Blicke (München, 1991), 65–91.

33. On programs and practices of social discipline and disciplining, see in particular the case study of R. Po-chia Hsia, *Society and Religion in Münster, 1535–1618* (New Haven and London, 1984). See also his more general account of the enormous impact of the (counter) reformations on disciplinary notions and practices: R. Po-chia Hsia, *Social Discipline in the Reformation: Central Europe 1550–1750* (London and New York, 1989). For the German discussion of theoretical concepts, see Stefan Breuer, "Foucaults Theorie der Disziplinargesellschaft. Eine Zwischenbilanz," *Leviathan* 15 (1987): 319–37. See also the balanced account of the historiographical debates by Robert Jütte, " 'Disziplin zu predigen ist eine Sache, sich ihr zu unterwerfen eine andere' (Cervantes): Prolegomena zu einer Sozialgeschichte der Armenfürsorge diesseits und jenseits des Fortschritts," *Geschichte und Gesellschaft* 17 (1991): 92–101.

34. Martin Dinges, " 'Weiblichkeit' in 'Männlichkeitsritualen'? Zu weiblichen Taktiken im Ehrenhandel in Paris im 18. Jahrhundert," *Francia* 18:2 (1991): 71–98.

35. On the changes of legal notions and strategies, see the concise summary by Michael Stolleis, *Geschichte des öffentlichen Rechts in Deutschland. Vol. 2: 1800–1914* (München, 1992). The emergence of a science of internal administration and the organizational changes of bureaucracy in the nineteenth century are treated in a comparative perspective in *Wissenschaft und Recht in der Verwaltung seit dem Ancien Régime,* ed. Erk V. Heyen (Frankfurt, 1984); *Formation und Transformation des Verwaltungswissens in Frankreich und Deutschland (18./19. Jahrhundert),* ed. Erk V. Heyen (Baden-Baden, 1989); and his *Profile der deutschen und französischen Verwaltungsrechtswissenschaft 1880–1914* (Frankfurt, 1989).

36. Norbert Finzsch, *Obrigkeit und Unterschichten: Zur Geschichte der rheinischen Unterschichten gegen Ende des 18. und zu Beginn des 19. Jahrhunderts* (Stuttgart, 1990). Generally on the various aspects of the reform of government and society, see *Reformen im rheinbündischen Deutschland,* ed. Eberhard Weis (München, 1984). The growing interventionist role of various (reformed) German states and the related struggles between social classes and officialdom on power relationships has been analyzed by Paul Nolte, *Staatsbildung als Gesellschaftsreform: Politische Reformen in Preussen und den süddeutschen Staaten 1800–1820* (Frankfurt am Main, 1990). For the introduction of the French civil law, the *Code Napoléon,* cf. Elizabeth Fehrenbach, *Traditionale Gesellschaft und revolutionäres Recht* (Göttingen, 1974).

37. See, in particular, the study by Reinhart Koselleck, *Preussen zwischen Reform und Revolution. Allgemeines Landrecht, Verwaltung und soziale Bewegung von 1791 bis 1848,* 2d ed. (Stuttgart, 1975); on the conservative and, in the 1790s, counterrevolutionary motivations of the authors of the Prussian codifications, see Andreas Schwennicke, *Die Entstehung der Einleitung des Preussischen Allgemeinen Landrechts von 1794* (Frankfurt am Main, 1993).

38. In addition Dirk Blasius studied an important branch of civil law and the respective jurisdiction for divorce in *Ehescheidung in Deutschland 1794–1945: Scheidung und Scheidungsrecht in historischer Perspektive* (Göttingen, 1987). In this book, he paid much attention to the public and political dimensions of divorce and marriage, thereby denouncing any sharp distinction between private and public.

39. Alf Lüdtke, *Police and State in Prussia, 1815–1850* (Cambridge and New York, 1989), and the German edition (Göttingen, 1982).

40. On the connection of pitiless philanthropy with rigid disciplining (leading toward the permanent threat and application of violence against the clients), see the intriguing case study on the "correction class" of the Hamburg work- and labor-house by Joachim Döbler, *Gezähmte Jugend. Regulierungsprozesse in der Strafklasse des Hamburger Werk- und Armenhauses (1828–1842)* (Münster and Hamburg, 1992).

41. Wolfram Siemann, *Deutschlands Ruhe, Sicherheit und Ordnung Die Anfänge der politischen Polizei 1806–1866* (Tübingen, 1985); and *Der Polizeiverein deutscher Staaten. Eine Dokumentation zur Überwachung der Offentlichkeit nach der Revolution von 1848–49,* ed. Wolfram Siemann (Tübingen, 1983). See also Walter Obenaus, *Die Entwicklung der Preussischen Sicherheitspolizei* (Berlin, 1940).

42. The classic summarizing account of the paradigm has been given by Hans-Ulrich Wehler, one of the founding fathers of the "Bielefeld School" of social history or of "historical social science" (as many adherents label themselves), in his *Das deutsche Kaiserreich* (Göttingen, 1973).

43. Albrecht Funk, *Polizei und Rechtsstaat: Die Entwicklung des staatlichen Gewaltmonopols in Preussen 1848–1914* (Frankfurt am Main, 1986).

44. Thomas Lindenberger, "Strassenpolitik: Zur Sozialgeschichte der öffentlichen Ordnung in Berlin, 1900–1914" (unpublished Ph.D diss., TU Berlin, 1993). Richard Evans has published pre–World War I reports from the Hamburg political police, dealing with the surveillance of the working class, in *Kneipengespräche im Kaiserreich: Stimmungsberichte der Hamburger Politischen Polizei 1892–1914,* ed. Richard J. Evans (Reinbek, 1989).

45. See, for instance, a book about the political police in the Prussian province of Hanover: Reinhard Wilms, *Politische Polizei und Sozialdemokratie im Kaiserreich. Zur Tätigkeit der Politischen Polizei in der Provinz Hannover von der Zeit der Reichgründung bis zum Ende des Sozialistengesetzes 1871–1890* (Frankfurt am Main, 1992).

46. Ralph Jessen, *Polizei im Industrierevier. Modernisierung und Herrschaftspraxis im westfälischen Ruhrgebiet 1814–1914* (Göttingen, 1991).

47. See also Herbert Reinke, "Armed As If for a War:" The State, the Military and the Professionalization of the Prussian Police Force in Imperial Germany," in *Policing Western Europe. Politics, Professionalization and Public Order, 1850–1940,* ed. C. Emsley and B. Weinberger (Westport, 1991), 55–73.

48. Current work on the topic is Elaine Glovka Spencer, *Police and the Social Order in German Cities. The Düsseldorf District, 1848–1914* (DeKalb, Ill., 1992); comparative aspects are discussed in Barbara Weinberger and Herbert Reinke, "A Diminishing Function? A Comparative Historical Account of Policing in the City," *Policing and Society* 1 (1991): 213–23.

49. Ralph Jessen, "Polizei, Wohlfahrt und die Anfänge des modernen Sozialstaats in Preussen wahrend des Kaiserreichs," *Geschichte und Gesellschaft. Zeitschrift für historische Sozialwissenschaft* 20 (1994): 157–80. However, the constant reliance on force and violence, least if not especially by these professional welfare institutions and their personnel, has to be kept in mind; cf. the thorough case study by Wolfgang Ayass, *Das Arbeitshaus Breitenau. Bettler, Lanstreicher, Prostituirte, Zuhälter und Fürsorgempfänger in der Korrektions- und Landarmenanstalt Breitenau (1874–1949)* (Kassel, 1992). See also, Joachim Fenner, *Durch Arbeit zur Arbeit erzogen. Berufsausbildung in der preussischen Zwangs- und Fürsorgeerziehung 1878–1932* (Kassel, 1991).

50. Herbert Reinke, " '. . . hat sich ein politischer und wirtschaftlicher Polizeistaat entwickelt.' Polizei und Grosstadt im Rheinland vom Vorabend des Ersten Weltkrieges bis zum Beginn der zwanziger Jahre," in Lüdtke, *"Sicherheit" und "Wohlfahrt,"* 219–42.

51. Karl Dietrich Bracher, *Die Auflösung der Weimarer Republik. Eine Studie zum Problem des Machtvergalls in der Demokratie* (Villingen, 1955).

52. Robert Harnischmacher and Arved Semarak, *Deutsche Polizeigeschichte. Eine Allgemeine Einführung in die Grundlagen* (Stuttgart, 1986).

53. Johannes Buder, *Die Reorganisation der preussischen Polizei 1918–1923* (Frankfurt am Main, 1986).

54. Jürgen Siggemann, *Die kaserneirte Polizei und das Problem der inneren Sicherheit in der Weimarer Republik* (Frankfurt am Main, 1980).

55. Peter Lessmann, *Die preussische Schutzpolizei in der Weimarer Republik: Streifendienst und Strassenkampf* (Düsseldorf, 1989).

56. Thomas Kurz, *"Blutmai." Sozialdemokraten und Kommunisten im Brennpunkt der Berliner Ereignisse von 1929* (Bonn, 1988); and Léon Schirmann, *Blutmai Berlin 1929. Dichtung und Wahrheit* (Berlin, 1991).

57. As, for example, in " . . . *durch polizeiliches Einschreiten wurde dem Unfug ein*

Ende gemacht." Geheime Berichte der politischen Partei Hessen über Linke und Rechte in Offenbach 1923–1930, ed. Bernd Klemm (Frankfurt am Main, 1982).

58. Patrick Wagner, "'Feindbild Berufsverbrecher' Die Kriminalpolizei im Übergang von der Weimarer Republik zum Nationalsozialismus," in *Zivilsation und Barbarei. Die widersprüchlichen Potentiale der Moderne. Detlev Peukert zum Gedenken,* ed. F. Bajohr et al. (Hamburg, 1991), 226–52.

59. David Crew, "Eine Elternschaft zu Dritt—staatliche Eltern? Jugendwohlfahrt und kontrolle der familie in der Weimarer Republik 1919–1933," in Lüdtke, *"Sicherheit" und "Wohlfahrt,"* 267–94.

60. Ursula Nienhaus, "Einsatz für die 'Sittlichkeit:' Die Anfänge der weiblichen Polizei im Wilhelminischen Kaiserreich und der Weimarer Republik," in Lüdtke, *"Sicherheit" und "Wohlfahrt,"* 243–66.

61. Herbert Reinke, ". . . hat sich ein politischer und wirtschaftlicher Polizeistaat entwickelt."

62. Cf. Bill Drews, Gerhard Wacke, Klaus Vogel, and Wolfgang Martens, *Gefahrenabwehr: Allgemeines Polizeirecht (Ordnungsrcht) des Bundes und der Länder,* 8th ed. (Cologne, 1977), 10ff.; see also the widely used textbook on police education in police history by Robert Harnischmacher and Arved Semerak, *Deutsche Polizeigeschichte: Eine allgemeine Einführung in die Grundlagen* (Stuttgart, 1986).

63. Benno Müller-Hill, *Todliche Wissenschaft* (Reinbek, 1984); Peter Weingart, J. Kroll, and K. Bayertz, *Geschichte der Eugenik und Rassenhygiene in Deutschland* (Frankfurt am Main, 1988). On the network of legal and administrative measures, see Hans-Werner Schmuhl, *Rassenhygiene, Nationalsozialismus, Euthanasie. Von der Verhütung zur Vernichtung 'lebensunwerten Lebens' 1890–1945* (Göttingen, 1987). Six biographical cases are discussed by P.E. Becker, *Zur Geschichte der Rassenhygiene. Wege ins Dritte Reich, Stuttgart* (New York, 1988). On the doctors of the concentration camps, see Robert Jay Lifton, *The Nazi Doctors: A Study in the Psychology of Evil* (London, 1986). The identity of the Nazi "politics of race" and antifeminist politics (enforcing abortion and/or general Nazi *Antinatalismus*) is at the center of the argumentation of Gisela Bock, *Zwangssterilisation im Nationalsozialismus. Studien zur Rassenpolitik und Frauenpolitik* (Opladen, 1986), 116ff. and 456ff.

64. For the gradual build-up of police competence after 1933 see Gerhard Worle, *Justiz-Strafrecht und polizeiliche Verbrechensbekämpfung im Dritten Reich* (Berlin, 1989).

65. Lothar Gruchmann, *Justiz im Dritten Reich 1933–1940. Anpassung und Unterwerfung in der Ara Gürtner* (München, 1988).

66. Gruchmann, *Justiz im Dritten Reich,* 535–694. See also Deimut Majer, "Zum Verhältnis von Staatsanwalt und Polizei im Nationalsozialismus," in *Strafjustiz und Polizei im Dritten Reich,* ed. U. Reifner and B.R. Sonnen (Frankfurt am Main and New York, 1984), 121–60.

67. On the academic discipline and collusion of leading theoreticians of law, see Bernd Rüthers, *Rechtslehren und Kronjuristen im Dritten Reich,* 2nd ed. (München, 1989). On the expelled professors of law, cf. Hermann Göppinger, *Juristen jüdischer Abstammung im "Dritten Reich:" Entrechtung und Verfolgung,* 2d ed. (München, 1990).

68. *"Für Fuhrer, Volk und Vaterland . . ." Hamberger Justiz im Nationalsozialismus,* ed. Justizbehörde Hamburg (Hamburg, 1992), in particular the contibutions by Hans-Christian Lassen, 216–89; Gunter Schmitz, 290–331; and Wolfgang Sarodnick, 332–81. For the legal reorganization of work and industrial relations and on the expansion and

range of a new system of administrative rulings (by the *Treuhänder der Arbeit*) pushing aside the special branch of the justice system designed to sanction this field, see Andreas Kranig, *Lockung und Zwang. Zur Arbeitsverfassung im Dritten Reich* (Stuttgart, 1983). Conflicts in this field, and workers' behavior in general, were considered as politically extremely sensitive by all Nazi and government authorities; cf. the comprehensive collection by Timothy Mason, *Arbeiterklasse und Volksgemeinschaft. Dokumente und Materialien 1936–1939* (Opladen, 1975).

69. Ralph Angermund, *Deutsche Richterschaft 1919–1945. Krisenerfahrung, Illusion, politische Rechtsprechung* (Frankfurt am Main, 1990). See also the contributions by Helge Grabitz, 21–73; Klaus Bästlein, 74–145; and Hans-Konrad Stein-Stegemann, 146–215, in Hamburg, *"Für Führer, Volk und Vaterland."*

70. Klaus Bästlein, "Sondergerichte in Norddeutschland als Verfolgungsinstanz," in *Norddeutschland im Nationalsozialismus,* ed. Frank Bajohr (Hamburg, 1993); and Anna Blumberg-Ebel, *Sondergerichtsbarkeit und "politischer Katholizismus" im Dritten Reich* (Mainz, 1990). See also the study by Klaus Marxen of the *Volksgerichtshof,* the infamous, national special court. Marxen reveals many links between its judges and the "ordinary" judiciary, notably with reference to recruitment and sentencing. He also emphasizes the amount of denunciatory participation by the people in "its" court, which made the people's court a veritable court of the people. Klaus Marxen, *Das Volk und sein Gerichtshof. Eine Studie zum nationalsozialistischen Volksgerichtshof* (Frankfurt, 1994).

71. As one of the rare studies so far, see Helmut Fangmann, Udo Reifner, and Norbert Steinborn, *"Parteisoldaten:" Die Hamburger Polizei im "Dritten Reich"* (Hamburg, 1987). The authors' main focus is on the organizational "takeover" after 1933 and the overwhelming personal continuity afterward. The actual practices of police officials and their exchanges with clients are not the issue of this study. See also the singular and rare case of police sergeant Franz Fischer, who was with the local police of public order (*Schutzpolizei*) in the Bavarian town of Eichstätt and who did not hesitate to intervene in cases he perceived as disturbances of public order: cf. Elke Fröhlich, "Ein katholischer Polizeiwachtmeister," in *Die Herausforderung des Einzelnen: Geschichten über Widerstand und Verfolgung. Bayern in der NS-Zeit* (München, 1983), 6: 157–71. This does not hold only for the first years of Nazi rule but also for the immediate participation in the administration of the Holocaust. Only a few individuals disrespected orders. One of them was a *Gestapo* official in 1943 in Bremen who, being responsible for preparing the list for the deportation of the Jews of the city of Bremen to the death camps in 1942 and 1943, withheld names of those who were not on the lists provided by the synagogues but who had been registered as "Jews" according to the racial norms of Nazi law. This official was transferred to another branch, but not punished, when some superiors discovered his practice: cf. Inge Marssolek and René Ott, *Bremen im Dritten Reich. Anpassung-Widerstand-Verfolgung* (Bremen, 1986), 341 ff.

72. The simultaneity of rule of law (or norms) and rule by decree was put forward by Ernst Fraenkel in his analysis of Nazi domination and published for the first time in 1942; the reedition of his book was published as *Der Doppelstaat* (Frankfurt am Main, 1984).

73. For a general account of the administrative networks and notional clues executing or legitimizing the Holocaust, see Raul Hilberg, *The Destruction of the European Jews,* vols. 1–3; rev. ed. (New York, 1985), the German translation appeared only in 1989. A first effort to analyze the role of police in this context was Heiner Lichtenstein, *Himmlers grüne Helfer. Die Schutz- und Ordnungspolizei im "Dritten Reich"* (Köln, 1990). He

discussed primarily the activities of police battalions recruited from the police of public order (*Ordnungspolizei*) and their participation in the killing actions designed by the police of security—especially the *SS-Einsatzgruppen* and SD Commandos during the war in the occupied territories of the East. The daily practices of local officials and their cooperation in the policing of the deportation—to take only one field of action—remain in the margins. See also Christopher J. Browning, *Ordinary Men: Reserve Police Battalion 101 and the Final Solution in Poland* (New York, 1992).

74. See Christoph Graf, *Politische Polizei zwischen Demokratie und Diktatur. Die Entwicklung der preussischen Politischen Polizei vom Staatsschutzorgan zum Geheimen Staatspolizeiamt des Dritten Reiches* (Berlin, 1983). According to Graf, the turning point toward a nondemocratic political police was marked by the "*Preussen-Schlag*" of von Papen and his reactionary supporters from the old elites of July 20, 1932. On the infights between the branches of organized Nazism and the emergence of the *Gestapo* complex (including the "selling of the police state" between 1934 and 1936), cf. Shlomo Aronson, *Reinhard Heydrich und die Frühgeschichte von Gestapo und SD* (Stuttgart, 1971); and George C. Browder, *The Foundations of the Nazi Police State* (Lexington, Ky., 1990), 163–71.

75. Reinhard Mann, *Protest und Kontrolle im Dritten Reich. Nationalsozialistische Herrschaft im Alltag einer rheinischen Grosstadt* (Frankfurt am Main and New York, 1987), 287ff. Due to the author's premature death in 1981, this study and particularly the chapter mentioned had to be published in a preliminary version.

76. Robert Gellately, *The Gestapo and German Society. Enforcing Racial Policy 1933–1945* (Oxford, 1990).

77. Ibid., 259.

78. Klaus-Michael Mallmann and Gerhard Paul, *Herrschaft und Alltag. Ein Industrierevier im Dritten Reich* (Bonn, 1991), chap. 5, 164–326.

79. On the organization of the police and its further orientation on policies of extermination of "others" during the war, see Rugh Bettina Birn, *Die Höheren SS-und Polizeiführer: Himmlers Vertreter im Reich und in den besetzten Gebieten* (Düsseldorf, 1986). On the *Gestapo* and, generally, the security police and their part in preparing and executing the Holocaust, see Helmut Krausnick and Hans-Heinrich Wilhelm, *Die Truppe des Weltanschauungskrieges: Die Einsatzgruppen der Sicherheitspolizei und des SD 1938–1942* (Stüttgart, 1980); Peter R. Black, *Ernst Kaltenbrunner: Ideological Soldier of the Third Reich* (Princeton, 1984); Richard Breitman, *The Architect of Genocide: Himmler and the Final Solution* (New York, 1991); and Hans Safrian, *Die Eichmann-Männer* (Wein, 1993).

80. *Polizei 1945—ein neuer Anfang*, ed. Hans-Werner Hamacher, 2d ed. (Hilden, 1989).

81. Falco Werkentin, *Die Restauration der deutschen Polizei. Innere Rüstung von 1945 bis zur Notstandsgesetzgebung* (Frankfurt am Main, 1984).

82. Norbert Steinborn and Karin Schanzenbach, *Die Hamburger nach 1945. Ein Neuanfang, der Keiner war* (Hamburg, 1990). Norbert Steinborn and Hilmar Krüger, *Die Berliner Polizei 1945–1952. Von der Militäreserve im Kalten Krieg auf dem Weg zur bürgernahen Polizei* (Berlin, 1993).

83. With the very recent exception of Richard Bessel, "Police and Society in Eastern Germany after 1945," in *German History* 10 (1992): 290–301.

84. The most prominent among the official police histories in the German Democratic

Republic is the two-volume edition of the *Geschichte der Deutschen Volkspolizei,* ed. Ministry of the Interior/GDR, 2d ed. (Berlin, 1987).

85. In the aftermath of the collapse of the German Democratic Republic and its political police, the STASI, a vast number of publications on the dissolution of the STASI have been published by members of the committees, which had been in charge of the STASI abolition.

86. Two groups organize regular meetings, one group on the history of early modern patterns of crime and a second one on police history topics.

87. The first volume, containing attempts to compare the most prominent political policies in German history (among them the *Gestapo* and the STASI), has recently been edited by Bern Florath, Armin Mitter, and Stefan Wolle, *Die Ohnmacht der Allmächtigen: Geheimdienste und politische Polizei in der modernen Gesellschaft* (Berlin, 1992).

7

Brigands, Mafiosi, and Others: Italy

Steven C. Hughes

Although there was originally some resistance among Italian scholars to the acceptance of criminality as a legitimate subject of historical research, a good deal of fruitful scholarship has recently appeared on Italy that clearly fits under the rubric of criminal justice history. Large conferences have been organized around banditry, police legislation, social control, and penal reform, while more and more historians are turning to related topics.[1] In particular, younger scholars in Italy are familiar with the literature on crime from elsewhere in Europe and North America and are carefully using a variety of methods to start a comparative framework that will serve the future well. In addition, a number of non-Italians have looked to Italy as a critically important area full of interesting and sometimes unique possibilities of investigation. Concentrating on the nineteenth and twentieth centuries, this chapter seeks to highlight some of the aspects of this recent historiography and suggest some possible directions for research which might prove useful.[2]

To date, the bulk of criminal justice history in Italy has been of the juridical variety, which has fed on the country's long tradition of historical idealism and legal exegesis. One of the best and most prolific authors of this school is Mario Sbriccoli, who is well known for an exhaustive technical study on the legal ideology of political crime at the start of the early modern period.[3] For the most part, Sbriccoli's works are rather rarified for the social historian, seldom touching ground as they discourse on internalist legalistic debate and penal theory. Some tend to the abstract and occasionally incorporate legal jargon that leaves the generalist gasping for air and reaching for Latin dictionaries.[4] On the other hand, anyone trying to understand the changing conceptions of criminality in late nineteenth-century Italy and its impact on legislation simply cannot ignore Sbriccoli's many articles on the development of legal culture after unity.[5] Above all, however, Sbriccoli has been a staunch proponent and defender of criminal justice history, and many people have entered the field under his tutelage. He has also become a major advocate for what he calls ''integrated criminal history,'' which combines the study of criminal action, repressive institutions, and legal theory.[6]

One of the best examples of such integreated history is Isabella Rosoni's *Criminalità e giustizia penale nello Stato Pontificio del secolo XIX. Un caso di banditismo rurale.*[7] Although archival sources provide the core of this fine monograph, Rosoni uses her obvious command of the secondary literature in anthropology, criminology, and juridical theory to offer a multilayered view of both rural crime and preunitary justice by meticulously dissecting a ''maxi'' trial of thirty-two peasants accused of brigandage in the Papal States during the early 1840s. She sets the social stage for her analysis—often reminiscent of the work of Carlo Ginsburg—with a penetrating examination of rural poverty and how it affected both crime and justice in the area. Elaborating on the now well-accepted theme of a ''Crisis in the Countryside,'' she describes the deteriorating position of the rural work force as the Papal States (like the rest of Italy) went through a massive agricultural transition starting in the 1750s. The key factors in this upheaval were the privatization of communal land and the gradual deterioration of sharecropping (*mezzadria*) in favor of new forms of land tenure based on a wage-based labor market. This created an ever-growing number of *braccianti* or day laborers, who had little security and who constantly competed for even the most poorly paid work. Often lacking the basics of survival, these rural proletarians, according to Rosoni, gradually slipped further and further into marginal lifestyles until they virtually lived on the edge between legal and illegal activities, often engaging in various forms of minor rural theft (particularly the pilferage of consumable food items). Interestingly, Rosoni asserts that despite their frequent complaints about such *furti campestri,* the owners seldom prosecuted the peasants involved—a phenomenon she calls ''landlord hospitality'' and which she variously attributes to sympathetic charity, fear of retaliation, and ignorance of exactly how much was actually disappearing. Likewise, the regime with its notorious judicial inefficiency allowed much illegal activity to slide by.

This tolerant attitude could change, however, as happened when *braccianti* around the town of Filottrano in the Marche organized themselves into a brigand band in the early 1840s and carried out a series of daring ''invasions'' in which local farmhouses were attacked and their inhabitants terrorized or even tortured into giving up their valuables. The collective nature of these crimes and their obvious threat to social hierarchy shocked the government and the landlords, transforming their hospitality into hostility and paving the way for massive judicial action. The arrest of a robber who had gotten drunk at the scene of the crime eventually led to a full-scale investigation and the round-up of some sixty-nine suspects who were implicated in fifty-three separate crimes, many of which carried the death penalty. After years of further inquiry by a papal official, who was assigned full time to the case, these were reduced to thirty-two suspects accused of twenty-seven crimes. The trial itself did not take place until 1850, when the court handed down seven death sentences and a variety of lesser penalties. Four years later, all but two of the death sentences were commuted on appeal. Although the trial clearly demonstrated all the problems and inefficiencies of inquisitorial procedure under papal rule, according to Rosoni the trial had its own logic, which was essentially political rather than judicial and which was designed to mollify public sentiment aroused by the crimes. Once the suspects were in jail and the invasions conveniently came to an end, papal officials could take all the time they needed in creating an elaborate paper portrait identifying those involved in the most violent crimes as leaders of a hierarchically organized gang: a portrait which Rosoni suggests probably had little to do with reality but which fit their particular conception of banditry in general. Without a counterbalancing view from the defense, the examining judge over time determined his own historical version of the truth, which was tied indirectly to the political exigencies of the moment.

Rosoni's most creative analysis, however, comes in her reconstruction—taken from the thousands of pages of testimony, of what one might call the criminology of extreme poverty. In a certain sense, the bandits were forced into collective crime if they were to escape their miserable conditions, but their own poverty as well as the relative poverty of their better-off neighbors helped lead to their eventual discovery and conviction. In short, there was little of the real "treasure" (cash and jewels) of which the robbers talked and dreamed, and they usually ended up emptying the targeted houses of their entire contents, including furniture, clothing, and even broken pots and pans. According to this logic people, who have nothing value everything. Conversely, this made it almost impossible for the robbers to fence their booty; and indeed it was the gradual accumulation of material evidence which finally led to their arrest and conviction. There is much here for those interested in material culture, and Rosoni relates how the most trivial objects could be described in the most amazing detail by people months and sometimes years after the event.

This was vitally important to the judicial procedure itself, because in contrast to their amazing memory for stolen objects, the victims were universally unable to provide even the sketchiest information about their assailants, even though they were sometimes with them for hours. This *omertà* of silence—mostly based on a fear of reprisal—forced the prosecution to rely overwhelmingly on circumstantial evidence and the written testimony of a wide range of "experts," who could discuss such evidence. Eventually, as the net of physical evidence drew tighter, the authorities were rewarded by the decision of one of the robbers to turn state's evidence, although this occasioned a complicated and lengthy reevaluation of the entire process, which contributed to the overall delay of seven years in getting to trial. It is in this painstaking re-creation of the inquisitorial procedure that Rosoni makes her most substantial contribution. Very little has been written about the mechanisms of preunitary criminal justice, and then only at the structural or legislative level. This is the first time, at least for the Papal States, that one can get a feel for how the system actually operated, and Rosoni uses her knowledge of legal theory to enhance the description.

Her book, however, is not without its flaws. The main theme is not well articulated, as evidenced by the lack of a formal conclusion; and for all her talk of the indirect political functions of the judiciary, Rosoni seems to ignore vital political events of the day that would have had an impact. Thus, the Mazzinian revolution of 1843 at Savigno, which incorporated the help of supposed brigands, and the revolution of 1848–1849 would have conditioned the judicial environment of the time, and yet Rosoni says nothing of them. On the other hand, the incorporation of so many different methodologies occasionally leads to somewhat superficial analysis, as when Rosoni attempts to place the trial within the framework of Hobsbawm's social banditry. Likewise, her lengthy section on how specific crimes within the Gregorian penal code lacked theoretical precedents will strike the general reader as both abstract and irrelevant. Despite these problems, however, Rosoni is to be congratulated for what is obviously an important and original book symbolizing both the rapprochement between juridical and social history in Italy and the growing acceptance of criminal justice history as a particular field of study.

That acceptance is already well established in mafia studies, wherein the recurring nature of the problem in Italy and popular fascination with its mystique have occasioned the publication of many historical and sociological works. One of the latest of these is Christopher Duggan's *Fascism and the Mafia.*[8] Despite the specificity of his title, Duggan devotes the first part of his book to an important discussion of the development of the idea of mafia in Sicily. Echoing the work of scholars such as Henner Hess, Anton Blok, and Peter and Jane Schneider, Duggan asserts that the popular perception of the mafia as a secret criminal organization—complete with highly articulated command structures, rites of initiation, and widespread networks of control—never existed. This picture was instead the invention of various criminologists, politicians, and administrators, who could not fathom the nature of Sicilian society after the island's incorporation into united Italy in 1861. Mafia then was never an organization per se, but rather a set of attitudes and power relations based on traditions of private justice, personal strength, dyadic clientelism, and universal silence (*omertà*) toward the authorities. These cultural habits had developed through centuries of weak government, economic exploitation, and agricultural decline, which had left the vast majority of Sicily's peasantry tied up in a war of every man for himself and one's family against all. Government was to be distrusted, associations eschewed, and fellow peasants exploited. Such a system served the absentee owners of the large *latifundia* and their *gabellotti,* or on site managers, all of whom profited from unfair labor practices and faced no concerted opposition from the peasants. In the absence of a strong state apparatus, personal connections and the ability to use violence substituted for formal mechanisms of justice. Thus, an unwritten code of honor and a system of private justice through vendetta had come to permeate Sicilian society but, by definition, had never given rise to an identifiable organization or even ritual association.

The idea of an organized mafia came as Piedmont attempted to introduce a new regime of formal centralized law backed up by the state's military, administrative, and judicial bureaucracies. Unable to account for the Sicilians' refusal to cooperate with the new system and unwilling to understand the basic social disparities that continued to promote such a culture, the Italian government blamed the region's problems on a secret organization of criminals, who seemed to be coordinating the resistance against the regime and enforcing their own alternative rule. This assumption set the program for government policy for years to come and contributed to the idea that all Sicily really needed was forceful police action, which would break the back of this criminal association and reassure people that the state could be relied on to protect them. It is this emphasis on the government's own perspective of Sicilian affairs rather than on the mafia per se that makes Duggan's book so creative. He shows how, by defining all disorder on the island in terms of a secret society, administrators could not only easily ignore the social and economic ills of the people but also employ Italy's rather illiberal laws of criminal association in order to perform large-scale arrests with relatively little evidence. Such harshness, however, only further alienated the Sicilians and reinforced their distrust of the central system. Although liberal governments more often than not found it expedient to use Sicily's informal networks of personal power to reinforce their own political position, they could on occasion mount highly publicized campaigns against the mafia as evidence of their commitment to good government.

This all leads into Duggan's analysis of Mussolini's celebrated attack on the mafia, which was spearheaded by the "prefect of iron," Cesare Mori. Using archival sources, Duggan meticulously reconstructs Mori's violent and often indiscriminate tactics during the campaign, which led to mass raids on towns, the arbitrary arrest of thousands of people, and show trials that made a mockery of judicial procedure. Convinced that the *gabellotti,* or agricultural middlemen, were the heart and soul of mafia organization, he also attempted to restructure rents and contracts to the advantage of the landlords, hoping that they would come to take a direct role in running their properties. Meanwhile, Mori had to deal with his fellow Fascists, many of whom doubted his sincerity to their cause. In turn, he felt that some sectors of the party had been infiltrated by the mafia and eventually accused his Fascist opponents of complicity. Through a series of machinations, Mori managed to secure the removal of the local Fascist Federale, Alfred Cucco, who opposed his policies as being misdirected at the *gabellotti* when the real brains and beneficiaries of the mafia were the elite landowners. Mori himself was removed in 1929, the result not only of his own administrative excesses but also of the consistent efforts of various enemies within the party.

Duggan's book is at its best in this description of the unending complexities and the personal intrigues of Fascist politics, which surrounded Mori as he sought to set his policies in action. Duggan concludes that for all his efforts, Mori had little chance of success because he misunderstood the amorphous nature of the mafia, and no amount of power or force could eliminate an organization which did not really exist.

Despite the obvious merits of his book, Duggan has not been without his critics. Adrian Lyttelton has accused him of relying too heavily on a purely rural model of mafia, with its emphasis on the influence of large estates, and not understanding the critical role of Palermo as an urban link between them.[9] Likewise, he suggests that Duggan's rebuttal of the organizational myth of the mafia downplays the possible kinds of relationships that could connect different networks of kinship and clientilism. Some groups in urban areas probably used secret society rituals, a commonplace of preunitary Italian politics, to reinforce personal ties, and some *mafiosi* seem to have spread their networks beyond local boundaries of geography and kinship. In a sense, he is suggesting that Duggan goes so far in debunking the myth of the mafia that he leaves very little reality to explain actions and events that are clearly mafia related. As he says, "Sea monsters may be mythical, but octopuses do exist."[10] Above all, however, Lyttelton stresses the importance of violence as a defining marker of mafia networks:

> In economic, political, and cultural terms the mafiosi acted as mediators between the various levels of Sicilian society and the national State. In this they were not essentially different from the other patron-client networks which operated in the South. But the Mafia was a system of *violent* clienteles, which was able to usurp a part of the State's functions, and even to function as a kind of "parallel system of justice."[11]

With this in mind, Lyttelton suggests that Duggan should make clearer how the *mafiosi* exploited the violent honor code of Sicily and stressed those aspects of it which suited their purposes.

Lyttelton bases much of his criticism on the work of Raimondo Catanzaro, a sociologist who stresses the continuity and adaptability of the mafia as clues to its nature.[12] Catanzaro accepts the central role of honor in explaining the mafia, but he combines it with the idea of "instrumental friendships" and argues that together they formed a code that was a modern hybrid rather than a feudal holdover. Such behaviors came to dominate Sicilian society because of its lack of internal economic development and its position on the periphery of first the Spanish Empire and later the Italian nation-state. Like Duggan, he sees the mafia emerging around the time of unification; but rather than a chimera of bureaucratic imagination, he portrays it as a series of "*ad hoc* temporary coalitions based on networks of instrumental friendship" which came to play a vital mediating role within the new government system.[13] Unable to penetrate the island both physically and mentally, afraid of social disorder among the peasantry, and bound to national politics based on local patronage, the new Italian government came to rely heavily on *mafioso* connections as a mechanism of rule:

> Thus the *mafia* represented a response to the strains among peasants, landlords and *gabelloti,* and between them and the central government. It was a way to manage these strains by means of a particular behaviour in which *mafiosi* specialized as power brokers. Once characterized as holders of the honour monopoly, the *mafiosi* were able to exercise social control legally, playing a role of political and economic intermediaries. Their functions of mediation and liaison were not limited to control of the electorate and prevention of peasants' rebellions (or their repression by violence), but were based on their position of supervision and management on the absentee landlords' estates.[14]

Anything but illegal, these competing networks came to supplant the authority of the state. In addition, the principles of honor, instrumental friendship, and personal violence were not tied to any particular philosophy or institution and thus proved themselves amazingly adaptable to both political and economic change. Consequently, after World War II, the networks shifted from legal, albeit informal, mediation for the state to the illegal, albeit more lucrative, organization of activities such as drug trafficking. Because the mafia has been a hybrid of modern institutions and traditional values from the beginning, it has continued to evolve along with Italian society.

This concept of evolution has also been a key theme in the work of Pino Arlacchi, whose *La mafia imprenditrice* has the double of advantage of bringing the story up to present day and of examining the mafia phenomenon on the southern Italian peninsula as well as in Sicily.[15] Based in part on his earlier sociological study of society in Calabria, Arlacchi postulates that "classic" or traditional mafia arose primarily in areas of "permanent transition," where there was "a marked asymmetry between the mercantile-capitalist economic structure and the traditionalism of the cultural structure."[16] In these areas, he suggests that social relations were dominated by a constant and deadly competition along vertical lines for honor and power. Rather than the product of class stasis and privilege, mafia behavior resulted from the violent struggle for upward mobility on the part of marginals who utilized the primitive practices of predatory vendetta and universal *omertà* to gain positions of unofficial authority within society. Ruthless and cunning, Arlacchi's ideal type *mafioso* rose from humble origins to become a respected arbiter and mediator of society, although such respect was always based ultimately on a willingness to resort to murder and physical intimidation. But, says Arlacchi, the classic *mafioso* did not adapt well to the changes occuring in postwar Italian society, particularly the emigration of workers to the north and the massive investment of the central government in the south. In addition, for the first time the state began to enforce its monopoly over coercion, bringing an end to the mediating role of *mafiosi* and thus criminalizing their previously tolerated activities. Indeed, Arlacchi suggests that in the 1950s and 1960s, the traditional mafia underwent a major crisis, making way for men who understood that wealth rather than old-time respect (or the articulation of mediating power in and of itself) had now become the basis of honor. Not wanting to lose his identity with the common people, the traditional *mafioso* had always stayed within the middle range of society, whereas the new *mafioso* clearly saw money, power, and honor as identical and ostentatiously displayed his wealth while seeking constantly to expand it. He frequently achieved this goal by investing illicit capital, gained from kidnapping, extortion, and the like, into licit enterprises such as construction, transportation, or the tourist trade, where his ultimate willingness to use violence gave him a number of critical advantages against competing firms. Thus, the new *mafioso* took the arcane practices of *omertà* and vendetta out of their traditional roles and applied them effectively toward new entrepreneurial goals. But as mafia business grew, it also eventually brought about encounters and competition among old groups over new enterprises, thus occasioning a widespread increase in mafia violence throughout the south. The entire process has since been complicated by the entrance of the mafia into the international drug trade, the profits of which have been so great as to alter the economy of Sicily and allow some families to try to challenge the state's legal apparatus, assassinating key figures of the judiciary and police. Thus, Arlacchi sounds a pessimistic note in his book, warning that "the entrepreneurial activity of the mafia is poisoning large stretches of territory, and entire sectors of production, with heavier and heavier doses of destructive anarchy and barbarism, and is proving one of the gravest threats to democracy and development."[17]

Leaving aside Arlacchi's appraisal of the current situation, it should be clear that the historiography of the mafia in Italy has reached a sophisticated level based on numerous highly researched monographs. This leaves one asking, however, why this interest in organized crime has not been extended to other parts of Italy. Many historians and sociologists, including Duggan and Arlacchi, refer with frequency to the Neapolitan *camorra,* but there is almost a complete dearth of solid secondary literature on the topic. Inevitably, claims about this infamous urban crime organization are based on a relatively limited number of rather sensationalistic contemporary descriptions—exactly the kind of evidence that current scholars of the mafia would question carefully. Clearly the *camorra* is a topic in need of investigation. It has been portrayed time and again as playing a vital role in the city's history, and it offers an important urban counterbalance to the rural emphasis of current mafia studies. Moreover, this obvious disparity of historical interest in the two phenomena, mafia and *camorra,* is in and of itself an interesting historiographical conundrum worthy of investigation.

One might even take the investigation of organized crime farther north. The Piedmontese did not restrict their use of the juridical device of criminal association to Sicily.[18] Indeed, the charge was brought against over 200 defendants in Bologna in 1862 and resulted in a rather classic show trial complete with a huge cage full of defendants, all of whom were predictably convicted and sentenced. The fact that organized crime was perhaps around in the north immediately after unity leads to a whole gamut of interesting questions about how it might have differed from its counterparts in the south and why, above all, it disappeared after this initial official onslaught. On the other hand, such criminal associations in the north may in fact have been no more than handy fictions utilized to lump perceived enemies of the regime into easily managed categories. In sum, comparative history would serve us well if some of the insights gained from studies on the mafia were applied elsewhere.

Another topic of major interest in Italy is brigandage, especially in the south. One of the best of the early works, Franco Molfese's *Storia del brigantaggio dopo l'unità*,[19] laid to rest the official Piedmontese story, which blamed the massive brigandage in the Kingdom of Naples following unification in 1860 on the political machinations of Bourbon and papal legitimists. Allowing that in some ways the brigands were fighting a *guerra contadina* to maintain peasant civilization against the incursions of the state, Molfese placed primary emphasis on the social roots of the movement, which combined massive unemployment and destitution with the peasants' desire for land—a desire first piqued by Garibaldi and then betrayed by the Piedmontese regime.[20] Although Molfese's book has been criticized effectively for its overly simplified analysis of the political forces in play at the time, his theme of social conflict has endured well and was, of course, reinforced by the publication of Eric Hobsbawm's *Primitive Rebels* and *Bandits,* which stressed the universal image of a Robin Hood style of bandit supported in myth if not in reality by peasant societies seeking to manifest their resistance to class oppression.[21] More recently, however, Hobsbawm's social bandit thesis has been under considerable attack. Expanding the investigation back before Italian unity, Marta Petrusevich has argued for the importance of the state and its attack on peasant culture as the primary cause of brigand activity in the south. She explains how the modernizing state's taxation, conscription, and unfamiliar forms of justice created more and more occasions for conflict with the traditional peasant norms, increasing the number of those forced into exile and opposition. This emphasis allows for the continuity of brigandage across various political regimes and helps differentiate it from more direct forms of peasant class struggle, such as land occupations, which were usually peaceful in content.[22]

Another important criticism of the idea of bandits as primitive rebels comes from John Davis, who emphasizes the many ties between brigandage and local notables.[23] Not only were brigands often connected with elite-sponsored smuggling, but, according to Davis, the patron client relationships and relative autonomy of the large landowners allowed them to act "not only as protectors and supporters but indeed as the organizers of brigand bands."[24] From such sponsorship, agrarian elites could gain large illicit profits, protection for their own property, and the status of having armed men at their beck and call. So, far from being heroes of lower class struggle, brigands usually preyed on the smaller landowners, peasant farmers, and poor shepherds. Davis logically argues that where state power was weakest and landowners most independent, as in

Sicily, the ties between brigands and elites were correspondingly stronger and more apparent. Davis's ideas have the added advantage of helping to explain the virulence of brigandage after unity, when the Piedmontese rather stupidly alienated southern elites out of fear of left-wing radicalism. Disbanding Garibaldi's army without thanks or reward and refusing to rely on local national guards who had been willing to help maintain order, the new government rebuked those classes which might have been able to restrain the brigands. Instead, Italy spent the next four or five years fighting a bloody guerrilla civil war that left the south and north at odds for years to come.

Davis's attempt to tie brigandage to the "rich and powerful" is less convincing for the north.[25] Here the connection revolved around contraband, which Davis assumes had to be coordinated by the elites, and he uses the smuggling of tobacco in the Veneto during the late eighteenth century to make his point.[26] But Furio Bianco's research on the same topic clearly emphasizes the connection between brigands and small village farmers, who used the smuggling of tobacco to supplement their otherwise meager incomes.[27] One should not assume that all or even most brigands were necessarily involved in smuggling and hence tied to the strings of powerful protectors. Indeed, during the nineteenth century in the Papal States, the loudest complaints against brigandage came from the upper crust landlords, who often complained that it was not safe for them to summer in their country villas.[28] Likewise, Piero Brunello relates how during the 1830s, brigands in the lower Po valley were particularly feared by the richest landowners.[29] His study also underscores the social side of banditry in that the areas most heavily affected by brigandage in the Veneto were those where thousands of sharecroppers were being forced off their farms into the uncertain and poorly paid existence of day laborers. One might consider an argument distinguishing between endemic or permanent brigandage, which had tighter connections to elite backers, and periodic brigandage, which would break out during political and economic crises; but it would be risky to do so with the evidence at hand.[30] Perhaps we should use Davis's own observations from the south and suggest that in the north, where the power of the state was already more highly articulated, the ties between elites and brigands were more tenuous. In particular, after the Napoleonic intervention, elites came to rely on the central government for the maintenance of public order, and brigands were seen more as a threat to property than as a bolster of personal authority. Conversely, the increasing strength of the state would have made the protection and use of brigands a perilous occupation, with the penalties outweighing the advantages. As with the mafia, however, this brings us back to the problem that more research has been done on brigandage in the south than the north, and this should be a direction of future investigation.

John Davis's ideas on brigandage form only part of his larger project, published under the title *Conflict and Control: Law and Order in Nineteenth-Century Italy,* which deserves its own category of discussion.[31] In this book, Davis focuses on the problems of criminality, policing, and public order as key issues that helped shape the entire political process in Italy during the nineteenth century. Courageously rejecting the standard temporal and geographic divisions of Italian history, he follows his subject from 1750 to 1900 and deals with the entire peninsula (and the islands) despite the difficulties presented by the lack of administrative and political unity during the Risorgimento period. Davis can do this because he has such a solid grasp on the vast social and economic changes that transcended political boundaries during the period, and he portrays the resulting issues of conflict and control as vital to understanding the complex interaction between local elites and state power both before and after unification.

His themes are best illustrated in the first part of the book, which deals with the Risorgimento period. In it, Davis describes thoroughly the disruptive impact of changing economic patterns and perceptions of property on the social, political, and administrative structures of the old order. He continues this analysis through the French occupation and subsequent restoration to show how preunitary Italy was embroiled in a deeply rooted social crisis marked by angry peasants dispossessed of their communal rights, hoards of displaced *braccianti* forced to compete for day labor, and disgruntled urban workers, who (although better off than their rural counterparts) faced stagnating industries and, after 1840, growing competition from abroad. All of these groups fed into the ranks of beggars and brigands, which helped create the perception among Italy's elites that they were living in dangerous times and provided an excuse for the expansion of the centralized state's power into previously untouched areas of administration. Although his analysis of the economic roots of this crisis is admirable, it is in his emphasis on the relationship between the state and the elites that Davis proves most creative. He shows how the absolutist governments of the Restoration failed for the most part to provide either the patronage or the power desired by Italy's notables and at the same time failed to put their fears of lower class upheaval, exacerbated by the social crisis, to rest. Following the Revolutions of 1848, it became clear that the old absolutist formula could not cope with the current problems of disorder, and Cavour was able to enlist the aid of many elites in pulling off an "administrative revolution" that promised, under the auspices of Piedmont's liberal constitutional government, to come to grips with the "social problem" while providing national prestige and patronage for local notables. Two unfortunate consequences, however, came out of this unitary solution. First, Piedmont, in its role as the champion of order, stability, and progress, created rather illiberal traditions of policing, politics, and administration that would carry on through the rest of the century. Second, the perceived necessity of extending the administrative revolution to the south in order to stop Garibaldi and the democrats created the circumstances for a bloody and protracted civil war as southern elites fought against each other and against the unified state in order to maintain their traditional status and power.

Having thus added an important social dimension to our understanding of the Risorgimento, Davis pursues the basic themes of disorder, elites, and the state through the postunitary period, although they occasionally get lost as he attempts to handle a wide variety of complex issues, such as political opposition, labor organization, and positivistic criminology. Nevertheless, he argues effectively that despite its pretensions of centralized power, the new state was not particularly strong and often depended on long-established patron/client relationships to maintain order. This was particularly true of the south and, as we have already seen, helps explain the continuing problems of private justice in that area and the growth of mafia culture in Sicily. These traditions of physical violence in the Mezzogiorno were a major contributor to what Italians perceived to be their "sad primacy" as one of the most crime-ridden countries of Europe, a constant source of embarrassment and a spur to illiberal police practices as well as racial theories of criminology. Indeed, the state often acted with excess precisely because it did not seem to have the administrative, political, or financial wherewithal to maintain order without abusive displays of force as Italy moved into an era of mass politics and labor unrest. Despite the social basis of his analysis, however, Davis does not see the law purely in terms of class conflict. He shows how peasants and artisans often resorted to the courts for protection and reparation and how the judiciary could act as a liberal counterbalance to oppressive police practices. In the end, it was the concept of law which helped the parliament maintain its power against monarchical encroachments during the public order crises of the 1890s.

Taken together, this all provides an original and persuasive panorama of relations between the state and society in Italy, but Davis's book is not without its faults. Although interesting and provocative, his epilogue on the 1890s, which sees a major shift in the perception of social realities, needs both more clarity and more evidence, especially in his claim that criminal anthropology faded into obscurity as common criminality became less important than public order during the decade.[32] One might also question his conception of the state as a historical actor. In his laudable attempt to stress the role of evolving administrative structures in altering the social and political relations of the region, Davis also tends to endow the state with almost animate characteristics. Thus, he talks about the "centralizing instincts" of the state as if it had a life of its own complete with definable behaviors. He therefore sees every disturbance of public order as a pretext for the state to extend its control farther out into society, whereas it is possible that administrators (who were, after all, humans) saw problems as just problems and solved them as best they could with the material forces and organizational tools at hand. This is not to deny that there existed a certain belief in the efficiency of centralization, but it is to question the reification of the state into some kind of autonomous, and obviously rapacious, entity devoid of human connections. These peccadillos do not, however, detract from the overall importance of Davis's work, and he is to be commended for bringing criminal justice into the spotlight as a vital element of Italy's history.

At the same time, however, his book has relatively little to say about criminal behavior, comparative amounts of crime, or even the visibility of crime in official statistics; and this points out an interesting lack of secondary literature in

Italy on these particular topics, especially for urban areas which have naturally escaped the ongoing investigations devoted to brigandage. There are a variety of reasons for this lacuna, including the aforementioned preponderance of the juridical school in Italy. There are also some historians who view criminal records with great suspicion and think them useful only as ancillary sources for more accepted topics of social history, such as gender, family, and work.[33] In addition, it may well be that Italian historians shy away from studying, especially quantitatively, criminal behavior because of the continuing memory of the positivist school of criminology and its often spurious collection and use of criminal statistics. Whatever the reason, it is not for lack of raw material. The police and the judicial archives of nineteenth-century Italy are overflowing with documents, and governments both before and after unity collected reams of statistics devoted to various forms of criminality. Granted, all of this needs to be weighed carefully, but in general the tendency has been not even to try.

There are various exceptions to this rule,[34] of which one of the most interesting is Mario Da Passano's *Delitto e delinquenza nella Sardegna Sabauda (1823–1844)*.[35] In some ways, his book also attempts to realize Sbriccoli's concept of "integrated criminal history." He begins by laying out the competing ideologies and traditions that contributed to the formulation of the Piedmontese law code of 1827, a code which he sees as still based on eighteenth-century "particularism" and severity despite its more modern format. He then moves on to a quantitative analysis of crime and delinquency in Sardinia between 1834 and 1844. Finally, he ends by examining the official interpretation of criminality on the island and the remedies that were proposed to deal with it. He thus covers legislative theory, criminal activity, and administrative policy over a relatively short period of time. Of these topics, the second stands out as particularly revealing. Acutely aware of all the caveats that should attend the use of judicial records to measure criminality (or the official "shadow" of criminality), Da Passano carefully compares three sets of official documents (1830–1834, 1835–1838, and 1839–1844) containing crimes denounced to the authorities throughout the island. Thus they deal with reported crimes rather than those which eventually came to trial or conviction. From this evidence, Da Passano draws a number of interesting conclusions. First he confirms Sardinia's reputation as a violent society. Reported personal crimes far outweighed reported property crimes, and for all three periods murder ranked as the single most reported crime in both real and adjusted terms by a substantial margin. Thus, between 1835 and 1838, 482 murders were reported for a yearly average of 2.32 for every 10,000 inhabitants, while 199 violent assaults amounted to 0.96 per 10,000. The latter category appears not to include 103 (0.49 per 10,000) gunshot wounds, which were recorded separately. In contrast, 239 recorded thefts only came to 1.15 per 10,000 and 130 robberies figured as 0.62 per 10,000.[36] Adding up the totals, crimes of personal violence were reported at an average rate of 3.77 per 10,000 as compared to an average rate of 1.77 per 10,000 for the most common property crimes.

While attesting to the violence of Sardinian culture, Da Passano also dispels some common notions about criminality on the island. Plotting the geographic distribution of crime, he finds that crimes in general were reported more or less uniformly throughout the island.[37] Even in the larger towns, reported personal violence still outweighed reported property crime, although here the disparity was not quite as striking. Thus, between 1839 and 1844 the towns reported 220 murders and assaults as opposed to 101 thefts and robberies, or 56.2 percent versus 27.6 percent of all crimes reported. Da Passano also suggests that the traditional wisdom that pastoral areas and the pastoral way of life accounted for more crime has to give way before this generalized distribution, and he categorically rejects the idea of a "fortress interior" acting as a center of banditry and resistance to outside interference.[38] Finally, he puts to rest the image of large stable bands of professional brigands in Sardinia, suggesting that such groups came together on an occasional basis to carry out one or two criminal acts before disbanding.[39]

Da Passano's data and analysis are impressive, but they also raise some interesting questions. In particular, one wishes that he had attempted to tie his results into the long-standing *violence/vol* debate on the transition from early modern to modern criminality. In contrast to the work of people such as James Sharpe, Da Passano's data would seem to breathe life into the idea that less economically developed societies tend to report, if not actually experience, more crimes against people than against property.[40] On the other hand, one also wishes that he had discussed this obvious discrepancy more fully. More than likely, property crimes were grossly underreported, but why should this be the case? What informal mechanisms existed to adjudicate theft and robbery, or do the high rates of violence suggest that such crimes were left to private justice with a concomitant increase in physical retaliation? Da Passano might also have done more with his statistics on who was involved in reported crime. Although he denies the preponderance of crime in pastoral areas, his data also reveal that shepherds tended to be the group most often involved in murders, at least in those cases for which information was available. This pastoral propensity for murder could easily help account for the more general reputation of herding society as the prime locus of criminality on the island. Likewise, one regrets that Da Passano is not more specific about how many people were involved as perpetrators in robberies and thefts. This would have helped gauge the extent of group banditry on the island and provided some interesting data for comparison with brigandage elsewhere. But these questions only underline the importance of Da Passano's work and advertise the need for more archival investigation.

Unfortunately, his example and the good work of others have recently been offset by the publication of Romano Canosa's *Storia della criminalità in Italia 1845–1945*.[41] Canosa is a prolific writer on judicial topics who is widely read and even occasionally undertakes archival research. In this case, however, he demonstrates a serious inability to differentiate between reliable and unreliable sources, and he tends to use statistics without questioning their provenance or applicability. Overall, his book lacks any unifying theme or argument as he jumps from one topic to another, and he occasionally slips into improbable generalizations based on thin or nonexistent evidence. Thus, he affirms that in contrast to Italy's illiterate criminals, delinquents in mid-nineteenth-century England, France, and Switzerland were more likely to read than other people.[42] He even suggests that Italians were not worried about crime in the cities of the north during the first half of the century because they were too busy dealing with the Risorgimento.[43] After unity he also sees no special concern for urban criminality and consequently misinterprets the theoretical works of policemen like Giovanni Bolis as well as Lombroso and the criminal anthropologists. Many of his statistics are from suspect sources, and he often fails to adjust the data for population. His concluding chapter does have adjusted statistics from 1887 to 1952, but he lumps together all forms of crime without regard to changing legislation or jurisdiction.[44] Canosa's book might be praised for drawing attention to the history of crime in Italy, but in fact he only makes the kinds of errors of judgment and methodology that will strengthen the position of those who disparage the discipline.

In contrast to criminality per se, the institutions of criminal justice have started to receive considerable attention in Italy. For instance, a number of doctoral dissertations have appeared in the last decade dealing with the Italian police, and Richard Bach Jensen has recently published a lengthy monograph on policing and its relationship to politics during much of the liberal period.[45] He examines the many attempts to reform the police and argues that lack of an efficient force—caused primarily by a dearth of economic resources—restricted the public control alternatives available to Italy's elites and consequently often resulted in overly repressive, not to say bloody, attempts to maintain order, especially during the violence-ridden decade of the 1890s.[46] Also of importance is Mary Gibson's excellent work on prostitution and its control in postunification Italy, which still remains the best example we have of the Italian police actually attempting to implement policy.[47] If one considers as well Livio Antonelli's painstaking reconstruction of the Napoleonic prefectoral system and Gabriella Santoncini's analysis of police legislation in the Papal States, it should be obvious that scholars have begun to sketch the basic outline of this important institution, which was one of the most prominent mediators between state and society in Italy.[48]

A key contribution to that outline can be found in Carlo Mangio's *La polizia toscana: organizzazione e criteri d'intervento.*[49] Although Mangio is primarily concerned with the impact on Tuscany's police system of Peter Leopold's Beccarian-style judicial reforms, he follows the story well into the nineteenth century up to the region's incorporation into Napoleon's Empire. Working his way through the rather labyrinthine paths of administrative politics in early modern Tuscany, he shows how the gradual disassociation of police power from judicial power served those who wished to provide greater guarantees for the rights of private citizens. Likewise, the centralization of police authority in a single minister of *Buon Governo* helped to eliminate confusion and abuse by various officials at the local level. In particular, he examines the changing use of *pene economiche,* or sanctions which could be employed without judicial review, as the government genuinely tried to balance freedom and efficiency (a task that became ever more complicated in the face of new political ideologies from France and an apparent increase in common crime). The key figure in all of this was Giuseppe Giusti, who served as the head of *Buon Governo,* with only minor breaks, between 1784 and 1805. Mangio, in what turns out to be a compelling intellectual biography, shows us how a man like Giusti could, on one hand, try to enforce religious compliance as a bolster to public order or plan a penal island to be peopled by suspects rather than convicts, yet on the other hand would fight for greater clarity of police legislation in order to protect the rights of citizens and argue for massive public works to provide the lower classes with work and food. In sum, Mangio has gone beyond simple definitions of conservative or liberal to create a complex and fascinating picture of late eighteenth-century illuminism as applied to the police.

But the larger theme that emerges from Mangio's book is how the regime needed to improve the image of the policemen in the street, who suffered from an extraordinary tradition of public disdain and hatred going far back into history. This was not only the case in Tuscany, and Mangio's depiction of the *sbirri,* or police guards, as being correctly regarded as violent, corrupt, arbitrary, and vexatious could be applied throughout the peninsula.[50] Realizing that such popular revulsion toward the police necessarily undercut any attempt at judicial change, the Tuscan government undertook to control its unfortunate agents with a number of initiatives, which included replacing the *bargello* or head *sbirro* with a minister of police, issuing standard uniforms, and raising the *sbirri*'s pay while eliminating the informal "gifts" which they previously had to provide to superiors in order to hold their jobs. Not only were precise lists of functions and duties drawn up, but they were also read aloud on a weekly basis to the *sbirri,* who, as Mangio suggests, were perhaps thought *poco intelligenti.*

Mangio's stress on the need to reform the *sbirri* confirms what is an enduring theme of current police historiography and one which needs to be pursued more openly for the later periods. For instance, I have argued elsewhere that so strong was the public antipathy toward lower police officials even after the restoration that it affected the continuity of police personnel during the Risorgimento.[51] Likewise, the many complaints of Italy's politicians after unity that the continuing traditions of the *sbirri* and the absolutist regimes hampered their efforts to create a fair and efficient police force should not be, as they often have been, simply shoved aside as special pleading or an excuse for inaction. Indeed, I would suggest that revulsion toward the *sbirro* was so deeply seated that it naturally affected police reform—including the way the Italian police enthusiastically embraced positivism and "scientific" policing—throughout the liberal period.[52]

This brings out as well the fact that although much good work has lately appeared on Italy's police, much remains to be done. Virtually nothing has been written on the municipal police, and there is not to my knowledge a single example of an urban case study of policing for the postunitary period. Perhaps even more surprising is the lack of interest shown in Italy's ubiquitous military police or *Carabinieri,* who form an almost sacrosanct institution of formidible importance yet who are universally derided as unintelligent. This could be the stuff of high historical drama, yet there is no serious history of the *Carabinieri* nor of their civilian counterpart, the *Guardie di pubblica sicurezza.* Much the same could be said of the judicial system. Although there are some excellent studies on the role of the judiciary in certain political arenas, such as Mario D'Addio's *Politica e magistratura (1848–1876)* and Guido Neppi Modena's outstanding *Sciopero, potere politico, e magistratura, 1870–1922,*[53] much needs to be learned about how the magistracy was recruited and how it functioned on a daily basis. One important initiative in this direction is the work of Pietro Saraceno, who is currently doing a painstaking reconstruction of the careers of 800 judges from before unity through the liberal period.[54] In addition, he is publishing a general history of the Italian judiciary and how it functioned, which will be a great help for those who desire to study criminal justice history in Italy but do not have the benefit of a formal degree in *giurisprudenza.*[55] One would further like to see much more on the preunitary courts of justice and their procedures along the lines of Rosoni's work on the Papal States.

In conclusion, criminal justice history is alive and well in Italy. Certain topics, such as the mafia and brigandage, have already attracted considerable attention and have reached a sophisticated and nuanced level of discussion. As for criminality, policing, and the courts, there are some good examples of what can be done, and new studies are appearing every year. Certain centers have started specializing in related topics, networks have begun, and Mario Sbriccoli is currently working on a cumulative bibliography similar to that which Eric Monkkonen has done for the United States, and this will be an enormous asset for everyone involved. Yet there is much still to do, as I hope this chapter has indicated. Above all, what is needed are people willing to do the kind of local archival research that will eventually allow patterns to emerge and paradigms to ripen. Italy has some of the richest police and judicial archives in the world, most of which are well organized and easily consultable. Combining this treasure of documentation with creative and well-informed scholars, Italy has much to offer in terms of modern criminal justice history.

NOTES

1. One particular conference held at Siena in December 1986, which was dedicated to the important penal reforms of Archduke Peter Leopold in eighteenth-century Tuscany, has given rise to no less than thirteen different volumes of monographs and articles coordinated by Luigi Berlinguer and published by Giuffrè.

2. I wish to thank Luigi Cajani and Mario Sbriccoli for their invaluable help in compiling information on the current state of criminal justice history in Italy. Unfortunately, my somewhat arbitrary temporal periodization leaves out of the discussion a number of recent works that deserve mention as part of the growing Italian literature. Specifically, Daniele Boschi, "I reati contro la persona a Roma alla metà del Settecento," *Archivio della società romana di storia patria* 112 (1989): 453–80; Irene Polverini Fosi, *La società violenta: Il banditismo dello Stato Pontificio nella seconda metà del Cinquecento* (Rome, 1985); Floriana Colao, *'Post tenebras spero lucem'. La giustizia criminale senese nell'età delle riforme Leopoldine* (Milan, 1989); and, in particular, the various excellent entries in *Criminalità e società in età moderna,* ed. Luigi Berlinguer and Floriana Colao (Milan, 1991).

3. Mario Sbriccoli, *Crimen Laesae Maiestatis: Il problema del reato politico alle soglie della scienza penalistica moderna* (Milan, 1974). For a similar study of the question during the modern period, see Floriana Colao, *Il delitto politico tra Ottocento e Novecento: Da "delitto fittizio" a "nemico dello stato"* (Milan, 1986).

4. Sbriccoli is aware of this problem and has commented on the need to improve communication between social historians and legal scholars. See, in particular, "Storia del diritto e storia della società: Questioni di metodo e problemi di ricerca," *Storia sociale e dimensione giuridica: Strumenti d'indagine e ipotesi di lavoro* (Milan, 1986), 128–37.

5. E.g., "Il diritto penale sociale: 1883–1912," *Quaderni fiorentini per la storia del pensiero giuridico moderno* (Milan, 1974–1975), 3: 557–642; "Il diritto penale liberale. La 'Rivista penale' di Luigi Lucchini: 1874–1900," ibid., (1987), 16: 105–83; "Dissenso politico e diritto penale in Italia tra Otto e Novecento," ibid., (1973), 2: 607–702; and, above all, "La penalistica civile: Teorie e ideologie del diritto penale nell'Italia unita," *Stato e cultura giuridica in Italia dall'unità alla repubblica* (Rome, 1990), 147–232.

6. In private correspondence, Professor Sbriccoli kindly provided the following examples: Giovanna Fiume, *La vecchia dell'aceto. Un processo di veneficio nella Palermo di fine Settecento:* Andrea Zorzi, *L'amministrazione della giustizia penale nella Repubblica fiorentina. Aspetti e problemi* (Florence, 1988); Massimo Vallerani, "Conflitti e modelli procedurali nel sistema giudiziario comunale. I registri di processi a Perugia nella seconda metà del XIII secolo," *Società e storia* 13 (1990): 267–99 n. 48. One should also include Patrizia Guarnieri, *L'ammazzabambini. Legge e scienza in un processo toscano di fine Ottocento* (Torino, 1988).

7. Isabella Rosoni, *Criminalità e giustizia penale nello Stato Pontificio del secolo XIX. Un caso di banditismo rurale* (Milan, 1988).

8. Christopher Duggan, *Fascism and the Mafia* (New Haven: Yale University Press, 1989). For a recent bibliography on mafia in Sicily, see Diego Gambetta's sociological treatise, *La mafia siciliana. Un'industria della protezione privata* (Torino, 1992), 383–98.

9. Adrian Lyttelton, "Breaking a Code of Honour," *Times Literary Supplement,* 3 March 1989, 211–13.

10. Ibid., 213.

11. Ibid.

12. Raimondo Catanzaro, *Il delitto come impresa. Storia sociale della mafia* (Padova, 1990). For an excellent English summary of Catanzaro's ideas, see his "Enforcers, Entrepreneurs, and Survivors: How the *Mafia* Has Adapted to Change," 36:1 *British Journal of Sociology* (1985): 34–57.

13. Ibid., 41.

14. Ibid., 43.

15. Pino Arlacchi, *La mafia imprenditrice* (Bologna, 1983); published in English as *Mafia Business* (New York, 1987).

16. Ibid., xiii.

17. Ibid., xvi. One might add that the spectacular assassination of the investigating judges, Luigi Falcone and Giovanni Borsellino, in 1992, only underscores the immediacy of Arlacchi's concern.

18. On the original development of this legislation under Napoleon, see Luigi Lacchè, *Latrocinium: giustizia, scienza penale e repressione del banditismo in antico regime* (Milan, 1988), 283–89.

19. Franco Molfese, *Storia del brigantaggio dopo l'unita* (Milan, 1964).

20. For an excellent review of Molfese and subsequent research, see Alfonso Scirocco, ''Il brigantaggio meridionale post-unitario nella storiografia dell'ultimo ventennio,'' *Archivio storico per le province napoletane* 21 (1983): 17–32.

21. One conference at the University of Venice focused on reaction to the ideas of Hobsbawm, who wrote the introduction to the published papers. See *Bande armate, banditi, banditismo e repressione di giustizia negli stati europei di antico regime,* ed. Gherardo Ortalli (Rome, 1986).

22. Marta Petrusewicz, ''Society Against the State: Peasant Brigandage in Southern Italy,'' *Criminal Justice History* 8 (1987): 1–20.

23. John Davis, *Conflict and Control: Law and Order in Nineteenth-Century Italy* (London and Atlantic Highlands, N.J., 1988), 80–90.

24. Ibid., 81. This interpretation fits in with evidence from other areas of the world. See, for instance, Richard Slatta, ''Banditry as Political Participation in Latin America,'' *Criminal Justice History,* 12 (1991): 180–82.

25. Davis, *Conflict and Control,* 80.

26. Ibid., 78.

27. Furio Bianco, ''Sbirri, contrabbandieri e le 'rie sette dei malfattori' nel '700 friulano,'' *Emarginazione, criminalità, e devianza in Italia fra '600 e '900* (Milan, 1990), 51–76.

28. This results from my own research contained in *Crime, Disorder, and the Risorgimento: The Politics of Policing in Bologna* (Cambridge, 1994).

29. Piero Brunello, *Ribelli, questuanti e banditi: proteste contadine in veneto e in Friuli, 1814–1866* (Venice, 1981), 207.

30. Another difference between brigandage in the north and the south is perhaps the nature of the crime itself. In the Papal States, it was clear that seldom if ever did the bands stay together. Rather, brigands would go their separate ways and then regroup for a job.

31. Parts of the following can be found in my review of Davis's book in *The Journal of Social History* 15:2 (1990): 612–14.

32. In contrast to Davis's views, Mary Gibson is currently working on a monograph that clearly shows the continuing influence of Lombroso and his disciples on policemen and jurists well after the turn of the century.

33. Indeed, there has been considerable debate in some of the most prestigious journals over whether criminality is worthy of historical study. See, for instance, Edoardo Grendi, ''Per lo studio della storia criminale,'' *Quaderni storici* 44 (August 1980): 580; ''Premessa'' to the issue of *Quaderni storici* entitled ''Fonti criminali e storia sociale,'' (1987): 695; Mario Sbriccoli, ''Fonti giudiziarie e fonti giuridiche. Riflessioni sulla fase

attuale degli studi di storia del crimine e della giustizia criminale,'' *Studi storici* 2 (1988); 491–501; Edoardo Grendi, ''Sulla 'storia criminale' risposta a Mario Sbriccoli,'' *Quaderni storici* 73 (April, 1990): 269–75.

34. Although for a slightly earlier period, three important examples are Dario Zuliani, ''Reati e pene nel vicariato di Prato prima e dopo la 'Leopoldina' (1781–1790),'' Laura Carli Sardi, ''Analisi statistica sulla criminalità nel 1700 (reati e pene) con riguardo allo Stato senese,'' and Luigi Cajani, ''Pena di morte e tortura a Roma nel Settecento,'' all in the aforementioned *Criminalità e società in età moderna,* 307–26, 327–476, and 517–48, respectively.

35. Mario Da Passano, *Delitto e delinquenza nella Sardegna Sabauda (1823–1844)* (Milan, 1984).

36. Ibid., 87. Note that no separate category was set aside for the theft of livestock (*abigeato*), as was done for the other sample period.

37. Ibid., 93–101.

38. Ibid., 102; cf. Davis, 88–90.

39. Ibid., 117.

40. James Sharpe, *Crime in Early Modern England* (London, 1984), 59.

41. Romano Canosa, *Storia della criminalità in Italia 1845–1945* (Torino, 1991).

42. Ibid., 42.

43. Ibid., 158–59. John Davis's book does not appear in his bibliography, and it shows. My own research indicates that fear of crime was so great among elites in the Papal States that it substantially contributed to the fall of the temporal power.

44. Ibid., 342.

45. Luigi Londei, ''Organizazione della polizia e giustizia penale a Roma tra antico regime e restaurazione, 1750–1820'' (Ph.D. diss., Università di Perugia, 1987); Richard Collin, ''The Italian Police and Internal Security from Giolitti to Mussolini'' (D. Phil., Oxford University, 1983); and Steven C. Hughes, ''Police, Public Order, and the Risorgimento in Bologna'' (Ph.D. diss., University of Michigan, 1984). These have done much to offset earlier works that substituted ideology for research, such as Domenico Tarantini, *La maniera forte: elogio alla polizia* (Verona, 1975) and Angelo D'Orsi, *Il potere repressivo* (Milan, 1972).

46. *Liberty and Order: The Theory and Practice of Italian Public Security Policy, 1848 to the Crisis of the 1890s* (New York, 1991). Also see ''Police Reform and Social Reform: Italy from the Crisis of the 1890s to the Giolittian Era,'' *Criminal Justice History* 10 (1989): 179–200.

47. Mary Gibson, *Prostitution and the State in Italy 1860–1915* (New Brunswick, N.J., 1986).

48. Livio Antonielli, *I prefetti dell'Italia napoleonica* (Bologna, 1983); Gabriella Santoncini, *Ordine pubblico e polizia nella crisi dello Stato Pontificio, 1848–1850* (Milan, 1981). One should also consider Fiorenza Fiorentino, *Ordine pubblico nell'Italia giolittiana* (Rome, 1978) and Steven C. Hughes, ''The Theory and Practice of Ozio in Italian Policing: Bologna and Beyond,'' *Criminal Justice History* 7 (1986): 89–103; ''Probing the Police in the Past, an Italian Case Study,'' *Criminal Justice Review* 13:2 (1988): 21–40; and ''La continuità del personale di polizia negli anni dell'unificazione nazionale italiana,'' in *Clio* (April–June 1990): 337–63. Also of importance is the series of conference papers on police powers during the Risorgimento period, which have been published under the title *Amministrazione della giustizia e poteri di polizia dagli stati preunitari alla caduta della Destra* (Rome, 1986).

49. Carlo Mangio, *La polizia toscana: organizzazione e criteri d'intervento* (Milan, 1988).

50. Steven C. Hughes, "Fear and Loathing in Bologna and Rome: The Papal Police in Perspective," 12:1 *Journal of Social History* (1987): 97–116; for the *sbirri* in the Veneto, see Furio Bianco, "*Sbirri,* contrabbandieri e le 'rie sette dei malfattori' nel '700 friulano," in *Stato società e giustizia nella Repubblica Veneta,* ed. G. Cozzi (1980), 66–72; and Claudio Pavolo, "Aspetti e problemi dell'amministrazione della giustizia penale nella Repubblica di Venezia, secoli XVI–XVIII," in ibid., 207–10.

51. Hughes, *La continuità,* 359–60.

52. Apropos, one might point out the weakness of the police novel in Italian literature. Although *gialli* or mysteries, including police procedurals, have long been popular in Italy, they were always imported from other countries. It was not until the 1970s that an Italian detective novel was written or accepted.

53. Mario D'Addio, *Politica e magistratura (1848–1876)* (Milano, 1966); and Guido Neppi Modena, *Sciopero, potere politico, e magistratura, 1870–1922* (Bari, 1969). Also important in this regard are Gian Carlo Jocteau, *La magistratura e i conflitti di lavoro durante il fascismo, 1926–1934* (Milan, 1978) and Fernando Venturini, *Un 'sindacato' di giudici da Giolitti a Mussollini: L'Associazione Generale fra i Magistrati Italiani 1909–1926* (Bologna, 1987).

54. For a preliminary report on his research, see *Alta magistratura e classe politica dalla integrazione alla separazione* (Rome, 1979). Also see *I magistrati italiani dall'unità al fascismo* (Rome, 1988). His study has important ramifications for all those studying administrative history in Italy since he is using his results to test the accuracy of the *Calendari Generali,* the single most important printed source for the reconstruction of bureaucratic careers.

55. Part of this survey has already been published as "dispense delle lezioni" entitled *Storia della magistratura italiana. Le origini: La magistratura del Regno di Sardegna* (Rome, 1991).

PART III

THE AMERICAS AND AUSTRALIA–NEW ZEALAND

8

Crime and Punishment in the Dominion of the North: Canada from New France to the Present

Jim Phillips

In a recent review of the literature on Canadian criminal justice history, I referred to the subject as "one of the most underdeveloped areas of Canadian history" and as a "poor relation in the burgeoning international family of studies in the history of crime and punishment."[1] That review provided a chronological account of institutional and social developments, often drawing on general works primarily concerned with other issues, and an analysis of major themes in the history of crime, state, and society. This attempt at comprehensive coverage meant that all sections were necessarily brief. For this volume, I have adopted a different approach. The primary focus is on the limited number of topics that have engendered a substantial literature and on which there is a lively, growing, and sophisticated body of work that merits more detailed exploration.

The five major sections of this chapter represent a somewhat eclectic collection.[2] They comprise, in order, New France/Quebec from the mid-seventeenth to the end of the eighteenth century; penal institutions; studies of crime, prosecution, violence, and social order in the nineteenth and twentieth centuries; policing; and women and the criminal law. Given its different early history under the French regime, its experience of adaptation to a foreign regime, the unusually comprehensive nature of the historical literature, and the fact that so little has been written about other Canadian colonies in the early period, New France/Quebec clearly deserves treatment separate from the other thematically defined sections. There is obviously some overlap between the other major topics selected, all of which are principally situated in the nineteenth century. But it seemed logical to deal with prisons, policing, and women separately from general discussions of crime, prosecution, violence, and social order. Despite the relationships among them, each has its own particular dynamics of historical evolution and historiographic interpretation. Regions and periods not included in these major sections (English Canada prior to 1800 and the twentieth century), as well as other topics such as criminal law, criminal procedure, and native peoples and the law, are discussed in a final section, which both reviews the existing literature and points out the more obvious *lacunae*.

Lamentation about the inadequacies of Canadian criminal justice history is commonplace. Yet the topic does present some special problems. It involves two European empires and languages, more than three and a half centuries of history, ten provincial jurisdictions, and relations with native peoples. Moreover, Canada lacks a tradition of historical scholarship by legal academics in this area that might have laid the institutional groundwork for later students concerned with broader sociolegal themes.[3] Despite these problems, substantial strides recently have been and continue to be made, and notwithstanding my earlier comment I intend this chapter to be in part an acknowledgment of that fact. Much of the best work reviewed here has been written in the last decade, very little of it before 1975. Indeed, given the current vitality of the field and the relative youth of many of its practitioners, I have chosen to include references to theses and to forthcoming publications where I am aware of the latter. Criminal justice history has come far enough to merit entry into the mainstream of Canadian historiography, as it has done in Britain and the United States, even if that mainstream does not yet seem to have grasped the fact.[4]

NEW FRANCE AND QUEBEC, CIRCA 1650–1800

The history of criminal justice in Quebec involves two successive transplantations of European systems, one in the early to mid-seventeenth century and the other in the 1760s following the British conquest. The historiography has tended to divide itself along these lines, with more detailed coverage of the earlier period. Indeed, we know a great deal about all aspects of the criminal process in New France, and a considerable amount has also been written on the social history of crime and punishment in that period, albeit by relatively few individuals.

Throughout the seventeenth and eighteenth centuries, jurisdiction over the criminal process at first instance was shared by seigneurial, company (prior to 1663), and royal courts (in Quebec and Trois Rivières from 1663 and in Montreal from 1693), although the royal courts were predominant. Few seigneurs appear to have actually exercised the power they had to establish criminal courts. The bulk of the substantive criminal law, as well as prosecution and trial procedures, was at all times derived from French law and procedure, with little room for local initiative.[5] While there may have been departures in fact before the later seventeenth century, this was much less the case thereafter. Procedure in Quebec from 1670 was governed by the metropole's *Grande Ordonnance Criminel* of that year, which categorized all crimes and minutely detailed procedures to be followed.[6]

Under the *Ordonnance*, a full inquisitorial and public prosecution system was established. Its operation from complaint through initial judicial inquiry, involvement of the public prosecutor, private judicial interrogation of the accused, the *reglement à l'extraordinaire,*[7] torture if necessary to obtain a confession, sentencing, and limited appeals has been described in great detail for the eighteenth century by André Lachance.[8] His various accounts, which stress the close adherence paid to the procedures laid down in the imperial *Ordonnance,* highlight the obvious differences between adversarial and inquisitorial systems of procedure. Not the least of these was that only fifty-eight accuseds were fully acquitted between 1712 and 1748 out of 796 cases that went through all stages of the process, with a further sixty-three cases leading to "temporary acquittals" and thirty-seven dismissed for lack of evidence.[9] Lachance also demonstrates, however, that torture, the feature of French procedure perhaps most notably different from English, was employed just six times in that same sample, although it was requested by prosecutors on a further eight occasions.[10] Lachance concludes by asserting *la dureté du système* and stressing the lack of procedural protections for the accused. He does, however, also acknowledge a relatively high rate of nonconviction compared to Metropolitan France, which he ascribes to a "softening" of the king's justice in Canada.[11]

There is also a substantial literature on crime and punishment in New France. Statistical studies all tend to show that prosecuted crime rates were relatively low, although this conclusion is based on limited records and conceals an apparent consistent decline in prosecutions in the first half of the eighteenth century which has not been satisfactorily explained. Much of the prosecuted crime was committed by soldiers. While the range of criminal activity appears to have been broad in all districts, regional differences are apparent in, for example, the prevalence of theft.[12] Other studies of crime demonstrate that prosecutions for verbal insults feature prominently in the court records and were by no means the exclusive preserve of the gentleman, that sexual offenses were relatively rare and became even more so in the eighteenth century, and that New France was no model of an orderly society, with food and price riots occurring in this part of the New World as elsewhere.[13] Women and the criminal process are specifically considered by two writers. Lachance offers a general account which demonstrates that women played a minor role in criminal activity, and Robert Seguin describes a number of witchcraft prosecutions.[14]

Studies of punishment demonstrate that they ran the gamut from fines and apologies for assaults and insults to corporal punishments like the pillory, whippings, the carcan (iron collar), amputation and branding, banishment, galley service, and death, any of which could be imposed for theft. The death sentence was inevitable in homicide cases, and religious and sexual offenses were treated with harsh corporal punishments. Executions—sixty-seven in all during the

French regime, according to Lachance[15]—were invariably carried out immediately after sentencing, and with much of the pomp and ceremony familiar to this process in the early modern world.[16] All accounts stress the wide degree of discretion available to sentencing judges, and it is clear from some that social class and race could be crucial determinants in a person's fate.

Despite these insights into the meaning and operation of the system, and despite the considerable information available on it, it is probably reasonable to criticize the historians of criminal justice in New France for not paying enough attention to an issue which has come to the fore in English-language historiography in recent decades—the links between prosecution and punishment, on the one hand, and social control and political authority, on the other. Lachance, for example, for all the breadth and painstaking research of his work, is generally content to comment on the harshness and blood-thirstiness of the system, which included terrible conditions for prisoners awaiting trial.[17] He does, however, acknowledge its temporal context and stresses the crucial importance of infamy to the meaning of punishment. Infamy and other aspects of public punishments might be more deeply explored to test their ideological meanings in a system which generally seems not to have had much need to rely on "ideology," as that term has been used by Douglas Hay, to lend support to state power. One article which does consider such issues is André Morel's account of sentencing, which offers a somewhat ambiguous conclusion about the arbitrariness of punishment and the nature and legitimacy of authority. On the one hand, Morel argues not only that formal and informal checks limited judicial discretion and that sentencing cannot simply be labeled "arbitrary" because it was well understood what factors relating to the crime and the criminal were to be taken into account. On the other hand, he is forced to conclude, from a review of appeals, that the Montreal seigneurial court probably did abuse its sentencing discretion.[18]

Following the conquest of New France, English criminal law and procedure was imposed on Quebec under military rule, a decision confirmed when civil government was fully established by the Quebec Act of 1774. Although the voluminous literature on the conquest has had little to say on this aspect of colonial imposition, it seems clear that Whitehall wanted English criminal law at least in part because of the eighteenth-century English faith in constitutional values like trial by jury and distrust of secretive, tyrannical, "continental" approaches to criminal procedure. Moreover, English law represented English order and political authority.[19] Here, therefore, we see the criminal law as a proxy for broader political values. The *canadiens* who had that law imposed on them appear to have seen it that way as well, for there is evidence that they resented the system and used it as little as possible.[20] In addition to detailing some of these reactions, Douglas Hay's stimulating essay also comes to grips with deeper issues of transplantation and adaptation. He argues that aspects of the system, such as equality before the law, public trial, and public prosecution, acted not to solidify English authority but to add to resentments already felt by the conquered elite—who now found themselves exposed to public humiliation at the hands of any who wished to launch a prosecution. The situation was compounded by language difficulties, struggles over jury composition, and the religious disabilities which prevented most colonists from serving on commissions of the peace. One result was a partial boycott of the courts. Another perhaps more important consequence was that the criminal law failed to enhance authority. If the law was effective ideology in eighteenth-century England, Hay argues, it was because its forms were "imbricated in the whole pattern of social belief and relations of power." When "so distinctive a cultural product was transferred to so different a society as Quebec, the forms prevailed but many of their social meanings did not."[21]

While other work has detailed the continuing reception of English criminal law after 1774 and charted the eventual adaptation of *canadien* society,[22] much less is known about the operation of the criminal law in Quebec in the decades immediately following the conquest than about its structure. Hay's article presents some statistics for the years prior to 1774, and Jean-Marie Fecteau considers its role in social control at the end of the century.[23] But the operation of the system on the ground and sociocultural reactions have not been charted in detail. Here the historians of criminal justice in the postconquest years have to yield primacy to their colleagues who have examined the earlier period.

PRISON HISTORY AND INCARCERATION

Accounts of Canadian prison history must begin with Kingston Penitentiary, the largest and most ambitious structure of its kind in the world when it was opened in 1835 and the most-studied institution since that time. While the standard histories offer slightly different emphases on the respective roles of crime control and reformation of criminals as motivations, Kingston's origins have generally been attributed to dissatisfaction with the state of the colony's local jails, to the search for penal alternatives given the inefficacy of the received English "bloody code," and to ideas—largely imported from the United States—about the need to reform and not merely to punish convicted criminals.[24] Other perspectives on the penitentiary have come from examining opposition to it from local trades organizations concerned about competition for their labor[25] and from a close analysis of the problems of existing carceral institutions.[26] Some recent work ambitiously links Kingston's construction to both the Tory paternalism that pervaded Upper Canadian politics and the rise of parallel state institutions of control, such as the asylum. Russell Smandych argues that the building of the penitentiary was much less a "reformist" initiative than a new strategy of social control adopted by an existing elite in a rapidly changing social and economic context. While he tends to exaggerate the reliance on mere reformism of previous historians of the penitentiary and perhaps fails to account for the extent to which received ideas contributed at least to the scale and ambition of the project, he does note the central role of Tory boosters. His approach thus has the virtue of situating Canadian developments in the context of Canadian society and politics.[27]

We also know a good deal about the history of Kingston's early years. Its initial failures, revealed by the Brown Commission of 1848–1849, have been well documented. The harshness of the silent regime, the extensive use of corporal and other physical punishments, mismanagement, and largely useless labor are all laid bare. The commission reaffirmed an official commitment to reform and called for a modification of the silent system by adding a period of solitary confinement on entry, although this was not implemented.[28] Regrettably, there is little published work on Kingston after midcentury. The same can be said for penitentiaries generally after Confederation, when such institutions became a federal concern. The one comprehensive study of the late nineteenth century argues that, whatever the official rhetoric, the federal institutional regime was always "more punitive than reformative."[29]

Studies of Kingston have been recently joined by accounts of nineteenth-century penitentiary building and regimes in Halifax and Saint John[30] and of the process by which the Montreal prison evolved slowly into a penitentiary-like institution from the mid-1830s onward.[31] Modified Auburn-style regimes were again chosen for Halifax and Saint John, with much apparent stress on labor and reform. But despite a good deal of innovation and flexibility in the Halifax penitentiary, including the introduction in 1851 of a "mark" system, these institutions provide further testimony to the profound failure of this great nineteenth-century experiment in penology.

Penitentiaries were never the only, or indeed perhaps the major, type of penal institution, and two studies of others stand out. Peter Oliver's rich account of the Ontario Central Prison demonstrates that at the local level reform ideas played a secondary role to punitiveness, a conclusion supported by Berkovits's work on labor in the institution.[32] Carolyn Strange's study of the origins of the Mercer Reformatory, Canada's first prison for women, represents an ambitious attempt to link a prison for women to the rise of maternal feminist ideology in the late nineteenth century.[33] A feature of these two accounts, and indeed to some extent also of work on the penitentiary, appears to be the crucial role played by particular individuals in their establishment and operation. A comprehensive study might reduce this emphasis on individuals by drawing links across disparate areas of nineteenth-century penal policy.

Completing our knowledge of the history of penal institutions are accounts of the development of various kinds of juvenile facilities, particularly the reformatory at Penetenguishene (opened in 1859) and the industrial schools movement of the later nineteenth century,[34] and some studies of provincial and municipal jails, bridewells, and prisons before and after the construction of penitentiaries.[35] Early jails deserve much more attention, given both the increasing dissatisfaction in the late eighteenth and early nineteenth centuries with the unreformed system reliant on capital and corporal punishments and the consequent search for alternatives, and the recent renewed interest in these institutions among criminal justice historians elsewhere. Two other topics, related to the history of prisons, bear mention. First, a number of authors have examined the development of the asylum in nineteenth-century Canada, significant given the fact that previously lunatics and the criminally insane were housed in jails. Some of this work also links the asylum and penitentiary as part of a broader process of introducing and enforcing "segregative control."[36] Second, a useful beginning has been made to the study of a closely related subject, probation. Canadian provinces were extremely slow in building probation systems, a fact that has been attributed to both a greater and a lesser emphasis on crime control in Canadian society than elsewhere.[37]

Despite recent writing, Kingston still tends to dominate the historiography of Canadian prisons, unreasonably so. In addition to the gaps in the literature already noted, the most striking *lacuna* is probably the lack of work on the twentieth century as a whole. The consequence is that we have little knowledge of the federal women's prison at Kingston, opened in 1925, or of four relatively recently created federal penitentiaries—Stony Mountain (Manitoba), Prince Albert (Saskatchewan), New Westminster (British Columbia), and Dorchester (New Brunswick), the last-named being founded in 1880 to replace Halifax and Saint John. This neglect of the modern period is surprising given the consolidation of penitentiary legislation of 1906, the founding of the Canadian Penal Congress in 1935, and the production of various major inquiries and reports in 1914, 1938, 1956, and 1969.[38] Our knowledge of the many smaller, often municipal, institutions for minor offenders which sprang up throughout the nineteenth century is also thin. Yet these facilities played an important role in imposing urban order and, at times, in supplementing inadequate welfare systems. They should not be neglected in favor of the more spectacular moments in penal history. Closer examination of these institutions might also offer insights into popular attitudes to incarceration. Indeed, a theme that is generally worth greater exploration is that of the relationship between punitiveness and Canadian legal and political culture, given the popular belief that Canadian society is more orderly and more respectful of authority than, for example, the United States.

CRIME, PROSECUTION, VIOLENCE, AND SOCIAL ORDER IN THE NINETEENTH AND TWENTIETH CENTURIES

Significant work has been done on the nature and prevalence of crime and violence and the social meaning to be attached to each of them. This work can be divided it into three subtopics: patterns of prosecution of crime; the extent and nature of violence; and attitudes toward deviance and the role of criminal law in the general process of social control. There is necessarily some overlap between these three, for topics like social control and prosecution are obviously closely linked. But analysis is made easier by this division. As with so much Canadian criminal justice history, work in these areas has generally been restricted to particular localities, and it tends to be concentrated primarily in the nineteenth century.

Patterns of Prosecution

There are relatively few statistical studies of changing patterns of criminalization, and those that are available reveal both similarities and differences with cognate jurisdictions. The early decades of the nineteenth century saw profound social and economic upheaval in central Canada, with large-scale pauper Irish immigration, early urbanization, the construction of large-scale transportation projects, and substantial economic fluctuations. John Weaver's study of crime and prosecution in the Gore district of Upper Canada/Canada West in the 1830s and 1840s is set against, and sensitive to, this background. It also acknowledges that the "crime rates" measured were "often the product not only of crime itself but also of changes in what society considers to be acceptable behaviour." Weaver shows both that property offenses can be linked to periods of distress and that increases in public order crime resulted in some measure from a new intolerance of pursuits previously considered acceptable. In addition, the district witnessed a general repression of Irish immigrants, which contributed to increases in prosecution rates.[39]

Many of the same points are made in Jean-Marie Fecteau's recent study of Quebec in approximately the same period. He demonstrates that prosecutions for property crime rose substantially while those for offenses against the person declined to some extent, a finding replicated for many other nineteenth-century societies. He also argues that in seigneurial, premodern Quebec, the overall increase in crime rates, and particularly the dramatic increase in the use of imprisonment in the 1830s, was the result of the destabilization of traditional methods of social control and the rise of new, state-based methods of repression.[40]

Other studies of long-term trends in crime rates examine the period from the mid-nineteenth to the mid-twentieth centuries. The evidence from police department and jail records in Toronto suggests that Canada experienced the familiar prolonged decline in crime rates between the mid-nineteenth and early twentieth centuries and a small increase thereafter—the "distended U-curve."[41] Yet the authors of these studies are less concerned with explaining this trend than they are with accounting for a consistently high if fluctuating incidence of public order offenses. From this they conclude that policing in Toronto did not substantially change its focus from "class control" to "crime control" but remained always concerned with the former. Unfortunately, the research into long-term trends has not been carried out for many other places. Extant studies suggest that while the overall trend in Montreal was also a downward one, it was much less pronounced than elsewhere and interrupted by a number of upward fluctuations, especially in the 1870s and 1880s.[42] Halifax and Saint John appear to have seen little fluctuation in prosecuted crime rates in the late nineteenth and early twentieth centuries,[43] while in the early years of settlement on the prairies rates moved up and down according to the vagaries of immigration levels, policing patterns, and economic change.[44]

Most of the aforementioned studies rely largely on evidence of generally "minor" offenses, either public order violations or simple theft and assault. We know less about the prevalence of the more serious offenses. If one wishes to look at homicide, for example, one must largely rely on accounts of particular *causes célèbres.*[45] Despite their particular merits, collectively they tell us little about the incidence of this or other serious offenses. There are some longer term studies of homicide for the twentieth century, which show a gradual decline from the 1930s to the 1960s, a steep rise thereafter, and a falling off from the early to mid-1970s.[46] Also dealing mainly with the modern period is an examination of criminal code offenses, which argues that, unlike either Britain or the United States, the more serious crimes were committed in ever-increasing numbers from the late nineteenth century on.[47] Moreover, those who have collected and analyzed information on crime rates, primarily sociologists, have not much augmented their quantitative evidence with qualitative work on official and popular policies and attitudes toward them. Overall, it is difficult to extract from all of this a sense of broad historical patterns. It is possible to conclude that Canada's nineteenth-century cities shared much of the experience of their counterparts in the eastern United States and that at many points in time those who pulled the strings of the criminal process were prepared to use it actively against particular groups. But this is a frustratingly general observation; much work still needs to be done to chart and explain broad trends in crime and prosecution rates.[48]

Violence and Order

Canadian political and popular culture contains a deep-rooted belief in the orderliness of Canadian society. This belief has been formed principally out of comparisons between Upper Canada's "peaceable kingdom" of the early nineteenth century and Jacksonian America, and the contrast in the western frontier experience of the two countries later in the century. I discuss later, in connection with the North West Mounted Police, some ways in which the latter distinction has been undermined. Other work has attacked the perception of an orderly Upper Canada, arguing that the image of the "peaceable kingdom" is a myth and that "the colonial social order was anything but cohesive and stable" but rather was "volatile and raucous."[49]

The image of a well-ordered Canadian past has been more generally undermined by a collective exposure of the substantial number of occasions in which Canadian towns and cities, and occasionally rural areas, saw riots or other disorders over a variety of issues.[50] Michael Cross has sought to explain some of the disorder, both "general" violence and that represented by a particular "riot," as "traditionalist" protest fueled by changing economies and the intrusion of centralized bureaucracies into local ways of ordering. The disorder emerges therefore as an expression of lower class political consciousness.[51] One must applaud the effort to situate violence and petty criminality in its social context and to consider it as something more than mere disorderliness or pathology. However, although some incidents do fit the broader interpretation imposed on them, the thesis is ultimately unconvincing. Violence was as much episodic as endemic, as much about conflict within rather than between the classes. Ruth Bleasdale's work on the Irish canal laborers of the 1840s, for example, shows that their violence was the result of tensions immigrants brought with them and of shortages of employment as well as an aspect of the laborers' efforts to exert control in their relationship with capital.[52]

Deviance and Social Control

The extent to which the criminal law was used as one aspect among middle-class strategies to deal with a perceived mid- to late nineteenth-century social crisis whose symptoms were intemperance, transiency, and sexual transgression as well as crime is considered by a number of historians. In an excellent but unfortunately unpublished study of Ontario in the third quarter of the century, Susan Houston shows how crime control, moral order, and poverty/unemployment merged in the minds of many of the elite, who saw causal links among poverty, ignorance, and crime. She demonstrates that urbanization and economic change altered a prior acceptance of unemployment as seasonal and affecting largely only transients and raised fears about a permanent class of dependent urban poor, dangerous to public morals and public order. The middle class responded with educational schemes as well as more repressive measures aimed particularly at delinquency.[53]

The same theme of the use of criminal law for social control purposes is raised in other studies of vagrancy, juvenile delinquency, and prostitution.[54] A direct link between class interests and prosecuted crime rates has been postulated (not successfully) for early twentieth-century Manitoba.[55] Not all authors, however, view the criminal law as a significant mechanism of state control or state response to social problems. Pierre Tremblay and André Normandeau deny a link between incarceration and economic change in their study of Montreal in the second half of the nineteenth century, although they do not offer alternative explanations for fluctuations. One might speculate that a solution may be found in perceptions of social unrest.[56] Jean-Marie Fecteau argues that the criminal law played a relatively minor role in the maintenance of social relations in early nineteenth-century Quebec. But it was important in that it was used primarily in the cities, where community mechanisms for ensuring lower class subordination were less effective than in rural areas. Migrants, servants, soldiers, and sailors were the particular targets of the law in Quebec City, he argues, because they lived at the margins of social life and it is at those margins that the criminal law operates to control and punish. As traditional methods of social control broke down with the advent of commercial and capitalist development, however, a more ''modern'' approach came to the fore, with criminal justice playing an increasing role in social ordering.[57]

Social control approaches have also been criticized for ignoring the ''popular legitimacy'' of many laws, legal institutions, and sociolegal practices.[58] These criticisms have some force. They are front and center in Judith Fingard's study of a selected sample of mid-nineteenth-century Halifax's most consistent petty offenders and the responses of municipal politicians, welfare groups, and institutions to them.[59] Revealing as that account is in many respects, however, particularly about the way institutions operated for what she calls the ''underclass,'' the implicit reliance on individual and family weakness provides little in the way of explanation about the wider society and the relationships among poverty, personality, police, prison, and philanthropy.[60] This and other accounts, by both proponents and opponents of a social control framework, have shown us who were the petty offenders subject to the concerns of prosecutors and reformers. A remarkable consistency over time has appeared, with the jails generally full of Irish, immigrants, prostitutes, native peoples (where appropriate), blacks (in communities like Halifax, where they were concentrated), the unemployed and underemployed, and recidivists.[61] This demonstrates that concern with providing a more complete picture of the criminal process at the petty and local level should not blind us to the fact that class and race relations played a role in the formation and operation of the law. Merely because the poor used prisons as winter shelters, for example, does not mean that those same institutions were not used for disciplinary purposes; nor does the fact of recidivism reduce all crime to pathology.

Two other works deserve mention in this section. First, there are a number of studies of crime and punishment in particular places at particular times which provide details and/or documents but regrettably little else. There is much information in the work of Peter McGahan, for example, but little effort to draw out the deeper meanings to be attributed to the stories told or the documents reproduced.[62] Second, and related to the issue of social control, there is a literature which deals not so much with crime itself but more with the emergence and operation of what has been called ''urban justice.'' Just as new police forces altered the law-enforcement landscape in the nineteenth-century city, so too did municipal magistrates' courts take over from the old sessions courts, disposing of the increasing volume of petty cases in a regular and routinized fashion. Paul Craven offers an ambitious assessment of the ideology of the Toronto police court. His account captures its intriguing mix of legal power and popular theater, although his reliance on newspaper sources may push the analysis in this direction.[63] No other such court has been so closely studied, although the evolution of the institution itself has been charted for a number of communities.[64]

THE POLICE IN CANADIAN HISTORY

Long dominated by the Royal Canadian Mounted Police (RCMP), the historiography of Canadian policing has in recent years concentrated on the rise, evolution, and functions of the "new police" in the nineteenth century. I will begin with that topic and then examine in turn the RCMP and other aspects of law enforcement.

There is no substantial general history of the new police,[65] but a relatively comprehensive coverage is available in a series of community studies. Writing in this area has been influenced by both social history approaches, which reflect a concern with class and moral order, and by the issues which are central to urban history—adaptation, reform, and modernization of governing institutions. In part as a result of this, the historiography of the police in Canada encompasses a lively debate about the motivations for police reform and the role played by the police. Nicholas Rogers's account of the Toronto force, for example, argues that reform and modernization represented not merely a bureaucratization which moved police policy out of the mainstream of sectarian city politics. They were also important elements in the "quest for moral reform," which cut across those religious-ethnic divisions. Thus, Rogers views the police not merely as the product of urban growth but also as resulting from a new concern to tame the immorality of the urban working classes.[66] In contrast, Greg Marquis's work on Saint John and Toronto argues that the police enjoyed a degree of popular legitimacy. They served a variety of purposes in the emerging cities, including welfare functions, and they frequently identified with the policed as much as with their political masters.[67] This debate about the nature and function of the new police has a place in a number of other community studies. John Weaver's work on Hamilton demonstrates some of the difficulties in sustaining a social control model, although there seems more evidence for this during the early years of policing experiments.[68] Helen Boritch, in perhaps the best single study of one urban force, acknowledges the complex nature of the police role and, in addition, provides an analysis of police evolution from within while stressing the importance of the force's search for autonomy.[69]

There are, perhaps, three weaknesses in the nineteenth-century literature. First, particularly for central Canada, the tendency has been to concentrate on major centers at the expense of other communities.[70] Second, while the introduction of urban forces in the prairie West has received some attention, this work is less attentive to broader debates about the social and political meaning of policing.[71] Third, relatively little has been done outside the prairie region on rural policing. One notable exception is Alan Greer's recent account of the early Lower Canadian experience, which situates rural policing within the process of mid-nineteenth-century "state formation."[72] Here we find an example of a quasi-military *gendarmerie,* whose functions were as much political as they were the maintenance of social and urban order. In some respects, like the North West Mounted Police (NWMP) (discussed later), the principal purpose of the early

Lower Canadian rural police was to "show the flag," to provide tangible evidence of the presence and power of the state among a rebellious population. Thus, Greer demonstrates one broad relationship between policing and state formation.[73] His work serves as an implicit call to put a little of the politics back into policing, although his, of course, is a different politics than that which found expression in middle-class concerns with class control and social order.

The most-studied institution of Canadian criminal justice is the Royal Canadian Mounted Police, although accounts of the force tend to be concentrated in its early years, when it was known as the North West Mounted Police. Founded in 1873 to police the newly acquired former territories of the Hudson's Bay Company, the "mounties" for many years received the best of reviews from historians, who stressed the force's crucial role in the orderly development of the Canadian West and its fairness in dealings with settlers and the native peoples of the plains. This historiography gave the force a near-mythic status in popular culture—a process which itself has been the subject of an impressive and fascinating study.[74] More recent work on many aspects of the organization and operation of the force has offered a much more balanced picture. Accounts of its establishment, for example, have stressed the fact that it was a political instrument, an element in the continentalist policy of Prime Minister John A. Macdonald.[75] It provided a method both of establishing a Canadian presence in the west and thereby forestalling American expansion, and of securing the area for white settlement and the railway, which would in turn provide a market and transportation for the new industry of central Canada. Of particular interest is the decision by the federal government to create not a force based on the urban models of eastern Canada but a quasi-military, *gendarmerie*-type organization, recruited from ex-servicemen, organized on military lines, and drawing for its inspiration on the Royal Irish Constabulary. It was very much a colonial police force, designed to achieve broader political ends as much as to fight crime and to bring not just white settlement and economic development but also eastern Canadian cultural values. The force was used in the same way a little later when settlement moved north to the Yukon.[76] The enormous power and discretion given to its members, especially before 1885, made them in some sense not representatives of the state, but the state itself.[77] It would be fruitful to link the NWMP to the Irish and similar colonial and state-building forces, including the much earlier Lower Canadian rural police.

A second theme in recent literature has been more detailed examination and assessment of the work and effectiveness of the force. From the great march west in 1874, which has been shown to be an ill-conceived and poorly executed venture that could well have turned into disaster, to the presence of dissatisfaction with the hard and lonely life, leading at times to desertion, the NWMP appears now as a more ordinary collection of imperfect men.[78] More importantly, much doubt has been cast on the centrality of their role in pacifying the prairies. Although its first decade or so saw the force principally concerned with an extensive treaty-making process,[79] it has been argued that the eventual absence of Indian wars once white settlement began had less to do with individual officers gaining the trust of the native peoples or with skill at treaty making and more to do with the fact that by the mid-1870s the plains Indians had fought and lost the battle to the south. They knew, therefore, that resistance was fruitless.[80]

Another aspect of the work of the NWMP, which implicitly also points up its political nature, is that it operated as much as an administrative body as a police service in its dealings with settlers. Fire prevention, quarantine enforcement, cartography, crop reporting, and even welfare work came under its effective mandate for a number of years. The NWMP was the settlers' principal link with government, broadly conceived, and whether willingly or not took on a number of government functions. It has also been argued that its enduring popularity derived in part from the fact that it demonstrated no particular partialities in its dealings with settler groups of different origins.[81]

Two further themes in the historiography deserve discussion. Some attention has been paid to the NWMP's generally procapital role in labor strife in the west, particularly in strikes which threatened the construction and operation of the Canadian Pacific Railway. When the railway builders struck in the Kootenay district of British Columbia in 1885, for example, the NWMP's response was to intervene decisively in favor of capital; troops were sent in with instructions to "use the very severest measures to prevent a cessation of the work of construction."[82] The force was prominent also in other conflicts, particularly in the suppression of the Winnipeg General Strike of 1919, with the historiography of their role on that occasion reflecting sharply divergent views.[83]

The second theme is that of relations between the force and native peoples, which arose in a variety of contexts—treaty making, control of the liquor trade, limitation of native peoples to reserves, the North West rebellions, and the operation of the pass system following the second Riel rebellion.[84] The traditional historiography is, not unexpectedly, an altogether laudatory one. Although reviews of pre-1885 activities tend still to be largely favorable, it is now clear that a breakdown in relations with indigenous peoples occurred thereafter. In part this was the product of the rebellion and consequent distrust, and in part it resulted from the intervention of a federal bureaucracy, which took power from local officers and tightened the screws of assimilation.[85] The force did not, however, always support these government policies. An account of its enforcement of pass laws, for example, demonstrates that concern with their legality affected operations.[86]

Finally, work on law enforcement in the early west should be noted, particularly that of Hamar Foster. He describes the law enforcement problems faced by the Hudson's Bay Company in its territories prior to annexation by Canada, and he has also given us a rich study of the work of the assizes in British Columbia's "frontier" communities.[87] The relationship between unofficial methods of ordering and state institutions in the far west and north is examined in a number of other works.[88]

This section has demonstrated that work on the history of policing in Canada has become substantial, diverse, and sophisticated. There are nonetheless still gaps to be filled. We need to know more about the twentieth-century history of the RCMP, in its municipal and provincial policing functions in communities where it fulfils such a role, in its work as an agent of central government in Canada's northward expansion,[89] and in its work as a state security agency, particularly during the 1950s.[90] Indeed, our knowledge of policing generally is still largely restricted to the nineteenth- and early twentieth-century city. Provincial forces, rural policing, the advent and evolution of detective work, and developments after 1920 are all topics worthy of much more comprehensive study than they have been afforded to date, although an account of the Canadian Association of Chiefs of Police sheds light on some of these issues.[91]

WOMEN AND THE CRIMINAL LAW

The recent explosion of interest in women's history in general has spawned a considerable literature on the history of women and crime. Most of this deals with what one might term "female-specific" areas of the criminal law—prostitution, rape, abortion, and infanticide. There is little that examines women generally as offenders or victims in the criminal process. André Lachance's study of female crime in New France is an exception and concludes, similarly to work on female offenders elsewhere, that women were considerably underrepresented among those brought to court. He attributes this in part to the demographic imbalance and to "the accepted traditional female role," which placed women "in the privacy of the home rather than in places of public gatherings."[92] Other studies based on the more serious offenses are this author's accounts of women and criminal justice in eighteenth-century Halifax, which also demonstrate that women were infrequently prosecuted.[93] Analyses of minor theft and public order prosecutions in the nineteenth century again reveal a low level of prosecution, although a higher one than for the more serious offenses. The most comprehensive of these studies also argues that "official rates of female crime were much higher in the nineteenth than in the current century" and attributes the decline to the effectiveness of informal social controls which accompanied urbanization and industrialization.[94] An account of the recent past argues that greater involvement by women in the public world has brought with it a higher rate of involvement in crime.[95] Much more work needs to be done on long-term trends in arrest and prosecution rates, but these represent a useful beginning.

Female offenders feature most prominently in accounts of infanticide, abortion, and prostitution laws. The operation of infanticide laws in Canada would be familiar to students of the subject elsewhere. While the English-derived presumption of guilt for the unmarried who concealed a birth was in force in the eighteenth and early nineteenth centuries, then and later the legal system treated those who committed the offense very leniently. Prosecutions were few, despite some evidence that the practice was at times widespread. Convictions for the principal offense were even rarer, and pardons were invariably granted to those who were found guilty.[96] Constance Backhouse is probably correct to conclude that society could treat these deviant women lightly in part because the exposure of their illegitimate pregnancies had already led to social disgrace, and in part because they represented no broader threat to social order and mores. The infanticide laws "functioned largely as symbolic pronouncements" and the young, single, and usually poor female offenders "provided a conspicuous and ideal platform upon which the courts could . . . exhibit compassion towards desperate women." Work on infanticide should probably take more account of the choices women made to bear and keep their children; the social disgrace does not appear to have been so overwhelming as once thought.[97]

Infanticide laws were obviously concerned in some degree with control of reproduction, and even more so was the criminalization of abortion. The development of the law from the first Canadian legislation in New Brunswick in 1810 is covered by a number of authors. They link the abortion prohibition to the later criminalization of contraception and consider both against the background of the eugenics movement and the turn-of-the-century concern about "race suicide."[98] They also attempt to quantify both the level of prosecution, which appears to have been very low and to have involved principally those who procured abortions for others, and the general extent of the practice of abortion, which was considerable.[99]

Prostitution has emerged as the most-studied female-specific area of women's criminal justice history in Canada. The development of the law during the social purity era of the late nineteenth and early twentieth centuries has been comprehensively examined, as have general patterns of enforcement in the same era.[100] John McLaren concludes that the substantial volume of antiprostitution legislation was at one and the same time "a genuine response to a domestic problem of the toleration of prostitution" and, to a considerable extent, an unnecessary aping of British and American social purity campaigns. This and other work, much of it locally focused, also has much to tell us about the composition of the prostitute population, and in places there are glimpses of the clientele.[101] Complexity and ambiguity abound. Both the substantial legislative activity in this pèriod and differential enforcement, across time and place and among prostitutes, procurers, and clients, demonstrate that the criminalization of prostitution acted as a proxy for broader concerns about the changing role of women—especially young, single women in a society undergoing rapid urbanization and industrialization. This general point is made, in different ways, in those studies that address the issue of prostitution as work and in an article not concerned with prostitution per se but with the genesis and operation of Toronto's early twentieth-century Social Survey Commission.[102]

Women as victims of crime are considered in accounts of rape, seduction, spousal assault, and spousal homicide. The history of rape involves a familiar story of unwillingness on the part of judges, juries, and prosecuting authorities to provide effective protection for rape victims.[103] Constance Backhouse's work demonstrates this story statistically and doctrinally. Her examination of particular cases also paints a vivid and compelling picture of the difficulties faced by complainants, whose very involvement in the crime made their morality suspect. Rape represents an example of the operation of law as ideology in the context of gender, for procedural and societal barriers to conviction for rape were combined with both additional sanctions in other areas of male predation (such as statutory rape, procuring, and seduction) and the retention of the death penalty for rape until 1954. According to Backhouse, the laws were "paternalistic," designed to signal societal disapprobation of violence against women but to protect only the "chaste." To Backhouse's work, which examines rape law only in the context of gender relations, should be added that of Carolyn Strange, which presents a sustained analysis of relationships among rape, gender, class, race, and legal process.[104]

Seduction has been examined in a number of studies, most comprehensively in a recent account, which argues that "the criminalization of voluntary sexual activity" served to "entrench the legal and parental regulation of women, and to punish women who transgressed cultural prohibitions of female desire."[105] Spousal assault is only now beginning to attract the direct attention of historians, although its nature and attitudes to it can also be traced in work on other aspects of family law.[106] There is a brief account of prosecutions in early twentieth-century Alberta and more widely researched studies on Halifax and late nineteenth-century Montreal. The latter attempts also to situate domestic violence in the context of working-class life and to examine both women's strategies for dealing with the problem and broader societal attitudes and responses.[107]

Two recent essays consider the ultimate example of violence against women—homicide. One demonstrates that women were the victims of deadly force far in excess of their numbers in eighteenth-century Halifax, although that violence was not principally "domestic" in origin but derived from the peculiar social and demographic conditions of the city.[108] The other essay traces the prevalence of spousal killings in Toronto and Vancouver in the twentieth century. While women represented only a small minority of homicide victims, their violent deaths came predominantly at the hands of their husbands and boyfriends. Employing primarily statistical analyses, the authors draw links between changing women's status and "victimization rates";[109] work of this kind for the more distant past would be invaluable.

The criminal law may have done little to protect women who were victims of violent assaults, but some recent work on the treatment generally of women in the criminal process shows that patriarchy has worked in complex ways at different times. We have seen that lenient treatment was the norm for infanticide offenders, while other studies suggest that generally female offenders were more harshly treated by the courts than men.[110] The importance of particular context is well illustrated by Karen Dubinsky and Franca Iacovetta's recent account of the campaign for clemency for a woman who murdered her abusive husband. They demonstrate that public sympathy and public outcry could be engendered if the correct appeal could be made to the virtues of "motherhood" and to the fear of foreigners and "sexual slavery."[111] This work, and some of the other articles already cited, demonstrates that, as in so many other areas of historical inquiry, work written with feminist concerns to the fore requires us to think differently about the historical meaning of aspects of the criminal law and criminal process.

OTHER TOPICS: A REVIEW AND AN AGENDA FOR FUTURE RESEARCH

The five preceding sections have obviously not covered all the issues that have been and still should be addressed by historians of Canadian criminal justice. This section completes the general picture, with a review of the strengths and weaknesses of the extant literature on a potpourri of other topics central to an understanding of the field as a whole.

In the last two decades, no period has been more closely explored by English criminal justice historians than the eighteenth and early nineteenth centuries, and it is therefore perhaps especially surprising that we know very little about the operation of the unreformed system in those areas of what is now English Canada where it was introduced—Upper Canada, the Maritime provinces, and Newfoundland.[112] The Maritimes and Upper Canada received, in different ways and at different times, English criminal law and procedure. A large measure of English ideology came with formal systems, and colonial communities had both the responsibility of operating those systems and the opportunity to alter them. Yet the large subjects of crime and the courts and of social attitudes and adaptations are largely unexplored for this period outside of Quebec. For Upper Canada, for example, one must rely on accounts of particular cases or court sessions, and some of these are antiquarian in approach, providing little more than brief description and/or anecdote.[113] There are a few exceptions, however, including John Blackwell's study of the effect of the major Upper Canadian reforms of 1833, which argues that the substantial reduction of capital punishment in the statute book did bring real change to the practice of the courts. This article also contains a brief survey of the movement for reform in that colony, a subject which nonetheless deserves a much more detailed account.[114] In addition, there is some useful institutional history, which traces the links between criminal justice and politics, and much instructive material in the work of Robert Fraser on early Upper Canadian society. Some insights into the approach to the criminal law of the colony's dominant legal personality, Chief Justice Sir John Beverley Robinson, can also be gleaned from a variety of studies.[115]

The Maritime provinces have also been largely ignored, despite their colonization by English-speaking settlers from the mid-eighteenth century onward. There is a general overview of the criminal justice system, and other work offers glimpses of the court process.[116] In addition, I have recently provided accounts of the operation of aspects of the unreformed criminal justice system in Nova

Scotia and have sought to trace the ways in which that system was molded by indigenous circumstances into a relatively unique local product. In a study of the pardon system, for example, an aspect of the criminal process that has engendered much controversy across the Atlantic, I argue that the structure of colonial society and government meant that connection to the military was a more crucial determinant in the decision-making process than any other consideration.[117]

Like the early period, the twentieth century as a whole has not received much attention, a point I have already made in relation to prisons and policing. This neglect is ironic given that recent writing on Canadian history generally has concentrated on the post-Confederation period. A few community studies provide qualitative accounts of crime, policing, and punishment.[118] There are some accounts also of the evolution of laws and prosecutorial practices surrounding particular activities. Much work has been done, for example, on drug offenses, where the increasing legal regulation and patterns of prosecution show the complex interplay of moral panics, racism, and the institutional interests of law-enforcement agencies.[119]

In addition to these two major periods, insufficient attention has been paid to a number of particular topics. We know very little about the process by which major changes to the criminal law were effected in the early nineteenth century,[120] and there is relatively little on the evolution of the law thereafter. The enactment of the Criminal Code in 1892 has received some attention, but the major account tends to be strong on parliamentary process and insufficiently attentive to the meaning of codification. It remains to be explained what deeper considerations about the legitimacy of law motivated that initiative at a time when central Canadian legal culture was suffering an attack of Anglophilia.[121] We know little also about the substance or the process of the pre-Confederation colonial statute revisions, although an excellent unpublished account now exists of some of the early work of the federal government after it took jurisdiction over the substantive criminal law in 1867.[122] The post-1892 evolution of the law has been largely ignored at the general level,[123] although there are a number of particular areas in which a good deal of attention has been paid to "law emergence." These include the laws relating to drugs and prostitution already discussed, specific regimes for juveniles,[124] and the criminal repression of homosexuality.[125]

The topic of capital punishment has surprisingly received short shrift. There are accounts of its prevalence on the statute books,[126] some statistical studies of modern commutation patterns which stress the importance of race,[127] and a smattering of other works on the pardon and particular cases.[128] An excellent beginning for a more comprehensive account of law and practice is provided by Carolyn Strange, who examines legislative change and patterns of executive commutations and points up the need to pay close attention to the interplay of gender, race, and politics in the evolution of capital punishment policies and practices.[129]

Like criminal law, criminal procedure is largely an unexplored topic in all periods of Canadian history. The insanity defense is the most comprehensively studied aspect of procedure.[130] One can also glean much about it, as well as some appreciation of trial tactics, from Martin Friedland's account of the trial of Valentine Shortis in 1895, although the same author's other foray into the procedure field is rather less instructive.[131] There are two useful studies of the institutional organization of prosecution and some unpublished work on Justices of the Peace, although we still know too little about this important subject on the ground, including the development of bail laws.[132] There is nothing on the operation of grand or trial juries, although Paul Romney's work on the constitutional and political significance of aspects of trial procedure is replete with imagination and insight.[133] Extradition has been treated only in the context of specific cases.[134]

Finally, an issue still largely unexplored but of much contemporary interest is that of the role of criminal justice in the processes of conquest and assimilation of Canadian native peoples. The most-studied aspect of this topic is the attempt in the late nineteenth and early twentieth centuries to apply southern laws relating to murder to the north. Sidney Harring's account of the spate of killings that occurred in Copper Inuit society around the time that Canadian sovereignty was being extended to their region is strong on demonstrating that the white justice system lacked any substantial understanding of what was happening. In two cases, natives were tried and hanged without a full appreciation on their part of the process, but by Harring's own admission he is not able to offer conclusive explanations of the central events in the story. Nonetheless, this is the best account we have of both indigenous methods of social ordering and of the process and policy that informed the extension of southern attitudes to crime and law into the north.[135]

There is a more scanty literature dealing with southern native peoples and the criminal law. The kind of interaction described by Harring and others took place in the south in an earlier period and was complicated in many regions by the process of extensive white settlement. Most of the standard accounts on native history in southern Canada do not concern themselves with criminal law, and indeed we do not know when colonial governments' justice systems actually began to extend their effective jurisdiction to include native peoples. The native peoples of eastern Canada, for example, do not appear at all in that colony's eighteenth-century criminal justice records. We have some glimpses of the process of cultural imperialism through the criminal law. John Dickinson discusses criminal sanctioning as an aspect of sovereignty disputes in early New France, while Tina Loo and Hamar Foster have looked at the same theme for the west in a later period.[136] Loo's study of potlach prosecutions in British Columbia is a model for this kind of work.[137] But while the west has received considerable recent attention, we need to continue systematic investigation into when, how, and with what consequences native peoples' own systems of social ordering were ousted in favor of European ones elsewhere in the country. Those indigenous systems are also little understood, although the recent campaign for native self-government has sparked an interest in them as it becomes obvious that they will in some degree be revived.[138]

CONCLUSION

It has long been commonplace for Canadian legal (including criminal justice) historians to lament the poverty and paucity of writing in their field.[139] It may still be right to do so, especially if one is drawing comparisons to the English and American literature. But it would be wrong to make too much of this. Despite all of the gaps in our knowledge, the field is much healthier, in both product and potential, than it was a decade ago. It is still perhaps too early to think about a comprehensive general study, for so much primary work still needs to be done in so many areas, and the difficulties of relying only on secondary sources are amply demonstrated by the one purported general treatment of the subject.[140] It is time, however, that major particular themes were addressed, such as policing, incarceration, or the relationship between the law-and-order emphasis in Canadian political culture and the operation of the criminal process. In this way, we can begin to indentify what is particularly Canadian about the history of crime, law, and order above the 49th parallel. Perhaps when that occurs, the problem referred to earlier in this chapter—the inability of criminal justice history to intrude itself into the general consciousness of the historical community—will also recede. Criminal justice is an integral part of state formation, and understandings of that process will benefit greatly from a focus wide enough to incorporate crime, courts, and punishment.

NOTES

I wish to thank Lise Favreau for her assistance with the literature on Quebec. For their comments on an earlier draft, I thank Jerry Bannister, Susan Lewthwaite, Tina Loo, Greg Marquis, Peter Oliver, Kent Roach, and Carolyn Strange, and the editors of this volume.

1. Jim Phillips, "The History of Canadian Criminal Justice, 1750–1920," in *Criminology: A Reader's Guide,* ed. Jane Gladstone, Richard Ericson, and Clifford Shearing (Toronto, 1991), 65. See also R.C. MacLeod's introduction to the only published collection of articles in the area, *Lawful Authority: Readings on the History of Criminal Justice in Canada* (Toronto, 1988), 4: "the scope for new and exciting research in this area is almost without limit."

2. Perhaps most notably I have not included a separate section dealing with "political crime," the offenses of treason and sedition. There is a rich literature on this, emanating primarily from the rebellions in the Canadas in 1837–1838 and the Riel rebellion of 1885; a multivolume *Canadian State Trials* project is in progress under the direction of Professors J.B. Wright and F.M. Greenwood. Given the shortage of space, however, I have elected to stay close to the mainstream of criminal justice history.

3. Just two decades ago, the leading Canadian legal historian wrote, with reference

to legal history generally (although his comment included criminal justice) that "[w]e have not even accumulated and organised most of the major facts, let alone thought about them": Richard C.B. Risk, "A Prospectus for Canadian Legal History," *Dalhousie Law Journal* 1 (1973), 227. See also the comment on the failure of "legal historians" in André Morel, "Réflexions sur la justice criminelle canadienne, au 18e siécle," *Revue d'histoire de l'Amérique Française* 29 (1975): 241.

4. As the leading historian of Canadian policing has recently noted, criminal justice history exists "on the fringes" of historians' concerns: Greg Marquis, "Law, Society and History: Whose Frontier," *Acadiensis* 21 (1992), 174. Not only do survey histories ignore the topic, two otherwise comprehensive bibliographic aids (*A Reader's Guide to Canadian History,* 2 vols., ed. J.L. Granatstein, Paul Stevens, and D.A. Muise [Toronto, 1984], and *Canadian History: A Reader's Guide,* 2 vols., ed. M. Brook-Taylor and D. Owram [Toronto, 1994]) contain no chapter on criminal justice history, and the subtopics that comprise it merit hardly a mention within chapters dealing with subjects such as social and urban history.

5. For the organization of the court system, see André Morel, "L'imposition et le contrôle des peines au Baillage de Montréal (1666–1693)," in *Etudes Juridiques en Hommage à Monsieur le Juge Bernard Bissonette* (Montreal, 1963); André Lachance, *Le Bourreau au Canada sous le régime français* (Quebec, 1966), 15–24; John A. Dickinson, "La justice seigneuriale en Nouvelle-France: le cas de Notre-Dame-des-Anges," *Revue d'histoire de l'Amérique Française* 28 (1974): 323–26; E.-Z. Massicotte, "Peines et châtiments sous M. de Maisonneuve," *Bulletin des recherches historiques* 45 (1939): 115–16, and "Les tribinaux et les officiers de justice a Montréal sous le régime français, 1648–1760," *Bulletin des recherches historiques* 37 (1931): 122–28, 179–92, 252–56, 302–13. For a general overview in English, see John A. Dickinson, "Law in New France," Canadian Legal History Project, University of Manitoba [hereafter CLHP], Working Paper No. 92–5. Local ordinances are discussed in John A. Dickinson, "Réflexions sur la police en Nouvelle France," *McGill Law Journal* 32 (1987): 497–522.

6. André Lachance, "Le procès criminel en Canada au XVIIIe siècle (1712–1748)," *Revue de Droit de l'Université de Sherbrooke* 5 (1974): 111–55, and "La criminalité à Québec sous le régime français: étude statistique," *Revue d'histoire de l'Amérique Française* 20 (1966): 409–14.

7. This was the process whereby witnesses' statements were first verified by further judicial questioning and the accused was then confronted with some or all of those witnesses.

8. Lachance, "Le procès criminel," *Le Bourreau au Canada,* and *La justice criminelle du Roi au Canada au XVIIIe siècle: Tribunaux et officiers de justice* (Quebec, 1978). On control of seigneurial courts, see also Massicotte, "Les tribunaux et les officiers de justice," and Morel, "L'imposition et le contrôle des peines," 424–25. There are also numerous older accounts of particular trials, which vary in length and usefulness, in the work of T.P. Bedard, G. Malchelosse, Y. Prevost, and P.G. Roy. These may be located in an excellent guide to a wide variety of literature: *Canadian Criminal Justice History: An Annotated Bibliography,* comp. Russell Smandych, Catherine Matthews, and Sandra J. Cox (Toronto, 1987) [hereafter *CCJH Bibliography*]. I will frequently use this method of referring to additional work published before 1987 rather than produce extremely lengthy notes.

9. Lachance, "Le procès criminel," 139–40. "Temporary acquittals" were made

on decrees of "*plus amplement informe*" and lasted for limited periods of time while more information was sought.

10. Ibid., 130–31, and see 131–36 for the torture process. This is also described in Lachance, *Le bourreau au Canada,* chap. 1, and in Raymond Boyer, "The Question: Judicial Torture in New France," *Canadian Journal of Criminology and Corrections* 5 (1963): 284–91.

11. Lachance, "Le procès criminel," 155.

12. This section on crime and punishment is drawn principally from Lachance, "La criminalité à Québec," and *Crimes et Criminels en Nouvelle France* (Montreal, 1984). See also Morel, "L'imposition et le contrôle des peines," and "Réflexions sur la justice criminelle"; Jacques Mathieu, "Les causes devant la prévoste de Quebec en 1667," *Social History-Histoire Sociale* 3 (1969): 101–11. For the records problem, see Morel, "L'imposition et le contrôle des peines." For regional differences, compare Morel's study of Montreal with that of Lachance, based on the Quebec district. For additional informative, but not always scholarly, accounts see the work of H. Bizier, R. Boyer, and P.G. Roy in *CCJH Bibliography.*

13. See, respectively, André Lachance, "Une étude de mentalité: les injures verbales au Canada au XVIIIe siècle (1712–1748)," *Revue d'histoire de l'Amérique Française* 31 (1977): 229–38; Peter Moogk, " 'Thieving Buggers' and 'Stupid Sluts': Insults and Popular Culture in New France," *William and Mary Quarterly* 36 (1979): 524–47; Morel, "Réflexions sur la justice criminelle," 248–51; Terrence Crowley, " 'Thunder Gusts': Popular Disturbances in Early French Canada," *Historical Papers* (1979): 11–32.

14. André Lachance, "Women and Crime in Canada in the Eighteenth Century," in *Crime and Criminal Justice in Europe and Canada,* ed. Louis A. Knafla (Waterloo, 1981), 157–77; Robert L. Seguin, *La sorcellerie au Québec du XVIIe au XIXe siècles* (Montreal, 1971).

15. Lachance, *Le bourreau au Canada,* 45–46, which generally gives the most detailed account of punishment. A further eighteen people were "killed in effigy," having been convicted in their absence.

16. See also Lachance's detailed description of the office of executioner and of the men who filled it in *Le bourreau au Canada,* chaps. 3–5.

17. André Lachance, "Les prisons au Canada sous le régime français," *Revue d'histoire de l'Amérique Française* 19 (1966): 561–65

18. Morel, "L'imposition et le contrôle des peines," 419–31. See also the suggestion that one earlier seigneurial court was in fact lenient with a familiar population in Massicotte, "Peines et châtiments."

19. The decision to retain English law and the structure of the systems established between 1760 and 1774 are variously discussed in André Morel, "La reception du droit criminel anglais au Québec (1760–1892)," *Revue juridique Thémis* 13 (1978): 450–51; Jacques L'Heureux, "L'organisation judiciaire au Québec de 1764 à 1774," *Revue générale de droit* 1 (1970): 226–331; John L. J. Edwards, "The Advent of English (Not French) Criminal Law and Procedure into Canada: A Close Call in 1774," *Criminal Law Quarterly* 26 (1984): 464–82; Louis A. Knafla and Terry Chapman, "Criminal Justice in Canada: A Comparative Study of the Maritimes and Lower Canada, 1760–1812," *Osgoode Hall Law Journal* 21 (1983), 258 et seq.; Hilda Neatby, *The Administration of Justice Under the Quebec Act* (Minneapolis, 1937).

20. Morel, "La réception du droit criminel anglais," 480–508; Douglas Hay, "The Meanings of the Criminal Law in Quebec, 1764–1774," in *Crime and Criminal Justice*

in Europe and Canada, 77–110. This reaction was even more strongly manifested in the civil courts when English law was applied there in the pre-1774 period: André Morel, "La réaction des Canadiens devant l'administration de la justice de 1764 à 1774: une forme de resistance passive," *Revue du Barreau de la Province de Québec* 20 (1960): 53–63.

21. Hay, "Meanings of the Criminal Law," 100. For an earlier observation that English practices must have invoked confusion and resentment among the *canadien* population, see E.-Z. Massicotte, "Les pendus encagés," *Bulletin des recherches historiques* 37 (1931): 427–32.

22. Morel argues that by the early nineteenth century, the criminal law was no longer contested cultural terrain even though the francophone legal profession was not much involved in its operation: "La réception du droit criminel anglais," 509–32.

23. Jean-Marie Fecteau, "Régulation sociale et répression de la déviance au Bas-Canada au tournant du 19e siècle (1791–1815)," *Revue d'histoire de l'Amérique Française* 38 (1985): 499–521. I discuss this and other work by Fecteau in more detail later. There is also some information on crimes and punishments in this period in Neatby, *The Administration of Justice.*

24. The principal narrative accounts of the founding of Kingston, which also effectively demonstrate its general adoption of New York's Auburn system, are Rainer Baehre, "Origins of the Penitentiary System in Upper Canada," *Ontario History* 69 (1977): 185–207; J. M. Beattie, *Attitudes towards Crime and Punishment in Upper Canada, 1830–1850* (Toronto, 1977); J. Jerald Bellomo, "Upper Canadian Attitudes Towards Crime and Punishment," *Ontario History* 64 (1972): 11–26; C. J. Taylor, "The Kingston, Ontario Penitentiary and Moral Architecture," *Social History-Histoire Sociale* 12 (1979): 385–408. In addition to these and the other work on Kingston noted later (notes 25–27), see the work of C.R. Adamson, B. Curtis and B. Edgington, J.A. Edmison, R. Gaucher, C.K. Joliffe, A.M. Kirkpatrick, and A.E. Lavell listed in *CCJH Bibliography.* Peter Oliver is currently preparing a monograph on prisons in nineteenth-century Ontario which contains the best account yet of the origins of Kingston.

25. Bryan Palmer, "Kingston Mechanics and the Rise of the Penitentiary, 1833–1836," *Social History-Histoire Sociale* 13 (1980): 7–32.

26. Peter Oliver, "From Jails to Penitentiary: The Demise of Community Corrections in Early Ontario," *Correctional Options* 4 (1984): 1–10.

27. See two recent articles by Russell Smandych: "Beware of the 'Evil American Monster': Upper Canadian Views of the Need for a Penitentiary, 1830–1834," *Canadian Journal of Criminology* 33 (1991): 125–47, and "Tory Paternalism and the Politics of Penal Reform in Upper Canada, 1830–1834: A 'Neo-Revisionist' Account of the Kingston Penitentiary," *Criminal Justice History* 12 (1991): 57–83; see also the forthcoming account by Oliver mentioned in note 24. For Tory paternalism and attitudes to the penitentiary, see Donald J. McMahon, "Law and Public Authority: Sir John Beverley Robinson and the Purposes of the Criminal Law," *University of Toronto Faculty of Law Review* 46 (1988): 390–423. For the asylum, see note 36 and the work by T. Brown and Smandych listed in *CCJH Bibliography.*

28. Beattie, *Attitudes Towards Crime and Punishment,* and the work of D.E. Chunn and W.G. Norman noted in *CCJH Bibliography.*

29. William A. Calder, "Convict Life in Canadian Federal Penitentiaries, 1867–1900," in *Crime and Criminal Justice in Europe and Canada,* 314. See also the same author's "The Federal Penitentiary System in Canada, 1867–1899: A Social and Insti-

tutional History'' (unpublished Ph.D. diss., University of Toronto, 1979). See also the forthcoming study by Oliver mentioned in note 24. For the jurisdictional arrangements consequent on Confederation, see H.G. Needham in *CCJH Bibliography.*

30. Rainer Baehre, ''From Bridewell to Federal Penitentiary: Prisons and Punishment in Nova Scotia Before 1800,'' in *Essays in the History of Canadian Law: Volume Three, Nova Scotia,* ed. Philip Girard and Jim Phillips (Toronto, 1990), 163–99, and ''Prison as Factory, Convict as Worker: The Saint John Penitentiary, 1841–1880,'' in *Essays in the History of Canadian Law: Volume Five,* ed. Susan Lewthwaite, Tina Loo, and Jim Phillips (Toronto, 1994), 439–77.

31. The development of the Montreal prison system can be variously traced in Pierre Tremblay, ''L'évolution de l'emprisonnement pénitentiare, de son intensité, de sa feremté et de sa portée: le cas de Montréal de 1845 à 1913,'' *Canadian Journal of Criminology* 28 (1986): 47–68; Jacques Laplante, *Prison et ordre social au Quebec* (Ottawa, 1989); Jean-Marie Fecteau, *Un nouvel ordre des choses: la pauvreté, le crime, l'Etat au Québec, de la fin du XVIIIe siècle à 1840* (Montreal, 1989), 198–206, and ''Between the Old Order and Modern Times: Poverty, Criminality, and Power in Quebec, 1791–1840,'' in *Essays in the History of Canadian Law: Volume Five.* See also the work of P. Landreville, G. Julien, F. Lefebvre, and D. Delisle in *CCJH Bibliography.*

32. Peter Oliver, ''A Terror to Evil-Doers: The Central Prison and the Criminal Class in Late Nineteenth-Century Ontario,'' in *Patterns of the Past: Reinterpreting Ontario's History,* ed. Roger Hall et al. (Toronto, 1988); Josef Berkovits, ''Prisoners for Profit: Convict Labour in the Ontario Central Prison, 1875–1915,'' in *Essays in the History of Canadian Law: Volume Five,* 478–515.

33. Carolyn Strange, ''The Criminal and Fallen of their Sex: The Establishment of Canada's First Women's Prison, 1874–1901,'' *Canadian Journal of Women and the Law* 1 (1985): 79–92. Strange's thesis is challenged in Peter Oliver, ''To Govern by Kindness: The First Two Decades of the Mercer Reformatory for Women,'' in *Essays in the History of Canadian Law: Volume Five,* 516–72. For other women's prisons, see Pierre Tremblay and André Normandeau, ''L'économie pénale de la société montréalaise, 1845–1913,'' *Social History-Histoire Sociale* 19 (1986): 180–81.

34. See the work of S. Shoom and A. Jones in *CCJH Bibliography.* See also Susan Houston, ''The Impetus to Reform: Urban Crime, Poverty and Ignorance in Ontario, 1850–1875'' (unpublished Ph.D. diss., University of Toronto, 1974) and ''School Reform and Education: The Issue of Compulsory Schooling, Toronto, 1851–1871,'' in *Egerton Ryerson and His Times,* ed. Neil MacDonald and Alf Chaiton (Toronto, 1978); Paul W. Bennett, ''Turning Bad Boys into Good Citizens: The Reforming Impulse of Toronto's Industrial Schools Movement, 1883–1920s,'' *Ontario History* 78 (1986): 209–32, and ''Taming Bad Boys of the Dangerous Class: Child Rescue and Restraint at the Victoria Industrial School, 1887–1935,'' *Social History-Histoire Sociale* 21 (1988): 71–96; Tremblay and Normandeau, ''L'économie penale,'' 188–99.

35. See variously Oliver, ''From Jails to Penitentiary'' and the same author's forthcoming study mentioned in note 24; Richard B. Splane, *Social Welfare in Ontario 1793–1833: A Study of Public Welfare Administration* (Toronto, 1965), chap. 4; Paul Romney, ''Rebel as Magistrate: William Lyon Mackenzie and his Enemies,'' in *Essays in the History of Canadian Law: Volume Five;* Baehre, ''From Bridewell to Federal Penitentiary''; Donald G. Wetherell, ''To Discipline and Train: Adult Rehabilitation Programmes in Ontario Prisons, 1874–1900,'' *Social History-Histoire Sociale* 12 (1979): 145–65; Fecteau, ''Régulation Sociale et répression de la déviance''; Judith Fingard, *The Dark*

Side of Life in Victorian Halifax (Porter's Lake, Nova Scotia, 1989). See also, on early jails, the work of J.E. Jones, R.E. Kroll, and C.K. Talbot listed in *CCJH Bibliography.*

36. Simon N. Verdun-Jones and Russell Smandych, "Catch-22 in the Nineteenth Century: The Evolution of Therapeutic Confinement for the Criminally Insane in Canada, 1840–1900," *Criminal Justice History* 2 (1981): 85–108. See also the entries under H. Stalwick, D. Francis, C. Krasnick, and R. Baehre in *CCJH Bibliography.*

37. For the former view, see John Hagan and Jeffrey Leon, "The Rehabilitation of Law: A Social-Historical Comparison of Probation in Canada and the United States," *Canadian Journal of Sociology* 5 (1980): 235–51, and "Philosophy and Sociology of Crime Control: Canadian-American Comparisons," *Sociological Quarterly* 49 (1977): 181–208. For the latter, see Peter Oliver and Michael Whittingham, "Elitism, Localism, and the Emergence of Adult Probation Services in Ontario, 1893–1972," *Canadian Historical Review* 68 (1987): 225–58.

38. Twentieth-century developments are usefully, if necessarily briefly, reviewed in John W. Ekstedt and Curt T. Griffiths, *Corrections in Canada: Policy and Practice* (Toronto, 1988), 48–57. There is some account of commissions of inquiry in the otherwise disappointing Michael D. Whittingham, "Criminality and Correctional Reformism in Ontario, 1831–1954" (unpublished Ph.D. diss., York University, 1980), chaps. 4, 5. The best single study of the modern period, albeit a relatively short one, is Shirley Skinner et al., *Corrections: An Historical Perspective of the Saskatchewan Experience* (Regina, 1981). See also the work of P. Goldring and J.T.L. James in *CCJH Bibliography.*

39. John Weaver, "Crime, Public Order and Repression: The Gore District in Upheaval, 1832–1851," *Ontario History* 78 (1986): 175–207. See also the same author's *Crimes, Constables and Courts: Order and Transgression in a Canadian City, 1816–1970* (Montreal and Kingston, 1994).

40. Fecteau, *Un nouvel ordre des choses,* and idem, "Between the Old Order and Modern Times."

41. Helen Boritch and John Hagan, "A Century of Crime in Toronto: Gender, Class and Patterns of Social Control, 1859–1955," *Criminology* 28 (1990): 567–99, and "Crime and the Changing Forms of Class Control: Policing Public Order in 'Toronto the Good', 1859–1955," *Social Forces* 66 (1987): 307–35; Helen Boritch, "Crime and Punishment in Middlesex County, Ontario, 1871–1920," in *Essays in the History of Canadian Law: Volume Five,* 387–438.

42. Tremblay and Normandeau, "L'économie penale," especially at 181–86.

43. Peter McGahan, "Reconstructing Patterns of Crime in Halifax and Saint John: A Preliminary Historical Analysis," in *Dimensions of Communities: A Research Handbook,* ed. Dan A. Chekki (New York, 1989).

44. The principal studies are those of T. Thorner and T. Thorner and N. Watson noted in *CCJH Bibliography.* A more recent study is Jon Swainger, "Dime Novel Toughs: Legal Culture and Criminal Law in Red Deer, Alberta, 1907–1920," *Criminal Justice History* 14 (1993):109–33.

45. There is an extensive populist and antiquarian literature dealing with murder cases, and some, though by no means all, of this work is noted in *CCJH Bibliography, passim.* Among the better scholarly accounts are the work of Dubinsky and Iacovetta, Strange, Romney, Strum, and Friedland (see notes 111, 113, and 131). Some useful material is contained in Neil Boyd, *The Last Dance: Murder in Canada* (Scarborough, 1988), chap. 1.

46. This summarizes the work of R. Charland and J.C. Gorman listed in *CCJH Bibliography,* Rosemary Gartner, "Homicide In Canada" (unpublished ms, 1991), and Rosemary Gartner and Bill McCarthy, "The Social Distribution of Femicide in Urban Canada, 1921–1988," *Law and Society Review* 25 (1991): 287–311.

47. P. and P. Brantingham, *Patterns of Crime* (New York, 1984), chap. 8. See also G. Won Lee, "Are Crime Rates Increasing? A Study of the Impact of Demographic Shifts on Crime Rates in Canada," *Canadian Journal of Criminology* 26 (1984): 29–42; J.P. Huzel, "The Incidence of Crime in Vancouver During the Great Depression," *BC Studies* 69–70 (1986): 211–48. It is rather surprising that more use has not been made of the national criminal code statistics, maintained since the 1870s. They are summarized in *Historical Statistics of Canada,* ed. M.C. Urquhart and K.A.H. Buckley (Ottawa, 1983).

48. Offenses specific to women have been more closely examined than most; I discuss later the literature on rape, infanticide, abortion, and prostitution.

49. W. Thomas Matthews, "The Myth of the Peaceable Kingdom: Upper Canadian Society during the Early Victorian Period," *Queen's Quarterly* 94 (1987), 385, 399. This work draws substantially on that of Weaver, Cross, and others noted elsewhere. See also, on rural violence, Susan Lewthwaite, "Violence, Law and Community in Rural Upper Canada," in *Essays in the History of Canadian Law: Volume Five,* 353–86.

50. In addition to the works specifically discussed, see the three articles on riots and other disorders by M.S. Cross and that by P.E. Roy in *CCJH Bibliography.* See also Frederick H. Armstrong, "The York Riots of March 23, 1832," *Ontario History* 55 (1963): 61–72; Gregory S. Kealey, "The Orange Order in Toronto: Religious Riot and the Working Class," in *Essays in Canadian Working Class History,* ed. Kealey and Peter Warrian (Toronto, 1970); Leo Johnson, "The Gore District Outrages, 1826–1829: A Case Study of Violence, Justice and Political Propaganda," *Ontario History* 83 (1991): 109–26; M. Galvin, "The Jubilee Riots in Toronto," *Canadian Catholic Historical Association Annual Report* (1959): 93–107; John Foster, "The Montreal Riots of 1849," *Canadian Historical Review* 32 (1951): 61–65; J.A. Wright, "The Halifax Riot of 1863," *Nova Scotia Historical Quarterly* 4 (1974): 299–310; George F. Stanley, "The Caraquet Riots of 1875," *Acadiensis* 2 (1972): 21–38; Tina Loo, " 'A Delicate Game': Law and Localism on Grouse Creek," *BC Studies* 96 (1993): 41–65; Scott See, *Riots in New Brunswick: Orange Nativism and Social Violence in the 1840s* (Toronto, 1993); Carol Wilton, "Conservative Political Violence in Upper Canada," *Law and History Review* 13 (1995).

51. Michael S. Cross, "The Laws are Like Cobwebs: Popular Resistance to Authority in Mid-Nineteenth Century British North America," in *Law in a Colonial Society: The Nova Scotia Experience,* ed. Thomas G. Barnes et al. (Toronto, 1984).

52. Ruth Bleasdale, "Class Conflict on the Canals of Upper Canada in the 1840s," *Labour/Le Travailleur* 7 (1981): 9–39.

53. Houston, "The Impetus to Reform." See also the same author's "School Reform and Education" and work by her and H.J. Graff in *CCJH Bibliography;* Michael B. Katz et al., *The Social Organization of Early Industrial Capitalism* (Cambridge, Mass., 1982).

54. Jim Phillips, "Poverty, Unemployment and the Criminal Law: The Administration of the Vagrancy Laws in Halifax, 1864–1890," in *Essays in the History of Canadian Law: Volume Five,* 174–206; James Pitsula, "The Treatment of Tramps in Late Nineteenth-Century Toronto," *Historical Papers* (1981): 116–32. On delinquency, see the work on juvenile institutions referred to in note 34, Susan Houston, "The Waifs and

Strays of a Late Victorian City: Juvenile Delinquents in Toronto,'' in *Childhood and the Family in Canadian History,* ed. Joy Parr (Toronto, 1982); Neil Sutherland, *Children in English-Canadian Society: Framing the Twentieth-Century Consensus* (Toronto, 1976), part 3; and the work of R. Coulter and H. Beaupre in *CCJH Bibliography.* I deal with prostitution in the section on women and the criminal law.

55. Darlene G. Kellough et al., ''The Politics of Incarceration: Manitoba, 1919–1939,'' *Canadian Journal of Sociology* 5 (1980): 253–71.

56. Tremblay and Normandeau, ''L'économie penale,'' 185–88. See also, to the same effect, Tremblay, ''L'évolution de l'emprisonnement.''

57. Fecteau, *Un nouvel ordre des choses,* ''Régulation sociale et répression de la déviance,'' and ''Between the Old Order and Modern Times.''

58. See the fine explication of this argument in Greg Marquis, ''Doing Justice to 'British Justice': Law, Ideology and Canadian Historiography,'' in *Canadian Perspectives on Law and Society: Issues in Legal History,* ed. J. Barry Wright and W. Wesley Pue (Ottawa, 1988). See also Lewthwaite, ''Violence, Law and Community.''

59. Fingard, *The Dark Side of Life,* and ''Jailbirds in mid-Victorian Halifax,'' in *Law in a Colonial Society.*

60. This point is made in a review by Bettina Bradbury in *Canadian Historical Review* 72 (1991): 601–3.

61. See Phillips, ''Vagrants and Vagrancy in Halifax,'' and the work of H.J. Graff, D. Delisle, and H.C. Klassen listed in *CCJH Bibliography.*

62. Peter McGahan, *Crime and Policing in Maritime Canada: Chapters from the Urban Records* (Fredericton, 1988), *Reconstructing Patterns of Crime in Charlottetown, 1875–1900* (Digby, Nova Scotia, 1988), ''Reconstructing Patterns of Crime: Crime and Policing in Late Nineteenth and Early Twentieth Century King's County, Nova Scotia,'' Atlantic Institute of Criminology Occasional Paper Series, No. 1, 1988, ''Crime and Policing in Late Nineteenth Century Halifax,'' ibid., No. 5, 1989, and ''Crime and Policing in Charlottetown,'' ibid., No. 3, 1988. See also Terry L. Chapman, ''Crime and Justice in Medicine Hat, 1883–1905,'' *Alberta History* 38 (1990): 17–24, and ''The Handling of Children in Sex Assault Cases in the Canadian West, 1890–1920,'' in *Dimensions of Childhood: Essays on the History of Children and Youth in Canada,* ed. Russell Smandych et al. (Winnipeg, 1991).

63. Paul Craven, ''Law and Ideology: The Toronto Police Court, 1850–1880,'' in *Essays in the History of Canadian Law: Volume Two,* ed. David Flaherty (Toronto, 1983): 248–307. For the Toronto court, see also Gene Howard Homel, ''Denison's Law: Criminal Justice and the Police Court in Toronto, 1877–1921,'' *Ontario History* 73 (1981): 171–86.

64. A brief general review of the phenomenon is Greg Marquis, ''The Contours of Canadian Urban Justice, 1830–1875,'' *Urban History Review* 15 (1987): 126–33. See also Philip V. Girard, ''The Rise and Fall of Urban Justice in Halifax, 1815–1866,'' *Nova Scotia Historical Review* 8 (1988): 57–71; Katz, *Social Organisation of Early Industrial Capitalism,* 202–41; Thomas Thorner and Neil B. Watson, ''Keeper of the King's Peace: Colonel G.F. Sanders and the Calgary Police Magistrates Court,'' *Urban History Review* 12 (1984): 45–55.

65. The broad contours of police force founding and development are traced in the works by C.E.S. Jayawardene, N. Kelly and W. Kelly, and C.K. Talbot noted in *CCJH Bibliography.* While the last is not always uncritical, none of them provide much more than a general overview. A good succinct summary may be found in the introduction to

Greg Marquis, *Policing Canada's Century: The History of the Canadian Association of Chiefs of Police* (Toronto, 1993).

66. Nicholas Rogers, "Serving Toronto the Good: The Development of the City Police Force, 1834–1884," in *Forging a Consensus: Historical Essays on Toronto,* ed. Victor L. Russell (Toronto, 1984). To similar effect, see Boritch and Hagan, "Crime and the Changing Forms of Class Control," which argues that "class control" remained an important aspect of the work of the Toronto force through the late nineteenth and twentieth centuries.

67. Greg Marquis, " 'A Machine of Oppression Under the Guise of the Law': The Saint John Police Establishment, 1860–1890," *Acadiensis* 16 (1986): 58–77, "Police Unionism in Twentieth Century Toronto," *Ontario History* 81 (1989): 109–28, "Working Men in Uniform: The Early Twentieth Century Toronto Police," *Social History-Histoire Sociale* 20 (1987): 259–77, and "The Police as a Social Service in Early Twentieth Century Toronto," *Social History-Histoire Sociale* 26 (1993).

68. John Weaver, "Social Control, Marital Conformity, and Community Entanglement: The Varied Beat of the Hamilton Police, 1895–1920," and "Introduction: Trends and Questions in New Historical Accounts of Policing," both in *Urban History Review* 19 (1990): 79–83, 113–27; "A Social History of Theft in Depression and Wartime: The Police Occurrence Books for Hamilton, Ontario, 1934–42," *Criminal Justice History* 12 (1991): 161–87, and "Crime, Public Order and Repression." The documentary evidence reproduced in the various studies published by Peter McGahan for a number of Maritime communities also demonstrates the variety of roles performed by the police: See the references in note 62, and also *The Saint John Police Story: The Clark Years, 1890–1915* (with William Higgins) (Fredericton, 1991); "The Police Commission and the Halifax 'Guardians', 1925–1931," Atlantic Institute of Criminology Occasional Paper Series, No. 10, 1989; "Disciplining the 'Guardians': Halifax Police Force, 1905–1913," ibid., No. 6, 1989; and "The Reorganisation of the Halifax Police Force–1893," ibid., No. 7, 1989.

69. Helen Boritch, "Conflict, Compromise and Administrative Convenience: The Police Organisation in Nineteenth-Century Toronto," *Canadian Journal of Law and Society* 3 (1988): 141–74. See also Bill Rawling, "Technology and Innovation in the Toronto Police Force, 1875–1925," *Ontario History* 80 (1988): 53–71.

70. Community-based studies other than those noted are Greg Marquis, "Enforcing the Law: The Charlottetown Police Force," in *Gaslights, Epidemics and Vagabond Cows: Charlottetown in the Victorian Era,* ed. D. Baldwin and T. Spira (Charlottetown, 1988); T. Acheson, *Saint John: The Making of a Colonial Urban Community* (Toronto, 1985); Michael McCulloch, "Most Assuredly Perpetual Motion: Police and Policing in Quebec City 1838–1858," *Urban History Review* 19 (1990): 100–112; F. Lefèbvre and J. Turmel in *CCJH Bibliography.* For a more general review see Greg Marquis, "Power from the Street: The Canadian Municipal Police," in *Police Powers in Canada: The Evolution and Practice of Authority,* ed. David Schneiderman and Roderick C. MacLeod (Toronto, 1994).

71. See the work of S. Donaghey, M. Gilkes and M. Symons, and R. Hutchinson listed in *CCJH Bibliography.*

72. Alan Greer, "The Birth of the Police in Canada," in *Colonial Leviathan: State Formation in Mid-Nineteenth Century Canada,* ed. Greer and Ian Radforth (Toronto, 1992). See also two still useful earlier pieces by E.K. Senior noted in *CCJH Bibliography.*

73. For the broader purposes of *gendarmeries* in nineteenth-century Europe, see

Clive Emsley, "Peasants, Gendarmes and State Formation," in *National Histories and European History,* ed. Mary Fullbrook (London, 1993), 69–93. The relationship between policing and politics is also noted in a study which perhaps does not belong here, but which is nonetheless fascinating reading: J. Keshen, "Cloak and Dagger: Canada West's Secret Police, 1864–1867," *Ontario History* 79 (1987): 353–81.

74. Keith Walden, *Visions of Order: The Canadian Mounties in Symbol and Myth* (Toronto, 1982). See also the articles by Walden, D. Harrison, and H.C. Klassen in *CCJH Bibliography.*

75. Stanley W. Horrall, "Sir John A. Macdonald and the Mounted Police Force for the Northwest Territories," *Canadian Historical Review* 53 (1972): 179–200, and Roderick C. MacLeod, "Canadianising the West: The NWMP as Agents of the National Policy, 1873–1905," in *Essays in Western History,* ed. Lewis H. Thomas (Edmonton, 1976). See also the fullest and still the standard account of the early years of the force, R.C. MacLeod, *The North West Mounted Police and Law Enforcement, 1873–1905* (Toronto, 1976).

76. Thomas Stone, "The Mounties as Vigilantes: Perceptions of Community and the Transformation of Law in the Yukon, 1885–1897," *Law and Society Review* 14 (1979): 83–114, provides an excellent account of this.

77. See MacLeod's comment in *The NWMP and Law Enforcement,* 36, that the force "occupied a position of power rarely, if ever, equalled by a police force in a free society" before 1885. Another author has noted that "[i]n essence the Canadian government . . . established a legal tyranny": John Jennings, "The Plains Indians and the Law," in *Men in Scarlet,* 58.

78. Stanley W. Horrall, "The March West," and Ian Getty, "The Role of Mounted Police Outposts in Southern Alberta," both in *Men in Scarlet.* Edwin Morgan, "The North West Mounted Police: Internal Problems and Public Criticisms, 1874–1883," *Saskatchewan History* 26 (1973): 41–62.

79. A process well described in MacLeod, *The NWMP and Law Enforcement,* chap. 3. See also J.R. Miller, *Skyscrapers Hide the Heavens: A History of Indian-White Relations in Canada* (Toronto, 1989), chap. 9.

80. Desmond Morton, "Cavalry or Police: Keeping the Peace on Two Adjacent Frontiers, 1870–1900," *Journal of Canadian Studies* 12 (1977): 27–37. For a similar argument, but one which stresses more the longevity of the process and the active participation and insistence on terms of the native people, see J.L. Tobias, "Canada's Subjugation of the Plains Cree," in *Sweet Promises: A Reader in Indian-White Relations in Canada,* ed. J.R. Miller (Toronto, 1991). For the same issues on the Pacific slope, see Robin Fisher, "Indian Warfare and Two Frontiers: A Comparison of British Columbia and Washington Territory During the Early Years of Settlement," *Pacific Historical Review* 50 (1981): 31–51. For a review of the "law and order" debate see R.C. MacLeod, "Law and Order on the Western Canadian Frontier," in *Law for the Elephant, Law for the Beaver: Essays in the Legal History of the North American West,* ed. Hamar Foster and John P.S. MacLaren (Regina and Pasadena, 1992), 90–105.

81. The administrative role of the force is described in detail in the work of C. Betke, D.H. Breen, W. Beahen, and D.M. McLeod in *CCJH Bibliography.* See also MacLeod, "Canadianising the West" and Getty, "The Role of Mounted Police Outposts."

82. Walter N. Sage, "The North West Mounted Police and British Columbia," *Pacific Historical Review* 18 (1949): 352. Although the force's writ did not generally run

in British Columbia, the province gave the federal government jurisdiction over a twenty-mile-wide "railway belt" through it.

83. Stanley W. Horrall, "The Royal North West Mounted Police and Labour Unrest in Western Canada, 1919," *Canadian Historical Review* 61 (1980): 169–90; A. Lorne and C. Brown, *An Unauthorised History of the RCMP* (Toronto, 1973), chap. 3; William M. Baker, "The Miners and the Mounties: The Royal North West Mounted Police and the 1906 Lethbridge Strike," *Labour/Le Travail* 27 (1991): 55–96.

84. See notes 79 and 80 and Brown and Brown, *Unauthorised History,* chap. 1; F. Laurie Barron, "The Indian Pass System in the Canadian West, 1882–1935," *Prairie Forum* 13 (1988): 25–42; S.W. Horrall and J. Jennings in *CCJH Bibliography.*

85. For this, see J.L. Tobias, "Protection, Civilization, Assimilation: An Outline History of Canada's Indian Policy," in *The Prairie West: Historical Readings,* ed. R.D. Francis and Howard Palmer (Edmonton, 1985).

86. Barron, "Indian Pass System."

87. Hamar Foster, "Long Distance Justice: The Criminal Jurisdiction of Canadian Courts West of the Canada, 1763–1859," *American Journal of Legal History* 34 (1990): 1–48; "Sins Against the Great Spirit: The Law, the Hudson's Bay Company, and the Mackenzie River Murders, 1835–1839," *Criminal Justice History* 10 (1989): 23–76; "Mutiny on the Beaver: Law and Authority in the Fur Trade Navy, 1835–1840," *Manitoba Law Journal* 20 (1991): 15–45; "Law Enforcement in Nineteenth Century British Columbia: A Brief and Comparative Overview," *BC Studies* 63 (1984): 3–28; "The Kamloops Outlaws and Commissions of Assize in Nineteenth Century British Columbia," in *Essays in the History of Canadian Law: Volume Two:* 308–64; and "The White Man's Law in the Far West: Establishing Legal Institutions in British Columbia," CLHP, Working Paper No. 92-12.

88. See especially Loo, "Law and Localism on Grouse Creek"; Thomas Stone, "The Mounties as Vigilantes," and *Miners' Justice: Migration, Law and Order on the Alaska-Yukon Frontier, 1873–1902* (New York, 1988); Barry C. Gough, "Keeping British Columbia British: The Law-and-Order Question on a Gold Mining Frontier," *Huntington Library Quarterly* 38 (1974–1975): 269–80.

89. William R. Morrison, *Showing the Flag: The Mounted Police and Canadian Sovereignty in the North, 1894–1925* (Vancouver, 1985), and "The North West Mounted Police and the Klondike Gold Rush," *Journal of Contemporary History* 9 (1974): 93–105; Stone, *Miners' Justice,* especially chap. 4.

90. The best work in this area has been done by scholars interested in labor and political radicalism: see particularly Gregory S. Kealey, "The RCMP, the Special Branch, and the Early Days of the Communist Party of Canada: A Documentary Survey," *Labour/Le Travail* 30 (1992): 169–204, and "The Surveillance State: The Origins of Domestic Intelligence and Counter-Subversion in Canada, 1914–1920," *Intelligence and National Security* 7 (1992): 179–210. See also the series of published *RCMP Security Bulletins,* edited by Kealey and Reg Whitaker. For other work on the RCMP as a security service, see Brown and Brown, *Unauthorised History,* chaps. 5–8, and the work of P. Campbell and J. Sawatsky listed in *CCJH Bibliography.*

91. Greg Marquis, *Policing Canada's Century.* A chronology of the development of provincial and municipal forces is provided by the works cited in note 65, and municipal forces are reviewed in Philip Stenning, "The Role of Police Boards and Commissions as Institutions of Municipal Police Governance," in *Organisational Police Deviance: Its Structure and Control,* ed. Clifford Shearing (Toronto, 1981). For provincial forces see

R.C. MacLeod, "The RCMP and the Evolution of Provincial Policing," in *Police Powers in Canada.* For other studies, many of the municipal ones being "in-house" histories, see *CCJH Bibliography,* chap. 1. See also, for provincial forces, Greg Marquis, "Policing in the Maritimes," *Urban History Review* 19 (1990): 84–99; Lynne Stonier-Newman, *Policing a Pioneer Province: The B.C. Provincial Police 1858–1950* (Madeira Park, 1989); John Phyne, "Prohibition's Legacy: The Emergence of Provincial Policing in Nova Scotia, 1921–1932," *Canadian Journal of Law and Society* (1993): 157–84.

92. Lachance, "Women and Crime," 109.

93. Jim Phillips, "Women, Crime and Criminal Justice in Early Halifax, 1750–1800," in *Essays in the History of Canadian Law: Volume Five,* 174–206; and idem, "Women and Crime in Halifax, 1750–1800," *Criminal Justice History* 16 (1995).

94. Boritch and Hagan, "A Century of Crime in Toronto," 594. See also B. Jane Price, "Female Petty Crime in Halifax, 1864–1890," in *Essays in the History of Canadian Law: Volume Three,* 200–231; M. Elizabeth Langdon, "Female Crime in Calgary, 1914–1941," in *Law and Justice in a New Land.*

95. John Fox and Timothy F. Hartnagel, "Changing Social Roles and Female Crime in Canada," *Canadian Review of Sociology and Anthropology* 16 (1979): 96–104. Lee, "Are Crime Rates Increasing," also charts the increase in female crime since 1949.

96. Constance Backhouse, "Desperate Women and Compassionate Courts: Infanticide in Nineteenth Century Canada," *University of Toronto Law Journal* 34 (1984): 447–78 (quotations at 475 and 478), and *Petticoats and Prejudice: Women and Law in Nineteenth Century Canada* (Toronto, 1992), chap. 4; Mary Ellen Wright, "Unnatural Mothers: Infanticide in Halifax, 1830–1875," *Nova Scotia Historical Review* 7 (1987): 13–29. Different legal structures do not appear to have made the Quebec experience much different: see Marie-Aimée Cliche, "Infanticide dans la région de Québec (1660–1969)," *Revue d'histoire de l'Amérique Française* 44 (1990): 31–59.

97. W. Peter Ward, "Unwed Motherhood in Nineteenth-Century English Canada," *Historical Papers* (1981): 34–56. Quebec, however, appears to have been different in this regard: see Andrée Levesque, "Deviant Anonymous: Single Mothers at the Hopital de la Misericorde in Montreal, 1929–1939," *Historical Papers* (1984): 168–83.

98. See the articles by C. Backhouse and Angus McLaren in *CCJH Bibliography,* and Angus McLaren and Arlene Tigar McLaren, *The Bedroom and the State: The Changing Practices and Policies of Contraception and Abortion in Canada, 1880–1910* (Toronto, 1986).

99. For a detailed treatment of one such prosecution for carrying out abortions, see Backhouse, *Petticoats and Prejudice,* chap. 5, and "Prosecution of Abortions under Canadian Law, 1900–1950," in *Crime and Justice in Canadian History.* The McLarens also present their statistical evidence in "Discoveries and Dissimulations: The Impact of Abortion Deaths on Maternal Mortality in British Columbia," *BC Studies* 64 (1984): 3–26. For a debate on the validity of those statistics, see George Emery, "British Columbia's Criminal Abortion History, 1922–1949: A Critique of the Evidence and Methods in the Work of Angus and Arlene McLaren," and Angus and Arlene Tigar McLaren, "The Forest and the Trees: A Response to George Emery," both in *BC Studies* 82 (1989): 39–64.

100. See particularly John P. McLaren, "White Slavers: The Reform of Canada's Prostitution Laws and Patterns of Enforcement, 1900–1920," *Criminal Justice History* 8 (1987): 53–119 (quotation at 109), "The Canadian Judiciary and the Anti-White Slavery Campaign, 1900–1920," in *Canadian Perspectives on Law and Society;* "Chasing

the Social Evil: Moral Fervour and the Evolution of Canada's Prostitution Laws, 1867–1917,'' *Canadian Journal of Law and Society* 1 (1986): 125–65, and ''Recalculating the Wages of Sin: The Social and Legal Construction of Prostitution in Canada 1850–1920,'' CLHP, Working Paper No. 92-4; Constance Backhouse, ''Nineteenth Century Canadian Prostitution Law: Reflection of a Discriminatory Society,'' *Social History-Histoire Sociale* 18 (1985): 387–423. See also John P. McLaren and Janet Lowman, ''Enforcing Canada's Prostitution Laws, 1892–1920: Rhetoric and Practice,'' in *Securing Compliance,* ed. Martin L. Friedland (Toronto, 1990); Graham Parker, ''The Legal Regulation of Sexual Activity and the Protection of Females,'' *Osgoode Hall Law Journal* 21 (1983): 187–244; Fay Farraday, ''The Debate about Prostitution: A History of the Formation and Failure of Canadian Laws Against the Sex Trade, 1867–1917'' (unpublished M.A. thesis, University of Toronto, 1991); Janice Newton, ''From Wage Slave to White Slave: The Prostitution Controversy and the Early Canadian Left,'' in *Beyond the Vote: Canadian Women and Politics,* ed. Linda Kealey and Joan Sangster (Toronto, 1989).

101. See especially Backhouse, ''Nineteenth Century Canadian Prostitution Law,'' and the same author's *Petticoats and Prejudice,* chap. 8. Useful local studies include Fingard, *Dark Side of Life,* especially chap. 4; Deborah Nilsen, '' 'The Social Evil': Prostitution in Vancouver, 1900–1920,'' in *In Her Own Right: Selected Essays in Women's History in British Columbia,* ed. B. Latham and C. Less (Victoria, 1980); Andrée Levesque, ''Eteindre le red light: reformateurs et la prostitution à Montréal 1865–1925,'' *Urban History Review* 17 (1989): 191–201; and the work of L. Rotenberg, J. Bedford, and L.W. Brooking in *CCJH Bibliography.*

102. Carolyn Strange, ''From Modern Babylon to a City Upon a Hill: The Toronto Social Survey Commission of 1915 and the Search for Sexual Order in the City,'' in *Patterns of the Past;* Marianna Valverde, *The Age of Light, Soap and Water: Moral Reform in English Canada, 1885–1925* (Toronto, 1991), especially chaps. 4–6; Backhouse, *Petticoats and Prejudice,* chap. 8; Newton, ''From Wage Slave to White Slave.''

103. Constance Backhouse, ''Nineteenth Century Canadian Rape Law,'' in *Essays in the History of Canadian Law: Volume Two,* 200–247, ''The Sayer Street Outrage: Gang Rape and Male Law in Nineteenth Century Toronto,'' *Manitoba Law Journal* 20 (1991): 46–48, and *Petticoats and Prejudice,* chap. 3. See also an earlier brief survey: Ruth A. Olson, ''Rape—An 'Un-Victorian' Aspect of Life in Upper Canada,'' *Ontario History* 66 (1976): 75–79.

104. Carolyn Strange, ''Patriarchy Modified: The Criminal Prosecution of Rape in Toronto, 1880–1930,'' in *Crime and Criminal Justice in Canadian History.*

105. Karen Dubinsky, '' 'Maidenly Girls' or 'Designing Women'? The Crime of Seduction in Turn-of-the-Century Ontario,'' in *Gender Conflicts: New Essays in Women's History,* ed. Franca Iacovetta and Marianna Valverde (Toronto, 1992). See also Backhouse, ''Nineteenth Century Canadian Rape Law,'' and *Petticoats and Prejudice,* chap. 2; McLaren, ''Chasing the Social Evil.''

106. See Kim Smith-Maynard, ''Divorce in Nova Scotia, 1750–1890,'' in *Nova Scotia Essays;* Constance Backhouse, ''Pure Patriarchy: Nineteenth Century Canadian Marriage,'' *McGill Law Journal* 31 (1986): 265–312, and *Petticoats and Prejudice,* chaps. 6 and 7.

107. Terry Chapman, '' 'Til Death Do Us Part': Wife Beating in Alberta, 1905–1920,'' *Alberta History* 36 (1988): 13–22; Fingard, *Dark Side of Life,* esp. chap. 8; Kathryn Harvey, ''To Love, Honour and Obey: Wife-Battering in Working Class Montreal, 1869–1879,'' *Urban History Review* 19 (1990): 128–40; ''Amazons and Victims:

Resisting Wife Abuse in Working-Class Montreal, 1869–1879,'' *Journal of the Canadian Historical Association* 2 (1991): 131–48; and André Lachance, ''Family Conflict and the Law in New France,'' in *Crime and Criminal Justice in Canadian History.*

108. Phillips, ''Women, Crime and Criminal Justice.''

109. Gartner and McCarthy, ''Social Distribution of Femicide.''

110. See Lachance, ''Women and Crime''; Helen Boritch, ''Gender and Criminal Court Outcomes: An Historical Analysis,'' *Criminology* 30 (1992): 293–325; Weaver, ''Crime, Public Order and Repression''; Phillips, ''Women, Crime and Criminal Justice.''

111. Karen Dubinsky and Franca Iacovetta, ''Murder, Womanly Virtue, and Motherhood: The Case of Angelina Napolitano, 1911–1922,'' *Canadian Historical Review* 72 (1991): 505–31. See also the exploration of the concepts of chivalry and female sexuality in Carolyn Strange, ''Wounded Womanhood and Dead Men: Chivalry and the Trials of Clara Ford and Carrie Davis,'' in *Gender Conflicts,* and of race and gender in the same author's ''Patriarchy Modified.'' See also, in a rather different context, Joan Sangster, ''Pardon Tales from a Magistrate's Court: Women, Crime and the Court in Peterborough County Court, 1920–1950,'' *Canadian Historical Review* 74 (1993): 161–97.

112. Newfoundland has been almost completely neglected, and for that province the reader should consult Christopher English, ''The Development of the Newfoundland Legal System to 1815,'' *Acadiensis* 20 (1990): 89–119.

113. The reader should consult the works by J.K. Elliott, J.E. Jones, W.R. Riddell, E. Shortt, and C.K. Talbot listed in *CCJH Bibliography.* More useful trial accounts include Paul Romney, ''The Ordeal of William Higgins,'' *Ontario History* 67 (1975): 69–89; Josephine Phelan, ''The Tar and Feather Case: Gore Assizes, August 1827,'' *Ontario History* 68 (1976): 17–24; Johnson, ''Gore District Outrages''; H. Strum, ''A Most Cruel Murder: The Isaac Underhill Affair, 1809,'' *Ontario History* 80 (1988): 293–310.

114. John D. Blackwell, ''Crime in the London District, 1828–1837: A Case Study of the Effect of the 1833 Reform in Upper Canadian Penal Law,'' *Queen's Law Journal* 6 (1981): 528–67. On the reform movement see also Beattie, *Attitudes Towards Crime and Punishment.*

115. Paul Romney, *Mr. Attorney: The Attorney-General for Ontario in Court, Cabinet and Legislature, 1791–1899* (Toronto, 1986); ''The Administration of Justice in Ontario, 1784–1900,'' CLHP Working Paper No. 91-1; *Provincial Justice: Upper Canadian Legal Portraits* (Toronto, 1992), ed. Robert L. Fraser, especially the introductory essay and the third section of portraits of ''The Accused''; ''Like Eden in Her Summer Dress: Gentry, Economy and Society in Upper Canada, 1812–1840'' (unpublished Ph.D. diss., University of Toronto, 1979); McMahon, ''Sir John Beverley Robinson''; Patrick Brode, *Sir John Beverley Robinson: Bone and Sinew of the Compact* (Toronto, 1984); Brendan O'Brien, *Speedy Justice: The Tragic Last Voyage of His Majesty's Vessel Speedy* (Toronto, 1993).

116. Louis A. Knafla and Terry Chapman, ''Criminal Justice in Canada: A Comparative Study of the Maritimes and Lower Canada, 1760–1812,'' *Osgoode Hall Law Journal* 21 (1983): 245–74; Thomas Vincent, ''Jonathan Belcher: Charge to the Grand Jury, Michaelmas Term, 1754,'' *Acadiensis* 7 (1977): 103–9; Lorna Hutchinson, ''Buggery Trials in Saint John, 1806: The Case of John Smith,'' *University of New Brunswick Law Journal* 40 (1991): 130–48. Less useful is the work of J. Chisholm, R.E. Kroll, J.W. Lawrence, and J.F. Smith listed in *CCJH Bibliography.*

117. Jim Phillips, ''The Administration of the Royal Pardon in Nova Scotia, 1749–

1815,'' *University of Toronto Law Journal* 42 (1992): 1–49. See also idem, ''Women, Crime and Criminal Justice''; ''Securing Obedience to Necessary Laws: The Criminal Law in Eighteenth Century Nova Scotia,'' *Nova Scotia Historical Review* 12 (1992): 87–124; and ''The Reform of Nova Scotia Criminal Law, 1832–1841,'' paper delivered to the Canadian Law in History conference, Carleton University, 1987, and ''The Criminal Trial in Eighteenth-Century Nova Scotia,'' paper delivered to the Atlantic Legal History Conference, Dalhousie University, 1995.

118. Peter McGahan, *Crime and Policing in Maritime Canada;* ''Crime and Policing in King's County, Nova Scotia, 1920s and 1930s,'' Atlantic Institute of Criminology Occasional Paper Series, No. 2, 1988; and ''Crime and Policing in King's County, Nova Scotia, 1940s–1960s,'' ibid., No. 3, 1988.

119. There are a number of accounts of the evolution of drug laws, the best of which include those of N. Boyd, M. Green, R. Solomon and M. Green, and S. J. Cook in *CCJH Bibliography.* An excellent recent account of enforcement is Clayton Mosher, ''The Legal Response to Narcotic Drugs in Five Ontario Cities, 1908–1961'' (unpublished Ph.D. diss., University of Toronto, 1992), which also provides a legislative history. See also P.J. Giffen et al., *Panic and Indifference: The Politics of Canada's Drug Laws* (Ottawa, 1991); G.F. Murray, ''Cocaine Use in the Era of Social Reform: The Natural History of a Social Problem in Canada, 1880–1911,'' *Canadian Journal of Law and Society* 2 (1987): 29–44; and the work of T.L. Chapman and C.L. Krasnick noted in *CCJH Bibliography.*

120. André Morel briefly outlines nineteenth-century French Canadians' attitudes toward capital punishment and the movement for its reform in ''Les crimes et les peines,'' 384–96. See also Phillips, ''The Reform of Nova Scotia's Criminal Law,'' and Romney, *Mr. Attorney,* 202–8.

121. Desmond H. Brown, *The Genesis of the Canadian Criminal Code of 1892* (Toronto, 1989). Graham Parker, ''The Origins of the Criminal Code,' in *Essays in the History of Canadian Law: Volume One:* 249–80, considers the meaning of codification at an elite rather theoretical level. On codification itself and its place in different legal cultures, see the excellent Nicholas Kasirer, ''Canada's Criminal Law Codification Viewed and Reviewed,'' *McGill Law Journal* 35 (1990): 841–79. For the turn to British sources in legal thought generally, see G. Blaine Baker, ''The Reconstitution of Upper Canadian Legal Thought in the Late-Victorian Empire,'' *Law and History Review* 3 (1985): 219–92.

122. Susan Binnie, ''Explorations in the Use of Criminal Law in Canada, 1867–1892'' (unpublished Ph.D. diss., Carleton University, 1991). The earlier period is briefly reviewed in Brown, *The Genesis of the Criminal Code,* chaps. 4, 5.

123. One general account for the postcodification period exists, but it tells us little and is more concerned with the reception of the 1892 Code: R.C. MacLeod, ''The Shaping of Canadian Criminal Law, 1892–1902,'' *Historical Papers* (1978): 64–75.

124. See the work of D. Gagnon and J. Leon noted in *CCJH Bibliography;* Jean-Marie Trepanier, ''The Origins of the Juvenile Delinquents Act of 1908: Controlling Delinquency through Seeking Its Causes and through Youth Protection,'' in *Dimensions of Childhood;* Dorothy Chunn, *From Punishment to Doing Good: Family Courts and Socialized Justice in Ontario, 1880–1940* (Toronto, 1992); Sutherland, *Children in English-Canadian Society.*

125. A. Gigeroff, ''The Evolution of Canadian Legislation Relating to Homosexuality, Pedophilia and Exhibitionism,'' *Criminal Law Quarterly* 8 (1966): 445–54; Hutchinson,

"Buggery Trials in Saint John"; Terry L. Chapman, "Male Homosexuality: Legal Restraints and Social Attitudes in Western Canada, 1890–1920," in *Law and Justice in a New Land,* and "An Oscar Wilde Type: The Abominable Crime of Buggery in Western Canada, 1890–1920," *Criminal Justice History* 4 (1983): 97–118. See also, in other areas of the law, Cyril Greenland, "Dangerous Sexual Offender Legislation in Canada, 1948–1977," *Canadian Journal of Criminology* 26 (1984): 1–12, and Martin L. Friedland, *A Century of Criminal Justice: Perspectives on the Development of Canadian Law* (Toronto, 1984), chap. 4, on gun control.

126. Claude Desaulniers, "La peine de mort dans le législation criminelle de 1760 à 1892," *Revue générale de droit* 8 (1977): 141–84; Carolyn Strange, "The Politics of Punishment: The Death Penalty in Canada, 1867–1976," *Manitoba Law Journal* 24 (1995). A useful short history of the abolition movement is provided in David Chandler, *Capital Punishment in Canada: A Sociological Study of Repressive Law* (Toronto, 1976).

127. K.L. Avio, "Capital Punishment in Canada: A Time Series Analysis of the Deterrent Hypothesis," *Canadian Journal of Economics* 12 (1979): 647–76, "Capital Punishment in Canada: Statistical Evidence and Constitutional Issues," *Canadian Journal of Criminology* 30 (1988): 331–49, and "The Quality of Mercy: Exercise of the Royal Prerogative in Canada," *Canadian Public Policy* 13 (1987): 366–79.

128. On the pardon, see Phillips, "Royal Pardon"; Dubinsky and Iacovetta, "Murder, Womanly Virtue and Motherhood"; Backhouse, *Petticoats and Prejudice,* chap. 4; Marvin K. Evans, "The Prerogative of Pardon in Canada: Its Development 1864–1894" (unpublished M.A. thesis, Carleton University, 1971). For particular cases, see Cyril Greenland, "The Last Public Execution in Canada," *Criminal Law Quarterly* 29 (1987): 415–20; Jim Hornby, "Capital Punishment in Prince Edward Island," unpublished paper, 1989; Tremblay and Normandeau, "L'économie penale," 183–85; Frank W. Anderson, *Hanging in Canada* (Calgary, 1973). It is hoped that the lack of work on the use of the death penalty before World War I will be remedied now that the comprehensive run of post-Confederation capital case files is open to researchers.

129. Strange, "The Politics of Punishment." Dr. Strange is currently engaged in a comprehensive study of capital punishment in Ontario between 1890 and 1930.

130. See S.N. Verdun-Jones in *CCJH Bibliography.*

131. Martin L. Friedland, *The Case of Valentine Shortis: A True Story of Crime and Politics in Canada* (Toronto, 1985), and idem, *A Century of Criminal Justice,* chap. 8.

132. Romney, *Mr. Attorney;* Philip Stenning, *Appearing for the Crown: A Legal and Historical Review of Criminal Prosecutorial Authority in Canada* (Cowansville, Quebec, 1986); J.H. Aitchison, "The Development of Local Government in Upper Canada, 1783–1850" (unpublished Ph.D. diss., University of Toronto, 1953); Susan Lewthwaite, "Keepers of the Peace: The Magistrates of Georgina Township, 1830–1850" (unpublished M.A. thesis, University of Toronto, 1987). Ms. Lewthwaite is completing a doctoral thesis on JPs, which will be a valuable addition to our knowledge of the prosecutorial process.

133. See Romney, *Mr. Attorney,* passim, and "From Constitutionalism to Legalism: Trial by Jury, Responsible Government, and the Rule of Law in Canadian Political Culture," *Law and History Review* 7 (1989): 121–74.

134. Patrick Brode, *The Odyssey of John Anderson* (Toronto, 1989), is a short but fascinating account involving an escaped American slave. See also Dale and Lee Gibson, "Railroading the Train Robbers: Extradition in the Shadow of the Law," *Manitoba Law Journal* 20 (1991): 69–90.

135. Sidney L. Harring, "The Rich Men of the Country: Canadian Law in the Land

of the Copper Inuit, 1914–1930,'' *Ottawa Law Review* 21 (1989): 1–64. See also Cornelia Schuh, ''Justice on the Northern Frontier: Early Murder Trials of Native Accused,'' *Criminal Law Quarterly* 22 (1979–1980): 74–111; Graham Price, ''The King v. Alikomiak,'' *Manitoba Law Journal* 20 (1991): 204–26. For the earlier period see Foster, ''Sins Against the Great Spirit.''

136. John Dickinson, ''Native Sovereignty and French Justice in Early Canada,'' Tina Loo, ''The Road from Bute Inlet: Crime and Colonial Identity in British Columbia,'' and Hamar Foster, ''The Queen's Law is Better Than Yours: International Homicide in Early British Columbia,'' all in *Essays in the History of Canadian Law: Volume Five:* 41–111. See also Hamar Foster, ''Killing Mr. John: Law and Jurisdiction at Fort Stikine, 1842–1846,'' in *Law for the Elephant, Law for the Beaver,* and idem, ''Long Distance Justice,'' and Barry M. Gough, ''Send a Gunboat: Checking Slavery and Controlling Liquor Traffic among Coast Indians of British Columbia in the 1860s,'' *Pacific Northwest Quarterly* 69 (1978): 159–68.

137. Tina Loo, ''Dan Cranmer's Potlatch: Law as Coercion, Symbol and Rhetoric in British Columbia, 1884–1951,'' *Canadian Historical Review* 73 (1992): 125–65. See also Douglas Cole and Ira Chaikin, *An Iron Hand Upon the People: The Law Against the Potlatch on the Northwest Coast* (Vancouver, 1990).

138. See Michael Coyle, ''Traditional Indian Justice in Ontario: A Role for the Present,'' *Osgoode Hall Law Journal* 24 (1986): 605–33; ''Aboriginal Concepts of Justice,'' in *Report of the Manitoba Aboriginal Justice Inquiry* (1989), chap. 2. A recent popular but useful account is Rupert Ross, *Dancing with a Ghost: Exploring Indian Reality* (Toronto, 1992). An older study is W.B. Newell, *Crime and Justice Among the Iroquois Nations* (Montreal, 1965).

139. See my own comment, with which this chapter began, and a recent review of the writing of legal history in the Maritime provinces, which suggested that while legal history remains ''one of the most neglected branches of social history in Canada,'' the history of criminal justice ''receives even less attention'': Marquis, ''Law, Society and History,'' 162.

140. D. Owen Carrigan, *Crime and Punishment in Canada: A History* (Toronto, 1991). I do not wish to suggest that the gaps in the secondary literature are more than marginally responsible for the numerous inadequacies of this volume.

9

The Urban Police in the United States

Eric H. Monkkonen

Historians working in the field of American crime and justice have produced a massive body of scholarship; a recent, selected collection of articles alone consumed over 7,000 pages in sixteen bound volumes.[1] A significant portion of this work deals with the police as opposed to a more holistic view of the criminal justice system, or, alternatively, of the whole city government. The police have attracted the historian's attention for many reasons, ranging from simple curiosity to questions about urbanization, crime control, and the history of society. Although no single concept or paradigm has guided this research, the result has been a rich and valuable set of empirical studies.

A decade ago, Roger Lane published in *Crime and Justice,* a synthetic article on urban policing that newer work expands on in several different directions.[2] This chapter follows the directions of the new research, emphasizing areas in which substantive gains have been made. The intention here is to examine the areas in which there is new knowledge rather than to write a completely new history of policing. That task grows ever more complex, especially for the years after World War I. Historians have, for the most part, concentrated on the earlier years for several reasons. First, the history of the nineteenth-century United States has captured intense research excitement in many fields, and the police have given historians an avenue of investigation with a unique perspective. Second, in most periodizations of U.S. history, the Progressive era, closed by World War I, culminates in many of the principles and issues which undergird the major intellectual, social, and political developments of the remainder of the twentieth century. Finally, modern social science has much better documented the post–World War II era, so the challenge of historical recovery and analysis has not been as great for more recent historical events.

The new studies have deepened our understanding of the origins of the police, their functional roles, their relationship to criminal behavior and public order, police organizations as employers and as well as controllers of labor, the police professionalization movement, the complex and unique situating of police in the larger political order, and the growth and change of nonurban police—private and federal, in particular. In addition, we now have a fuller picture of police as they became regular components of the urban service sector and essential participants in the criminal justice system.

The first two sections of this chapter summarize my book on the police, supplementing its research and analysis with other new and relevant work.[3] The first section stresses the social and political innovation represented in policing, while the second section emphasizes that the fundamental aspect of U.S. policing as components of local government has made police a part of urban services. In the third section, the chapter turns to new research publications focusing on police as employers and police relations with organized labor. The fourth section turns to those issues in police reform which have attracted historical research, while the fifth section focuses on policy issues in the context of a federal political system. The final section delineates future research needs and directions.

POLICE AS AN INNOVATION

Police are relative newcomers to the Anglo-American criminal justice system. The Constitution does not mention them. Early city charters do not mention them either, for the simple reason that as we know them, police had not been invented. Instead, cities had loosely organized night watches and constables who worked for the courts, supplemented by the private prosecution of offenders through lower level courts.[4] The night watch and day constable, dating from the Middle Ages, were familiar comic figures in Shakespeare's plays and were not replaced until the 1820s, when London police were reorganized by Robert Peel. The police precedent for the United States, as is well known, came from the Metropolitan Police of London (1829). Peel used his military experience in Ireland to create a social control organization midway between a military and a civil force.[5] The new police solved both tactical and political problems: They were cheaper than a military force; they created less resentment; and they were more responsive to civil authorities.[6]

Constables were responsible to civil and criminal courts. They supported themselves by fees, which came from serving warrants and civil papers to arresting offenders. The victim of an offense had to seek a constable, paying for his or her actions. Ferdinand's study of Boston showed that a few constables often took the initiative in making drunk arrests, apparently to make a continuous income.[7] The fees for catching an offender or for restitution could often be higher than the value of a stolen object, but Steinberg's new work suggests that these fees were no deterrent to many poor people using the criminal justice system. His work also shows that the constables could be sidestepped, with victims going directly to local aldermanic courts.

Night watch did just that: Raise the hue and cry in case of an offense or sound an alarm for a fire. The usual criticism of them was that they slept, used their noisy rattles to warn off potential offenders, and ran from real danger. The *New York Gazette* asserted that the watch were a " 'Parcel of idle, drunken, vigilant Snorers, who never quelled any nocturnal Tumult in their lives; but would, perhaps, be as ready to join in a Burglary as any Thief in Christendom.' "[8] These criticisms are difficult to evaluate, but they do suggest that the night watch, who were either citizens doing required volunteer service or, more likely, their paid substitutes, were not in any way a serious crime-fighting organization.

There are four important innovative features of the new police as created in the United States. First, the new police had a hierarchial organization, with a command and communications structure resembling the military. This gave them an ordered and centralized hierarchy with an immediate communication superiority to all other urban organizations as well as the preceding constable watch system. Even without an electronic communications system (call boxes or police telegraphs first, then the telephone, which came a little later in the nineteenth century), the simple chain of command meant that a citizen could report an offense to an officer, who would in turn relay the information to headquarters, which could then distribute the information back down the line. While no doubt the system operated with less than perfect precision, in the traditional constable watch system, this was even less likely to happen. Haller's work on Chicago shows that after 1930, centralization increased further, especially as with the introduction of radio cars, and the local station house decreased in importance.[9] Since under the prepolice constable watch system the constables had gained their incomes from fees, the structural incentive encouraged them to follow up promising (that is, high fee generating) leads themselves.

Second, increasing functional differentiation in revised city governments located the police under the executive rather than judicial branch—previous constables and watch had been part of the lower courts. As a part of the mayor's executive office, the police were no longer general factotums for courts, which freed them from civil court activities. This shift had to accompany the abandonment of fees for service, for civil fees had been a part of the constabulary incomes.[10] This shift also sent the American police down a different developmental path from the English police, who remain much more active and involved in preparing and prosecuting criminal cases than do their American counterparts. It also ensured a structural antagonism between the courts, prosecuting attorneys, and the police as the divide in responsibilities took on greater ideological content in the twentieth century. This antagonism, usually characterized as an aspect of adversarial justice, was not at all intended and sets the United States off from other nations.

Third, the uniforms made the police visible and hence accessible to all—whether neighbors or strangers—and this essentially made them the first and for a long time only officials easily seen by the public. Uniforming, an integral part of the new organizational model, generated consternation and some amusing anecdotes for police historians. At first the uniforms were mocked by commentators and shunned by police officers. Called "popinjays" in Boston; ridiculed as "expensive and fantastical" in New York; derided as "livery" in Chicago; and refused by an officer in Philadelphia as "derogatory to my feelings as an American," uniforms were a difficult part of the transformation.[11] Americans valued greatly their freedom to wear what they pleased. Previously, only soldiers and servants of the wealthy had been seen on the streets in such outfits. But the uniforms instantly increased citizen access to patrol officers, now visible for the first time. This visibility, for instance, combined with a centralized communication system, accounted for the sudden turn to the police by parents of lost children: Prior to the police, they had had to conduct frantic, random community searches.[12] In addition, uniformed officers were easier for their superiors to find and control.

Fourth, the police were conceived to be active: This entailed patrol (expected to discover and prevent), regular salaries and lines in the city budget, and free prosecution of criminal offenders. Conceptualized as bringing regular and more effective crime prevention to the city, this new activity contrasted with the constables' specifically responsive, fee-based work. City officials hoped that regular patrol would prevent crime by scaring would-be offenders. If successful, of course, then fees for catching offenders would no longer be a fair way of paying for police services. So the new police had to have regular salaries and be part of the city budget. An unexpected consequence of this was free prosecution of offenders: No longer did a victim have to calculate the value of a stolen pair of boots before calling a constable. Steinberg's research in the Philadelphia aldermanic court records suggests that people may have been willing to pay a fee to prosecute neighbors: He argues that one reason for creating the Philadelphia police was to stop frivolous private prosecution. The regularity of the salaries made the police jobs more attractive (hence their almost immediate seizure as political plums to be handed out by the political party gaining the mayor's position). From this, then, developed the use of police in political control, with police officers sometimes deterring voters and generally working for a partisan control of the ballot boxes.[13] This, in turn, meant that as immigrant voting machines grew, immigrants had access to these city jobs early on: The image of the Irish cop had a genuine basis in reality, even in cities like New Orleans.

Allen Steinberg's important work on Philadelphia (see note 4) shows that prior to the police, a vigorous system of private prosecution had kept the aldermen and mayor busy adjudicating minor criminal offenses. He argues that this system, though corrupt, kept the citizenry in easy and constant contact with the law and that the police, for their first two decades, mainly pursued arrests for public order offenses (the petty larcenies and assaults were handled by these lower and more neighborhood courts). His book adds an additional dimension to what local criminal justice looked like prior to the police, revising the work on the constable watch by Ferdinand, who emphasized their inefficiency and unsystematic entrepreneurialism. It raises new sets of complex questions for further analysis in the history of crime control and policing, in its argument that the police deliberately, albeit slowly, eroded the vigorous involvement of the urban poor and laboring classes in the justice system. That is, regular patrol by salaried officers in theory reduced corruption, increased the availability of the police for consistent service, and removed the opportunity for frivolous complaints and prosecution by those with the money to pay fees. Did the modern police in fact decrease crime control and make the justice system less easily accessible?

Steinberg's work depends in part on a scholarly find, the fragmentary logs of three aldermen. Apparently, almost all of the numerous aldermen kept no written records, which means that a more systematic comparison than he has essayed will depend on historians discovering new records. Nevertheless, until Steinberg's book, no historian even had the idea of looking for such materials, and his work opens an exciting new set of questions. In addition to such logs, police historians have already uncovered a rich lode of systematic sources.[14] These include detailed annual reports, internal records, less regularly preserved blotters (the daily log of station activities), and, for the nineteenth century, detailed newspaper accounts. Most police departments have written histories which vary widely in quality and coverage.[15] In addition to these specifically police-oriented sources, there are records produced by courts, coroners, and carceral institutions. Most of these are manuscripts, but state governments produced annual summaries of court, prison, and jail activities. In addition, the federal censuses have interesting data, rendered difficult to use by its inconsistency from decade to decade.

POLICE AS AN URBAN SERVICE

The new kind of police came as costly service innovations to American cities, and stingy city governments often resisted the transition specifically because of their new claim on city budgets.[16] Uniformed police spread across the United States to most cities in the three decades between 1850 and 1880. It sometimes seemed that local incidents, most typically riots, "caused" a city to change its police to the modern form. But in general, a city's rank size in the U.S. city system determined the order of police adoption, and the spread of police innovation followed a diffusion curve typical for all sorts of innovations.[17] Some historians have argued that police were created in response to increasing crime, but there is little empirical evidence to support this: Most social scientists now assume that the long-run trends in crime have been downward.[18] More to the point, those creating police would have had little way of detecting increases in crime. Riots had long been a part of American urban life, and historians have been able to describe in considerable detail the political ends of riots as conscious social forms.[19] New York City, for instance, had major nineteenth-century riots in 1806, 1826, 1834, 1837, 1849, 1855, 1857, 1863, 1870, 1874, and 1900.[20] At best, one could say that the creation of the police reflected a growing intolerance for riots and disorder rather than a response to an increase in crime. Gallman has shown that this was the case for Philadelphia, a city with a long tradition of rioting; he argues that citizens no longer accepted public outbursts.[21]

The police grew in per capita strength from around 1.3 per thousand in the 1860s and stabilized at 2 per thousand in 1908, still around the current ratio. Examined more carefully, the data suggest two eras of growth, the first up to about 1890, when police became permanent fixtures of city government, and the second the decade of the 1890s, when they again and finally expanded in strength. As a reciprocal to the increasing number of police per capita, the proportion of patrol officers fell from around 95 percent to about 75 percent by 1920. Toward the end of the nineteenth century, the actual patrol hours may have declined also, for not only did the proportion of patrol officers decrease, but the two-shift system (twelve hours on, twelve off) yielded to the more humane three-shift system in this era.[22] Certainly, the twentieth century saw declining patrol hours per officer. Watts, using more precise data for the St. Louis police department, has estimated police hours available for patrol since 1900, accounting for vacation and work-week changes. He concludes that since the nineteenth century, police have consistently declined in the hours per officer on the street, as one might expect given the general decrease in the length of the working day. Using hours worked in 1958–1962 as a base, police worked about 80 percent more at the end of the nineteenth century, about 20 percent more between 1907 and World War II, about 10 percent less after 1962.[23] At least for time allotted to patrol, police presence began declining within four decades after their introduction to cities.

Once in place, city police almost immediately began doing things unexpected by their original creators, whose expectations were more along the lines of crime prevention. Along with arresting offenders, the police took in tramps, returned lost children by the thousand, shot stray dogs, enforced sanitation laws, inspected boilers, took annual censuses, and performed a myriad of other small tasks. Their unique communications organization and street presence virtually forced them to become city servants as well as crime control officers. Simultaneous with a pull toward urban service came a surprising inability to fulfil other crime-related functions—most notably riot control and catching of offenders whose crimes crossed many local government districts (e.g., thieves on railroads)—and unpredictability in controlling strikes, with police sometimes siding with strikers (e.g., Homestead). Robert Fogelson shows that urban elites created armories in response to strikes and riots beginning in the post–Civil War era, signaling their clear recognition that police skills did not include antiriot mobilization.[24] Or, as the contributor to the *Cyclopedia of American Government* stated, "Labor riots, particularly against strike breakers, sometimes have the sympathy of the police."[25]

From very early on, police did something for which they had not been created: dispensing forms of welfare in response to the pressing demands of citizens. It is important to be clear about this particular transformation: In the mid-nineteenth century, all welfare was a local responsibility. The federal government took no such responsibility until the early twentieth century. State governments accepted limited responsibility for the blind and mentally ill and juveniles in need of reform.[26] County governments accepted responsibility for paupers, a group confined to the severely disabled, the old and infirm, and pregnant, destitute women.[27] City governments took on all others, from orphans to the homeless. Police departments were the front line of encounter for many of such needy people. Station houses contained separate dorm type rooms to house overnight "lodgers." Each city varied in what it provided, but the accommodations were primitive and limited to a few nights. A police officer recorded each person's name and sometimes rather detailed information (age, place of birth, occupation, "whither from," and destination). Such police service did not go unnoticed, either by the poor or by city officials.

Toward the end of the nineteenth century and into the 1920s, many reformers worked to dismantle station house lodging. Jacob Riis, in his autobiography, complained bitterly about his and his dog's maltreatment by the police when he stayed in stations in New York City and Camden, New Jersey, after his arrival in the United States in the 1870s.[28] Later, his bitterness fused with the critique of police commissioners like Theodore Roosevelt, who argued that the presence of tramps was degrading and threatened police officers with contagious diseases. At the same time, other reformers in major eastern cities worried about the consequences of the indiscriminate giving of overnight lodging. This, they argued, did nothing to reform the bad habits of the poor: Scientific charity should not be indiscriminate. Instead, they encouraged cities to substitute for police lodging municipal lodging houses, which required delousing and work from the overnight lodgers. Such reforms carried through at least in Boston and New York, much to the unhappiness of the lodgers, who preferred dirty but no-strings-attached shelter. By the 1920s, police were out of the lodging business, and only rarely have social welfare histories shown an awareness of this important role taken on by the police.

It seems almost natural to ask today why this simple police activity should have been allowed to disappear, especially since there is no evidence suggesting that the police themselves complained. But in the context of the original impetus behind the creation of police forces—crime control—and the changing focus of their range of activities, the disappearance of lodging makes more sense. Social welfare reformers, and some police chiefs, began to differentiate the components of the "dangerous class," and tramps became, to them, the unemployed rather than dangerous. After the 1890s, police did focus more and more on crime control. So did the other loose components of the criminal justice system: Friedman and Percival, in their study of Alameda County, California, show that in this period "criminal justice shifted away from amateurs and part-timers toward full-time crime handlers."[29]

Other tests confirm the change in police focus from a broad, welfare-as-well-as-crime-control focus to more concentration on actual crime control: For instance, in most major cities the correlation between arrests for criminal offenses (as opposed to public order offenses) and numbers of police per capita increased after 1890. A recent analysis of arrests for murder, other felony crimes, lodgers, and police strength in the twenty largest U.S. cities more precisely confirms 1894 as the turning point, the moment when police began to respond more directly to crimes of violence—measured by murder arrests. At the same time, they focused their attention on other felony crimes, continuing to slough off their burden of housing homeless lodgers and even reducing the numbers of people arrested for order misdemeanors.[30]

The narrowing focus of police on crime in turn came with a new set of external pressures, including demands for efficiency, for honesty, and for crime control. Coordination of departments began at the modest scale of sharing information. The Police Chiefs Union, founded in 1893 (to become the IACP), started a modest bureau of identification at some point in the 1890s. Its efforts did not meet with success because of the nature of the federal system: Voluntary contributions from city police departments could not provide an adequate or consistent funding base for this national activity. Not until the United States had a president with experience in local policing, Theodore Roosevelt, were police leaders to see the creation of the Federal Bureau of Identification, some twenty years later.[31] A range of local changes paralleled these fledgling national coordinating efforts.

In this context, the question of the police and public order gains new significance. Miller argued that compared to their British predecessors, the new police in the United States envisioned their role as keepers of public order, dispensing summary justice immediately, on the street.[32] Police organizations had high turnover on the job, in part because of their nature as political plums in cities with rapid regime transitions and in part because high residential mobility characterized all of urban America. Turnover ensured that police professionalization issues never mattered for the nineteenth-century officer. For the whole police organization, the keeping of lodgers had no logical role conflict with arresting drunks and felons: All of these activities involved control of what was then called the "dangerous class." The cessation of control of the dangerous class came with the first reforms of police corruption in the 1890s, followed by new emphases on investigative techniques like fingerprinting (around 1905) and by the slow change of the job from political plum to career occupation. By the end of World War I, police were in the business of crime control: Other city- or state-run agencies had taken over their former non–crime-control activities.

In this chapter, the dating of the turn to crime control is based on police behavior: Additional evidence suggests that over the decades of the early twentieth century, the crime control model became more explicitly drawn. Douthit, for instance, presents evidence that in the 1920s and 1930s, an effort to create a professional police force brought with it an even more refined focus on crime control which excluded all other forms of social conflict. In the mid-1920s, the concept of a "war against crime" was popularized by businessman Mark Prentiss, who wrote in the popular magazine *Current Opinion,* as somewhat more serious work was being conducted by crime commissions or crime surveys in twenty-four states.[33] President Coolidge's National Crime Commission (1925) brought national attention to the movement; President Hoover created a better known National Commission on Law Observance and Enforcement, usually referred to as the Wickersham Commission, which published fourteen reports and had research conducted by such experts as August Vollmer, Zechariah Chafee, Jr., Newton Baker, Edith Abbott, Mary Van Kleeck, Sam B. Warner, Miriam Van Watters, Clifford Shaw, and Henry Mackay.[34] These national commissions and the high publicity earned by J. Edgar Hoover marked an image-setting finale to the much longer swing of the police mission of crime control.

Not all scholars agree with the 1890s dating of the transition to a crime control model for the police. In a debate over policing practice and public order arrests, Watts has argued that crime control–oriented policing was not finalized until the 1940s, an argument based on internal documents as well as quantitative evidence from the St. Louis police.[35] On the other hand, Wertsch, in a close documentary analysis of the Des Moines police department, argues for a change in the 1920s, a "methodological change in policing that drew its attention away from public disorder offenses toward the more urgent task of protecting lives and property."[36] Therefore, while there is agreement that a shift from order control to crime control did in fact occur, the precise timing remains disputed. Several factors probably affected this transition and its city-to-city variability, just as several factors affected the initial adoption of uniformed police. More precise examination may well establish a parallel: an early but longer lasting transition (e.g., from 1890 to 1920) in those large cities with both progressive reform movements on many fronts and with innovative police departments, with a later but quicker transition in smaller cities.

A declining per capita rate of arrests for drunkenness offenses may also have resulted solely from this shift in emphasis, although there is strong, if contested, evidence suggesting that drinking itself has been in a long decline since the mid-nineteenth century.[37] For instance, the complexity of the topic and the question of policy is most dramatically illustrated by the articulated policy change in the Cleveland police in 1908 (see Figure 1). Under Chief Fred Kohler, the police adopted the "golden rule" in 1908, assisting drunks home or ignoring them. As the seventh largest U.S. city, Cleveland was often looked to as a model for reform. Arrests for drunkenness offenses plummeted from 18,743 in 1906 to a low of 909 in 1912, the most visible impact being between 1907 and 1908, when the arrests fell by 80 percent. Patrol officers arrested about thirty-seven per year in 1906 and less than two per year in 1912. But this dramatic policy

Figure 1
Cleveland Drunk Arrests per Thousand, 1872–1915

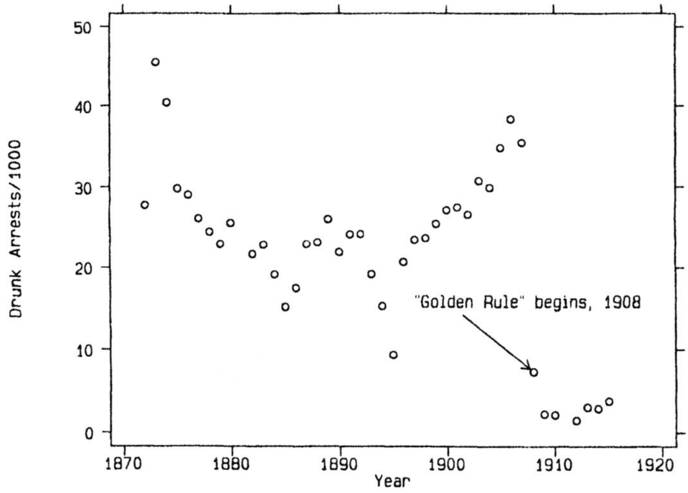

change simply followed a more complex trend in Cleveland: Arrest rates for drunkenness had fallen from as early as 1873 until the mid-1890s, and the peak in 1906 was the result of a decade of increased aggressiveness. Kohler's policy could actually be interpreted as a return to an established pattern. Thus a probable scenario, one linking policy to public behavior, is that for decades more decorous behavior had begun to prevail on the city streets, with the nineteenth-century campaign against excessive drinking slowly spreading its influence. In the larger context of growing urban order and political progressivism, the police themselves shifted toward a crime control orientation and simultaneously reconsidered the effectiveness of arresting drunks. Kohler also called his golden rule "common sense," so for the drinking world, nonarrests were a golden rule while for temperance advocates they were just common sense.

Whether or not public behavior became less disorderly, it is clear that the policing of drunkenness had been in a long downswing prior to the movement in the 1970s to decriminalize public drunkenness. When the question of drunkenness is considered in the context of public order, more broadly defined, the notion of a shift in police action from order maintenance to crime control remains a major argument from the past decade's research. It should still be considered as a hypothesis worth more systematic exploration. At least one pair of scholars is doing this. A project by Weinberger and Reinke has been designed to compare two industrial locations—Manchester, England, and Wuppertal, Germany—for the period 1890–1930.[38] (See Figure 2.) Based on the American work and on work for England, which argues that urban policing had aggressively reduced criminal offenses until the 1890s, these authors seek to expand and make more precise the relationship between police, public order, and issues of social welfare. They have already found important differences from the American experience and evidence which suggests that the shift away from welfare concerns may not have occurred until after World War I. In Britain, police orientation toward class control was "self-evident."[39] In Germany, the police explicitly focused on controlling worker politics and unions, and at the same time separate health and sanitary police were created to implement growing expertise in these fields.[40]

POLICE AS EMPLOYERS AND ORGANIZED LABOR

Police as Employers

In the United States, through their organizational tie to the mayor's office and to local partisan politics, police have been important as employers of some immigrant groups, most notably the Irish. This held true even for southern cities; in 1850, over one-third of New Orleans's police force had been born in Ireland (as opposed to about one-fourth of the city population).[41] Rousey quotes northern visitor Frederick Law Olmstead's encounter with a police officer in New Orleans in 1854: Asking him for directions, " 'a policeman, with the richest Irish brogue, directed me back to the St. Charles.' "[42] Nativist politicians purged the police of most of their immigrant officers in the late 1850s, but by 1870 the Irish were back in the department. Summarizing the experience of seventeen southern cities, Rousey discovered that Vicksburg and Memphis both had 50 percent of their officers born in Ireland as late as 1880 (if children of immigrants were included, this proportion would probably have been much higher). He concludes that "a large Irish role in southern urban policing was the rule" for most of the nineteenth century.[43]

Several recent studies by Watts analyze police hiring practices in St. Louis in great detail, using personnel data which include persons not hired. The results of his work provide a unique source of information on twentieth-century police departments. Between 1917 and 1969, one-third of St. Louis's recruits had had a previous local arrest record. The median age of recruits, around thirty at the beginning of the twentieth century, dropped slowly as policing changed from a job, typically one of several in a man's life, to a career.[44]

As the twentieth century began, even a heavily German city like St. Louis had an Irish police force: Only a slight 3 percent of its population had been born in Ireland, as contrasted to one-third of its police force. Of more importance, at the turn of the century the total ethnic composition of police, fire, and watch reflected the immigrant heritage of the city, three-fourths of whom were immigrants or children of immigrants, a figure somewhat less than that for Milwaukee, New York, or Chicago.[45]

Figure 2
Juveniles before the Courts in Manchester, 1890–1930

Relevant legislation: Employment of Children Act 1903
Children Act 1908
Education Act 1921
Manchester Corporation Act 1901 (juvenile street trading)
City of Manchester By-law 1922

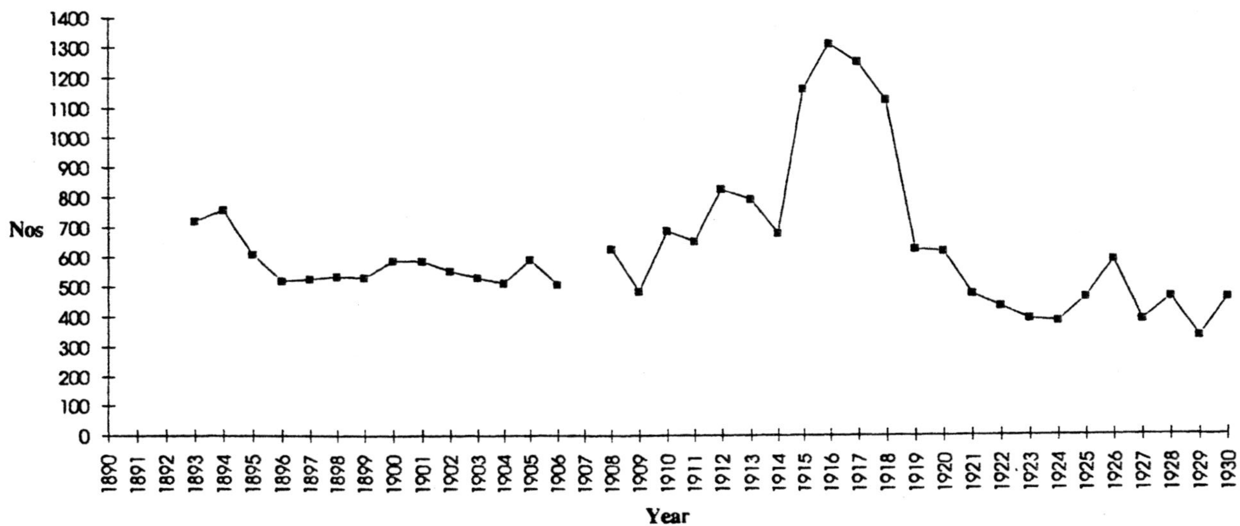

At the turn of the century, 6 percent of St. Louis's population was black; its police department appointed its two first police officers in 1901. Watts points out that Democrats controlled the police department and that virtually all of the city's black voters were Republicans, which suggests that politics combined with racial exclusion.[46] A Republican governor in 1920 admitted fifteen black officers to the department, and in the immediate post–World War II era, when black voters shifted to the Democratic party, 10 percent of all new recruits were black. Watts argues that many changes in the racial and ethnic composition of the St. Louis police in the twentieth century were actually not the result of reform but of larger "societal changes," such as the black shift to Democratic politics.[47]

Probably the most significant result to come from Watts's intense analysis of the individual career patterns of police officers is his discovery that over the course of the twentieth century, "no truly 'typical' pattern ever emerged." The average tenure of police officers varied highly at the beginning of the century and continued to vary through the 1970s. Moreover, actual individual careers belied the seemingly clear structural reforms and the appearance of a transformation of the police from a relatively simple and unpredictable internal structure to a highly structured and rationalized bureaucracy. Watts's conclusion that the "police in St. Louis failed to establish a uniform, coherent career pattern for its members" provides a cautionary note to the strong impression most scholars carry of the police as a Weberian bureaucracy in the process of professionalization.[48]

Police and Labor

Police control of labor in the United States has been much less direct and open than in Germany, and the recent historiography reflects a surprisingly ambiguous though still incomplete picture, one tied in large part to issues in private policing. In spite of notorious incidents, like the Memorial Day Massacre in Chicago in 1937, when police killed demonstrating workers, most recent labor history does not paint a completely antilabor picture of American police and organized labor. In fact, until the defeat of striking police officers in Boston in 1919 ended police unionization efforts for almost a half century, police themselves were often a part of the American labor movement.[49] One of the best-known labor historians, Herbert Gutman, pointed out that police sometimes sided with striking workers.[50] Usually this occurred in smaller cities, where police budgets depended on taxes paid by workers. Additionally, in small cities, police officers were often related directly to strikers or were literally from the same labor pool. Finally, in small cities, labor parties often gained considerable political power: Terrence V. Powderly, the founder of the Knights of Labor, also gained the mayor's seat of Scranton, a town racked with antilabor violence (not by the police). According to Walker, as far as the police were concerned, "Powderly resembled his predecessors," making the police a part of his political machine in an attempt to get the city council to enlarge the force.[51] In larger cities, police officers did not know or were not related to strikers, so at least the personal element of police/labor amicability was missing.

By far the most systematic and wide-ranging examination of police labor relations has not come from labor historians but from a police historian, Sidney Harring.[52] In a study of Great Lakes cities, he has identified a strong antiunion bias of the police in Buffalo, Chicago, and Milwaukee (under a socialist government). He argues vigorously that the police in these and other cities acted as shock troops for local capitalists, pacifying and controlling local labor under the dictate of local businessmen. In Chicago, for instance, Harring has identified extensive strikebreaking activities by the city police, especially after 1910. Though his evidence for Chicago is persuasive, it is less so for other cities, where his arguments remain widely disputed and highly controversial. For instance, in Chicago in 1905, in Oshkosh in 1898, and in Akron in 1913, police "weakness" failed to curb strikes, and either private guards or the militia intervened.[53] But until further systematic research is completed, Harring's stands as the best study of police and labor to date.[54]

In one of the most famous labor disputes in the United States—the lockout in Homestead, Pennsylvania—local police sided with the locked-out workers; Carnegie's plant officials had to hire nearly 400 Pinkerton agents to support them. The agents attacked the strikers from barges in the river: Three agents and ten strikers were killed. This incident highlights two long traditions: (1) that the police have local political ties by virtue of their local funding, and (2) that their responsiveness to local circumstances created an opportunity for private enterprise, the private police.

In a careful institutional history of the Pinkerton National Detective Agency, Frank Morn has provided a badly needed narrative history of the most visible and oldest form of private policing, the detective. Morn shows how this famous agency quickly moved from "detection to protection," becoming a "private army of capitalism." He argues that "railroad expansion [in the 1850s] quickly exposed the weaknesses of police work in a country enamored of federalism."[55] Once a train left a city, it had no police protection: In a long-distance trip, it passed through many small police regions. Pinkerton capitalized on this gap in governance in the railroad industry first, "testing" employee honesty (e.g., theft by conductors) as trains rolled across the countryside. Later his business expanded to capture similar opportunities in other industries and began to include strikebreaking in instances for which neither local police nor militia could or would provide assistance. In all situations, the private sector either filled in governmental interstices or took on possibly illegal actives. (An example is employee testing involving "sting" operations whereby Pinkerton agents tried to bribe conductors to let them ride without tickets and then filed reports to the companies, who fired corruptable conductors. Did the Pinkerton operatives in fact blackmail or extort money on occasion?)

Reviewing Morn's book, Jeffreys-Jones observes that it is "the first serious monograph on private detective agencies."[56] Jeffreys-Jones clarifies how Allen

Pinkerton's prolabor radicalism was also antistrike and anticommunitarian; how in the United States he could be a reformer yet also work against all labor violence. Moreover, Jeffreys-Jones sets a research agenda for more work to be done in the history of private detective agencies as part of the history of private policing, including divorce work and family law, with a suggestion of new primary sources. His brief but important essay provides the starting point for the next round of historical research.

Yet the role of such private armies did not pass unscrutinized: The Homestead incident shocked the nation and prompted a federal investigation, which resulted in no federal legislation but in widespread antidetective legislation in many states.[57] The irony of the Pinkerton agency's antilabor reputation came from Allan Pinkerton's widely publicized prolabor radicalism, which had forced him to leave Scotland in the 1840s. The company was embarrassed by the Homestead fiasco and actually did little strike work for ten years after it. However, antilabor activity could include more than strikebreaking, and by the 1930s the company was a leader in the industrial espionage field, with over 1,000 operatives in all major unions. Again the focus of an embarrassing federal investigation and exposé, the Pinkerton agency left these activities by 1940, slowly moving into the private security business.[58]

Private police like the Pinkerton and Burns agencies gained their economic advantage by moving across political regions, using means of dubious legality and working only for the monied. But they were not the only private police, for another form of nonmunicipally controlled police has been present in American cities since the 1890s: privately employed off-duty police officers and, more important, public officers appointed and employed solely by private organizations. Reed's work on Detroit has shown how these officers and their commissions issued by the police department grew in numbers as crime (indicated by the homicide rate) and population increased while the per capitized police budget decreased. About a fourth of these officers were employed by other municipal agencies, and about two-thirds were employed by businesses; in essence, businesses hiring these officers simply eliminated the services of detective agencies. Reed also has evidence that the police department was reluctant to let the police be used in strikes and that these privately employed police may have been business's response to the official aversion to strikebreaking.[59]

Recent work on a famous teamsters strike in Minneapolis in 1934 supports Reed's insights. The so-called Citizen's Alliance was in fact a group of businessmen vigilantes who supplemented the police in the strike. Formed in 1917 to keep Minneapolis open shop, it successfully "eliminated the political threat of the Municipal Nonpartisan League of the Minneapolis trade unions and the NPL [Nonpartisan League], deunionized the Minneapolis police, maintained an effective intelligence service, and helped establish a Highway Patrol and a Bureau of Criminal Apprehension headed by men it could trust."[60] Its political clout and credibility ended when its members tried to drive and guard trucks to keep goods flowing in the strike: Armed with clubs and guns, they actually got into armed conflict with the strikers, and their amateurish aggression resulted in many deaths. After this misadventure, one in which the governor intervened on the side of the strikers, the Citizen's Alliance did not disband but instead hired parapolice to do investigative and patrol work. In essence, this private group used force of dubious legality to supplement the legitimate police when they were unwilling to step over the bounds of legitimate action.

REFORMING POLICE

Often police have stepped over the bounds of legitimate action, and corruption has been a persistent problem in U.S. policing. The Lexow Commission (1894, of the New York state legislature) gained national prominence during its investigation of the New York City police and subsequent exposé of corruption: Subsequent investigative reforms occurred in other large cities for the next three decades.[61] Sherman has observed that waves of scandal and reform have run in twenty-year cycles since 1894 and the Lexow committee's investigation of New York City police corruption. He argues that "virtually every urban police department in the United States has experienced both organized corruption and a major scandal over that corruption."[62] Reforms following scandal, he contends, have often been successful, but control of scandal, like control of crime itself, is hampered by fundamental freedoms. As opposed to most crime, however, scandal arises under fairly predictable conditions, usually surrounding vice operations. Historians have shown the long connection of police corruption with prostitution and drugs (including alcohol, when illegal).[63] The potential for scandal is made most clear in those episodes when cities tried, for health reasons, to regulate prostitution without legalizing it. By the turn of the century, local political machines depended on these semilegitimate vice districts, and the bribes from vice entrepreneurs funded the machines. (In some cases, elected nonmachine governments depended on the revenues from such fines—for example, the small city of East Grand Forks, Minnesota, in the pre–World War I era.)[64] Since the 1960s, federal investigations of police corruption have reduced the ability of local vice entrepreneurs to control police.

Earlier, police historians had envisioned the first decades of the twentieth century as the dawn of scientific policing, a notion associated with Berkeley's famous chief August Vollmer; Richard Sylvester of Washington, D.C. and the IACP; and the serious communication among scholars and various segments of the crime control community through the pages of the *Journal of Criminal Law and Criminology,* which began publication in 1909.[65] Yet recent work has made this clean, Progressive Era picture more complex. For instance, as Watts's work has shown, the emergence of a more professional police force did not result in more orderly career paths for St. Louis police officers, implying that the bureaucracy did not have the organizational rationality earlier observers had envisioned.[66]

Nor did shedding by police of service activities and a focus on crime-related arrests conform to the professional picture being painted by prominent police officers like August Vollmer. Vollmer, elected Town Marshall of Berkeley in 1905, where he supervised a force of three nonuniformed officers, soon became famous and influential. He achieved publicity in local and national newspapers, wrote extensively in the professional journals, and published several well-respected books. His innovations included a counseling clinic with a psychiatric social worker, Elisabeth Lossing, and an aggressive policing policy, which emphasized intervention in personal affairs and prevention through methods prescribed by the latest ideas of the mental hygiene movement. The most recent scholarship on Vollmer denies his widely acclaimed genius without denigrating his considerable achievements:

> Rather than an original thinker, Vollmer's strengths lay in finding ingenious practical applications of ideas he borrowed from others, in carefully supervising the implementation of a wide variety of technical and procedural innovations, and, perhaps, most importantly, in maintaining high personal involvement and exercising decisive leadership in community affairs that impinged on police functions.[67]

It is important to see the shift Vollmer represented and advocated as not directly countering the narrowing police function or as a return to the multi-service police of the nineteenth century. All of his intervention and social work orientation and his genuine sympathy for, and stern guidance of, troubled people was directed toward the end of crime prevention. Earlier, police had taken in the homeless as a sort of municipal housekeeping, which was in fact technically implied by the legal notion of "police power" (which meant the power of a state or its local governments to do housekeeping, from cleaning streets to creating an orderly public arena[68]). Vollmer's new and generous vision of policing was all oriented toward the prevention of individual criminal actions.

This same vision enabled police to respond in new ways to old problems. During World War II, vicious race riots in several cities took the lives of African Americans and Mexican Americans. More to the point, the police not only failed to control the riots but were in many cases part of the problem. Thurgood Marshall compared the Detroit police to the gestapo, and some police officers saw the events and attitudes as providing fuel for Nazi anti-American propaganda.[69] From these experiences, Milwaukee police chief Joseph Kluchesky earned a national reputation for his race relations training program in Milwaukee in 1944. In the same year, the International City Manager Association published a manual on police relations with minority groups that became widely used throughout the United States. Walker found twenty-two cities adopting some race relations training between 1943 and 1950 (in some cities, this involved little more than a two-hour lecture). However, the lack of urban riots after World War II until the 1960s never really tested the effectiveness of these programs or their companion antiriot strategies, leaving the police with untested and feebly implemented programs when the urban riots of the 1960s began.[70]

While much has been written about the urban riots and the civil rights movement, no historian has yet tackled these episodes and the police roles in them in a systematic way. For instance, the Little Rock police attained considerable notoriety in 1957 and 1958 for their morally repugnant refusal to protect black children in the school integration crisis. Did such outrages as these, exposed on national television, prompt public support for stronger federal standards in all areas of law enforcement? Did the question of racial fairness make an impact in other cities which did not gain media attention? Atlanta marketed itself as the "city too busy to hate" at the same time; did other urban boosters strive to make their cities and police fairer for latent economic incentives? In the 1960s, did the impact of seeing riots on national television have an equal if different impact?[71]

FEDERAL-LOCAL POLICY ISSUES

As these visible urban problems in which the police were inextricably involved gained public attention, scholars turned to researching local police departments. The work of the 1960s and 1970s focused intensely on local aspects of policing, on detailed studies of individual police departments, and on questions about the social side of policing.[72] Implicit in all of the work was the recognition that policing in the United States was an activity done by local governments. Historians ignored issues of larger political entities to assess the details of the actual local systems. But now some historians whose earlier work began in the arena of the local have turned toward these other issues relating to the nature of the federal system and policing. In so doing, they bring their sensitivity to the all too often ignored importance of the local and its imbeddedness in the federal. The significance of these historians' work is clear in its comprehension of the high visibility of federal levels of policing and of federal policing's relatively small scope compared to the local. This work represents only a beginning. The working out of the appropriate theoretical context has only begun.[73] The work of Athan Theoharis has focused on the issues of "intelligence and legality" and the long conflict they represent within the FBI mission.[74] Alix has published a unique study on a single criminal offense, kidnapping, which includes an examination of the federalization of this crime and its incorporation into the purview of the FBI.[75] But most work on the FBI has not considered the context of policing or the nature of criminal law in the United States (and as a result it is too often journalistic, attending to particular aspects without relating them to any larger context) or it deals with abuses, in particular FBI abuses of power.

Miller's work represents a pioneering approach to federal law enforcement.[76] Examining the issue of collecting federal revenue on alcohol production in the South, he highlights both the scope and limits of this early form of federal policing. While he draws no explicit comparison with drug enforcement today, the contemporary comparison with the too often romanticized illegal production of the nineteenth-century drug of choice, liquor, is obvious. The revenue collectors were sometimes corrupt; moonshiners often resisted violently, killing ten revenue collectors between July 1877 and June 1878. There was also internal violence in the moonshine business; after 1879, federal troops accompanied revenue collectors; and people in rural communities, often women, did not all approve of the illegal liquor and secretly informed the revenue collectors of illicit activity. The question of moonshine, Miller makes clear, is the question of state penetration into illegal business, just as it is today with nonalcohol drugs. Successful federal efforts were characterized by consistent and fair prosecution, a system of fines and suspended sentences which could be revoked if the defendant resumed illegal alcohol production. By the end of the nineteenth century, popular support for moonshine had dramatically eroded because of the consistent and judicious federal effort, so moonshiners were often denounced as " 'gangs of lazy, bad men . . . of general worthlessness.' "[77] While for Miller the important contrast in the research is with the federal failure to enforce civil rights, he might well have made the contrast with current efforts on drug enforcement.

One hopes that further work on federal policing will supplement Miller's work so we may begin to understand the nature of policing across the American social and political landscape. Miller's central argument is perhaps of more interest to historians and political scientists than to those in the criminal justice fields: The historiography which emphasizes the failure of reconstruction to protect black citizens in the South "overlooks the internal revenue system, a product of the Civil War that became a permanent element of expanded national authority."[78] This insight suggests that "expanded national authority" and policing do have an important connecting link: Federal laws are enforced through a wide variety of organizations, and too often writers attend only to the FBI as a unique institution. One hopes that Miller's recentering of thinking about national law enforcement by highlighting a forgotten aspect of national policing will provoke other historians into looking at other federal policing systems—the park police, for instance (as examined by Mackintosh in an internal history which does not link this agency to the broader context of police history) or the police of Washington, D.C., which, in spite of their federal mandate, have a past like that of other cities.[79]

David R. Johnson's work in progress on federal policing combines two approaches, one emphasizing federal crime (counterfeiting) and the other focused on large bureaucracies and state building. He argues that the "fitful" and "obscure" process behind the creation of a federal police followed from the creation of federal authority over currency during the Civil War.[80] Subtly using currency and counterfeiting as his topic, Johnson directly relates the question of state building to the chasing of counterfeiters, showing how the creation of a nation-state required a strong currency, which in turn boosted the creation of a small national police. He details how both criminals and federal agents operated in a local and highly irregular manner. Traub, writing on the use of rewards in the West, has evidence that both local governments and U.S. marshalls, reporting directly to the attorney general, used rewards as an attempt to compensate people for catching, and often killing, known offenders. He argues that rewards were a rational way to communicate and provide crime control in lieu of an efficiently organized state, although he notes that the system encouraged murder rather than trials.[81] Unlike Johnson, he links his analysis neither to theoretical questions surrounding local and federal policing nor to state building, clearly the essential missing element in the U.S. West.[82]

Uchida's work on the early FBI clarifies its origins in the Bureau of Investigation, begun by President Roosevelt in 1908. He provides a clear bridge to local policing by showing how this federal organization was begun by a politician expert in the ways and limitations of city police from his term as New York City police commissioner. Roosevelt mandated that the Bureau of Investigation initiate criminal investigations for crimes spreading beyond local felonies—beginning with political land frauds. While not explicitly understood as a structural problem related to the federal system, Roosevelt's agency indeed focused on those felonies simply beyond the scope of local police. Rather than seeing Roosevelt's actions as purely politically motivated, one might draw a comparison with progressive reformers in the late nineteenth and early twentieth centuries, who, Jeffreys-Jones contended, exaggerated the amount and fear of labor violence in order to accomplish their electoral and legislative goals.[83] In other words; reformers exaggerated fears to accomplish somewhat different ends.

Some of this recent police history has raised policy issues which cut across other features of local governments and services. Police, like schools, provide labor-intensive services which do not seem to be easily replaced by technology. Greater bureaucratic complexity has not broken down tasks to simple elements easily performed by machines, and this does not seem to be a realistic expectation. Local governments have the potential to do some things much better (e.g., traffic control), but policing and schooling do not have such rosy futures. Perhaps this is one reason why they both remain at the center of controversy: The jobs get no easier and the bureaucracies no more efficient with the passage of time and the growth of expertise. Equally important, the efficiency of these labor-intensive services seems to have an inverse relationship to city size: At some size, the bigger the city, the more costly and perhaps less efficient the service, whether school or police.[84]

The history of police raises some difficult theoretical questions about urban government and has unclear implications for policing. Paul Peterson, in *City Limits,* argues that policing is an "allocational" function of city government, meaning that it is neutral vis-à-vis increasing or decreasing the city's long-run expectations for revenue.[85] As the history of the police makes clear, the functional change of police over time renders Peterson's analysis problematic while at the same time making his overall model even more useful. In the nineteenth century, police clearly performed part of the city's welfare or distributional function. As the police shifted to a crime control emphasis, police officers became essential to the city's promotional functions in that they helped provide a safer environment for urban economic activities.

Following Peterson's larger argument, that distributional activities migrate to the highest—that is, geographically most capacious—level of government while promotional activities stay at the lowest—that is, the smallest geographical units—of government, then Peterson's theory could help describe and explain why policing changed from broad class control to more narrow crime control. Given the historic limitations of U.S. policing to small locales and the strong tradition prohibiting the creation of a state or national police system as in Europe, the police came under steady pressure to change what they did. As distributional actors, cities were under competitive constraints to spend less on welfare services, including those accomplished by the police, while at the same time they were under pressure to attract revenue-enhancing activities by providing crime-free environments. The fixed location of American police would then account for their turn to crime control and away from welfare, in contrast to the continued welfare and broader service orientation (class control) of European police. This constraint would also help account for the relatively low amount of development of crime control policing at the state and federal level in spite of tremendous political and social pressure to have more effective crime control. Crime control, then, would not migrate to the national level until local revenue enhancing disappeared, an unlikely scenario given the long history of local government. If one can imagine an international scenario in which the United States will have to make itself crime free to attract investment, then crime control might move to broader levels of government.

CONCLUSION: FUTURE RESEARCH NEEDS

The research of the past decade gives scholars a much deeper context and much greater empirical knowledge with which to understand current policing. As Lane's essay of 1980 synthesizes the pioneering generation of police historians, this chapter builds on a maturing field. This generation has had the advantage of a growing body of research and a broad spectrum of theoretical perspectives, from the Marxism of Harring to the interdisciplinary approach of Schneider. It has been much more synthetic than that of the pioneering generation. My overview and history in 1981 pulled information from dozens of late nineteenth- and early twentieth-century local police histories. In addition, it and the articles of Watts introduced new levels of statistics to the field. Friedman and Percival's study of Alameda county (1981) looked at the whole criminal justice system—police, the courts, law, lawyers, offenders, jails, and the media. Schneider's work on Detroit (1980) mapped arrests and police distribution and tied the social and economic geography of the city to the nineteenth-century development of its police and crime. Emsley published the first scholarly history of policing in Europe and England, enabling American scholars to begin to appreciate more deeply the complex differences between North America and Europe.[86]

This new stage of sophistication was matched on another level, too. On the international scene, a loose affiliation of scholars known as the Dutch Group had put together international scholarly conferences on crime history. Organizing a larger meeting in conjunction with the Seventh International Economic History Congress in Edinburgh in 1978, this group created a new, more formal organization and publication, the *International Association for the History of Crime and Criminal Justice Newsletter.*[87] Published by the Fondation de la Maison des Sciences de l'Homme in Paris, the *Newsletter* began the complex task of coordinating and informing researchers about the varied and rich research being conducted around the world in criminal justice history.[88] The work of this group introduced Americans to the historical sociology of Norbert Elias, whose generous theoretical approach underwrites much of the contemporary European scholarship. One year later in the United States, in 1980, the journal *Criminal Justice History* appeared: An annual serial, it publishes international scholarship and with its first issue established itself as a serious scholarly journal.

The research developments discussed in this chapter suggest a diverse research agenda. For instance, Steinberg raises the challenge to find sources which will permit the documentation of prepoliced modes of criminal justice. He has found fragmentary evidence on aldermen's courts. We need similar sources on church courts: Kasserman has documented the Methodists' exclusion of a young woman for prostitution, while Waldrep has systematic evidence on church trials and county court trials for a rural county in late nineteenth-century Kentucky.[89] He argues that a decline in church trails preceded a rise in felony court prosecutions. Similar work also must be done in labor union court records. Garlock, for instance, has documented the Knights of Labor courts in the late nineteenth century, showing that the expulsions mainly were for offenses having to do with union affairs but that the court structure of the union was specifically designed as a fairer alternative to the existing police and judicial machinery. He quotes Terrence Powderly: " 'They [workingmen] have long perceived that at the hands of advocates, justices and police, they get an immense amount of *law,* but no *justice.*' "[90] Finally, excellent recent studies of vigilantism and crime show the need for further systematic work on the power of the state and crime control.[91]

We also need comparable, systematic research on the constable watch system. These are all essential if we are to understand the transition to the police and a formal, state-run, justice system. Steinberg argues that in many ways the quantity as well as quality of local crime control decreased after the introduction of the police. This is a challenging assertion and should attract the research efforts of historians.

The work of Loftin and McDowell provides a model for research design in historical studies.[92] Constructing a long (fifty-year) data series of police behavior and expenditures and paying careful attention to the population denominator, they reexamine the role of expenditures on policing in Detroit. While they find a weak relationship between expenditures and apprehension rates, the article is of more importance for its demonstration of the feasibility of long-time series. Its research design is clearly generalizable to other cities, and it should provide a beginning orientation for future research.

How do police relate to issues of public order, from misdemeanors to riots? In spite of all the research, there has yet to be a research design capable of convincingly testing counterfactuals—that is, asking what would cities have been (or would be) like without the police. Schneider has systematically examined the relationship of police to riots in the mid-nineteenth century, looking as well at cities in which there were no riots (he argues that Detroit Germans and Irish had residential and journey-to-work patterns that minimized the friction which caused riots in other cities).[93] No historian has examined twentieth-century riots and police in such a systematic way. If urban rioting declined with the introduction of policing, did this reflect effective riot control, the consequence of a visible control mechanism, or an independent increase in urban order? The late nineteenth-century decline in violent crimes and in accidental deaths suggests the latter, but the project specifically designed to test these alternatives has yet to be conducted.[94]

We still need to know far more about the police themselves. Were nonurban police and private police so active in labor control that the local police could remain relatively absent? What has been the impact of police training and civil service rules? Did the slow change in police technology indicate a resistance to innovation detrimental to crime control? Did the transition from more generalized class surveillance and control to crime control wipe out an important urban welfare service? The question of productivity in a labor-intensive service like policing (and also school teaching) implicitly plagues most analyses: Little has been done to estimate the contributions of technological change to productivity and then to estimate the total changes in policing.

The question of police and order has special significance for southern cities; the work of Rousey on New Orleans suggests a very different development path from that in the North. Rousey has also shown how New Orleans in the second half of the nineteenth century was far more violent than northern cities. This extended to the police, often with disastrous results. In the period 1863–1890, police officers more often shot bystanders than did civilian shooters: In addition, police officers were more likely to be killed by fellow officers than by civilians.[95] In an unpublished article, Rousey shows how the police of New Orleans were essentially a military force, patrolling the city primarily to control slaves.[96] It is not yet clear whether we should even call the "city guard" police, for with their swords, armory, and uniforms, they represented a European-style urban military: They were at first called, in 1805, the *Gendarmerie.* The New Orleans police were demilitarized later in the century, and the post–Civil War police represented the city's first modern police system. The contrast between the South and the North in the pre–Civil War era suggests that an unfree society cannot support a modern police system. Systematic comparison both of organization and behavior can make clearer these regional differences and, in the process, show how the issues of liberty, partisan politics, and the legitimacy of the state directly affect policing. Thus, further opportunities for police history go in several directions; from policy to urban political theory to fundamental issues of democracy and liberty.

NOTES

I wish to thank the participants at the conference on Modern Policing (Washington, D.C., 1990) for their extensive and useful comments. In addition, Mark Haller has helped me rethink many issues posed in this chapter, and I thank him.

1. Eric H. Monkkonen, *Crime and Justice in American History* (Westport, 1990).
2. Roger Lane, "Urban Police and Crime in Nineteenth-Century America," *Crime and Justice: An Annual Review* 2 (1980): 1–44.
3. Eric H. Monkkonen, *Police in Urban America, 1860–1920* (New York, 1981); see also Monkkonen, "From Cop History to Social History: The Significance of the Police in American History," *Journal of Social History* 15 (1982): 575–91.
4. Allen Steinberg, *The Transformation of Criminal Justice: Philadelphia, 1800–1880* (Chapel Hill, 1989).
5. Stanley H. Palmer, *Police and Protest in England and Ireland, 1780–1850* (New York, 1988).
6. Wilbur R. Miller, *Cops and Bobbies: Police Authority in New York and London, 1830–1870* (Chicago, 1976).
7. Theodore N. Ferdinand, "Criminality, the Courts, and the Constabulary in Boston, 1702–1967," *Journal of Research in Crime and Delinquency* 17 (1980): 190–208.
8. Quoted in Arthur E. Peterson and George W. Edwards, *New York as an Eighteenth Century Municipality* (1917; Port Washington, N.Y., 1967), 324.
9. Mark H. Haller, "Civic Reformers and Police Leadership: Chicago, 1905–1935," in *Police in Urban Society,* ed. Harlan Hahn (Beverly Hills, 1970), 39–56; "Historical Roots of Police Behavior: Chicago, 1890–1925," *Law and Society Review* 10 (1976): 303–23.
10. Steinberg, *Transformation.*
11. Roger Lane, *Policing the City: Boston, 1822–1905* (Cambridge, Mass., 1967), 105; James F. Richardson, *The New York Police: Colonial Times to 1901* (New York, 1970), 65; David R. Johnson, "The Search for an Urban Discipline: Police Reform as a Response to Crime in American Cities, 1800–1875" (Ph.D. diss., University of Chicago, 1972). Published as *Policing the Urban Underworld: The Impact of Crime on the Development of the American Police, 1800–1885* (Philadelphia, 1979), 172–76.
12. Monkkonen, *Police,* 109–28.
13. Laylon W. Jordan, "Police and Politics: Charleston in the Gilded Age, 1880–1900," *South Carolina History Magazine* 81 (1980): 35–50.
14. Eric H. Monkkonen, "The Quantitative Historical Study of Crime and Criminal Justice in the United States," in *History and Crime: Implications for Contemporary Criminal Justice Policy,* ed. James Inciardi and Charles Faupel (Beverly Hills, 1980), 53–73, trans. in *Rechtsgeschichte, Rechtssoziologie und Historische Kriminologie,* ed. M. Rehbinder and M. Killias (Berlin, 1985), 169–94; idem, "Municipal Reports as an Indicator Source: The Nineteenth Century Police," *Historical Methods* 12 (1979): 57–65.

15. See Monkkonen, *Police,* 164–68, for a bibliography.

16. John C. Schneider, *Detroit and the Problem of Order, 1830–1880: A Geography of Crime, Riot, and Policing* (Lincoln, Nebr., 1980).

17. Monkkonen, *Police,* 49–64.

18. For the response argument, see Bobby L. Blackburn, "Oklahoma Law Enforcement since 1803" (Ph.D. diss., Oklahoma State University, 1979); Felix Rippy, "Crime and the Beginnings of the Muncie Police Force," *Indiana Social Studies Quarterly* 38 (1985): 5–18; Ted Robert Gurr, "Historical Trends in Violent Crime: Europe and the United States"; for the other argument, see *Violence in America: Volume 1: The History of Crime,* ed. Ted Gurr (Beverly Hills, 1989), 21–54.

19. Paul A. Gilje, *The Road to Mobocracy: Popular Disorder in New York City, 1763–1834* (Chapel Hill, 1987).

20. Monkkonen, *Police,* 196.

21. James M. Gallman, "Preserving the Peace: Order and Disorder in Civil War Pennsylvania," *Pennsylvania History* 55 (1988): 201–15.

22. Monkkonen, *Police,* 144–45.

23. Eugene J. Watts, "Police Priorities in Twentieth Century St. Louis," *Journal of Social History* 14 (1981): 671 n. 15.

24. Robert Fogelson, *America's Armories: Architecture, Society and Public Order* (Cambridge, Mass., 1989).

25. Ibid.; Andrew C. McLaughlin and Albert B. Hart, *Cyclopedia of American Government* (New York, 1914), 3: 584.

26. Barbara M. Brenzel, *Daughters of the State: A Social Portrait of the First Reform School for Girls in North America, 1856–1905* (Cambridge, Mass., 1983); Ellen Dwyer, *Homes for the Mad: Life Inside Two Nineteenth-Century Asylums* (New Brunswick, N.J., 1987); Steven Schlossman, *Love and the American Delinquent: The Theory and Practice of "Progressive" Juvenile Justice* (Chicago, 1977).

27. Michael B. Katz, *In the Shadow of the Poorhouse: A Social History of Welfare in America* (New York, 1986); Joan Underhill Hannon, "The Generosity of Antebellum Poor Relief," *Journal of Economic History* 44 (1984): 810–21; idem, "Poverty in the Antebellum Northeast: The View from New York State's Poor Relief Rolls," *Journal of Economic History* 44 (1984): 1019–31.

28. Riis, cited in Monkkonen, *Police,* 92.

29. Lawrence M. Friedman and Robert V. Percival, *Roots of Justice: Crime and Punishment in Alameda County, California, 1870–1910* (Chapel Hill, 1981), 194.

30. Erik H. Monkkonen and Catrien Bijleveld, "Cross-sectional and Dynamic Analyses of the Concomitants of Police Behavior," *Historical Methods* (1991): 16–24.

31. Donald C. Dilworth, *Identification Wanted: Development of the American Criminal Identification System, 1893–1943* (Gaithersburg, Md., 1977); Craig D. Uchida, "Policing the Politicians: Theodore Roosevelt and the Origins of the F.B.I," paper presented at the Academy of Criminal Justice Sciences annual meeting, San Antonio, 1983.

32. Miller, *Cops and Bobbies;* see also Friedman and Percival, *Roots of Justice,* 80–81.

33. Nathan Douthit, "Police Professionalism and the War against Crime in the United States, 1920s–1930s," in *Police Forces in History,* ed. George L. Mosse (Beverly Hills, 1975), 317–33.

34. Samuel Walker, *Popular Justice* (New York, 1981), 173–75.

35. Eugene J. Watts, "Police Response to Crime and Disorder in Twentieth Century St. Louis," *Journal of American History* 70 (1983): 340–58.

36. Douglas Wertsch, "The Evolution of the Des Moines Police Department," *Annals of Iowa* 48 (1987): 448; see also Eugene Watts, "Police Priorities in Twentieth Century St. Louis," *Journal of Social History* 14 (1981): 658.

37. Erik H. Monkkonen, "A Disorderly People? Urban Order in Nineteenth and Twentieth Century America," *Journal of American History* 68 (1981): 539–59; William J. Rorabaugh, *The Alcoholic Republic: An American Tradition* (New York, 1979); Jack S. Blocker, Jr., *American Temperance Movements: Cycles of Reform* (Boston, 1989); Erik H. Monkkonen, "Toward an Understanding of Urbanisation: Drunk Arrests in Los Angeles," *Pacific Historical Review* 50 (1981): 234–44.

38. Clive Emsley and Barbara Weinberger, eds., *Policing Western Europe, 1850–1940: Politics, Professionalization, and Public Order* (Westport, 1990).

39. V.A.C. Gatrell, "The Decline of Theft and Violence in Victorian and Edwadian England," in *Crime and the Law: The Social History of Crime in Western Europe since 1500,* ed. V.A.C. Gatrell, Bruce Lenman, and Geoffrey Parker (London, 1980), 238–370.

40. Barbara Weinberger and Herbert Reinke, "A Diminishing Function: A Comparative Account of Policing the City," *Policing and Society* (1991) part 1, p. 14; part 2, pp. 8–9.

41. Dennis Rousey, "Hibernian Leatherheads: Irish Cops in New Orleans, 1830–1860," *Journal of Urban History* 10 (1983): 62.

42. Ibid., 61.

43. Ibid., 80.

44. Eugene J. Watts, "St. Louis Police Recruits in the Nineteenth Century," *Criminology* 19 (1981): 82, 84.

45. Ibid., 100, 99; see also Robert Fogelson, *Big City Police* (Cambridge, Mass., 1977).

46. Eugene J. Watts, "Blue and Black: Afro-American Police Officers in Twentieth Century St. Louis," *Journal of Urban History* 7 (1981): 131–68; Watts, "St. Louis Police Recruits," 105–6.

47. Watts, "St. Louis Police Recruits," 107, 109; Watts, "Patterns of Promotion: The St. Louis Police Department, 1899–1975," *Social Science History* 6 (1982): 233–58, also demonstrates in an analysis of promotion practices that the only meaningful variable for promotion is seniority.

48. Eugene J. Watts, "Continuity and Change in Police Careers: A Case Study of the St. Louis Police Department," *Journal of Police Science and Administration* 2 (1983): 224.

49. Samuel Walker, *Popular Justice* (New York, 1980), 166–69.

50. Herbert G. Gutman, *Work, Culture, and Society in Industrializing America,* "Part IV. Local Behavior and Patterns of Labor Discontent in Gilded Age America" (New York, 1977), 293–343; Bruce C. Johnson, "Taking Care of Labor: The Police in American Politics," *Theory and Society* 3 (1976): 89–117.

51. Samuel Walker, "The Police and the Community: Scranton, Pennsylvania, 1886–1884, A Test Case," *American Studies* 19 (1978): 79–90.

52. Sidney Harring, *Policing a Class Society: Police and Labor in Buffalo, Chicago, and Milwaukee* (New Brunswick N.J., 1982).

53. Ibid., 125–31.

54. Richard J. Terrill, review of Harring in *Criminal Justice History: An International Annual* 7 (1986): 206–7; Roger Lane, review of Harring, *Policing a Class Society, Journal of American History* 71 (1984): 650–51; for a new look at police and labor, see Thomas Clark, "Police and Labor in California, 1870–1930" (Ph.D. diss., University of California, Los Angeles, 1993).

55. Frank Morn, *"The Eye That Never Sleeps": A History of the Pinkerton National Detective Agency* (Bloomington, 1982), 24.

56. Rhodri Jeffreys-Jones, "The Defictionalization of the American Private Detective," *Journal of American Studies* 17 (1983): 266.

57. Morn, *"The Eye,"* 91–109.

58. Ibid., 187, 192.

59. Rebecca Reed, "Private Employees/Public Badges: 'Additional Patrolmen' in the Policing of Detroit" (paper read at the Social Science History Association Annual meeting, St. Louis, 1986), 5, 10, 11.

60. William Millikan, "Maintaining 'Law and Order': The Minneapolis Citizen's Alliance in the 1920s," *Minnesota History* 51 (1989): 219–33, at 233.

61. Jay S. Berman, *Police Administration and Progressive Reform: Theodore Roosevelt as Police Commissioner of New York* (Westport, 1987), 23–29.

62. Lawrence W. Sherman, *Scandal and Reform: Controlling Police Corruption* (Berkeley, 1978), xxiii.

63. Joel Best, "Keeping the Peace in St. Paul: Crime, Vice, and Police Work, 1869–1874," *Minnesota History* 47 (1981): 240–48; Clare McKanna, "Hold Back the Tide: Vice Control in San Diego," *Pacific History* 28 (1984): 54–64; Mark H. Haller, "Illegal Enterprise: A Theoretical and Historical Interpretation," *Criminology* 28 (1990): 207–35.

64. Stephen G. Sylvester, "Avenues for Ladies Only: The Soiled Doves of East Grand Forks, 1887–1915," *Minnesota History* 51 (1989): 291–312.

65. David R. Johnson, *American Law Enforcement: A History* (St. Louis, 1982), 70.

66. Watts, "Continuity and Change."

67. Julia Liss and Steven Schlossman, "The Contours of Crime Control in August Vollmer's Berkeley," *Research in Law, Deviance and Social Control* 6 (1984): 81.

68. Erik H. Monkkonen, "Regional Dimensions of Tramping," in *Walking to Work: Tramps in America, 1790–1935,* ed. Monkkonen (Lincoln, 1984), 189–211.

69. Samuel Walker, "The Origins of the American Police-Community Relations Movement: The 1940s," *Criminal Justice History: An International Annual* 1 (1980): 231.

70. Ibid., 236–38, 242.

71. Hubert Williams and Patrick V. Murphy, "The Evolving Strategy of Police: A Minority View," *Perspectives on Policing* 13 (1990).

72. George L. Kelling and James K. Stewart, "The Evolution of Contemporary Policing," in *Local Government Police Management,* ed. William A. Geller (Washington D.C., 1991).

73. Wilbur R. Miller, "Police and the State: A Comparative Perspective," *American Bar Foundation Research Journal* 2 (1986): 339–48.

74. Athan G. Theoharis, *Spying on Americans: Political Surveillance from Hoover to the Huston Plan* (Philadelphia, 1978); idem, "The Presidency and the Federal Bureau of Investigation: The Conflict of Intelligence and Legality," *Criminal Justice History* 2 (1981): 131–60.

75. Ernest K. Alix, *Ransom Kidnapping in America, 1874–1974: The Creation of a Capital Crime* (Carbondale, 1978).

76. Wilbur R. Miller, "The Revenue: Federal Law Enforcement in the Mountain South, 1870–1900," *Journal of Southern History* 55 (1989): 195–216.

77. Ibid., 201, 206–8, 212.

78. Ibid., 196.

79. Barry Mackintosh, *United States Park Police: A History* (Washington D.C., 1985); n.a., *A Statutory History of the United States Capital Police Force, Ninety-ninth Congress, First Session* (Washington D.C., 1985).

80. David R. Johnson, "Crime and Power: Counterfeiters, the Secret Service, and the Nation State, 1865–1900" (unpublished work in progress, 1989), 1, 7.

81. Stuart H. Traub, "Rewards, Bounty Hunting and Criminal Justice in the West: 1865–1900," *Western Historical Quarterly* 19 (1988): 299.

82. For the best description of local violence in the west, see Roger McGrath's study of mining towns, *Gunfighters, Highwaymen, and Vigilantes: Violence on the California Frontier* (Berkeley, 1984).

83. Rhodri Jeffreys-Jones, *Violence and Reform in American History* (New York, 1978).

84. Erik H. Monkkonen, "The Organized Response to Crime in the Nineteenth and Early Twentieth Centuries," *Journal of Interdisciplinary History* 14 (1983): 113–28.

85. Paul Peterson, *City Limits* (Chicago, 1981).

86. Clive Emsley, *Policing and Its Context, 1750–1870* (London, 1983).

87. *IAHCCJ Newsletter,* 1979, 1: 4.

88. Erik H. Monkkonen, "The History of Crime and Criminal Justice after Twenty-five Years," *Criminal Justice History* 5 (1984): 161–65.

89. Christopher Waldrep, " 'So Much Sin': The Decline of Religious Discipline and the 'Tidal Wave of Crime,' " *Journal of Social History* 23 (1990): 535–52.

90. Jonathan Garlock, "The Knights of Labor Courts: A Case Study of Popular Justice," in *The Politics of Informal Justice,* ed. Richard Abel (New York, 1982), 29.

91. Larry D. Ball, "Military Posses: The Territorial Militia in Civil Law Enforcement in New Mexico Territory, 1877–1883," *New Mexico History Review* 55 (1980): 47–69; Phillip J. Ethington, "Vigilantes and the Police: The Creation of a Professional Police Bureaucracy, 1847–1900," *Journal of Social History* 21 (1987): 197–227; Craig B. Little and Christopher Sheffield, "Frontiers and Criminal Justice: English Prosecution Societies and American Vigilantism in the Eighteenth and Nineteenth Centuries," *American Sociological Review* 48 (1983): 796–808; Roger McGrath, *Gunfighters, Highwaymen, and Vigilantes.*

92. *David McDowell and Colin Loftin, "Conflict, Crime and Budgetary Constraint: Police Strength in Detroit, 1927–1976," in The Politics of Urban Fiscal Policy,* ed. Terrence McDonald and Sally Ward (Beverly Hills, 1984), 101–24.

93. Schneider, *Detroit and the Problem of Order.*

94. Roger Lane, *Violent Death in the City: Suicide, Homicide, and Accidental Death in Philadelphia* (Cambridge, Mass., 1979).

95. Dennis C. Rousey, "Cops and Guns: Police Use of Deadly Force in Nineteenth-Century New Orleans," *American Journal of Legal History* 28 (1984): 57.

96. Dennis C. Rousey, "Out of the Orbit of Mars: Demilitarizing the New Orleans Police, 1805–1836" (unpublished manuscript).

10

Bandits, Real and Imagined: An Introduction to the Theme in Mexican History

Paul Vanderwood

Bandit heroes flourish in many cultures because they symbolize a virtually universal belief: that at times it is necessary to break the law in order to obtain justice.[1] These heroes (and occasionally villains) have come down to us through the ages in ballads, folklore, and the popular imagination; then literature; and more recently in comic books, on radio and television, and through academic scholarship. Bandits, crafted and reworked by their admirers and critics making judgments sculpted by the context of their own particular times, have been used by people to measure the fairness of kings, ponder the boundaries of freedom, weigh the law, and protest abuses by the powerful and redistribute their wealth. Robin Hood probably never lived except as an ideal, but few doubt his capacity to excite emotions and provoke passions. If people persistently regenerate their Robin Hoods, the image, despite its variants, generally must speak to unfulfilled yearnings—perhaps for social justice or for getting something for nothing. Bandits may not incite revolutions (although they often join them); but their exploits, as fashioned and embellished by public perception, reflect the desires and fears, even obsessions, of the populace at large as well as its myths and fantasies (i.e., culture). They also may be reminders of societal bills long overdue.

People of all ethnicities and social groups seem to have their cherished bandit heroes and villains, and some of them cut across national and cultural boundaries. A good many of these bandits may have actually lived and others have been invented, but it makes no difference, for all are designed and periodically reshaped to fit the needs and imagination of the users. Most of these images are imbued with so much ambiguity and so many contradictions (which makes them that much more human) that they can be interpreted to symbolize almost anything. There is nothing strange about such looseness. Claude Levi-Strauss tells us that all such myths by their very nature are nebulous and open ended,[2] a point confirmed by Victor Turner, who says that myths have "many meanings and each is capable of moving people at many psycho-biological levels simultaneously."[3] In short, we may manipulate our bandits to fulfil any of our fantasies, and in doing so we make them our heroes, although certainly not our only ones. Joseph Campbell insists that we come by such heroes naturally, although there is considerable controversy over why this is so.[4]

Mexico's late nineteenth century produced its share of bandit heroes. They were real and are etched in public memory through folklore, ballads (*corridos*), literature, and occasionally gossip (*chismes*). Meet Jesus Arriaga, alias Chucho el Roto, who kidnapped priests and demanded ransom from the bishop, or picked the pockets of parishioners attending mass: in the popular memory, perhaps a comment on the official Church and its followers? A journalist called Chucho a "civilized bandit" and nominated him for the federal congress, where he would be right at home wallowing in the trough of the national treasury: a comment on the corrupt congress? When Chucho died in prison, the public demanded an investigation. The government insisted that he had died of dysentery, but many people, including some lawyers, did not trust the explanation.

Next we encounter the heralded Thunderbolt of Sinaloa, Heraclio Bernal. When his main antagonist, the state governor, arranged a banquet for a visiting dignitary, Bernal did the same for friends in a nearby rural village, but he provided an even more sumptuous feast and celebration. On another occasion, he invited the governor to a dance arranged for his compadres. Naturally, in his stead the governor sent troops, but by the time they arrived, Bernal was long gone. Mexicans of all social entities enjoyed the cavorting of the Thunderbolt; no doubt his jousting with the governor was exaggerated and perhaps even invented, but nonetheless "real." For a ransom, a companion eventually betrayed Bernal to the military, which shot him dead; but the Thunderbolt lives on in some thirty-odd *corridos* and as the star of several movies and of television programs.

Just down the historical path we encounter the bold and haughty Santana Rodriguez Palafox, nicknamed Santanón. His targets were the owners of sugar mills in southern Veracruz, and he may have had some radical politics on his mind, so the government particularly labored to apprehend him. But after a couple of years this mission had failed, so Santanón grew into a centaur protected by the shadows of the night, a mirage that no one had ever really seen. Moreover, he was amphibious, which explained how he raided cargo ships on the local rivers.[5] Finally, we encounter one of my favorites, *La Carambada,* a woman dressed in male clothing. After robbing a victim, *Carambada* waived her pistol in one hand and bore a bare breast with the other: "Look who has robbed you," she crowed in a devastating blow to Mexican machismo.[6] Here we have bandits who like most brigands, plied the tensions between legitimate authority and conceptions of justice, between fantasy and reality. Let us explore how they played out such dynamic roles in society and continue to do so today.

BANDITS AS REAL

Of course, brigands really lived, and not always at the margins of society. Over the last several decades, scholars have been especially aggressive in their search for the contours and rhythms of banditry in a variety of cultures, time periods, and geographical settings. In the late 1960s, the distinguished British economic and social historian, Eric Hobsbawn, who in large part based his conclusions on ballads and legends, threw down the gauntlet before academia with his concept of ''social banditry'' as mediated by his Marxist bent. For him, these social bandits were the disoriented products of modernizing impulses, which disrupted traditional peasant lifestyles mainly in the last century. Protected in their activities by their local communities, Hobsbawn found these bandits both prepolitical and ineffective motors of social change.[7] However, he celebrated them, and so did many of his readers. Hobsbawn's work was initially published in the late 1960s, a time of protest by students and others; people appreciated and apparently identified with the concept of social banditry, which legitimated crime in the name of justice. The cinematic resurrection of *Bonnie and Clyde,* who robbed banks in the 1930s ''because [according to the movie] they are there,'' seemed to resonate with student activists who were stoning and bombing the Bank of America in California. Social banditry was ''in'' then, and it still is to some degree. But academics have been picking away at its foundations.

Today, Hobsbawm's portrait of the social bandit stands severely defaced, if not defamed. It is not that such social types have never existed, or are not now among us, but, if so, researchers have found them exceedingly hard to come by. There has been no shortage of brigands, but historians plying the archives have found most of them to be pragmatic, opportunistic, aspiring self-promoters who robbed their fellow peasants along with people of better means. Moreover, bandits (through research) have developed into wily sorts of beings who established linkages with the powerful as well as with their village kin. At times, bandits had strong political convictions and ambitions and aimed more to enter society than to change it. Few Robin Hoods were to be found among the bandits, although a number (to ensure their welcome) had the good sense to sprinkle some of their booty among the local folk. Linda Lewin, in her study of a late nineteenth-century Brazilian bandit, Silvino, argues that the brigand's occasional distribution of stolen money, merchandise, and foodstuffs among the needy spectators of his sorties ''made good sense as well as bandit justice, for brigands who alienated the common people could be finished off by them.''[8] And they often were. Furthermore, in her study of crime and conflict in fourteenth-century England, two centuries or so after the supposed escapades of Robin Hood, Barbara Hanawalt assures that bandits robbed from the better off and poor alike, although they naturally preferred the rich, who had something worth the risk of stealing: "Bandits, like peasants, picked their victims from their own group or the next highest above them . . . the poor."[9] Hanawalt assumes that the social consciousness of the brigands she encountered was no more finely honed than that of the bulk of the peasantry. There was no particular reason why they should rob the rich to pay the poor.[10]

Nor in their adventures could bandits necessarily rely on peasant cooperation. Bandit chiefs, for example, constantly faced possible defection and, worse yet, betrayal by their followers, especially when the opposition offered substantial rewards for the head of the gang leader. Examples abound, including Santanón and Heraclio Bernal for nineteenth-century Mexico and Jesse James in the United States. When the mother of James identified the body of her assassinated son, she turned on one of the betrayers who had belonged to the gang: "Traitor! Traitor! Traitor! God will send vengeance on you for this. . . . Oh you villain; I would rather be in my boy's place than in yours."[11] Whatever their social attributes, bandits rarely died at a respectable old age in their own bed in their home town.

Who were these bandits? And what were their backgrounds? Can a social profile of bandits be drawn (here we are speaking of brigands in their heyday, mainly during the past century with some chronological spillover on either end)? New scholarship is providing some promising leads. The setting for our purposes is principally rural Mexico, but in comparison with other countries and cultures. Stereotypes (some in scholarly works) picture bandits as young, rootless males, unmarried but not devoid of family connections. No doubt, a good many teenagers joined bandit gangs. In China, the victims of brigands particularly noted the youth of their captors, mostly boys in their teens but also even younger lads among them.[12] But empirical research has begun to age the bandit and make him more mature and stable. For example, Eric Van Young surveyed rebel/criminal activities (the state routinely labels insurgents as bandits) in central Mexico about the start of the nineteenth century and found that while a good third fell into a young adult category, with ages of fifteen to twenty-four, nearly two-thirds should be considered mature adults between the ages of twenty-five and fifty. This is especially noteworthy at a time when life expectancy ran from only thirty-six to forty years.[13] William Taylor, working in the same general region about the same period, found most bandits in their late twenties or early thirties, "with experience [defined as with steady work and a family] as adults."[14] Ranajit Guha, studying peasant restlessness and rebellion in India in the 1860s, discovered in trial records that 85.7 percent of convicted bandits were twenty-five to forty years of age.[15] Of course, there are numerous examples of individual, high-profile bandits who flourished into their thirties—Jesse James comes to mind—or even their forties, as did the Thunderbolt of Sinaloa, Heraclio Bernal. Furthermore, both Van Young and Taylor found nearly 60 percent of their sample married, and Van Young concludes that most were family men.[16]

Nor do bandits seem to have been as rootless, parasitical, or underachieving as imagined. When one speaks of "rootless" in the context we are examining, it normally equates with "landless." In fact, Phil Billingsley states that landlessness characterized China's brigands.[17] But Taylor listed the daily work of more than 50 percent of his sample as *labradores,* and Van Young listed nearly 30 percent as such. While *labrador* ordinarily denotes simply "peasant farmer," the term did not exclude landowners or peasants with access to land through rentals, sharecropping, and other tenancy arrangements.[18] Carlos Aguirre confirms the pattern in Peru for the same period; 45 percent of his sample gave *chacarero/labrador* as their work.[19] Of course, before they turned to banditry, individuals held a variety of rural occupations: cowhands, woodcutters, sugar cane and hay cutters, charcoal makers, daily wage laborers, and the rest; but linked with *labrador,* occupational status indicates that a good many of those who became brigands did not necessarily run with any floating population visible at the time. In fact, large percentages of brigands came from the ranks of skilled laborers and craftsmen—carpenters, smithies, wheelwrights, shoemakers, bakers—an endless line of diversity, a good deal of which smacks of lower class urban work. Taylor found 41 percent in urban jobs, and Aguirre found nearly 30 percent in such. Van Young categorized 30 percent of his sample as skilled workers and craftsmen and another 10 percent as small merchants and muleteers.[20] Taylor even uncovered a doctor and a lawyer among his highwaymen. Later in the century, especially in countries beset by civil war and foreign invasion (such as Mexico and China), ex-soldiers—deserters, the defeated, and discharged—bloated bandit gangs, but early on former soldiers comprised only a small percentage of those who became brigands. So at least for this earlier period, we can agree with Van Young that bandits seem to have been not only mature chronologically but economically and socially as well; that bandits were "likely to be established family men with land and access to a steady means of livelihood."[21]

So why did bandits shed such apparent security? Of course, endless combinations of motivations pushed and attracted people into banditry. Billingsley quotes one Chinese bandit to the effect that " 'no one gets into this life for the fun of it,' "[22] but these seem like the words of a bandit down on his luck with little prospect of profit. Banditry, like all such endeavors, rarely lived up to its expectations. For Billingsley, the common denominator of banditry was poverty, a proposition echoed by Guha, who blames hunger and British colonial injustice for "turning mature adults into criminals and then cutting them off from their families."[23]

No doubt natural disasters, dearth, injustice, war, and all sorts of pressures on traditional community life propelled people into banditry, but pushes need to be pondered along with the pull of opportunity, ambition, blood feuds, feelings of manliness and adventure, boredom at home, escape from unhappy personal entanglements, and luck, both good and bad depending on how the individual viewed his circumstances. Because wives in Chinese peasant families typically tended to be independently minded and frequently hypercritical of their husbands, men sought "relief" in banditry;[24] and in an entirely different cultural setting, Ethiopian nobles struggled for power and higher office through banditry.[25] In Mexico, a captured brigand told authorities he had opted for banditry *sacarse de pobre* (to get out of poverty), and another *Vamos a ver lo que Dios nos da* (just to see what God would grant him).[26] Argentina's famous gauchos turned to brigandage to protect what they saw as their traditional rights to kill, sell, and otherwise utilize loose cattle roaming the Pampa.[27] Some contend that banditry resulted from a centralizing state's intrusions on local rights and practices; it represented a defense of local autonomy. Others see bandits as ambitious opportunists in search of a profitable niche in a changing society. Some bandits were driven by personal consideration, others by necessity or tradition. Whatever the motivation, in many cases it was powerful enough to jar or entice bandits from accustomed security.

In response to such a bewildering diversity of motives which might have inclined individuals and groups toward banditry, academics have constructed hypotheses to tame the bothersome contradictions, disparities, and inconsistencies normal to human thought and activities. At the turn of this century, Julio Guerrero found the criminal predilections of Mexicans embedded in their morals and character; while for Peru, Enrique López Albújar loosely linked banditry to climate, geography (coastal/mountain), land tenure, and labor relationships. More recently, Eric Mayer relates banditry in the Andes to seasonal ecology, while Benjamin Orlove discusses how geography shaped traditional cattle rustling in the same general region. Billingsley believes that banditry developed in areas where the soil was not productive enough to sustain a local population; while for Mexico, Alan Knight proposes that banditry flourished in regions dominated by haciendas as opposed to those areas in which villages retained a good deal of their autonomy from the centralizing designs of the state.[28]

This overview of theoretical propositions represents but a small and incomplete sampling of the impressive variety being put to empirical tests; the results and remains provide lively debate at professional conferences. However, these theses seem more correct than true. They attempt to force a symmetry on something that is characteristically amorphous, and they tend to rob banditry of its humanness, to dedicate a profoundly human activity to quantification and professional approval. Bandits, beyond personal and material motivation, are making a statement, and a bold one at that, about power which transcends artificial models and for some becomes a kind of religious expression. They do so at great risk to themselves, which only emphasizes their determination to be heard. Furthermore, bandits jailed in any scholarly paradigm sooner or later are bound to escape it as academic fashions change.

Gilbert Joseph, himself a discerning observer of Yucatecan society, has urged us to get on with our bandit business by broadening our perspectives to treat banditry as part of much larger historical processes, such as wars, state building, and peasant protest—those broad sea changes in history which disrupt the way things are and, in doing so, challenge the mind and move the feet.[29] Even before Joseph's recent well-taken advice, some academic explorers had begun to probe the influences of broad socioeconomic change on those power relationships which seemed to sustain banditry. However, the precise nature of those relationships is in dispute. Hobsbawm ties social banditry to local community support for protection and intelligence and to village issues. Alan Knight calls this the "defining" leitmotif of social banditry.[30] Many others, however, more or less agree with Billingsley that villagers supported brigands not only out of admiration but out of fear and necessity and perhaps even self-gain.

The feelings of locals toward bandits were, in fact, ambivalent, "reflecting a need for protection in a violent world and the knowledge that at any time their protectors could become aggressors."[31] Unable or unwilling to do their own farming, bandits approached peasants for their staples and often took them by force. On the other hand, peasants might willingly receive bandits because the brigands paid them out of their plunder for any support.[32] Nonetheless, bandits rarely let the villagers forget who was in charge, so the relationship between them was one of power, with the bandits holding the guns and the better reasons to use them: "Local people regarded them [brigands] as rulers, to whom a debt of gratitude might be owed for the relative protection they did bring, but who still demanded tribute and other ritual obeisances in return and took harsh revenge on those not forthcoming."[33] In sum, the respect that villagers showed to bandits was often built on fear, even terror.

Bandits much preferred to ally themselves to influential power groups, which had the wherewithal to hire their services, genuinely shield and protect their activities, and purchase their booty. These were people of means less tempted to turn bandits in for ransom, at least as long as the brigands continued to serve their pretensions and ambitions. It must be remembered that bandits, once committed to the game, do not have many exits. Death is one of them, the most common but least preferred. To return to one's village means a return to those circumstances which probably made banditry an option in the first place, a condition now worsened by the threat of reprisal. It made much more sense for brigands to chance their luck and fate to those who could best guarantee them what they seemed most to have wanted: material gain with a chance of social mobility, both cloaked with as much personal security as possible. Linda Lewin carefully describes how new economic and political forces from the "outside" broke down long-held patron/client relationships in Brazil's northwest and led to the emergence of individuals like the "good" bandit, Antonio Silvino, who made his compact with a new breed of power broker.[34]

Brigands may not only change their minds about preferred patrons but also their goals and style. In his detailed survey of the Mexican Revolution, Knight notes that bandits seemed to have switched roles during the course of the decade of fighting. Bandits who began as "social" (à la Hobsbawm)—that is, with genuine popular support and representative of peasant grievances—turned to terrorists, hostile to village interests, as represented by José Iñez Chávez García, a marauding cutthroat if there ever was one. Chávez did not lead a band; he led an army which pillaged drought-ridden parts of central Mexico in 1915 after all semblance of central government had collapsed and the movements of leaders like Pancho Villa and Emiliano Zapata been contained or scattered. The difference that Knight perceives in the motives and goals of bandits led him to categorize bandits as ''social'' or ''popular'' as opposed to ''professional.'' The former seem to have justice and grievances on their minds and peasant support to back them up, while the latter focus on the prospect of material gain. In Knight's opinion, the former can at times degenerate into the latter, and ''even the most hardened professionals by continuing bandit activities acquired 'social' characteristics,'' meaning political import.[35] So along with most others examining the nature and peculiarities of banditry, Knight keeps his options fluid.

Different time periods and geographical locations can lead to different sorts of banditry, or perhaps we are noticing the great varieties of banditry that may occur within any historical circumstances. Linda Lewin sees Silvino as a ''transitional'' bandit, preceded in the 1870s by a more ''social'' bandit (exemplified by Jesuino Brilhante) and succeeded by the politically charged and nationally oriented gang of Lampiao in the 1920s and 1930s. What had changed over this period in Brazil's northwest was the relationship of the *cangaco* (the bandit phenomenon related to the Northeast) and the nation's political structure.[36] For China, turbulence earlier in the twentieth century allowed banditry to break its localistic ties and move on to the national platform, where the brigands formerly linked to local power brokers now allied themselves to ambitious politicians and then patrons, the war lords.[37] Much the same process can be observed in nineteenth-century Mexico. Bandits emerging from the turmoil of Independence and the succeeding political instability served as retainers for power rural lords (*caudillos*) who aimed to keep the central government at bay. During the midcentury wars—Liberals versus Conservatives, Republicans versus Imperialists—bandits served all contenders for pay and later made their demands on the victors. Toward the end of the century, when provincial elites calculated that their future lay more with the federal government than against it, bandits lost their patrons. In fact, their former protectors turned against them and helped hunt them down. But bandits did not disappear. Instead they became isolated and forlorn figures like Chucho el Roto, Heraclio Bernal, and Santanón: pesky and widely appreciated for their pluck, but hardly a threat to the new consolidating regime, except as some might shape them into symbols of protest and resistance.[38]

Bandits may well have become more political over the nineteenth century and on toward present times. That is, they became much more attuned to how politics are played up to the national level, and their activities gained a strong political bent. Charles Walker noticed this new awareness among Peruvian brigands who marauded in the post-Independence period,[39] and Billingsley noted the same for China, in the ways that brigands involved themselves with the Japanese earlier in this century.[40] Mexican bandits supported the government as rural policemen; and in Brazil, Silvino's band collected political ''contributions'' and distributed campaign literature for its favorite gubernatorial candidate.[41] By the 1950s in Colombia, bandits endorsed the political platforms of political parties.[42] All of these tendencies place brigands just one short step from public office itself. Pancho Villa may be a case in point. History could undoubtedly provide examples of ex-bandits who made it to high office; at least plenty have found security in lower echelons of government.

Civil strife, which encourages political and social realignments, naturally breeds banditry. First, it forces the contenders to assemble and build up armies, and bandits have proven to be ready recruits. Booty is the business of bandits, and frequently the right to pillage was the only payment that political contenders could offer their adherents. As power changed hands during the turmoil, entire military units could be declared deserters, and then bandits, as happened in Roman times: ''Soldiers, therefore, offer an excellent illustration of the creation of bandits by the shifting frontiers of the definition of authority within the state itself.''[43] But bandits, if they chose to do so, resolved the matter simply by swearing in with their former foes. Second, once the dispute was more or less settled, the victors needed armed police to enforce the peace in their behalf. Bandits turned police helped fulfil the necessity, and it was good employment for them because it allowed them to work both sides of the law. Powerful losers in national disputes also had need for retainers to fend off their enemies. For Mexico, the high tide of banditry occured at midcentury during the Wars of the Reform and the succeeding French Intervention. Gangs of brigands made their demands on contending adversaries: Pay us, and pay us well, or we will fight for the other side. Regardless of the response, the brigands changed sides at will. Benito Juárez, the president of the beleaguered Mexican Republic during the French Intervention, had to apologize to foreign friends for his need to employ bandits in defense of the nation.[44] Billingsley describes well the same sort of context for China, as part of the convulsion created as the country moved from its imperial past toward political modernity: war lords fighting it out and recruiting bandits to do much of the work. Then in the 1930s came the Japanese invasion, and some of China's greatest bandit leaders took their support to the Japanese, because doing so enabled the bandits to go where they had always wanted to be: inside the political power structure.[45] Bandits also jockeyed for such positions during Mexico's Independence movement and then a century later in the Mexican Revolution.

The propensity of bandits to join or in some way become involved in rebellions of various stripes is one of the more fascinating aspects of their activities, although there is a continuing dispute over their aims and motivations. Rosalie Schwartz found the well-known bandit gang of Manuel García actively participating in the planning, financing, and armed struggle of Cuba's late nineteenth-century break with Spain. Indeed, almost everywhere bandits are well represented in this century's decolonization wars. These kinds of involvements have led scholars to designate brigands as ''patriot-bandits,'' ''guerrilla-bandits,'' and ''political-bandits.'' The ambiguity in such labeling indicates that bandits can, and often do, play dual roles and can switch back from one to the other with relative ease. The Cuban García is an especially interesting example of such a Latin American bandit. During the 1880s, after an initial armed insurrection for independence had been frustrated, García worked with a support system of kin, long-time companions, local officials, well-to-do entrepreneurs, and ranking politicians and managed to prosper in the Province of Habana, the site of the island's capital and major urban center. He kidnapped and held for ransom wealthy entrepreneurs and sent the proceeds to the defeated independence conspirators, who were licking their wounds in Florida. García's forays kept Spanish authorities off guard and concerned about domestic security, while the politicians regrouped and planned a new offensive. Then in 1895 he became part of the new military movement itself, which culminated in independence. In fact, García became a martyr to the cause, though largely unappreciated both today and at the time; he was assassinated, as are so many bandit leaders, when a member of his own band betrayed him.[46]

Christon Archer coined the term *guerrilla-bandits* to describe the activities of two families, the Villagráns and the Anayas, who, in order to "improve their fortunes," joined the Mexican Independence insurgency near their hometown of Huichapan in the state of Mexico. Says Archer, "They embarked upon careers of violence designed to redistribute the wealth and power of the existing elites mostly among themselves."[47] Employing guerrilla tactics, they raided in the name of patriotism and soon had the Spanish royal army on their necks. Even the insurgent leadership disavowed the Villagráns for their terrorist tactics. However, the bandits enjoyed considerable popular support around their home base at Huichapan and until well into 1813 continued to bedevil royalist pacification schemes. Even though the Spaniards finally managed to pluck the Villagrán and Anaya thorns from their flanks, they could not quell other guerrilla-bandits, who kept the independence stew stirred.[48]

Scholars such as the political scientist James Scott and the historian Ranajit Guha see banditry as part of the ongoing peasant struggle against their potent and relentless exploiters. In this sense, brigands have been injected into the class war. Scott is most interested in everyday forms of peasant resistance, those weapons employed by the weak in their daily lives to resist oppression—things like foot dragging, behind-the-back slurs, gossip, grumbling, and excuses to avoid compliance. He contends that peasants developed a whole agenda, much of it hidden from official surveillance, toward this end. This was the way in which common people ordinarily negotiated with elites, but occasionally and unpredictably under certain circumstances (e.g., when the negotiation process breaks down or becomes overloaded in favor of the power brokers), peasant frustrations may boil over into rebellions, millenarian movements, jacqueries, and banditry. Constant struggle is at the heart of Scott's thesis, in which even accommodation becomes a peasant strategy for survival. Banditry was simply one way in which common people stated their case.[49]

The historian of India under the Raj, Ranajit Guha, even more explicitly views banditry as social protest and sees it as a kind of stepping stone, a liminal or liberating in-between stage in a developing peasant consciousness. Banditry reflects social perceptions and can prod participants toward full-scale rebellion against the master. Banditry becomes a preliminary to revolution. Guha asks, "Why do 'foolish and ignorant villagers' who are usually so peaceful and adverse to crime and often preyed upon at other times by clubmen, dacoits [bandits] and 'bad Characters of the Country' join the latter on such occasions [peasant revolts]?" He replies, "Because a powerful and sustained class struggle . . . [as evidenced by sporatic outbursts of peasant unrest] tends to invest the disparate [bandit] attacks on property and person with new meanings and rephrase them as a part of a general discourse of rebellion."[50]

Through both Guha and Scott, we have class struggle undergirding banditry. We have leaped into the subtleties and vagaries of intent and consciousness from which there may be no satisfactory exit, not the least because peasants themselves may well be unable to distinguish or articulate the difference between activities they undertake simply to sustain and advance themselves in their everyday lives as opposed to resistance or protest. Or are such elements intertwined? Many scholars who have researched banditry doubt that it represented class conflict. In Cuba, Rosalie Schwartz found little evidence of class consciousness and conflict.[51] Nor did Linda Lewin among the *congacero* in Brazil.[52]

The social and political alliances forged by bandits, so necessary to their success and survival, seem to have been more vertical, cross-cutting classes, than horizontal. Billingsley states, "Banditry in practice was an adaptation to, not a protest against, the local power structure."[53] Political scientist Peter Singleman argues that in Brazil, banditry "was essentially not a reaction against, but an adaptation to, the politics and society of the interior Northeast."[54] As for the "good" thief Silvino, Lewin concludes,

> Depending on whether local family power was collectively shared, evenly divided between two warring factions, or extremely concentrated in one powerful *coronel,* Silvino accommodated himself accordingly. He either served specific family political interests for reciprocal favors or remuneration, advantageously exploited two factions against each other, or wisely submitted himself to superior authority and bought his own protection.[55]

Ethiopians may have considered the *shifta* to be their heroes, but bandits there "did not exert class vengeance, nor did they redistribute wealth. They usually robbed for their own gain."[56] In China they attacked the rich "not because of class hatred but because only they [the wealthy] possessed the resources worth stealing."[57] Taylor, Archer, and myself found similar evidence for Mexico. George Rudé, who examined crime in three British counties during the first half of the nineteenth century, reminds us that even if it was true that criminals and victims tended to belong to different, if not opposing classes, they were not engaged in class war.[58] Billingsley concludes that it seems unlikely that Chinese bandits "would ever become coordinators of peasant wrath, or even an independent vanguard of peasant resentment against their oppressor. In troubled times, bandits turned to those very oppressors, not to peasants, to sustain their existence."[59] In essence, banditry seems to have detracted from any potential coherence in peasant protest and reinforced in rural society the accustomed framework of power relationships and social inequalities, as obvious and unjust as they were.

Nor do bandits seem to be truly revolutionary. We have already indicated that they appear more anxious to join than to change the system which has excluded them. Basically, what they want is a share of the proceeds of that system. Billingsley states that "revolutionaries begin from an awareness of the need for an alternative, better society; bandits saw the better prospects in the world they knew."[60] The Chinese communists managed to integrate bandits into their ranks not by appeals to their patriotism or social consciousness but by portraying themselves as representatives of a new order which promised more return than even that of the Japanese. In this way, the communists " 'harnessed the bandits' essentially reactionary and self-aggrandizing traits to a forward looking policy of social change."[61] Of course, and in a healthy way, not all scholars agree. Louis Pérez finds Cuban banditry earlier in the century integral to peasant protest, which later nourished Castro's movement. To stretch our historical perspective in the other chronological direction, Horsley and Hanson stress that genuine social banditry played a crucial, if not pivotal, role in the struggle of the Jews against the Romans about the time of Jesus.[62]

Regardless of its nature, class oriented or otherwise, revolutionary or not, did banditry leave a socially significant residue on the social landscape or in the peasant mind? Again, there is a difference of opinion. For Scott and Hobsbawm, banditry made no difference and left no mark. To borrow Hobsbawm's concept, bandits were "primitive" rebels doomed by their disorganization and lack of political sophistication to failure. Others, like Guha, believe that bandits contributed to peasant political awareness; but Billingsley thinks the opposite, that bandits through their aggressive activities only undermined "the sense of futility which most peasants shared."[63] These differences are argued elsewhere with much sophistication and passion, and proof is hard to come by; however, I have been impressed by the manner in which the idea of banditry—much more so than the reality—seems to rattle regimes and excite expectations for change among subjects, a theme to which we now turn.

BANDITS AS IMAGINED

Bandits are not only real; they are also imagined—both by the official state, which normally seeks to repress them (although we have seen examples of authorities who encourage and cooperate with brigands as well as coopt them into government service), and by the public at large, which reshapes bandits to suit its liking and then proclaims them its heroes. The propensity of dominant groups to label its enemies bandits is well known. Terence Ranger informs us that the tactic is still widely used in Southern Africa, in places like Angola, Zimbabwe, and Mozambique. In fact, 1984 was "Crush the Bandits Year" in Mozambique.[64] Sociologist Howard S. Becker, a prominent labeling theorist, notes that "a major element in every aspect of the drama of deviance is the imposition of definitions . . . by those powerful enough or sufficiently legitimated to be able to do so."[65]

Banditry as a label is especially useful to authorities because it can be stretched so far: from common criminal, to rebellious upstart, and on to dedicated revolutionary. While in the written law of some countries the term may obtain some specificity, in practice it is ordinarily used by the state to sap the activities of its enemies of political intent or simply to bring the legitimacy of those activities into doubt.[66] That is, regimes seek to discredit acts which obviously are or could be conceived as being protest against the policies and politics of those in command, or, even more importantly, to defuse visions of radical social change which bandits may inspire. Rosalie Schwartz writes that during Cuba's independence movement, Spanish authorities "blew sand across the bandit trail, lumping politically motivated lawbreakers together with the myriad robbers, petty thieves, cutpurses and assassins . . . , although government agents knew that members of some robber gangs met with [political] separatists and contributed the proceeds of their extortions and kidnappings to rebel officers [seeking independence]."[67]

According to Brian Hamnett, Spanish propagandists employed similar tactics during Mexico's wars for independence: The officials "deprived them [the rebels] of a political existence and reduced them to the level of common criminals."[68] Alan Knight reports the same for the Mexican Revolution, and Hobsbawm states that "for the law, anyone belonging to a group of men who attack and rob with violence is a bandit, from those who snatch pay-rolls at an urban street corner to organized insurgents or guerrillas who happen not to be officially recognized as such."[69] Billingsley concludes for China that

> to the framers of the law, the police, and all those with a modicum of power, this image [created by the label "bandit"] provided the ideal means of drawing attention away from any genuine peasant grievances [that] bandits might represent, and of defaming or belittling political adversaries. The word "banditry" could be used to subsume the whole range of stealing, from a chicken to a kingdom, from petty thieving to political rebellion—and the effort was to tar all those to whom the term was used.[70]

So in the hands of the state the word *bandit* can be, and usually is, used instinctively to blanket a threat to its interests by declaring bandits outside the law and outside the bounds of accepted society as understood by "the nation," "the people," or "all of us." Elsewhere, in earlier times, bandits were portrayed as enemies of a divinely appointed social order, who mocked the Lord God by attacking peaceful citizens and churches. They were deemed to be outside the realm of God Himself.[71] That is what the word *bandit* means: to banish, to force the accused outside the boundaries of acknowledged society—not to the margins, but out.

Bandit did not always mean "outside." Brent D. Shaw, who studied banditry in Roman history and researched the etymology of the word, notes that the principal Latin word for bandit was *Latro,* and for banditry *latrocinium.* The root *latr* stems from a whole family of Greek words used from the seventh to the fourth centuries B.C., words which do not seem to have had any connection with banditry at all, insofar as we use and understand the term today. For example, *Latreia* carries the connotation of working for someone for compensation. By the fifth or perhaps the sixth century B.C., *lesti* and *lestes* seem to have referred to brigandage; but, according to Shaw, not as crime but more as a way of making a living, of acquiring material possessions, which, as we have seen, is the way numerous bandits seem to envision themselves.[72] Whatever the precise meaning and its daily usage, the word for *bandit* in those earlier epochs does not seem to have meant "outsider." By the time of Christ, Hyam Mccoby asserts that *lestai* could be interpreted as "rebel" as well as "bandit," so it appears that either two rebels died with their political leader on Calvary or that two bandits flanked a religious zealot at the execution site.[73]

The term *bandit* is extremely slippery, even puzzling: Scholars continue to interpret it; governments and their agents use it at whim to disparage their antagonists; it connotes different ideologies at different levels of society; its meaning changes over time. David Moss in the case of Sardinia agrees with the difficulty of assessing any useful meaning of the term; he asks whether it is a particular offense defined by law or a group of offenses, some of which appear or disappear from the set? He notes that in the past century, the word *bandit* pertained to an individual, and now *banditry* applies to an entire region of Sardinia, and a sizable territorial unit has been declared bandit infested and removed (for political purposes) from the national polity.[74] Under the circumstances, perhaps we should not attempt to define *banditry* with any preciseness, not so much because of the difficulty of the task but because in practice people of various social stamps do not limit banditry to a process or thing. They consider it more an idea—and therein lies its enormous potency to conjure up images of challenges and change. Hence, at least at that level, its threat to the state becomes clear.

The claim of legitimacy so dear to the state seems pertinent to its reliance on the label "bandit" to debunk its foes. Legitimacy, another elusive term, generally connotes the right to rule. In places like Mexico during the mid-nineteenth century, that right meant republicanism (as interpreted by Liberals of the epoch) or rule of the people, not that the Liberals ever intended that the people should rule or even be heard in any meaningful way. In fact, in places like southern Italy, a long history of banditry conferred a kind of legitimacy on the practice itself.[75] Legitimacy was much more claimed than realized by the Mexican government, but while engaged in consolidating its power (the real basis of domination), the government sought to extirpate its adversaries by labeling them bandits, which meant to exile them from normal society as defined by themselves and to strip the outlaws of their national citizenship.

To deprive bandits of their citizenship, the state enacted laws or invoked those all-purposeful clauses embedded in virtually all "Liberal" constitutions of the period (beginning with the Spanish Liberal Constitution of 1812) which gave executives (presidents and constitutional monarchs) extraordinary authorizations. These authorizations went well beyond constitutional restrictions meant to tether central authority in order to deal with domestic crises, which ranged from public disorder to foreign invasion. National congresses, especially those wary of kings and dictators, did not always grant these special powers without considerable debate. So in Mexico during the 1860s and 1870s, with legitimacy of government still contested in the public mind both through urban newspapers and political conclaves as well as banditry and rebellion in the countryside, the issue was joined.[76]

Simply put, the government and its supporters sought to suspend judicial procedures constitutionally accorded to citizens accused of banditry. Instead of guaranteeing to them the normal protections of the law, they wanted brigands subjected to military tribunals which utilized summary judgment and permitted no appeals, no pardons, and no amnesties. A military council heard the case, and a military commander confirmed its verdict. Those caught in the act of banditry could be executed on the spot. At various times, the promulgation of other suspensions also curtailed travel (one needed a passport or safe conduct pass), limited freedom of the press, and allowed military units in pursuit of duty to occupy private homes and to confiscate private property. The laws were draconian in concept and worse in practice. Attempts to soften the laws so that bandits received only ten years' imprisonment with no chance of pardon failed, and one may only measure the impact of the new procedures by the intensity of the public outcry against them.

Those who favored the suspensions argued that incessant civil war had produced numbers of soldiers and militiamen who deserted or were dispersed in battle and subsequently turned to brigandage. Local judges who heard bandit cases faced the vengeance of the culprit or his kin, as did those who accused people of banditry as well as witnesses who came forth to testify. Banditry affected the prestige of the government, highlighted its weaknesses, damaged public confidence, and paralyzed commerce. It caused a loss of public spirit. For those favoring suspension, legitimacy not only involved the right to govern but the capacity to do so: "We have laws to protect people in tranquil times, but these times are not tranquil, and so we need special laws."[77] They accused their adversaries of putting the cart before the horse: individual liberties ahead of public peace.

The opposition thundered that suspensions permitted authorities to confuse bandits deliberately with political enemies and to eliminate the latter in the name of the former. A deputy noted that nearly 80,000 countrymen had served the republic during the recent domestic wars: "We educated nearly all of them, from age twenty one, in the revolutions of the country. Banditry is the heritage of revolution, and we educated them in the school of revolution. Now we want to choke them off, people who are dying of misery, who have no food. We must not hang those who we needed yesterday and may need tomorrow."[78] Another declared that Mexicans would never learn about the viability of their new constitution (it had been promulgated in 1857 but never really been put into effect due to war) "if at the first disturbance the government asks for extraordinary powers."[79] But the suspensions went into effect anyway, reinforced by the organization of a national constabulary, Mexico's Rural Police Force (the famed *Rurales*), which, as previously noted, incorporated some bandits into its ranks, turning the poachers into police.[80] As a result, the suspensions were so abused and so many political antagonists were executed or imprisoned as bandits that even supporters of the program eventually agreed to curtail its use.

Laws of exception, such as those introduced in Mexico, tell us a good deal about how dominant groups view banditry. First, it threatens them beyond all apparent reason. Governments do not seem to fear individual bandits or even groups of brigands. They are a nuisance, especially as they wreck the image of an orderly state and make their arrangements with potentially powerful groups not yet committed, or in opposition to, the program of the national government. Moreover, bandits do tend to nourish the ideal of social justice beyond the law, although those in power have long understood how to defuse the concept by acknowledging its veracity to a point. Something much more powerful is at work here; it seems to be the very idea of banditry which so threatens the state, which explains why those in power customarily treat it as a serious crime against the state rather than a common misdeed, such as robbery, or even a serious felony, such as rape or murder. In fact, in Mexico bandits were not even codified in law. They are not mentioned as such in regulations for criminal procedures. We have thieves, robbers, rapists, and even kidnappers all mentioned in law along with specific regulations for dealing with them. We have rebellion and sedition defined right down to the level of individuals, but again no bandits, even though we have already noticed how bandits are attracted by rebellions against the state.[81]

Amnesty is the way the state normally prefers to deal with rebels. It may prefer amnesty to execution because amnesty, from the state's point of view, sets a salutary example to the rest of the populace; it brings rebels back into the fold along with a public and frank admission of governmental authority. In this manner, amnesty becomes a new swearing of allegiance to authority and thereby acknowledges its legitimacy, which is the kind of obedience that those who govern really desire of their subjects. But bandits do not seem to be eligible for amnesty; governments want them banished for good, which constitutes forceful testimony about the apprehension the state feels for bandits—but not brigands as individuals or bands, or even some vague social ideal. Once again, it seems that it is the idea of banditry which possesses a potency to threaten the state.

National governments recognized that banditry underscores their weakness and therefore undermines their legitimacy. Those who favored the suspension laws in Mexico were right: Legitimacy not only involves the right to rule but, perhaps even more indispensable in public thought, the ability or power to rule. Banditry flourishes in those geopolitical interstices in which central control and influence holds limited sway and in which its judicial influence is weakest. Many academics have relegated banditry mainly to the outlands, distant from the so-called seat of power, normally the national capital. They treat banditry as a defensive strategy. But banditry can be aggressive and challenging; it is not nearly as defensive as some think, and it frequently tests the limits of state control, at times within eyeshot of the capital itself, where brigands often have important contacts.

Banditry thrives during those disruptive periods in which state building takes place not only because it directly challenges the political legitimacy of the rulers and interdicts lines of communication which are essential to the process of national integration, or because it disrupts the commercial development designed to funnel profits into the pockets of the power brokers, or even because brigands may ally themselves with political dissidents. Banditry per se also wrecks the image of public peace and national consensus so vital to the shaky national project under construction. Boundaries do not make a nation; a sense of national community does and, as Benedict Anderson informs us, nations as community are more imagined than real.[82] The term *nation* more than anything else is simply another label which overlays distinct and frequently competing communities distinguished by their ethnicity, class, cultures, and history. It is now well recognized that people traditionally accustomed to one form of community may decline or only grudgingly acknowledge the invitation to join another configuration, especially when it is suggested by outsiders and is not perceived to be in their traditional community's best interests. Therefore, the state must manufacture national consensus, create a nationalism, and peddle it through image as well as formalized education and the invention of traditions. Bandits blemish the oneness of the image and prick at the imagined nation, so they need to be coopted or eliminated. Governments would normally prefer to vanquish the brigands, but the public pulse may give them pause. Bandits to them may be heroes to others.

Who can resist these kinds of heroes? Ivan Olbracht provides one possible answer and a rationale:

> Man has an insatiable longing for justice. In his soul he rebels against a social order which denies it to him, and whatever the world he lives in, he accuses either that social order or the entire material universe of injustice. Man is filled with a strange, stubborn urge to remember, to think things out and to change things; and in addition he carries within himself the wish to have what he cannot have—if only in the form of a fairy tale.

That is perhaps the basis for the heroic sagas of all ages, all religions, all peoples and all classes.[83]

One may look around our world or read Jerzy Kosinski's *The Painted Bird* and wonder about humankind's "insatiable longing for justice," although there is probably less doubt about his "wish to have what he cannot have." Our bandit-heroes may symbolize social justice, but only as perceived and patterned by ourselves, the myth makers. Paul Kooistra explains all too well how we create laudable motivation for the unsavory acts of our heroes and how we neutralize their reprehensible attributes. His examples from the American frontier and middle America include Jesse James, the Dalton boys, Billy the Kid, and Pretty Boy Floyd. First we ensure that our hero sees himself as a victim of his environment. Then, as a result of his or her activities, no one gets hurt or, if they do, it is what the victims deserved. Third, the real criminals are the law and politicians; and finally, we convince ourselves that our bandit-hero did what he did for a higher cause—for instance, in the name of social justice.[84] Once these matters are in line, we may concentrate on our hero's manliness, righteousness, cleverness (especially in outwitting the law), justice (notably in redistributing the wealth, preferably to us), womanizing (although some have pondered the relationship between male bonding and sexuality), violence, heart of gold, toughness, sense of humor, meanness, and whatever else tailors the mythic image to our liking, which may reflect our perceived needs and/or fears.

To this point, we have many examples of how both the state and its subjects may conceive of and utilize bandits for their immediate and practical purposes. As Kooistra observes, people may also involve bandits in an old morality play involving the law, justice, and the individual.[85] But none of this approaches the idea of banditry, which can so enthuse masses of people and frighten governments. The idea of banditry seems to conjure up notions of high-minded and ultimate power embedded in human spirituality and thought. We are speaking here of a kind of religious power which people sense is available to them, not only to right wrongs but to reconfigure their entire world more to their liking.

In the endeavor of humans to utilize such power, bandits may become their inspiration and then their guides. Richard Slatta has discovered in Argentina some gaucho bandits who have long been revered by common people as supernatural beings who could perform miracles, and devout pilgrims still visit the grave sites of these "miraculous gauchos."[86] Moreover, pious Mexicans in search of justice still light votive candles to the bandit Pancho Villa.[87] Billingsley enters this domain when he notes the manner in which people so readily imbue their bandit-heroes with courage, good deeds, a refusal to compromise, and myths of invulnerability and rebirth. Invulnerability and rebirth get very close to cultural heroes and religious configurations embedded in human thought. These matters suggest to Billingsley that "even the hopelessly oppressed dreamed of a world in which power was not always something to be used against the weak." Brent Shaw refers us to Roman legends which pit bandits against emperors, in which the bandit "is a symbol of what the emperor should be."[88] The bandit is no simple rebel merely opposed to the regime (we have already indicated that governments, through their laws, know how to classify and otherwise deal with such rebels), but in these tales the bandits mean to "reform and remodel society."

How far bandits aim to go may be a scholarly issue. Shaw believes they only intend "to fit an ideal pattern already imparted by its [society's] dominant class structure,"[89] but just as likely bandit-heroes may represent that sort of religious belief which promises new relationships of power. Danker says as much when he writes that bandits represent humankind's "secret desire for restraint from [the] rules and constraints" set by others—a utopian refrain echoed in so much religious thought.[90] Charles W. Long, who has examined the power of popular religion to produce social movements which aim "to turn the world upside-down," places prophets and bandits at the forefront of those activities—which, of course, have everything to do with power and the right to rule.[91] Perhaps this explains why bandits seem to have such an affinity for prophetic movements, like the one that occurred at Tomochic in northwestern Mexico in the 1890s, where among the general populace of the region only Pedro Chaparro and his gang of ten or so bandits joined the faithful, who had sworn to die for their religious beliefs.[92]

No wonder that governments so fear the idea of banditry, especially as rooted in that strain of religious inspiration which envisions an entirely new world about to come, one which strips the government of its power and delivers it to those the state meant to dominate. For right behind that idea itself stalks an impatient cultural hero—the long promised return of the just king, perhaps a secular ruler or a messiah, who will set things right, punishing the wicked and rewarding the righteous. This is no innocent hope; for many it is an indisputable promise, and only a question of when. The idea of banditry may not herald the moment, but it can invigorate the thought.

NOTES

My grateful appreciation to Professors Rosalie Schwartz and Eric Van Young for their helpful comments on an earlier draft of this chapter.

1. For example, this theme highlights advertisements for the 1991 version of the motion picture *Robin Hood.*

2. Claude Levi-Strauss, "Overture to *le Cru et le Cuit,*" in *Structuralism,* ed. Jacques Ehrmann (Garden City, N.Y., 1970), 38.

3. Victor Turner, *The Ritual Process* (Ithaca, 1966), 128–29.

4. A popular starting place on the work of Jospeh Campbell is Joseph Campbell, *The Power of Myth* (New York, 1988).

5. Paul J. Vanderwood, *Disorder and Progress: Bandits, Police, and Mexican Development* (Lincoln, 1981), 95–102.

6. Ibid., 8.

7. Eric Hobsbawm, *Bandits*, rev. ed. (New York, 1981).

8. Linda Lewin, "The Oligarchical Limitations of Social Banditry in Brazil: The Case of the 'Good' Thief Antonio Silvino," in *Bandidos: The Varieties of Latin American Banditry*, ed. Richard W. Slatta (Westport, 1987), 85.

9. Barbara A. Hanawalt, *Crime and Conflict in English Communities, 1300–1348* (Cambridge, Mass., 1979), 204–5.

10. Ibid., 204.

11. Paul Kooistra, *Criminals as Heroes: Structure, Power and Identity* (Bowling Green, 1989), 65.

12. Phil Billingsley, *Bandits in Republican China* (Stanford, 1988), 75.

13. Eric Van Young, from his manuscript in preparation titled "The Other Rebellion: Popular Violence and Ideology in Mexico, 1810–1817 (Berkeley, forthcoming), chap. 5, "A Social Profile." Professor Van Young concludes that the line between insurgent and criminal behavior can be faint. My thanks to him for allowing me to cite his manuscript in progress.

14. William B. Taylor, "Bandit Gangs in Late Colonial Times: Rural Jalisco, Mexico, 1794–1821," *Bibliotheca Americana* 1 (November 1982): 46.

15. Ranajit Guha, *Elementary Aspects of Peasant Insurgency in Colonial India* (Delhi, 1983), 95.

16. Van Young, "Social Profile"; Taylor, "Bandit Gangs," 42.

17. Billingsley, *China*, 73.

18. Taylor, "Bandit Gangs," 14; Van Young, "Social Profile," 21–23.

19. Carlos Aguirre, "Cimarronaje, bandolerismo y desintegración esclavista," in *Bandoleros, abigeos y montoneros; Criminalidad y violencia en el Perú, Siglos XVIII–XX*, ed. Carlos Aguirre and Charles Walker (Lima, 1990), 181.

20. Taylor, "Bandit Gangs," 44; Aguirre, "Cimarronaje," 181; Van Young, "Social Profile," 21–23.

21. Van Young, "Social Profile."

22. Billingsley, *China*, 70.

23. Ibid., xv; Guha, *Elementary Aspects*, 95.

24. Billingsley, *China*, 78.

25. Timothy Fernyhough, "Social Mobility and Dissident Elites in Northern Ethiopia: The Role of Bandits, 1900–69," in *Banditry, Rebellion and Social Protest in Africa*, ed. Donald Crummey (Portsmouth, 1986), 152.

26. Taylor, "Bandit Gangs," 46.

27. Richard W. Slatta, "Images of Social Banditry on the Argentina Pampa," in *Bandidos*, ed. Slatta, 51–52.

28. Julio Guerrero, *La Génesis del crimen en México: Estudio de psiquiatría social* (Mexico, 1901); Enrique Lopez Albujar, *Los Caballeros del delito*, 2d ed. (Lima, 1973); Eric Mayer, "Ecología, crimen y rebelión en los Andes," in *Bandoleros*, 185–212; Benjamin S. Orlove, "La Posición de los abigeos en la sociedad regional. El Bandolerismo social en Cusco en vísperas de la reforma agraria," in *Bandoleros*, 279–305; Billingsley, *China*, 5; Alan Knight, *The Mexican Revolution*, 2 vols. (Cambridge, 1986), 1: 351–52.

29. Gilbert M. Joseph, "On the Trail of Latin American Bandits: A Reexamination of Peasant Resistance," *Latin American Research Review* 25 (1990): 7–53. Responses to Joseph's stimulating essay and his report appear in *Latin American Research Review* 26 (1991): 145–74.

30. Knight, *Mexican Revolution*, 1: 354.

31. Billingsley, *China,* 186.
32. Hanawalt, *Crime and Conflict,* 204–5.
33. Billingsley, *China,* 192.
34. Lewin, "Silvino."
35. Knight, *Mexican Revolution,* 2: 392–406.
36. Lewin, "Silvino," 72–73.
37. Billingsley, *China,* 281–82.
38. Vanderwood, *Disorder and Progress.*
39. Charles Walker, "Montoneros, bandoleros, malhechores: Criminalidad y política en las primeras decadas republicanas," in *Bandoleros,* 118–25.
40. Billingsley, *China,* 224–25.
41. Lewin, "Silvino," 83.
42. Gonzalo G. Sanchez and Donny Meertens, "Political Banditry and the Colombian *Violencia,*" in *Bandidos,* 151–70.
43. Brent D. Shaw, "Bandits in the Roman Empire," *Past and Present* 105 (November 1984): 3–52.
44. Vanderwood, *Disorder and Progress,* 56.
45. Billingsley, *China,* 224–25.
46. Rosalie Schwartz, *Lawless Liberators: Political Banditry and Cuban Independence* (Durham, 1989).
47. Christon I. Archer, "Banditry and Revolution in New Spain, 1790–1821," *Bibliotheca Americana* 1 (November 1982), 74.
48. Ibid.
49. James C. Scott, *Weapons of the Weak: Everyday Forms of Peasant Resistance* (New Haven, 1985) and Scott, *Domination and the Arts of Resistance* (New Haven, 1990).
50. Guha, *Peasant Insurgency,* 107–8.
51. Schwartz, *Lawless Liberators,* 11–12, 88, 142.
52. Lewin, "Silvino."
53. Billingsley, *China,* 151.
54. Quoted in Richard Slatta, "Banditry as Political Participation in Latin America," *Criminal Justice History* 11 (1990): 175–76; Peter Singelmann, "Political Structure and Social Banditry in Northeast Brazil," *Journal of Latin American Studies* 7 (1975): 60.
55. Lewin, "Silvino."
56. Fernyhough, "Ethiopia," 166.
57. Billingsley, *China,* 125.
58. George Rudé, *Criminal and Victim: Crime and Society in Early Nineteenth-Century England* (Oxford, 1985), 117–18.
59. Billingsley, *China,* 282.
60. Ibid., 226.
61. Ibid., 283–84.
62. Louis A. Pérez, Jr., *Lords of the Mountain: Social Banditry and Peasant Protext in Cuba, 1878–1918* (Pittsburgh, 1989); Richard A. Horsley and John S. Hanson, *Bandits, Prophets, and Messiahs: Popular Movements in the Time of Jesus* (New York, 1985).
63. Billingsley, *China,* 231.
64. Terence Ranger, "Bandits and Guerrillas: The Case of Zimbabwe," in *Social Protest in Africa,* 373.

65. Howard S. Becker, "Labelling Theory Reconsidered," in *Deviance and Social Control,* ed. Paul Rock and Mary McIntosh (London, 1974), 62.

66. Shaw, "Roman," 33.

67. Schwartz, *Lawless Liberators,* 3.

68. Brian R. Hamnett, *Roots of Insurgency: Mexican Regions, 1750–1824* (Cambridge, 1986), 59.

69. Hobsbawm, *Bandits,* 17.

70. Billingsley, *China,* 9–10.

71. Uwe Danker, "Banditi and the State: Robbers and the Authorities in the Holy Roman Empire in the Late Seventeenth and Early Eighteenth Centuries," in *The German Underworld: Deviants and Outcasts in German History,* ed. Richard J. Evans (London, 1988), 101.

72. Shaw, "Roman," 24–29.

73. Hyam Mccoby, *The Mythmaker: Paul and Invention of Christianity* (New York, 1986), chap. 6 n. 1, 213.

74. David Moss, "Bandits and Boundaries in Sardinia," *Man* 14 (September 1979): 479–84.

75. Marta Petrusewicz, "Society Against the State: Brigandage in Southern Italy," *Criminal Justice History* 8 (1987): 1.

76. For a full discussion of the Mexican debate, see Daniel Cosío Villegas, ed., *Historia moderna de México: La república restaurada: La vida política* (Mexico, 1959), 227–359. Article 29 of Mexico's Constitution of 1857 permits the exceptions. See *Constitución federal de los Estados Unidos Mexicanos sancionada y jurada por el congreso general constituyente el día 5 de febrero de 1857* (Mexico, 1883), 20.

77. Cosío Villegas, *Historia moderna,* 252.

78. Ibid., 259.

79. Ibid., 232.

80. Paul J. Vanderwood, "Genesis of the Rurales: Mexico's Early Struggle for Domestic Security," *Hispanic American Historical Review* 50 (May 1970): 323–44.

81. For examples, see *Ley general para juzgar a los ladrones, homicidas, heridores y vagos* (Mexico, 1857); *Código penal del estado de Jalisco* (Guadalajara, 1885); and *Código de procedimientos en materia penal del estado de Tabasco* (San Juan Bautista, 1890).

82. Benedict Anderson, *Imagined Communities: Reflections on the Origin and Spread of Nationalism* (New York, 1983).

83. Hobsbawm, *Bandits,* 133–34.

84. Kooistra, *Criminals as Heroes,* 154–58.

85. Ibid., 38.

86. Slatta, "Banditry as Political," 172.

87. Noted at the Pedro Jaramillo shrine, Los Olmos, Texas, visited by the author on 5 December 1991.

88. Billingsley, *China,* 276; Shaw, "Roman," 30.

89. Shaw, "Roman," 47–49.

90. Danker, "Banditi and the State," 103.

91. Charles H. Long, "Popular Religion," in *The Encyclopedia of Religion,* ed. Mircea Eliade (New York, 1987), 448–49. Long's notion of religion as power is briefly discussed in his book *Significances: Signs, Symbols, and Images and the Interpretation*

of Religion (Philadelphia, 1986), 115–17. He fleshed out these ideas in several telephone conversations with the author of this chapter in the fall of 1991.

92. For Chaparro, see Plácido Chávez Calderón, *La Defensa de Tomochi* (Mexico, 1964), 33–35.

11

Slaves, Free Poor, and Policemen: Brazil

Marcos Luiz Bretas

The founding fathers of social science in the nineteenth century had crime as one of their major concerns. They saw it as one of the most visible signs of social disorder and believed that the increase of social knowledge would contribute to its control, or even to its elimination.[1] Crime was presented as the opposite of normal behavior. The last thing they expected to find in its study was the pattern of day-to-day life. Recent research in social history has moved crime into the core of societies, stressing the proximity between daily life and criminal behavior. Brazilian historians have found criminal records to be a valuable source in investigating daily life. Neglected for a long time by traditional historians, the free poor of the slave society, or the common laborers at the turn of the nineteenth century, had their daily activities recorded in police or judicial records. It is in this way that "the history of the dominated groups comes to the surface through the pen of the police clerk."[2]

The historian interested in criminal justice records will find a great diversity of sources available. Unfortunately, they cannot be trusted for serial studies since they have been collected haphazardly, but they do offer rich qualitative material. Police archives[3] have administrative documents that may prove valuable. The archives from courts are irregular in their contents, and most of the remaining older records are kept in the state's archives. Where they exist, however, the criminal justice files are extremely detailed since the structure of criminal procedure had the witnesses testify in court, and their depositions were registered.

Frequently, the records also had the statements made to the police, which provide detailed and often contradictory versions.

The criminal procedure developed since the Code of Criminal Procedure of 1832 created detailed records. After the police had notice of a crime being committed, they would hold an investigation, hearing victims, accused, and witnesses. The evidence gathered would be sent to a court,[4] where a prosecutor could return it to the police for further investigation or call for a trial. The evidence of the witnesses had to be repeated in court to be accepted. The Code of 1832 prescribed trials by jury, but during the century the powers of the jury were restricted, and cases in district courts were increasingly heard before a single, professional judge acting alone.

This discovery of the voice of the dominated through these criminal justice records raises many new questions for the historian. In what way did the writers of these discourses (e.g., the police clerks) work? How trustworthy can the documents be? Did people speak the truth before the agents of justice? If these reports are to be taken as trustworthy, how representative of popular culture are they? Can the criminal records provide us with helpful quantitative data? Questions such as these have provoked a debate among historians that is far from a solution. Some of them believe that criminal justice sources offer only hints about popular behavior and that they give voice only to a particular stratum of the poor—that is, those who deal with the police.[5] Arguing that these records come from a special kind of poor supposes a special control over certain groups among them. All groups on the lower levels of society were exposed to the possibility of meeting the police and probably knew how to present their discourses to the authorities. If we take as an example crimes involving morality, such as defloration, we will certainly find parts of the poorest groups trying to ascribe themselves some respectability and offering narratives of what was supposed to be proper behavior. A second group of historians believes that criminal records show a version of behavior produced for those in charge of justice.[6] Discourses are thus produced especially to support their expectations. The study of these sources will provide us with a useful knowledge of judicial procedures but with little about the actual behavior of the lower classes. Yet whether the stories presented were real or not, they had to make sense. To be presented in court, they must have been at least plausible and described behavior that actually existed.

The historians who tried to approach day-to-day life through criminal records also had problems. Justice archives are presented according to behavior classified as criminal, following the articles of the Penal Code, and by the name of the defendants. They are a challenging source when we try to locate other sorts of behavior. Looking for culture, gender, or religion across the files has proved difficult.

The production of useful quantitative data with criminal sources is still to be done. The nineteenth-century statistics are scarce and unreliable. The files at the National Archives and the courts' archives are not complete and cannot be relied on for accurate statistical accounts. Only prison records have made possible complete serial studies about color, age, and gender.[7] Since studies based on criminal justice records have been produced about different periods of Brazilian history, I will divide them into studies of crimes related to slavery, to the free poor during the period of slavery, and at the turn of the nineteenth century to the creation of a free labor market. In the last section, I discuss the emergence of a new set of agencies of social control to enforce the emerging social values.

SLAVERY AND CRIME

Violence has always been a central category for the study of slavery. From the days of the struggle for abolition, violence has been presented as essential for the survival of the economic system. Nineteenth-century critical accounts of slavery always stressed its violent character and even used violence to explain its survival for three centuries, until 1888. To present master-slave relations only through the violence of that relationship has become a rooted tradition in Brazilian history.[8]

If, on the one hand, violence is presented as the basis of the social order, on the other hand, violence is also seen as the way of breaking that order. Criminal acts committed by slaves were presented as acts of resistance and were understood as part of a collective fight against slavery.[9] It was the study of that resistance that provided us with research on slave crime. The few studies that are available discuss slave crime in different periods and regions of Brazil. They are all aware of the incompleteness of their data and present the difficulties they have found in dealing with them. Even the proportion of slaves in the colonial period is difficult to assess: The official census of 1821 presents, for the city of Rio de Janeiro, 36,182 slaves in a population of 79,321.

The first study to focus on crime during slavery was Patricia Aufderheide's "Order and Violence."[10] In an extensive study from 1780 until 1840, she dealt with data from many different cities and villages. In her view, apart from the street policing functions which controlled slaves, the judicial apparatus grew to repress the increasing number of mixed-blood free men. Local justice in the 1800s illustrated the failure of adapting European liberal and utilitarian policies to a society organized by slavery and racial values. "Modern" judicial institutions were spoiled by local interests and political control.

It might be of greater interest to try to compare some of the data and results produced in studies of crime in the nineteenth century. We compare the analysis by Leila Algranti, obtained from police files from Rio de Janeiro in the beginning of the nineteenth century, to data from the midcentury, collected by Maria Helena Machado from court files in small towns of São Paulo province, and to data from prison records in late nineteenth-century Recife—an old town of the Brazilian northeast—presented by Martha Huggins.[11] The studies of slave crime produced by Algranti and Machado depend on the enlarged notion of resistance that encompasses crime with rebellions, runaways, abortions, and suicide as forms of protest against slavery.[12] By getting drunk, beating people, or stealing, the slaves were developing forms of survival within the oppressive regime.[13] A considerable amount of slave crime was thus a natural concomitant of the colonial period. With the expansion of cities in the nineteenth century, which made surveillance over the slaves a harder task, crime again naturally increased. The files of arrests produced by Rio de Janeiro's police between 1810 and 1821 show 5,078 detentions, mainly of slaves (80 percent) and freed men.[14] These records seem to have been produced by street patrol arrests of people caught in the act, which explains the total absence of murders (only attempts) and sexual crimes. The main occurrences are those against public order (32 percent) and runaway slaves (20.8 percent). This pattern of slave crime is consistent with the data from Recife provided by Huggins (62 percent from public order violations, including runaway slaves).

Another important finding by Algranti is that the victims of slave crime did not belong to the higher levels of society but were fellow slaves and the free poor. Algranti argues that crimes against persons are underrepresented in these files, but it is clear that the victims were often individuals caught in the frequent street fights. Carrying weapons was a common habit in nineteenth-century Rio and was found in 15 percent of the cases. The main threat on the streets were the so-called *capoeiras*—street fighters (usually slaves) armed with razors, who terrorized Rio until the end of the century.[15] Police control over slaves increased through the century, replacing the owners as rule enforcers. Police provided the cities with a better surveillance system and rationalized the punishment of slaves by taking the responsibility out of the owners' hands. With the end of the slave trade in 1850, the price of slaves increased and the loss of a slave could cost the owners. The arrest of a slave became a financial problem to the owners, and, where possible, they resisted police action against their slaves even when they themselves were the victims.[16]

The disorganization of the slave system encouraged an increase in some slave crimes and widened the slaves' margin of negotiation with the owners. This can be seen in Machado's data for the 1870s. Using justice records, she shows an increase of crimes against the person, especially owners, on the coffee farms of São Paulo. Judicial records do not include the main occurrences found in police and prison files; disorderly conduct or curfew breaking seldom appear in courts. In contrast to Algranti's data, the presence of slaves is small—less than 20 percent of the cases brought to court. From the 1,274 cases that survived in the archives of the court in Campinas for the period between 1830 and 1889, only 144 were crimes committed by slaves. In the smaller villages, at least as implied by Celeste Zenha in her study of Capivary, the number of slave crimes is also low.[17]

M. K. Huggins is not interested in exploring crime as a means of resistance to slavery but in the criminalization of the free poor in the transition from slavery to free labor at the end of the nineteenth century. She argues that state action against crime increased with the need to control free workers, something which had been relatively unimportant during slavery. Huggins collected samples from the files of Recife's House of Detention from 1860 to 1922 and found that "even before Abolition, free people were more commonly arrested in the House of Detention than slaves. The proportion of slaves in the detained population was 18 percent in 1860, declining to 7 percent in 1855."[18] This result is in keeping with the conclusion from São Paulo, presented by Machado, but with a noticeable difference in the types of crime: Public order violation is the cause of 62 percent of the arrests in Recife, while crimes against persons account for only 3 percent.

Trying to compare the various statistics of slave crime in the nineteenth century has become a challenging task since we have only scarce data from diverse areas of the country for different periods. From the data already gathered and supported by the evidence of Algranti, Holloway, and Huggins, we may say that the main causes of slave arrests were public order violations and runaways. This seems to be true throughout the nineteenth century. But we still need to verify whether the increase in crimes against the person that occurred in the late 1880s in São Paulo also occurred elsewhere in the country.[19] The large coffee farms of São Paulo and the largest city of Brazil (also its capital), Rio de Janeiro, appear to show some common characteristics in the relation between masters, slaves, and the state. But we need to know more about other regions.

Another main point is the difference between researchers regarding approaches to slavery and the transition to free labor. While researchers of slavery, like Algranti and Machado, accentuate the role of the state in the control of slavery, others, like Huggins and Neder, consider the emergence of crime as a main problem in Brazilian society closely involved in the building of a free labor market from the 1870s onward. The creation of state forces to deal with crime took place in the nineteenth century worldwide. Until then, slave owners had been able to control crime without the interference of the state. The links between slavery and the creation of police still need to be better established. The number of arrests of free men suggests that they were in fact the main problem for state law enforcement. Of course, slave crimes did exist, but they could be dealt with by the owners.[20]

THE EMERGENCE OF THE FREE POOR

The existence of a significant group of free poor in slave societies was revealed in the 1960s through the classic study of Maria Silvia de Carvalho Franco. Using trial records from the *comarca* (judicial division of the province) of Guaratinguetá, she described the living conditions of the free poor in the coffee region of the São Paulo province in the second half of the nineteenth century, stressing how violence was a regular part of their lives. Problems brought to court had their origin in community relations that usually involved neighbors, kinship, or fellow workers. The factors that were traditionally used in social sciences to stress the strength of communal ties were also significant in the emergence of violence.[21]

During slavery, the position of the free poor in the social structure was delicate. While slaves had an effective cost to their owners, the use of free workers required no initial financial outlay, and consequently they proved to be very useful in accomplishing dangerous tasks. Free workers—either small farmers producing for subsistence or itinerants—were present in Brazilian society from the eighteenth century. It was then that the public authorities in the mining region of Minas Gerais asked for harsher measures to deal with vagrancy. The same authorities were also aware of the advantage they could gain from itinerants, either for the occupation of new territories or for recruitment as a military force,[22] and during the nineteenth century the number and the importance of the free poor increased. They had an influential role in the development of agriculture for the internal market and supplied the growing demand generated by the successful coffee farms. The expansion of the cities, especially Rio de Janeiro, also allowed the emergence of new groups of urban poor working in services and commerce.

The study of violence among the free poor in the rural areas is still to be done. The only research that has been produced with sources comparable to Franco's study is that of Celeste Zenha, who has analyzed the court files from Capivary, a small nineteenth-century village near Rio de Janeiro. The portrait of slave life in an impoverished economic environment shows the importance of daily activities in the production of conflicts—as shown by Franco and in the production of trials. Justice was a political resource that could be used by different groups in the small society, except for the slaves. Villagers developed strategies for presenting their cases to the courts, using witnesses and statements to win judicial officials to their side. Those who could show honor, morality, and respectability were the most likely to succeed in the courts, especially when supported by similar individuals. Thus, trials were the arena in which both the truth and the criminal were reconstructed.

But the urban poor received much more attention. The final crisis of slavery and the growth of immigration in the second half of the nineteenth century made the control over urban poverty a major concern for the elites. The growth of the cities (between 1872 and 1886, the city of São Paulo saw its population increased by 52 percent) created the opportunity and even the necessity for slaves and the free poor to live and work together. When slaves and the free poor came together in their daily activities, this provoked both disputes and the development of solidarity. In Rio de Janeiro, slaves and the free poor used to gather in the organized groups of *capoeiras;* they also shared the same houses and the same bars. Despite the existence of laws forbidding slaves to engage in many urban activities, the expansion of the cities blurred the distinction between themselves and the free poor.[23] An urban slave could live among the free poor for a long period without being identified as such. The city provided runaway slaves with a wonderful place to hide.

The elite's concerns about the social pathologies that developed in modern societies directed their attention to the behavior of the urban poor. Those poor were undisciplined, lazy, and immoral and had to be changed in order to place the nation on the right road to progress. Contemporary physicians and jurists produced many books and articles on urban social problems, which have attracted the attention of those historians interested in how the new capitalist groups established their power over the urban poor.[24] While the studies of the 1970s privileged organized labor and the repressive action of the state,[25] many studies are now focused on social control and the production of deviance as capitalist strategies.[26]

These newer studies focus on the control of particular social groups in an industrializing city. They deal with crime as a way of exploring the problems faced by nonwhites, immigrants, and females in the city. But the available statistics for urban crime, gathered through court files, prison records, or published statistics, do not easily allow many general conclusions.[27] Groups associated with poverty, such as blacks and immigrants, seem to be overrepresented among the offenders. Most records deal with public order violations such as vagrancy, disorder, and drunkenness. The relationship between violent crimes and property crimes, frequently associated with the development of capitalist society, is not clear. Arrests on charges of theft were common, outnumbering those for violent crimes. But many of those arrested and charged as "known thieves" never went to court. Trial records show violent crimes as the most frequently prosecuted in the courts.[28]

The criminalization of nonwhites had its origins in the culture of slavery. Slave owners justified slavery as a means of educating the blacks, who were seen as lazy, corrupt, and immoral. This argument found support in biological theories that asserted the inferiority of blacks.[29] Toward the end of the nineteenth century, even those involved in the abolitionist movement shared the idea of the blacks' lack of preparation for the modern society.[30] After the abolition of slavery, nonwhites were subject to police control as usual suspects of vagrancy, theft or the new kind of crime denominated *capoeiragem* (an increasingly organized kind of street fighting), created by the Penal Code of 1890.

Concerns about the behavior of nonwhites, together with the prevalence of European cultural values, led to a campaign against the cultural practices of that group. Afro-Brazilian music—sambas and batuques—as well as religion were criticized by the elite's intellectuals and put under the surveillance of the police. Musical gatherings had to be registered at the police stations and were frequently prohibited as a meeting place for criminals.[31] The repressive policy is treated by Adamo as a way of controlling nonwhite culture, and he considered that "sects constituted a much greater danger to the status quo than any other segment of nonwhite culture."[32] Only in the 1940s did elite intellectuals start to study Afro-Brazilian religions as part of a cultural tradition which deserved to be respected and preserved. According to Adamo, the acceptance of nonwhite samba and religion was "part of a larger effort to coopt and control non-whites in Brazil.'' This analysis follows the conclusions of Roger Bastide, who detected a ''whitening'' of Afro-Brazilian religion in São Paulo through an increase in the number of whites accused of witchcraft.[33]

A recent study on the repression of Afro-Brazilian religions by Yvonne Maggie[34] makes it more difficult to sustain the hypothesis of white control or cooptation of black culture. With data ranging from 1912 to 1945, Maggie also found whites overrepresented in police inquiries into complaints of witchcraft or the false practice of medicine. However, the trial records show that more nonwhites were accused and that all seven white defendants were acquitted. Only four of the thirty-four defendants analyzed were convicted.[35] Justice seemed to be very little concerned with repressing Afro-Brazilian cults, and complaints were not the resource of the controlling elite against poor sorcerers but stemmed from disputes among the lower orders. They appealed to the police to stop what they considered as the evil deeds of some sorcerers in a religion which was not regulated by a proper ''orthodoxy.''[36]

Among the defendants, there was also a great number of immigrants. From the end of the nineteenth century, the immigrants were presented as an alternative work force to substitute for the lazy slaves. They started to arrive in the 1870s from impoverished areas of Portugal, Spain, and Italy to work in the coffee farms; between 1890 and 1900, the state of São Paulo received 412,297 immigrants, and Rio received 70,298, comprising around half of the working force.[37] These immigrants, however, did not fulfil the expectations of that part of the elite who wished for a ''Europeanization'' of Brazilian labor. Among the working immigrants, they soon detected the scum of European society, members of the dangerous classes and anarchists, who were attracted by the possibilities of the new nation. In São Paulo between 1894 and 1916, immigrants were 55.5 percent of those arrested. This was the proportion of immigrants in the population as a whole in the mid-1890s, but it had declined to 36 percent by 1920.[38]

The immigrants played an important part in the social conflicts of the beginning of the twentieth century. Their place in such conflicts was not always the same, changing according to the foreign groups involved[39] and the social structure to which they belonged. In São Paulo and Belo Horizonte, the immigrants were treated as a threat to customs and public order, though clearly underrepresented in charges of vagrancy.[40] At the turn of the century, they were a constant concern of the public authorities and made up more than half of those arrested by the police. Intense conflicts developed between native Brazilians and alien workers and also involved the police.[41] In 1896, during the construction of a railroad in Sabará, a city near Belo Horizonte, 1,200 workers (most of them Italians) fought against both the local population and the police, resulting in fourteen arrests and two deaths. The railway company had to move the group to another city some 40 kilometers away. The Chief of Police illustrated the general state of mind: ''The people of Minas are the most peaceful in the world. The police in this good land would have almost nothing to do if it weren't for the foreigners.''[42]

The position of immigrants in Rio de Janeiro's society was different. Since Independence, there existed a strong prejudice against the Portuguese among the city's population. Some riots against them occurred in the 1830s. The ownership of food stores and house rentals was supposed to be in the hands of the Portuguese, and Rio's people always blamed the Portuguese for any increase in prices. In the 1890s, massive immigration increased to 20 percent the number of Portuguese in the city population. Republican radicals branded Portuguese exploitation as a leftover of the colonial period. Immigrants in Rio were the target of complaints from the urban worker; but many employers considered them as a better work force. Important political conflicts emerged in the 1890s against the Portuguese led by "Jacobin" politicians.[43] In the criminal records of homicide or assault, it is common to see immigrants as victims and prosecution witnesses and native Brazilians as defendants and defense witnesses. The battle was for the control of the labor market, where native Brazilian workers were replaced by "better" ones of Portuguese origin.[44] As expressed by the popular saying of the period, "Who kills Portuguese commits no crime" (*Quem mata galegos não tem crime*).

The other issues that have received some attention from researchers are sexual and female crimes. The number of crimes of these types is much less significant than those concerning nonwhites or immigrants. The Penal Code of 1890 enlarged the number of sexual crimes, creating the crime of defloration (i.e., obtaining consent for sexual intercourse with a woman under twenty-one years of age, who was virgin, by fraud or seduction). This was to become the main figure in the criminal statistics of sexual crimes in the following years, reaching, in Fausto's data, 51.4 percent.[45] Trials in these cases were transformed into investigations of the victim's honor and good behavior. In the cases analyzed by Martha Esteves, in the discourse of judges and lawyers a remarkable degree of emphasis was placed on the behavior of women. In some cases, the simple fact of going out without an escort or even being fond of dancing was enough to have a complaint of defloration denied. The victims had to prove their morality in order to win the case. This, in turn, prompted the appearance of other sorts of prejudice—most notably the complaints by white victims, who had much higher rates of success than those of nonwhites.[46] Overall, however, the rate of conviction for sexual crimes was the smallest found by Fausto: 21.3 percent versus 45.5 percent in homicides and 48.5 percent in property crimes. Esteves has interpreted these trials as a frustrated attempt to control the behavior and culture of working-class women. She argues that the sexual values of the poor resisted the imposition of a different sexual morality. Nevertheless, she does not account for the fact that defloration cases originated in complaints by the same poor women. These women agreed with the law and its values, or at least were prepared to use it when they felt that they had been wronged. Legal marriages and common law marriages coexisted in the cultural universe of the poor, and the appeal to justice seemed to be a strategy available and frequently used.[47]

The same concern for the morality of the female victims was shown in crimes of passion.[48] Though the cases of murder involving couples were far from a significant number (less then 10 percent in Fausto's data, counting eighteen for the period 1880–1924), they were the cases that attracted the attention of press and society.[49] They offered one of the focal points for questioning the boasted modernization of Brazilian society. In the prevalent view of modern culture, women were expected to have proper domestic behavior, centered on the family unit; but also, modern husbands were not expected to kill their wives. These values were confronted in courts when lawyers sucessfully justified murders by the behavior of the victims, which caused the defendant to be "momentarily deprived of his senses."[50] A reaction to the legitimation of murder came from members of the legal profession and from feminist groups, increasing the number of convictions in the 1930s; however, subsequent experience showed that the general view of a moral right of the husband to kill an unfaithful wife remained largely untouched.[51]

The more extensive researches of trial records for the beginning of the century have been made by Sidney Chalhoub on murder cases and by Rachel Soihet on crimes committed by women.[52] They invite us to return to the original work by Maria Silvia de Carvalho Franco. Crimes were mostly committed in circumstances involving family, work, or leisure; the defendant and the victim were often acquainted. New studies, however, include those crimes in "the process of expropriation of the free men or the effort to insert them in the emerging capitalist social order."[53] Establishing such a general link to the study of crime impoverishes the analysis by introducing an external element of power—a dominant class capable of building social order. The importance of recognizing violence as part of a common culture loses much of its significance when such external factors are stressed. Sidney Chalhoub's book must be considered the most successful attempt to incorporate criminal justice records in Brazilian social history. He uses the records of murder trials to reconstruct the lives and experiences of Rio de Janeiro's poor, achieving extremely vivid images of daily life in the city in a very good example of the use of anthropological resources in historical research.

THE FORCES OF ORDER

The study of police history has not attracted much attention in Brazil. For a long time, the study of São Paulo's military police made by Heloisa Fernandes remained the only point of reference. As a study of the organization of a military police force, its recruitment and career patterns, it is still the only one available.[54] In most studies produced on violence and crime, the police have been presented as the instrument of the dominant class, exercising their power according to external wishes. That is still the view of many researchers and the central approach of Neder and her collaborators in their study of Rio's police.[55] Changes in the city structure and the emergence of capitalist domination required reinforcement of police power to control the working class. The ambivalent behavior of dominated groups, frequently appealing to the police, and the differentiated response of police officers do not seem to be a major concern for these researchers. They find that the role of the police was merely instrumental.[56]

A critical history of police institutions in Brazil has yet to be written. The first police force was created when the country was still under Portuguese domination at the beginning of the nineteenth century. Following the model of Lisbon police, it was a force to protect the state and maintain order, composed of an administrative body with large functions—the *Intendência Geral de Polícia*—and a military force. These two bodies, during the century, would develop into the current police structure in Brazil, divided into a civil and a military police. From Rio, this model spread to other local forces over the century.[57] Toward the end of the century, an increasing concern over crime, together with the victory of federalism in the new Republic, stimulated the enlargement of police forces. The government of the now powerful states saw their military police as potential state armies.[58] Reformers tried to improve the police in order to cope with the emerging perception of a criminal problem, but they were unable to change the police forces because of political interference, bad recruitment, and conflicts over policing authority.[59] The state governments were more concerned with having a militarized police than an instrument to deal with crime.

At that time, the intellectual effort to cope with the crime problem was much broader. Some congresses were held, including some of Latin American scope, about police work and crime repression,[60] and periodicals and books were published on the problem. Many reforms of the law were made following the new Penal Code of 1890, and there was considerable discussion about crime, its causes, and the ways it should be dealt with. Innovations from European criminal anthropology and positivist approaches to law also caused many changes in criminal law,[61] increasing the concern about the criminal. This led to the development of systems of identification—by criminal records, identity cards, and fingerprinting—which soon became a general requirement.[62] The causes of criminal behavior were always present in the discussion, and many intellectuals associated the problems with alcohol and drug consumption.[63]

The state agencies to handle criminals experienced an increased development in the beginning of the twentieth century. The emphasis was on the scientific approach, with improvements in medical exams and the creation of an agency for criminal identification. The growing importance of scientific expertise opened the way to concerns about the treatment of criminals and inspired an expansion of the prison system, which had experienced a very slow development—impeded by the lack of funds—during the nineteenth century, even though long discussions about the new penitentiary models were conducted by the elite intellectuals.[64] Among the new developments in prisons came a particular concern with criminal insanity; and an institution to deal with the criminally insane, the Manicomio Judiciário, was created in Rio de Janeiro in the 1920s.[65]

CONCLUSION

While several studies have used the criminal justice records of Brazil, many problems remain. Not the least of these is the problem of the archives themselves, which, like most Brazilian archives, suffer from a lack of organization, perhaps the more so since they have scarcely attracted any attention for a long time.[66] The historical archives of the military police in Rio are placed in rooms over the petrol pumps of one of the barracks, and the documents are piled up without any order, with the exception of the books of correspondence of the commanders in the nineteenth century. But these archives contain rich material still to be uncovered.[67] Sadly, when postgraduate students have investigated these sources, the product of their research has usually remained unpublished, ignored by an editorial market in crisis and characterized by restricted access.[68]

Most of the work done in criminal justice records, however, has used these records as sources for analyzing other subjects, especially the lifestyle of the working class or slaves. The theoretical framework of research usually does not consider the investigation of violence and crime as independent subjects with a significant meaning in structuring society. Criminal offenses are treated either as natural expressions of class conflicts or as marginal elements in which the central concerns may be verified. But if we move from history to contemporary social science, we can find a concern with crime prevalent in Brazilian society.[69] The use of violence is a central piece in the organization of relational societies, not only as an instrument of domination but as part of generally accepted ways of structuring life, which have been extremely resistant to change.

Though we cannot be sure of the future of research about crime in Brazil, some points can be suggested for an agenda. From a macrosociological point of view, it would be very useful to have the development of instruments of social control—especially police, criminal justice, and prison—linked to a general discussion of the role of the state and its exercise of coercion. If centralization is a general trend in twentieth-century history, experienced by police forces in many different countries, central administration in Brazil has remained largely aloof from the criminal problem. At a regional level, where the problem of public order is dealt with, we need comparative studies in which historical experiences may be compared to see if there is a common trend in the development of the agents of social control. The study of criminal justice in the different Brazilian states is clearly needed, and the study of rural areas, almost unexplored to date, may offer new ideas.

Researchers need also to look closely at the social practices defined as criminal and the building of social order. Furthering the uses of anthropology in historical research, we may be able to acknowledge the social role of violence, drinking, vagrancy, and other practices labeled as criminal in societies that resist analysis according to the models defined in the study of modern Western civilization. Perhaps historians need to reconsider their attitude to violence, to understand it as a pervasive force in society and accordingly place it in their social explanations. Its use and existence are not only instruments to produce or prevent social change. Violence must be examined as a central part of social life and as a resource that can appear and be utilized in many different situations.

NOTES

I would like to thank José Murilo de Carvalho, Diana Palma, and the editors for their comments.

1. This concern can be found in French sociologists as Durkheim and Tarde or, later, in the Chicago school of sociology. See the examples in Joseph E. Jacoby, *Classics of Criminology* (Oak Park, 1979).

2. João José *Rebelião Escrava no Brasil. A História do Levante dos Malês 1835* (São Paulo, 1987), 8.

3. Brazilian police forces were organized at provincial level, and each province must have its own records. The case with which I am familiar is that of Rio de Janeiro, where the Military Police administers its own historic archive, largely untouched by researchers; the Civil Police, as far as I know, only has records from the beginning of the twentieth century (in microfilms; the original documents were destroyed). The Arquivo Nacional has an enormous collection of documents from the Civil Police, from which I have consulted the first 20 percent for my M.A. thesis; the rest remain unexplored.

4. Except in very small cases, when the case was judged by a Justice of the Peace or, after 1841, by the Chief of Police himself. The judicial power of the Chief of Police finished in 1871, after which all cases had to be sent to court. In 1898, a law authorized the police to act in the place of the public prosecutor for trials of some *contravenções* (misdemeanors). For a description of the court's system in the nineteenth century, see Thomas Flory, *Judge and Jury in Imperial Brazil, 1808–1871* (Austin, 1981).

5. Thomas H. Holloway, "The Brazilian Judicial Police in Florianópolis, Santa Catarina, 1841–1871," *Journal of Social History* 20 (1987): 733–56; idem, "A Healthy Terror: Police Repression of Capoeiras in Nineteenth Century Rio de Janeiro," *Hispanic American Historical Review* 69 (1989): 637–76.

6. M. Correa, *Morte em família: representações Jurídicas de Papéis Sexuais* (Rio de Janeiro, 1983), analyzing murders among couples in the 1950s, is the main source of this argument, using V. Propp's notion of fable.

7. S.C. Adamo, "The Broken Promise: Race, Health, and Justice in Rio de Janeiro 1890–1940" (Ph.D. diss., University of New Mexico, 1983).

8. When the abolition celebrated its centenary in 1988, many studies of slavery were published. More recently, the debate had been sharp; see the attack on the views that deny the main oppressive character of slavery made by Jacob Gorender, *A Escravidão Reabilitada* (São Paulo, 1992) and, as an example of the new views that point to a large extent to negotiation as well as oppression, see João José Reis and Eduardo Silva, *Negociação e Conflito* (São Paulo, 1992).

9. The large bibliography on slave rebellions and the so-called *quilombos* will not be discussed here. A major concern will be with the acts of slaves that could be classified as common crimes—that is, those that could be considered crimes even if committed by free men. A recent view of the duality violence/resistance can be found in Humberto Fernandes Machado, "Violência e resistência na cafeicultura escravista do Rio de Janeiro," *Revista do Rio de Janeiro–UERJ* 1 (1993): 24–34.

10. P.A. Aufderheide, "Order and Violence: Social Deviance and Social Control in Brazil 1780–1840" (Ph.D. diss., University of Minnesota, 1976).

11. L.M. Algranti, *O Feitor Ausente* (Rio de Janeiro, 1988); and idem, "Slave Crimes: The Use of Police Power to Control the Slave Population of Rio de Janeiro," *Luso-Brazilian Review* 25 (1988): 27–48; M.H.P.T. Machado, *Crime e Escravidão* (São Paulo, 1987); M.K. Huggins, *From Slavery to Vagrancy in Brazil: Crime and Social Control in the Third World* (New Brunswick, N.J., 1985).

12. L.L. de Gama Lima, *Rebeldia Negra e Abolicionismo* (Rio de Janeiro, 1981), 28–40.

13. On analyzing investigations into slave suicides, Zenha stresses that courts seemed to share this view, usually attributing suicide to the condition of captivity. Celeste Zenha, "As Práticas da Justiça no Cotidiano da Pobreza: Um estudo sobre o Amor, o Trabalho e a Riqueza Através dos Processos Penais" (M.A. diss., Niterói, 1984), 83.

14. On slave crime in Rio de Janeiro, see also Mary C. Karasch, *Slave Life in Rio de Janeiro 1808–1850* (Princeton, 1987), chap. 10.

15. On *capoeiras,* see Thomas H. Holloway, "A Healthy Terror: Police Repression of Capoeiras in Nineteenth Century Rio de Janeiro" and Marcos Luiz Bretas, "A Queda do Império da Navalha e da Rasteria: A República e os Capoeiras," *Estudos Afro-Asiáticos* 20 (1991): 239–56.

16. S. Chalhoub, *Visões da Liberdade* (São Paulo, 1990).

17. Zenha, "As Práticas da Justiça no Cotidiano da Pobreza," chap. 2.

18. Huggins, *From Slavery to Vagrancy in Brazil,* 88.

19. This question is essential for the discussion of the abolition of slavery in 1888. Some researchers have been arguing that abolition occurred when slavery was already collapsing through the resistance of slaves. This idea looks a little exaggerated, but the controversy continues. For this point of view, see, for example, the description of slave crimes in São Paulo, through official reports, made by C.M. de Azevedo, *Onda Negra Medo Branco. O Negro no Imaginário das Elites-Século XIX* (São Paulo, 1987), chap. 3.

20. Patricia Aufderheide insists that slaves were the main problem in street law enforcement and thus of the police: "In one year, 1818, Rio police suspects were nearly three-fourths slaves. . . . The police in the city had to substitute, with a curfew, for the lack of a master's vigilance." The free population were mainly to be found in the courts that were out of reach for the slaves. "Order and Violence," 137.

21. M.S. de Carvalho Franco, *Homens Livres na Ordem Escravocrata,* 3d ed. (São Paulo, 1983). Franco is dealing with the classical Tonnies's categories for community.

22. Laura de Mello e Souza, *Desclassificados do Ouro: A Pobreza Mineira no Século XVIII* (Rio de Janeiro, 1986), 71–74; P. Aufderheide, "Order and Violence."

23. In 1872, the population of Rio was 274,972, including 48,939 slaves. Chalhoub, *Visões da Liberdade,* and Sandra L. Graham, "Slavery's Impasse: Slave Prostitutes, Small-Time Mistresses, and the Brazilian Law of 1871," *Comparative Studies in Society and History* 33 (1991): 669–94.

24. Among the main names in the medical profession are Nina Rodrigues and her followers, analyzed by M. Correa, "As Ilusões da Liberdade: A Escola Nina Rodrigues e a Antropologia no Brasil" (unpublished Ph.D. diss., São Paulo, 1982). Among the jurists there was the Recife school, led by Tobias Barreto; positivists, such as Viveiros de Castro; and socialists, such as Evaristo de Moraes. On the intellectual discourse on social problems, see M. Engel, *Meretrizes e Doutores. Saber Médico e Prostituição no*

Rio de Janeiro (1840–1890) (São Paulo, 1989); and M.A. Esteves, "Em Nome da Moral e dos Bons Costumes: Discursos Jurídicos e Controle Social," *Seminário Crime E Castigo* 2 (Rio de Janeiro, Fundacão Casa de Rui Barbosa, 1986).

25. Paulo Sérgio Pinheiro, "Violência do Estado e Classes Populares," *Dados* 22 (1979): 5–24.

26. Maria Angela Borges Salvatore, "Probes, porém livres: a construção da noção do ócio"; and Marcelo Badaró Mattos, "Contravenções no Rio de janeiro do início do século," both in *Revista do Rio de Janeiro*–UERJ 1 (1993).

27. Statistical material can be found in B. Fausto, *Crime e Cotidiano: A Criminalidade em São Paulo (1880–1924)* (São Paulo, 1984) for São Paulo; Adamo, "The Broken Promise: Race, Health, and Justice in Rio de Janeiro 1890–1940," and Huggins, *From Slavery to Vagrancy in Brazil,* 88 for Recife; and L.T. de Andrade, "Ordem Pública e Desviantes Sociais em Belo Horizonte (1897–1930)" (unpublished M.A. diss., Belo Horizonte, 1987).

28. Arrests without charges were illegal but common. A "known thief" could spend, through different small arrests, 180 days a year in jail without being charged or tried. See M.L. Bretas, "A Guerra das Ruas: Povo e Polícia na Cidade do Rio de Janeiro" (unpublished M.A. diss., Rio de Janeiro, 1988). In the police statistics published for Rio de Janeiro between 1908 and 1918, violent crimes averaged more than 60 percent, while crimes against property were around 15 percent.

29. M. Correa, "As Ilusões da Liberdade: A Escola Nina Rodrigues e a Antropologia no Brasil."

30. C.M. de Azevedo, *Onda Negra*; L.M. Schwarcz, *Retrato em Branco e Negro. Jornais, Escravos e Cidadãos em São Paulo no Final do Século XIX* (São Paulo, 1987).

31. R. Moura, *Tia Ciata e a Pequena África no Rio de Janeiro* (Rio de Janeiro, 1983).

32. Adamo, "The Broken Promise: Race, Health, and Justice in Rio de Janeiro 1890–1940," 257.

33. Bastide's research covers the period from 1938 to 1941. Roger Bastide, "O mundo dos candomblés e macumba paulista," in *Estudos Afro-Brasileiros* (São Paulo, 1973), quoted by Yvonne Maggie.

34. Maggie, "Medo do Feitiçõ: Relações Entre Magia e Poder no Brasil" (unpublished Ph.D. diss., Rio de Janeiro, 1988).

35. Fausto found an average of 40.4 percent of defendants convicted in cases of murder, theft, and sex crimes. In cases involving nonwhite defendants, the rate of such convictions rose to 57.4 percent. Fausto, *Crime e Cotidiano,* 233–36.

36. It is not difficult to find evidence of police officers involved in Afro-Brazilian sects. For example, Orestes Barbosa reports the participation of the secretary of police headquarters in a *macumba. Ban-Ban-Ban* (Rio de Janeiro, 1923), 195.

37. Boris Fausto, *Trabalho Urbano e Conflito Social* (Rio de Janeiro, 1977), 27.

38. B. Fausto, *Crime e Cotidiano,* 59.

39. An example of what might be called "national culture" in the thought of the period is the analysis made by Evaristo de Morais, a workers' lawyer, on how the different national groups behaved during strikes. E. de Morais, *Reminiscências de um Rábula Criminalista* (Rio de Janeiro, 1989).

40. They were only 28.7 percent of those arrested for vagrancy between 1904 and 1906. In cases of murder, between 1880 and 1924, they were 61.3 percent. B. Fausto, *Crime e Cotidiano,* 44, 62.

41. B. Fausto, *Crime e Cotidiano,* 59–69. L.T. de Andrade *Ordem Pública e Desviantes Sociais em Belo Horizonte (1897–1930),* 13–17.

42. Ibid., 16.

43. J. Hahner, "Jacobinos versus Galegos, Urban Radicals versus Portuguese Immigrants in Rio de Janeiro in the 1890's," *Journal Of Interamerican Studies and World Affairs* 18 (1976): 125–54; G.S. Ribeiro, " 'Cabras' e 'Pés-de-Chumbo': Os Rolos do Tempo: O Antilusitanismo na Cidade do Rio de Janeiro (1890–1930)" (unpublished M.A. diss., Niterói, 1987).

44. Many newspaper advertisements offered jobs for Portuguese only.

45. The other sexual crimes Fausto considered were rape (29.3 percent), kidnapping (5.1 percent) and immoral behavior (14.2 percent). See Fausto, *Crime e Cotidiano,* 179.

46. M.A. Esteves, *Meninas Perdidas, Os populares e o cotidiano do amor no Rio de Janeiro da Belle Epoque* (Rio de Janeiro, 1989); and S. Caulfield and M.A. Esteves, "Fifty Years of Virginity in Rio de Janeiro: Sexual Politics and Gender Roles in Juridicial and Popular Discourse, 1890–1940," *Luso-Brazilian Review* 30 (1993).

47. R. Soihet, *Condição Feminina e Formas de Violência: Mulheres Pobres e Ordem Urbana 1890–1920* (Rio de Janeiro, 1989), 247–52.

48. The social views of sexuality, morality, and their connections with the urban underworld are the subject of Margareth Rago's study of prostitution in São Paulo, *Os Prazeres da Noite: Prostituição e códigos da sexualidade feminina em São Paulo (1890–1930)* (Rio de Janeiro, 1991). How the police expressed the general view of morality is the subject of S. Caulfield, "Getting into Trouble: Dishonest Women, Modern Girls, and Women-men in the Conceptual Language of *Vida Policial,* 1925–1927," *Signs* 19 (1993):146–76.

49. Maybe this can be explained by the persons involved. Of the seventeen wife killers in Fausto's data, they were all white and three were from the middle class.

50. Evaristo de Morais, *Reminiscências,* discusses cases in which he acted successfully as attorney for the defendant. The "deprivation of senses" would develop later in the "legitimate defense of the honour," still in use in courts. See Susan K. Besse, "Crimes of Passion: The Campaign against Wife Killing in Brazil, 1910–1940," *Journal of Social History* 22 (1989): 653–66; and Marisa Correa, *Morte em Família.*

51. M. Correa, *Morte em Família,* studies these crimes in the city of Campinas in the 1950s.

52. S. Chalhoub, *Trabalho, Lar e Botequim. O Cotidiano dos Trabalhadores no Rio de Janeiro da Belle Époque* (São Paulo, Brasiliense, 1986); and R. Soihet, *Condicão Feminina.*

53. S. Chalhoub, *Trabalho, Lar e Botequim,* 30.

54. H.R. Fernandes, *Política e Segurança: Força Pública do Estado de São Paulo: Fundamentos Histórico-Sociais* (São Paulo, 1973). See also S.B. Baggio, "A Força Pública de Minas na Primeira República," *Revista Brasileira De Estudos Politicos* 49 (1979): 201–32; and M.L. Bretas, "A Guerra das Ruas: Povo e Polícia na Cidade do Rio de Janeiro" (unpublished M.A. diss., Rio de Janeiro, 1988).

55. G. Neder et al., *A Polícia na Corte e no Distrito Federal 1831–1930* (Rio de Janeiro, 1981). Two recent studies take a similar line, Thomas H. Holloway, *Policing Rio de Janeiro: Repression and Resistance in a Nineteenth-Century City* (Stanford, 1994), and Elizabeth Cancelli, *O Mundo da Violência:* A *polícia da era Vargas* (Brasília, 1993).

56. The same view is shared by P. Tortima, "Polícia e Justiça de Mãos Dadas: A Conferência Judiciário-Policial de 1917" (unpublished M.A. diss., Niterói, 1989).

57. M.G.M. Brasil, *A Genealogia da Instituição Policial no Brasil e no Ceará* (Fortaleza, 1990); and Holloway, "The Brazilian Judicial Police in Florianópolis, Santa Catarina, 1841–1871."

58. In this case, the police force of the city of Rio de Janeiro seems to be an exception because it was controlled by the federal government.

59. State police forces came into conflict with the army and the National Guard, which exercised many police activities. Bretas, "A Guerra das Ruas."

60. Tortima, "Polícia e Justiça de Mãos Dadas."

61. P. Fry and S. Carrara, "As Vicissitudes do Liberalismo no Direito Penal Brasileiro," *Revista Brasileira De Ciências Sociais* 1 (1986): 48–54.

62. S.L. Carrara, "A Sciencia e Doutrina da Identificação no Brasil: ou do Controle do Eu no Templo da Técnica," *Religião E Sociedade* 15 (1990): 82–105.

63. J.C. Adiala, "A Criminalização dos Entorpecentes," *Seminário Crime E Castigo 1* (Rio de Janeiro, Fundacão Casa de Rui Barbosa, 1986). Drinking in Belle Epoque culture is a subject that deserves attention from historians.

64. Curiously, the Foucaultian trend of Brazilian historiography in the 1980s left the history of prisons almost untouched. On this theme, and not from a Foucaultian point of view, see the paper presented by Ricardo D. Salvatore at the meeting of the American Historical Association, Chicago, 1992, "Penitentiaries, Visions of Class, and Export Economies. Brazil and Argentina Compared." I would like to thank Professor Salvatore for a copy of his article.

65. On the criminally insane, see S.L. Carrara, "Crime e Loucura: O Aparecimento do Manicômio Judiciário na Passagem do Século" (unpublished M.A. diss., Rio de Janeiro, 1987). In the Manicomio, the criminally insane could be incarcerated for as long as the doctors considered necessary. In the 1970s, Peter Fry met there Febronio Indio do Brasil, accused of the murder of a child fifty years earlier.

66. The Arquivo Nacional in Rio de Janeiro has been indexing the files of trial records. For some courts the work is ready, and we should expect that research will be easier from now on.

67. I am presently working on the books of daily registers of police stations kept by the Civil Police in Rio de Janeiro since the beginning of the century.

68. Brasil's article is part of a dissertation which I could not obtain. Similarly, I have not been able to see Rejane Penna Monteiro, "A Nova Polícia. A Guarda Civil em Porto Alegre (1929–1938)" (unpublished M.A. diss., Porto Alegre, 1991). I would like to thank Cláudia Mauch for this reference.

69. This is not the place for a review of Brazilian sociology of crime. The interested reader may see the works of sociologists such as Edmundo Coelho, Antonio Luiz Paixão, and Luciano de Oliveira; anthropologists such as Alba Zaluar and Roberto Kant de Lima; and the works of the Núcleo de Estudos da Violência of the Universidade de São Paulo. For a general view, see the special volume on police of *Revista OAB-RJ* 22 (August 1985).

12

The Convict Taint: Australia and New Zealand

Stephen Garton

Crime is the seed-bed for European colonization of Australia, and assessments of the nature of this colonization, the society that grew from these beginnings, and the national character bred from such suspect "stock" have been central questions in Australian history. Although some historians have sought to place colonization within broader contexts of British mercantile and imperial expansion, the origin of European colonization as a series of penal settlements for Britain's convicts has clearly marked the development of Australian history in significant ways. More ink has probably been spilled on the "convicts" than any other theme in Australian history. This represents an unparalleled moment in which the concerns of crime history overlap significantly with those of national history. But, perhaps ironically, this conjuncture has been to the detriment of crime history. The concern with national identity has subsumed questions about the nature of crime, policing, and punishment to those of morality and character. Moreover, the overwhelming focus on the convict period has deflected attention from the history of crime, policing, and punishment in Australia since the cessation of transportation in 1868. Many have benefited from the pioneering work of Alex Castles on the history of the criminal justice system. More recently, works by David Neal on the rule of law, Alastair Davidson on the colonial state, Hilary Golder on magistrates, and Mark Finnane on policing and government, have made major contributions to the historical analysis of the criminal justice system. However, Australia still lacks any general administrative or social histories of crime, the police, or punishment practices.[1]

Although New Zealand has the benefit of a good administrative and social history of the police, and Peter Spiller's forthcoming general legal history promises much, for different reasons crime history in New Zealand has been similarly retarded.[2] New Zealand began not as a convict colony but as a site for commercial exploitation in the 1820s and 1830s. From the beginning, European traders, missionaries, and colonizers faced considerable opposition from the aboriginal inhabitations—the Maoris—and this story of often violent conflict, culminating in the Maori Wars of the 1860s, has dominated New Zealand historical scholarship. As a consequence, other historical questions and fields of inquiry have been marginalized. In the case of both Australia and New Zealand, however, the narrow focus of their dominant historiographical traditions also reflects the fate of national history in a colonial settler society context. Until recently, national history in Australia and New Zealand has been seen as inferior to that of the metropolitan center (in this case Britain), leading to a concentration of professional power and prestige in the field of European history.

The emerging postwar nationalism in Britain's former dominions, however, found its echos in the academy, with a renewed struggle to assert the significance of national history. In the last three decades, increasing numbers of undergraduate and graduate students have become interested in Australasian history, fueling a significant growth in the historical analysis of these settler societies. The first wave of interest, however, was concerned with ''national'' history—settlement, economic development, national identity, and the evolution of distinctive social and political institutions. In this wave, there was little focus on major historical specializations, such as crime or criminal justice history, except insofar as they added to the national story (which in the case of Australia meant a concern with the convicts). Only in the last two decades, with the increasing influence of social and cultural history throughout the history discipline internationally, have Australian and New Zealand historians developed an interest in the history of crime. Nonetheless, as with national history, social and cultural histories of crime, policing, and punishment have been less specializations in their own right and more the means for raising questions within the fields of labor, and women's, urban, and black history.

I am suggesting that crime history has been marginalized and neglected in Australia and New Zealand and, more importantly, when it has been studied it has been subsumed to the concerns of other historiographical traditions. This problem has begun to be redressed in recent years, but much of the best work is lying, largely dormant, in unpublished postgraduate theses. This is not to say that important work has not been done. Australasian historians have been particularly open to the historiographical currents of British, European, and North American crime and criminal justice history and have explored important themes in the social history of crime, policing, and punishment in the colonial context. Equally, new historiographical questions have led to some important reassessments in traditional areas, such as convict history. As these areas open up, the Australian context is becoming an increasingly fruitful area for comparative crime history. It offers an opportunity to analyze the transformation and evolution of British institutions and practices in frontier settler societies, and these transformations stand to illuminate the history of the metropolitan center as they do the colonial periphery. Although crime and criminal justice history in Australia and New Zealand is largely in its infancy, there are indications that its future is promising. The remainder of this chapter seeks to explore the evidence for this optimistic prognosis, examining four areas in particular—convicts and bushrangers, policing, imprisonment, and women and crime.

CONVICTS AND BUSHRANGERS

No historiographical analysis of crime history in Australia could begin without a discussion of the convicts. European colonization of Australia began with the decision to establish penal colonies there to relieve the overcrowding in the hulks after the American colonies declared their independence. The first convict transports arrived in 1788 and the last in 1868. In these eighty years, 160,000 convicts arrived in the Australian colonies; they and their descendants formed an important part of the colonial population. Equally, major social institutions and structures were determined by the demands of governing a captive population. It is not surprising, then, that Australian historians have examined extensively the nature of the convicts and the potential inheritance that they bequeathed the nation. A central question since the 1920s concerned the morality of the convicts: Were they victims of enclosures and industrialization or professional criminals from an urban subculture of "ne'er do wells" and prostitutes? Advocates of the former idea drew their inspiration from the work of the Hammonds, but it is the latter argument that has held sway since the 1950s.[3] Drawing on the evidence in the convict indents, the views of contemporary commentators and concepts derived from functionalist sociology historians such as Manning Clark, Lloyd Robson, and A.G.L. Shaw have mounted a convincing argument that the majority of convicts were from urban areas and arrested, often more than once, for petty property crimes. From this they have concluded that the convicts were not the "village hampdens" of popular myth but denizens of an urban criminal subculture.[4]

These conclusions have been bolstered by the pioneering work on political protesters by George Rudé and Eric Hobsbawm. They found that a number of convicts were transported for political protest crimes—Captain Swing rioters, Luddites, Tolpuddle Martyrs, and Irish republicans—but that overall these men only accounted for 4,000 of all the convicts transported to Australia.[5] The vast majority were urban criminals and prostitutes of the type described by Clark, Robson, and Shaw. Other historians, notably Portia Robinson, have carried forth the assumptions of this historiography into assessments of the nature of early colonial life. Robinson has concluded that early colonial life was far more peaceful and ordered than conventional accounts of the convict system have assumed, and from this she has argued that the convicts, driven to "depravity" through want, were reformed in the more hospitable colonial environment, which offered greater scope for social mobility.[6]

This rather sterile debate has floundered in questionable assessments of the moral character of the convicts, influenced more by concerns with national character than with criminological debates about the causes of crime, the role of policing practices in the construction of deviant populations, and the function of "moral entrepreneurs" in creating images of depraved convicts.[7] It has added much to our knowledge of the social characteristics (age, occupation, religion, conjugal condition, charges, places of trial) of the convicts, but the historians arguing that the convicts were a professional criminal class have interpreted these characteristics by taking as fact the views of moral entrepreneurs. Only recently has this dominant tradition been challenged in a controversial and pathbreaking collective project headed by Stephen Nicholas.[8] The *Convict Workers* project has drawn its theoretical and historiographical inspiration from the flourishing tradition of recent British social histories of crime.[9] The researchers have sought to use these works to place the convicts within broader and more accurate social contexts which produced crime and gave it specific social and cultural meanings. Empirically, they have reassessed the convict indent evidence using more sophisticated statistical techniques.

The findings of the *Convict Workers* group have challenged previous accounts in significant ways. The researchers concluded that far from being the criminal subclass of traditional accounts, the convicts were healthier, more literate, and more skilled than the general British working class of the same period. Their work on occupations has been particularly important. Clark, Robson, and Shaw dismissed the occupation evidence in the indents as unreliable, but the *Convict Workers* group has examined it more closely and found not only a great variety of occupations (suggesting that it is more reliable than has previously been supposed) but that, using Armstrong's work force and skill classifications, three-quarters of the convicts were skilled or semiskilled. In a refreshing reassessment of the female convicts, Deborah Oxley's sophisticated analysis of women convicts in *Convict Workers* challenges the notion that female convicts were prostitutes whose morality was worse than the men. She points to the masculinist assumptions underpinning representations of the female convicts and provides evidence of the work skills possessed by many female convicts.[10] Overall, this project has concluded that the convicts were part of a mobile, displaced, skilled labor force whose crimes were largely workplace related. They were workers who, through want and underemployment, stole. They were not professional criminals and frequent offenders who preferred crime to work. The procedures, methods, and conclusions of the *Convict Workers* project have been questioned by some historians, and although some of the evidence is not as tight as one might hope, it remains the most sophisticated and exciting intervention in convict historiography of the last thirty years.[11]

The focus of the Nicholas group and much of the historiography so far has been on the "moral chacter" of the convicts. A few recent studies have moved beyond this rather restricted focus to examine the processes of legal regulation in the colonies, particularly the social history of criminal justice in the convict period. Alan Atkinson and John Hirst have explored the complex forms of cultural resistance to the rule of law. Convicts resorted to "go slows," sabotage, and petty crime to frustrate abusive masters and overseers, often extracting concessions in return for work, or they overbally abused magistrates when masters sought to enforce labor obedience. Both David Neal and Paula Jane Byrne have also examined the nature of the criminal justice system in this period but more significantly have investigated how the convicts responded to, and sometimes negotiated these structures of power. They have shown that convicts, and former convicts, were avid users of the criminal justice system when it was possible to use it to their advantage. They embraced the idea of the rule of law when it offered an opportunity to place restrictions on their exploitation by masters, or a means of seeking redress against other convicts and colonists. Here they have demonstrated that much crime was intraclass, local, and in the case of crimes against the person, within the family. The law was a favored means of negotiating these difficult local and personal tensions and conflicts.[12]

Bushranging, the contemporary Australian expression for rural banditry, has been the other great theme in Australian crime history. But unlike the convicts, the bushrangers have been shrouded in a populist romanticism—colorful rebels expressive of Australian male values of mateship and antiauthoritarianism—that has also influenced academic representations. This romantic idealization of the bushrangers is all the more remarkable because many of them were escaped convicts.[13] From the 1820s to the 1880s, bushrangers created widespread alarm on the frontier and were condemned, hunted, imprisoned, and sometimes hung by authorities. Despite this, bushrangers—especially the Kelly Gang—were assisted by local settlers, frustrating the efforts of authorities. They have also become the subject of popular poems, songs, plays, novels, and, more recently, films. The sources of this popular fascination and support were largely ignored until John McQuilton's study of the Kelly Gang, which attempted to adapt Eric Hobsbawm's notion of "primitive rebels" to the colonial context. McQuilton situates the popular support for the Kellys in the simmering tensions between impoverished small, agricultural producers, known as selectors (similar to homesteaders or yeomen), and wealthy pastoralists determined to maintain their control over the land. Inadequate government protection of the rights of selectors and widespread suspicions that police and officials supported squatters underpinned popular support for the Kellys.[14] Both McQuilton and the *Convict Workers* group have demonstrated the potential of adapting British social history perspectives and theories to the colonial situation. Each has attempted to place crime in broader social, political, and economic contexts to move beyond the simplistic moralism and romanticism of earlier historiographical conventions.

POLICING

Some of the best work of recent years has been in the field of policing. Here Australian and New Zealand historians have had the opportunity to explore the nature of policing in unique settler society contexts. As British colonies, Australia and New Zealand adopted British styles of policing but had to adapt them to the particular demands of colonial life. Australasian historians, like their British and North American counterparts in recent years, have been particularly concerned with the social history of policing. Unfortunately, good administrative histories to establish the institutional context for the social impact of policing have been few. Mark Finnane has written some suggestive essays, and more recently a major book, examining (among many other themes) aspects of police administration, and there are some reasonable administrative histories for specific periods and particular colonies and states. The best are Hazel King's pioneering study of police administration in New South Wales from 1825 to 1856, Robin Walker's useful study of the New South Wales police in the late nineteenth century, and Robert Haldane's lively account of the Victorian force.[15] New Zealand is better served with Richard Hill's monumental four-volume (only two published so far) history of the police and police practice.[16] Although few in number, these histories agree on the general character of the colonial police forces. They drew on the models of both the London Metropolitan Force and the Royal Irish Constabulary; the London model is preferred in urban areas and the Irish model on the frontier. Despite this paucity of institutional and administrative accounts, there have been some important studies of colonial policing that focus on the impact of policing on crime rates, the demands of frontier control, and the role of policing in the structuring of social relations.

Michael Sturma's *Vice in a Vicious Society* was one of the first studies of policing which attempted to examine the social impact of policing.[17] He focuses on New South Wales from the 1830s to the 1850s, bridging the transition of that colony from penal settlement to self-governing colony, and he attempts to assess the impact of convictism and the peculiarities of colonial life on the character of colonial policing. He found that widespread fears of the convict taint were responsible for higher levels of policing in colonial society in comparison to Britain. There were more police per head of population in New South Wales than Britain and consequently a higher crime rate, which in turn bolstered colonial fears that the population was particularly unruly due to the convict and ex-convict element. Sturma's study problematizes traditional ideological accounts of the depraved character of the colonial populace by arguing that crime rates are in part a function of levels of policing and that these levels were high in the colonial period.

Sturma has also argued convincingly that whereas most British and American forces were formed in response to urban problems, the important dynamic in colonial policing was the frontier.[18] In New South Wales until 1862, there were six separate forces. The Metropolitan and Water forces were responsible for policing the city and tended to adopt the concern for orderly, discrete control and prevention characteristic of the London force. The remaining four—Rural, Border, Mounted, and Native—were closer to the military style of the Royal Irish Constabulary and maintained a rigid and often violent control on the frontier, facilitating the dispossession of the Aborigines and the orderly pastoral exploitation of the land. Studies by Suzanne Davies, Andrew Gill, J.E. Thomas, and McQuilton have raised similar issues in other colonies.[19] Frontier policing has also been a significant theme in New Zealand history. The works of Alan Ward and Richard Hill have pointed to the considerable difficulties New Zealand colonial authorities had in maintaining order, especially with respect to racial clashes between Maoris and settlers encroaching on their land. In this context, New Zealand adopted the Royal Irish Constabulary police model and retained it until after the Maori Wars of the 1860s. Gradually, as the frontier began to recede and the problems of order there diminished, authorities shifted to the London model of policing.[20]

One of the features that distinguished colonial policing from British practice was the policing of Aborigines and Maoris. A central theme here, particularly in relation to Aborigines, has been the important role of police in dispossession. Police often turned a blind eye to settler massacres, and when Aborigines retaliated, police quickly (although sometimes unsuccessfully) crushed their opposition forcing them off traditional lands or rounding them up onto reserves and missions. But some Aborigines and Maoris were also complicit in the process of dispossession. Aborigines joined the Native Police Force and were among the most vigilant in the suppression of aboriginal resistance. This force has been the focus of an illuminating study by Marie Fels, which attempts to analyze the complex processes involved in aboriginal participation in policing. For many displaced Aborigines, the force offered a means of social mobility in colonial society, and officers in charge were quick to exploit tribal rivalries to ensure the success of the force.[21] In New Zealand, Ward has shown that Maoris had an even more significant role in the criminal justice system. Frontier conflict was so intense that colonial authorities there appointed Maoris as assessors in special native magistrate courts. Until the 1870s, this system encouraged Maoris to assist the police and magistrates to determine the justice of Maori land claims and complaints against settlers.[22]

The peculiarities of the frontier affected policing in other ways. Some historians have sought to examine the specific character of frontier life on the types of crimes policed. In both Australia and New Zealand, the rough pastoral laboring life, excessive numbers of single men, and a male culture centered on drink and violence had an important impact on crime. Certainly this culture was the object of considerable police scrutiny. As Mark Finnane and Stephen Garton have shown, the scattered population and its male character increased the intensity of policing on the frontier, with police concentrations four times those of London or other major cities. Rates of arrest were correspondingly high, particularly for drink-related public order offenses but also for assault and property crimes.[23] Race was clearly a factor in arrest decisions, particularly in Queensland (according to Finnane, Garton, and Clive Moore), where Aborigines and Melanesians were much more likely to be arrested and given longer sentences than those of British background.[24] Finnane has also examined the higher incidence of arrest for those of Irish descent in Australia.[25] The complex intersections between policing, ethnic prejudice, and economic and social vulnerability are important themes that warrant further study. Similar themes have been explored by Miles Fairburn and Stephen Haslett for New Zealand.[26] This latter study is a complex statistical comparison between arrests for violent crime in New Zealand and V.A.C. Gatrell's figures for similar offenses in England. They conclude that a greater level of social anomie on the frontier was responsible for the higher incidence of violent crime and drink-related offenses in New Zealand. This welcome comparative dimension does much to illuminate the particularities of the colonial context and the effect of specific social contexts on crime and policing.

Urban crime has received far less attention in Australia and New Zealand. In part, this reflects a broader historiographical concern with the distinctive frontier character of these settler societies. The frontier seemed to many the heartland of these national cultures and the cradle for social development. Urban history itself emerged late in Australasia as a distinct historiographical specialization. But there were other factors in the neglect of urban crime. Integral to the emerging national identity in these cultures was the belief that the "New World" of Australasia was a workingman's paradise and a social laboratory, free from the entrenched problems of the Old World—slums, poverty, destitution, and crime. Nineteenth-century visitors, such as Anthony Trollope and J.A. Froude, remarked on the egalitarian nature of Australasia and the absence of poverty and slums. The context for crime did not seem to exist, and this image was one of remarkable longevity in popular and professional discourse. It was not until the 1970s that historians began to challenge seriously these dominant representations. Much social history of the last twenty years has focused on the historical recovery of poverty and destitution in the colonial cities.[27] Histories of urban crime have been one product of this historiographical challenge.

The first serious study of urban crime, however, had its origins in an American project of comparative urban crime. Peter Grabosky's *Sydney in Ferment* was a contribution to the project, with T.R. Gurr and R.C. Hula, on crime in four cities.[28] It is still the only general history of crime in an Australasian city. It carefully charts the changing patterns of crime and the response to crime over a long period. Its breadth is its great strength, but as a pioneering study, with little other work to assist, it is largely descriptive and overly reliant on official statistics for its account. It explores few patterns in detail, except for exceptional cases and patterns which generated significant newspaper comment, and largely ignores the archival evidence that is essential to any examination of the social meaning and complex criminal justice dynamics in the policing and prosecution of particular types of crime. Grabosky's study is further hampered because his object is Sydney, and unfortunately almost all the Police Department archives for Sydney districts in the nineteenth century have been destroyed. This has hampered the historical investigations of urban crime in one of Australasia's two largest cities. A few, such as Russell Hogg and Hilary Golder, have made suggestive excursions into the few remaining Sydney police sources, but most have to rely on the magistrate court records, which are rich but largely untapped except for the studies of Sturma and Byrne, who mainly concentrate on Sydney before 1860.[29]

Historians in other cities in Australia and New Zealand are better served. There are significant police and court archival holdings in most states for the nineteenth and early twentieth centuries, but these still remain neglected, especially for urban crime. Some of the best work has not come from crime historians but from urban historians such as Tom Stannage, Raymond Evans, and Chris McConville, who have used crime patterns and particular crimes to exemplify the social dynamics of inner-city urban life: poverty, conflict, and the secondary economy and culture which emerged to sustain those excluded from the general labor market.[30] Others, however, have attempted to use archival sources to explore more systematically the policing of particular crimes and the nature of policing work.

Finnane and Garton have sought to examine in detail the function of policing in specific contexts in late nineteenth- and early twentieth-century Queensland. They have charted changing levels of policing, crime rates, and, more importantly, the complex social relations between police and local communities. Central to their concerns have been the problems of selective policing, intraclass and interclass crime, and nonpolicing. They have used this material to exemplify theories of police as "managers of the social order." Although based on only preliminary work, they have demonstrated that police often ignored directives from centralized police administrations and implemented policing priorities that were in greater accord with local social problems, such as stricter policing of Melanesian laborers. Equally, they found that many crimes, particularly drinking and prostitution-related offenses, were not vigorously policed. Alternatively, some police did attempt to implement the full letter of the law, and this created local disputes and resentments, which eventually undermined police effectiveness. From this they have pointed to the ways in which policing was inscribed within local social contexts and how policing decisions played an important role in regulating local social relationships. Through detailed local studies, it is possible to gain a more precise understanding of the relationship between police, policing, and the wider social relationships in which these practices were inscribed.[31]

Similar insights have been developed in Suzanne Davies's important study of vagrancy in Melbourne. Using magistrate court records supplemented by other archival sources, she carefully charts how police and magistrates intervened in a variety of illicit practices and underground economies to construct a class of vagrants.[32] Concepts of selective policing have also been evident in the regulation of other criminal activities, notably liquor, drug, and gambling activities. Al McCoy, Charlie Fox, and John O'Hara have revealed how these illicit trades flourished and how their survival and profits often depended on police toleration and the targeting of particular enterprises to maintain the profitability of other enterprises.[33] These studies highlight the importance of examining police corruption in the regulation of criminal activity, particularly in the twentieth century. Few of these studies, however, have attempted to integrate an analysis of all levels of the criminal justice system into their project. Davies goes some way to exploring the different levels—police, magistrates, higher courts, and legislatures—in the policing of vagrancy, but only suggestive works by David Neal on the criminal justice system in the convict period, Pat O'Malley on Australian crime and legal order, David Philips on law and crime in 1888, and J.E. Thomas on crime and society in Western Australia have successfully sought to map the articulations between the different levels of the criminal justice system in the social regulation of criminal activities.[34] More recently the contributors to an illuminating volume of essays by David Philips and Suzanne Davies have canvassed many of these issues, but more detailed local studies are needed before major works of social history synthesis are possible.[35] The archives are rich for this type of research and most remain largely untapped.

Another important trend of recent years has been the history of policing social crises and political policing. Labor historians have begun to pay greater attention to the role of police in the suppression of strikes, building on arguments about the central role of police in cementing particular social and economic relationships.[36] Studies by Walker, Finnane, and Garton, however, have moved beyond mapping the repressive role of police in labor conflicts and speculated on the failure of the labor movement to develop a political critique of police and policing.[37] They argue that such insights were inhibited by a broader acceptance of a legitimate role for police in everyday life. The repressive policing of political organizations (usually socialist) and radical protests, such as Vietnam moratorium demonstrations, has been the focus of illuminating studies by Raymond Evans, Verity Burgmann, and Barry York.[38] More significant, however, have been the analyses by Andrew Moore, Frank Cain, and Les Lewis of the history of secret police, spying, and the links between these forces and secret right-wing neo-fascist groups, especially since the First World War.[39] Such studies highlight the complex intersections between governments, conservative ideologies, and the suppression of radical dissent in Australia and New Zealand. Also important have been studies of the role of the police in ensuring order in times of crisis, such as the Great Depression and World War II. Nadia Wheatley has shown the important role of the police in facilitating eviction of Depression victims and the suppression of the Unemployed Workers Movement. Others have highlighted the important role of the police in easing conflict between Australians and American servicemen stationed in Australia during World War II. Violent conflicts sometimes erupted in this context. But police and military police also regulated sexual practice during the war by segregating black servicemen from Australian women.[40]

The strength of these recent studies of frontier, urban, and political policing has been their emphasis on the social impact of policing. They examine in specific instances how police practice is formed not only by centralized administrative and political directives but also by local power structures and conflicts. They highlight how police are implicated in a variety of social and political relationships and how these facts impact on the decision to arrest, prosecute, and sentence people for particular types of crime. Here social historians of crime and policing are equally alive to the problems of nonpolicing as policing in understanding the historical role of police activity. They also raise the important problem of the effect of policing on social relationships; how policing decisions sanction some relationships, regulate others, and thus affect the labor market, urban economies, leisure, and sexual life. Much of this work is focused on specific crimes, times, and places, and much more archival work is needed before broader patterns and practices can be confidently described and theorized. However, there is considerable scope for future work in this field.

PUNISHMENT

European colonization of Australia is inscribed in the history of punishment. Colonization began as an open gaol, and these colonies were an important point of transition between two economies of punishment: from one predicated on the deterrent effect of public spectacles focused on the body to the rationalized, panoptic, moral reform practices of modern imprisonment. The penal colonies represented the last gasp of the older political economy of punishment. In its worst manifestations—notably special punishment colonies (the secondary convict colonies) for refractory convicts such as Norfolk Island, Port Arthur, and Moreton Bay—the Australian penal system represented the apotheosis of the brutal physical tortures symbolized by Tyburn Tree. But as the new ideals of imprisonment gained ground in Britain, so the Australian colonies changed and new model prisons began to be built in the colonies, often in the colonies of secondary punishment, from the 1840s. There have been a number of studies of the harsh convict system, particularly of the colonies of secondary punishment and the female factories; what is surprising is the lack of attention to the history of punishment since the convict period.[41]

The penal settlements have been used to exemplify the brutality of the convict system. More recently, historians such as John Hirst have questioned whether this image can be used to characterize the whole convict system.[42] Hirst has examined the power of resistance that convicts possessed, which allowed them to extract better working conditions and rations from masters. In fact, they helped forge an embryo free labor market almost from the beginnings of colonization. But in the colonies of secondary punishment and the female factories, arduous work in chains, confinement, and liberal use of the lash were the defining features. These patterns have been the focus of numerous studies, most graphically in the popular work of Robert Hughes.[43] The only counterpoint to this bleak history was the efforts of Alexander Maconochie, a disciple of Elizabeth Fry, to introduce a work incentive scheme on Norfolk Island to encourage reform. His failure, however, has been taken by historians to confirm the irredeemable nature of both the convicts and the convict system.[44] The harshness of the system, however, is often romanticized as Australia's colorful past and the point of departure for the nation's transformation into a civilized society. Most accounts have failed to situate the convict system within the broader history of punishment and thus perpetuate anachronistic whig notions of progress.

Historical interest in punishment after the cessation of transportation has been slight. Perhaps this reflects the loss of Australia's uniqueness in the history of punishment. Thereafter, as interesting studies such as that of Mead have shown, the history of punishment in Australia and New Zealand is the selective adoption of British practices developed by reformers and administrators, such as Crofton and Du Cane. Chris Mead, drawing on the work of David Garland, Michel Foucault, and Michael Ignatieff, examines the introduction of the separate, public works, intermediate, and restricted association systems in New South Wales, carefully criticizing whig theories of imprisonment by situating these changes within a humanist moral reform rhetoric of "tough but fair," which bore little on actual penal practice. The intersection between colonial systems of punishment and broader imperial programs of reform has also been explored usefully for New Zealand by John Pratt.[45]

New Zealand history has been better served for general histories of punishment and imprisonment. The work of P.M. Webb, and more specific studies such as those of R. Burnett and Pratt, have helped chart the general contours of punishment in that colony.[46] In Australia, there are a few recent criminological studies of punishment, such as those of David Brown and George Zdenkowski, which have useful historical introductions; but detailed general accounts do not exist, except for a study of imprisonment in Western Australia, despite the wealth of archival resources for such studies. In Australia there have, however, been some interesting studies of the place of prisons within local communities, notably Richard Broome's study of the Melbourne suburb of Coburg, where Pentridge gaol is located.[47] More recently, the history of particular groups in prison—notably women and Aborigines—has become the subject of important investigations, highlighting the different experiences of these groups from the ordinary prison population. The high incidence of aboriginal deaths in custody, in particular, has become a modern policy concern, and historical analyses have been used to provide the framework for policy development.[48]

Few historians have sought to investigate the variety of punishments for criminal offenses, the changing patterns in their use, or the experience of both warders and prisoners of institutionalization. Some studies have touched on these questions. R. Douglas and Kathy Laster have surveyed aspects of the history of capital punishment.[49] Mead and Garton have attempted to assess the impact of prison reform on the regime of punishment, the discourses of reform and their organization of penal space, the articulation of daily reform routines, the construction of particular prison populations, and the impact of these reforms on the experience of imprisonment.[50] But these are only preliminary excursions into this rich area of research. Some of the best work comes out of recent criminological studies, such as those of Janet Chan, Zdenkowski, and Brown on deinstitutionalization, warder brutality, prisoner resistance, and the emergence of prisoner action groups.[51] In a suggestive essay, Mark Finnane has outlined many of the important questions that need to be addressed in any comprehensive study of punishment in Australia: the shift from convict regulation to a more complex system of civil regulation, the diversity of imprisonment experiences, the use of alternatives such as floggings or fines, and the social experience of imprisonment. He points to the sources available for such studies, carving out an ambitious research agenda which, it is hoped, will be realized soon.[52]

Another important area of recent concern has been the relationship between imprisonment and other forms of incarceration. This comparative dimension is central to any historical understanding of the changing patterns of imprisonment. Stephen Garton has done some preliminary work here, mapping the increasing diversion of serious offenders in the early twentieth century from the criminal justice system to the mental hospital system. In this process, the McNaughton Rules were circumvented and offenders were sent to mental hospitals before being brought to trial. Another focus of Garton's work has been the marked decline in prison admissions in the late nineteenth century. Garton attempts to demonstrate that seeing the prison in isolation fails to grasp the complexity of the process of institutionalization. Although fines and first offenders legislation played a part in this decline, other traditional prison populations—such as lunatics, drunkards, prostitutes, and juveniles—were diverted to other medicalized institutional spaces. Overall institutionalization did not decrease but was articulated in a more complex carceral ensemble. Garton has used these arguments to mount a broad-ranging critique of labor market theories of incarceration, such as those of Rusche and Kirchheimer, Melossi, Quinney, and Jankovics.[53] But as with the other questions in the historiography of punishment in Australasia, these remain partial and specific studies. More comprehensive and general studies wait to be written.

WOMEN AND CRIME

One of the most significant fields of criminal justice history in Australia and New Zealand in recent years has been that of women and crime. Crime has generally been seen as overwhelmingly a male practice, but historians of women and crime have pointed to the significant place of women in this field as both victims and perpetrators. Much of the impetus for this work has come from women's history rather than crime history. Women's historians concerned with recovering the history of women have turned to criminal justice sources—police, court, coroner's, and morgue and prison records—to chart important dimensions of women's experience, such as domestic violence, desertion, incest, prostitution, and reproduction-related crimes. Nonetheless, these studies have yielded important insights into the nature of crime and the criminal justice system, and some have challenged central preoccupations in the discipline. There has been the important work of Deborah Oxley on women convicts, but the bulk of recent work has focused on prostitution.

Prostitution is the women's crime that has been most policed. The majority of women brought before the courts were arrested on drunk and disorderly charges usually associated with the regulation of prostitution. For many women's historians in Australia and New Zealand, prostitution was one of the few viable employments for women in restricted colonial labor markets, where women were the bulk of the poor.[54] But the emphasis on policing prostitution points to the importance of sexuality in the definition of women's deviance. It also marks the centrality of the double standard in the regulation of women's lives, because although the prostitution relationship involved two parties, the women (not their male clients) were the focus of police attention. Equally, male pimps and brothel owners were rarely the subject of prosecution. This concern with sexuality was most apparent in the introduction of contagious diseases legislation. Despite the widespread protests against such legislation in Britain, two Australian colonies (Queensland and Tasmania) and New Zealand followed the British example and introduced contagious diseases regulations to ensure that prostitutes were free of disease, especially in army and navy garrison towns and ports. New Zealand went further by making its contagious diseases regulation applicable to the whole colony.[55] Rather than suppressing and deterring prostitution, the effect of much prostitution-related policing was to provide clean women for men.

These studies have used prostitution as a means of understanding the position of women in society, but the examination of the history of prostitution also raises important problems for more general studies of policing. The fact that prostitution has been tolerated, even promoted, rather than suppressed by criminal justice authorities points to the importance of social regulation by police, magistrates, and politicians. Prostitution is only one of a range of illicit activities that continue to flourish under the gaze of the criminal justice system. Such insights have been common in other social histories of policing; but women's historians, such as Judith Allen and Hilary Golder, have moved beyond concern for the regulation of prostitution to more general conclusions about the industrial functions of policing.[56] In their study of prostitution, police regulated the prostitution market by extracting regular revenue, in the form of fines, from prostitutes and more rigorously policed particular types of prostitutes to ensure that they could no longer ply their trade. In this way, police removed aged and diseased prostitutes from the market and allowed other prostitution enterprises to flourish, providing the context for the growth of organized crime control of the prostitution market. This in turn raises important questions concerning the character and operation of police corruption. Such questions have been most forcefully developed in this field of women's history.

Some women's historians have explored women's other criminal offenses, such as murder, assault, reproduction crimes, larceny, and petty property crimes. Allen, Laster, Robyn Anderson, and Georgina Hall have each tried to examine a broader range of women's crimes in the hope of exploring further dimensions of women's economic and social vulnerability and recovering the experience of poorer women normally excluded from the historical record.[57] Equally, some historians (notably Philips and Allen) have explored similar issues through crimes, such as rape and femicide, in which women were the victims of men.[58] These crimes, whether women were the offenders or victims, have generally been seen as marginal to the main concerns of crime history or criminology because so few people have been arrested and sentenced for such offenses. But women's historians have taken this issue to be a central problem for crime history, especially as other evidence suggests that some of these crimes have been particularly prevalent. Why have crimes involving women been of low priority for the criminal justice system? In addressing this question, women's historians have raised pertinent issues and problems not only for women's history but also for crime history. The most sophisticated and comprehensive effort to tackle these issues has been the work of Judith Allen.

Allen's *Sex and Secrets* has examined the history of crimes involving Australian women since 1880.[59] Her concern is with women as both victims and offenders, particularly in such crimes as rape, abortion, infanticide, homicide and femicide, prostitution, carnal knowledge, and sexual assault. Each of these crimes is used as a means to explore Australian sexual culture and its effects on the lives of women. But this work also challenges the traditional marginalization of women in criminology and crime history. Allen shows that many crimes involving women—notably reproduction and prostitution crimes, rape, and sexual assault—are far more prevalent than crime statistics suggest. She argues that the systematic underpolicing of these crimes is integrally related to the sexual culture which produced them. The crimes themselves and their avoidance by the criminal justice system originated in and helped maintain complex relations of sexual inequality and conflict between men and women. Allen argues that criminal justice history has been hampered by a narrow concern with policed crime arising out of concerns with class and ethnic conflict and failed to theorize about the masculinism embedded in the criminal justice system.

CONCLUSION

This selective overview of crime and criminal justice history in Australia and New Zealand hardly does justice to the range and complexity of recent research in these fields. But on an international scale, as with much Australasian history, these fields are in their infancy. There have been a number of insightful pioneering studies of convicts, bushrangers, policing, punishment, and women and crime, but much of this work has barely touched the rich volume of archival sources relevant to these fields. As a consequence, there have been few works of synthesis, and it is difficult to see any such works in the future until many more detailed local studies have been undertaken. Nonetheless, although these fields may be empirically undernourished, theoretically and historiographically they are rich. Australasian historians have been quick to adapt the latest British, European, and North American historiography to the colonial situation, leading to valuable research and speculation. Moreover, in some instances (notably Allen's work on women and crime), the Australasian contribution has been at the forefront of international research and theoretical innovation. But regardless of the current state of research, the history of crime and criminal justice in Australia and New Zealand (as in other settler societies, such as Canada and South Africa) offers an opportunity to examine the transformation of British and European structures and practices in unique contexts. Some of the best research in the future will emerge when there is a greater recognition of the importance of comparative histories of crime and criminal justice systems.

NOTES

1. A.C. Castles, *An Australian Legal History* (Sydney, 1982); David Neal, *The Rule of Law in a Penal Colony* (Melbourne, 1992); Alastair Davidson, *The Invisible State* (Melbourne, 1990); Hilary Golder, *High and Responsible Office: The New South Wales Magistracy 1787–1986* (Melbourne, 1991); and Mark Finnane, *Policing and Government: Histories of Policing in Australia* (Melbourne, 1994).

2. R.S. Hill, *Policing the Colonial Frontier: The Theory and Practice of Coercive Social and Racial Control in New Zealand 1767–1867* (Wellington, 1986), and *The Colonial Frontier Tamed: New Zealand Policing in Transition 1867–1886* (Wellington, 1989).

3. See G.A. Wood, "Convicts," *Journal of the Royal Australian Historical Society* 8:4 (1922): 177–208.

4. C.M.H. Clark, "The Origins of the Convicts Transported to Eastern Australia 1787–1852," *Historical Studies* 7:26–27 (1956): 121–35, 314–27; Lloyd Robson, *The Convict Settlers of Australia* (Melbourne, 1965); A.G.L. Shaw, *Convicts and the Colonies* (London, 1966).

5. George Rudé, *Protest and Punishment: The Story of the Social and Political Protesters Transported to Australia 1788–1868* (Oxford, 1978); Eric Hobsbawm and George Rudé, *Captain Swing* (London, 1969).

6. Portia Robinson, *The Hatch in the Brood of Time: A Study of the First Generation of Native Born White Australians 1788–1828* (Melbourne, 1985).

7. For a critical survey of this debate, see Stephen Garton, "The Convict Origins Debate: Historians and the Problem of the Criminal Class," *Australian and New Zealand Journal of Criminology* 24:2 (1991): 66–82.

8. *Convict Workers: Reinterpreting Australia's Past,* ed. S. Nicholas (Melbourne, 1988).

9. Notable influences have been the works of Douglas Hay, Peter Linebaugh, E.P. Thompson, David Jones, David Philips, and Clive Emsley.

10. Deborah Oxley, "Female Convicts," in Nicholas, *Convict Workers.* See also Deborah Oxley, "Women Transported: Gendered Images and Realities," *Australian and New Zealand Journal of Criminology* 24:2 (1991): 83–98.

11. For some critical perspectives, see Garton, "The Convict Origins Debate."

12. See Alan Atkinson, "Four Patterns of Convict Protest," *Labour History* 37 (1979): 28–51; John Hirst, *Convict Society and its Enemies* (Sydney, 1983); Neal, *Rule of Law in a Penal Colony;* Paula Jane Byrne, *Criminal Law and the Colonial Subject* (Melbourne, 1993).

13. For a critical review of this mythologizing of the bushrangers, see R.B. Walker, "Bushranging in Fact and Legend," *Historical Studies* 11:42 (1964): 206–21.

14. John McQuilton, *The Kelly Outbreak: The Geographical Dimensions of Social Banditry* (Melbourne, 1979).

15. Mark Finnane, "Governing the Police," in *Ireland, England and Australia: Essays in Honour of Oliver MacDonagh,* ed. F.B. Smith (Canberra, 1990); "Writing about Police in Australia" and "The Politics of Police Powers: The Making of the Police Offences Acts," in *Policing in Australia: Historical Perspectives,* ed. Mark Finnane (Kensington, 1987). Also Hazel King, "Some Aspects of Police Administration in New South Wales 1825–51," *Journal of the Royal Australian Historical Society* 42:5 (1956): 205–27; R.B. Walker, "The New South Wales Police Force 1862–1900," *Journal of Australian Studies* 15 (1984): 25–38; Robert Haldane, *The People's Force: A History of the Victoria Police* (Melbourne, 1986).

16. Hill, *Policing the Colonial Frontier,* and *The Colonial Frontier Tamed.*

17. Michael Sturma, *Vice in a Vicious Society: Crime and Convicts in Mid-Nineteenth Century New South Wales* (St. Lucia, 1983).

18. Ibid. See also Michael Sturma, "Policing the Criminal Frontier in Mid-Nineteenth Century Australia, Britain and America," in Finnane, *Policing in Australia.*

19. Suzanne Davies, "Aborigines, Murder and the Criminal Law in Early Port Phillip 1841–51," *Historical Studies* 22:88 (1987): 313–35; Andrew Gill, "Aborigines, Settlers and Police in the Kimberleys 1887–1905," *Studies in Western Australian History* 1 (1977): 1–28; John Thomas, "Crime and Society," in *A New History of Western Australia,* ed. C.T. Stannage (Nedlands, 1981); John McQuilton, "Police in Rural Victoria: A Regional Example," in Finnane, *Policing in Australia.*

20. Hill, *Policing the Colonial Frontier;* Alan Ward, "Law and Law Enforcement on the New Zealand Frontier 1840–93," *New Zealand Journal of History* 5:2 (1971): 128–49.

21. Marie Fels, *Good Men and True: The Aboriginal Police of the Port Phillip District* (Melbourne, 1988).

22. Ward, "Law and Law Enforcement in New Zealand."

23. Mark Finnane and Stephen Garton, "The Work of Policing: Social Relations and the Criminal Justice System in Queensland 1880–1914," Parts 1 and 2, *Labour History* 62–63 (1992).

24. Ibid. Mark Finnane and Clive Moore, "Kanaka Slaves or Willing Workers? Melanesians and the Criminal Justice System in Queensland in the 1890s," unpublished conference paper, Australian Historical Association Conference, University of Queensland (September 1990).

25. Mark Finnane, "The Irish and Crime in the Late Nineteenth Century: A Queensland Study," unpublished conference paper, Ireland/Australia Conference, Canberra (1988).

26. Miles Fairburn and Stephen Haslett, "Violent Crime in Old and New Societies—A Case Study Based on New Zealand 1853–1940," *Journal of Social History* 20:1 (Fall 1986): 89–126.

27. See Stephen Garton, *Out of Luck: Poor Australians and Social Welfare 1788–1988* (Sydney, 1990).

28. Peter Grabosky, *Sydney in Ferment: Crime, Dissent and Official Reaction 1788–1973* (Canberra, 1977).

29. Russell Hogg and Hilary Golder, "Policing Sydney in the Late Nineteenth Century," in Finnane, *Policing in Australia;* Sturma, *Vice in a Vicious Society;* Paula-Jane Byrne, "Women, Men and Criminal Law in New South Wales 1810–30" (unpublished Ph.D. diss., University of New South Wales, 1988).

30. C.T. Stannage, *The People of Perth* (Perth, 1979); Raymond Evans, "Charitable Institutions of the Queensland Government to 1919" (unpublished M.A. thesis, University of Queensland, 1969); Chris McConville, "Outcast Melbourne: Social Deviance in the City 1880–1914" (unpublished M.A. thesis, University of Melbourne, 1974).

31. Finnane and Garton, "The Work of Policing."

32. Suzanne Davies, "Vagrancy and the Victorians: The Social Construction of Vagrancy in Melbourne 1880–1907" (unpublished Ph.D. diss., University of Melbourne, 1991).

33. Al McCoy, *Drug Traffic: Narcotics and Organised Crime in Australia* (Sydney, 1980); Charlie Fox, "Policing the Dangerous Bookie: Off-Course Betting and the Law in Western Australia," in *Workers and Intellectuals,* ed. Richard Nile and Barry York (London, 1992); John O'Hara, *A Mug's Game: A History of Gaming and Betting in Australia* (Kensington, 1988).

34. Neal, *Rule of Law in a Penal Colony;* P. O'Malley, *Law, Capitalism and Democracy: A Sociology of Australian Legal Order* (Sydney, 1983): David Philips, "Sex, Race, Violence and the Criminal Law in Colonial Victoria: Anatomy of a Rape Case in 1888," *Labour History* 52 (1987): 30–49; Thomas, "Crime and Society."

35. *A Nation of Rogues? Crime, Law, and Punishment in Colonial Australia,* ed. David Philips and Suzanne Davies (Melbourne, 1994).

36. See, for example, the studies in *Strikes,* ed. John Iremonger, Graeme Osborne, and John Merritt (Sydney, 1973).

37. Finnane and Garton, "The Work of Policing"; R.B. Walker, "Violence in Industrial Conflicts in New South Wales in the Late Nineteenth Century," *Historical Studies* 22:86 (1986): 54–70.

38. Raymond Evans, "Radical Departures: Paul Freeman and Political Deportation from Australia following World War One," *Labour History* 57 (1989): 16–26; Verity Burgmann, "The Iron Heel: The Suppression of the IWW during WWI," in *What Rough Beast? The State and Social Order in Australian History,* ed. Sydney Labour History Group (Sydney, 1982); Barry York, "Baiting the Tiger: Police and Protest during the Vietnam War," in Finnane, *Policing in Australia.*

39. Andrew Moore, *The Secret Army and the Premier: The Old Guard in New South Wales 1931–32* (Kensington, 1990); Frank Cain, *The Origins of Political Surveillance in Australia* (Sydney, 1983); Les Louis, "Operation Alien and the Cold War in Australia 1950–53," *Labour History* 62 (1992).

40. Nadia Wheatley, "Meeting Them at the Door: Radicalism, Militancy and the Sydney Eviction Campaign of 1931," in *Twentieth Century Sydney: Studies in Urban and Social History,* ed. Jill Roe (Sydney, 1980); Michael Sturma, "Loving the Alien:

The Underside of Relations between American Servicemen and Australian Women in Queensland 1942–45," *Journal of Australian Studies* 24 (1989): 3–17; and Kay Saunders and Helen Taylor, "The Impact of Total War Upon Policing: The Queensland Experience," in Finnane, *Policing in Australia.*

41. For example, M. Hazzard, *Punishment Short of Death: A History of the Penal Settlement of Norfolk Island* (Melbourne, 1984); Annette Salt, *These Outcast Women: The Parramatta Female Factory 1821–48* (Sydney, 1984).

42. J.B. Hirst, *Convict Society and its Enemies* (Sydney, 1983). Some of Hirst's conclusions have been challenged in David Neal, "Free Society, Penal Colony, Slave Society, Prison?" *Historical Studies* 22:89 (1987): 497–518.

43. Robert Hughes, *The Fatal Shore: A History of the Transportation of Convicts to Australia 1787–1868* (London, 1987).

44. J.V. Barry, *Alexander Maconochie of Norfolk Island: A Study of a Pioneer in Penal Reform* (Melbourne, 1958).

45. Chris Mead, "Tough But Fair: Some Practices of Imprisonment in New South Wales 1866–1914," *Journal of the Royal Australian Historical Society* 77:3 (1991): 57–79; J. Pratt, "Punishment, History and Empire," *Australian and New Zealand Journal of Criminology* 24:2 (1991): 118–38.

46. P.M. Webb, *A History of Custodial and Related Penalties in New Zealand* (Wellington, 1982); R. Burnett, "Penal Servitude in New Zealand" (unpublished paper, Institute of Criminology, Victoria University of Wellington, 1988); Pratt, "Punishment, History and Empire."

47. David Brown and George Zdenkowski, *The Prison Struggle* (Ringwood, 1979); J.E. Thomas and A. Stewart, *Imprisonment in Western Australia* (Nedlands, 1978); Richard Broome, *Coburg: Between Two Creeks* (Melbourne, 1987).

48. See, for example, Adrian Howe, "A Prologue to a History of Women's Imprisonment," *Social Justice* (1990); R. Broadhurst, "Imprisonment of the Aborigine in Western Australia," in *Ivory Scales: Black Australians and the Law,* ed. K. Hazelhurst (Kensington, 1987).

49. R. Douglas and K. Laster, "A Matter of Life and Death: The Victorian Executive and the Decision to Execute 1842–1967," *Australian and New Zealand Journal of Criminology* 24:2 (1991): 144–60.

50. Mead, "Tough But Fair"; Stephen Garton, "Frederick William Neitenstein: Juvenile Reformatory and Prison Reform in New South Wales 1878–1909," *Journal of the Royal Australian Historical Society* 75:1 (1989): 51–64.

51. Janet Chan and George Zdenkowski, "Just Alternatives," *Australian and New Zealand Journal of Criminology* 19:2–3 (1986): 67–90, 131–62; Brown and Zdenkowski, *The Prison Struggle.*

52. Mark Finnane, "After the Convicts: Towards a History of Imprisonment in Australia," *Australian and New Zealand Journal of Criminology* 24:2 (1991): 105–17.

53. Stephen Garton, "The Rise of the Therapeutic State: Psychiatry and the System of Criminal Jurisdiction in New South Wales 1890–1940," *Australian Journal of Politics and History* 32:3 (1986): 378–88; "Bad or Mad? Developments in Incarceration in New South Wales 1880–1914," in Sydney Labour History Group, *What Rough Beast?;* "The State, Labour Markets and Incarceration: A Critique," in *Understanding Crime and Criminal Justice,* ed. Mark Findlay and Russell Hogg (North Ryde, 1988).

54. Judith Allen, "The Making of a Prostitute Proletariat in Early Twentieth Century New South Wales," Kay Daniels, "Prostitution in Tasmania during the Transition from

Penal Settlement to Civilized Society,'' Raelene Frances, ''Prostitution in Western Australia,'' and Susan Horan, ''Prostitution in South Australia 1836–1914,'' in *So Much Hard Work: Women and Prostitution in Australian History,* ed. Kay Daniels (Melbourne, 1984); Meg Arnot, ''The Oldest Profession,'' in *Constructing a Culture,* ed. Verity Burgmann and Jenny Lee (Melbourne, 1988); Charlotte Macdonald, ''Crime and Punishment in New Zealand 1840–1913: A Gendered History,'' *New Zealand Journal of History* 23: 1 (1989): 5–21; Jan Robinson, ''The Oldest Profession,'' in *Public and Private Worlds: Women in Contemporary New Zealand,* ed. Shelagh Cox (Wellington, 1985), and ''Canterbury's Rowdy Women: Whores, Madonnas and Female Criminality,'' *Women's Studies Journal* 1:1 (1984): 6–25; Heather Lucas, ''Square Girls: Prostitutes and Prostitution in Dunedin in the 1880s'' (unpublished B.A. thesis, University of Otago, 1985).

55. See Kay Daniels and Mary Murnane, ''Prostitutes as Purveyors of Disease: Venereal Diseases Legislation in Tasmania 1868–1945,'' *Hecate* 5:1 (1979): 25–56; Charlotte Macdonald, ''The Social Evil: Prostitution and the Passage of the Contagious Diseases Act (1869),'' in *Women in History: Essays on European Women in New Zealand,* ed. Barbara Brookes, Charlotte Macdonald, and Margaret Tennant (Wellington, 1986).

56. Hilary Golder and Judith Allen, ''Restructuring an Industry: Prostitution in New South Wales 1870–1932,'' *Refractory Girl* 18–19 (1980): 17–24.

57. Judith Allen, ''Octavius Beale Reconsidered: Infanticide, Babyfarming and Abortion in New South Wales 1880–1939,'' in Sydney Labour History Group, *What Rough Beast?;* Kathy Laster, ''Infanticide: A Litmus Test for Feminist Criminology,'' *Australian and New Zealand Journal of Criminology* 22:1 (1989): 151–66; Robyn Anderson, ''The Hardened Frail Ones: Women and Crime in Auckland 1845–1870'' (unpublished M.A. thesis, University of Auckland, 1981); Georgina Hall, ''Female Crime in New Zealand 1950–80: Characteristics and Trends'' (unpublished M.Sc. thesis, University of Canterbury, 1985).

58. Philips, ''Sex, Race, Violence and the Criminal Law''; Judith Allen, ''The Invention of the Pathological Family: An Historical Study of Family Violence in New South Wales 1880–1939,'' in *Family Violence in Australia,* ed. Carol O'Donnell and Jan Craney (Melbourne, 1982).

59. Judith Allen, *Sex and Secrets: Crimes Involving Australian Women Since 1880* (Melbourne, 1990).

Bibliographical Essay

This short bibliographical essay concentrates on works in English since it has been prepared, first and foremost, with English-speaking readers in mind. The notes for each chapter in this volume are the best bibliographical guides to the respective national/regional experiences, and they have been designed as such. There is also an extensive bibliography divided by both periods and regions in Xavier Rousseaux, "Criminality and Criminal Justice History in Europe, 1250–1850: A Select Bibliography," *Criminal Justice History* 14 (1993): 159–81.

Of all the countries and regions discussed in the above chapters, France is probably the best served for bibliographical and research guides thanks to the work of Jean-Claude Farcy. His Deux siècles d'histoire de la justice (1789–1989), *Eléments de bibliographie* (Paris, 1990) and *Guide des archives judiciaires et Pénitentiaires, 1800–1958* (Paris, 1992) are exhaustive and invaluable. They provide models for what might be done for other countries or regions. Following next, perhaps, is Canada, where the most complete bibliography is that of Jim Phillips, *A Bibliography of Crime and Criminal Justice in Canada* (Toronto, 1989).

Broad survey texts are available for several countries or regions synthesizing the recent research, but also drawing on that of the individual authors. For the United States there is Lawrence M. Friedman, *Crime and Punishment in American History* (New York, 1993). For England there is J.M. Beattie, *Crime and the Courts in England 1660–1800* (Oxford, 1986) and the two survey volumes, J.A. Sharpe, *Crime in Early Modern England 1550–1750* (London, 1984) and

Clive Emsley, *Crime and Society in England 1750–1900* (London, 1987, 2nd ed, forthcoming, 1996). Sweden is the best covered of the Scandinavian countries with Eva Österberg and Dag Lindström, *Crime and Social Control in Medieval and Early Modern Swedish Towns* (Uppsala, 1988), and Jan Sundin, *För Gud, Staten och Folket: Brott och rättskipning i Sverige 1600–1840* (Lund, 1992). Rather more limited in its period sweep, but of considerable value, is John A. Davis, *Conflict and Control: Law and Order in Nineteenth-Century Italy* (London and Atlantic Highlands, N.J., 1988).

There are several essay collections exploring aspects of crime and/or criminal justice either for individual countries, or more generally. Among the first of these was V.A.C. Gatrell, Bruce Lenman, and Geoffrey Parker (eds.), *Crime and the Law: The Social History of Crime in Western Europe since 1500* (London, 1980) in which V.A.C. Gatrell's "The Decline of Theft and Violence in Victorian and Edwardian England" (pp. 238–370) is of particular value. A similarly wideranging collection, but with its main focus on France, is Benoît Garnot (ed.), *Histoire et Criminalité de L'Antiquité au XXe siècle. Nouvelles Approches* (Dijon, 1992). Bernard Schnapper's articles collected as *Voies nouvelles en histoire du droit. La justice, la famille, la répression pénale (XVIe-XXe siècles)* (Paris, 1991) provide a broad overview for France. Useful collections, spanning long periods and relating respectively to Germany and Italy are Richard J. Evans (ed.), *The German Underworld: Deviants and Outcasts in German History* (London, 1988) and L. Berlinguer and F. Colao (eds.). *Criminalità e società in età moderna* (Milan, 1991). Australian crime and policing over the period since white settlement are covered in Mark Finnane (ed.), *Policing in Australia: Historical Perspectives* (Kensington, 1987) and David Philips and Suzanne Davies, *A Nation of Rogues? Crime, Law, and Punishment in Colonial Australia* (Melbourne, 1994). While for the metropolitan areas of Canada see Susan Lewthwaite, Tina Loo, and Jim Phillips (eds.), *Essays in the History of Canadian Law: Volume Five* (Toronto, 1994).

Monographs on specific topics abound, but several may be read with profit for the light they can throw beyond their precise focus. Thus for women and crime the reader can usefully consult Elaine S. Abelson, *When Ladies Go A-Thieving* (New York, 1989), Judith Allen, *Sex and Secrets: Crimes Involving Australian Women Since 1880* (Melbourne, 1990) and Lucia Zedner, *Women Crime and Custody in Victorian England* (Oxford, 1991). Judith R. Walkowitz, *City of Dreadful Delight, Narratives of Sexual Danger in Late Victorian London* (New York, 1992) is suggestive of what might be done for other countries in other periods with the careful employment of gender and cultural critiques.

Debates on punishment are valuably explored by, among others, Patricia O'Brien, *The Promise of Punishment: Prisons in Nineteenth-Century France* (Princeton, 1982), Pieter Spierenburg, *The Spectacle of Suffering. Executions and the Evolution of Repression. From a Preindustrial Metropolis to the European Experience* (Cambridge, 1984), Richard Van Dülmen, *Theatre of Horror: Crime and Punishment in Early Modern Germany* (Cambridge, 1990), V.A.C.

Gatrell, *The Hanging Tree: Execution and the English People, 1770–1868* (Oxford, 1994), Alexander W. Pisciotta, *Benevolent Repression: Social Control and the American Reformatory-Prison Movement* (New York, 1994), and John Pratt, *Punishment in a Perfect Society; The New Zealand Penal System, 1840–1939* (Wellington, 1992).

The starting point for studying bandits and brigands probably remains Eric J. Hobsbawm, *Bandits* (London, 1969) though its arguments have been much criticized. Gherardo Ortalli (ed.), *Bande armate, Banditi, Banditismo e repressione di giustizia negli stati europei di antico regime* (Rome, 1986) is a collection of essays focusing on the problem across Europe (and with chapters in English, French, and Italian) Stephen Wilson, *Feuding, Conflict and Banditry in XIXth-Century Corsica* (Cambridge, 1988) provides a model of how a historian can contextualize the problem, though it would be dangerous to assume that his carefully drawn conclusions are necessarily relevant for elsewhere. Florike Egmond, *Underworlds. Organized Crime in the Netherlands 1650–1800* (Cambridge, 1993) provides a model of a different kind; her careful analysis of the gangs of bandits and robbers in both town and country draws out the significant roles played by ethnic minorities, demobilized soldiers and other "marginal" groups.

For the history of police Wilbur R. Miller's *Cops and Bobbies: Police Authority in New York and London, 1830–1870* (Chicago, 1977) is a stimulating and important comparative analysis. Clive Emsley, *Policing and its Context, 1750–1870* (London, 1983) attempts even broader comparisons, while his *The English Police: A Political and Social History* (Hemel Hempstead, 1991) concludes with a discussion of what, if anything, makes the English police different. A much more theoretical perspective focusing on the Prussian experience is to be found in Alf Lüdtke, *Police and State in Prussia, 1815–1850* (Cambridge and New York, 1989). The collection of essays edited by Lüdtke, *"Sicherheit" und "Wohlfahrt." Polizei, Gesellschaft und Herrschaft im 19. und 20. Jahrhundert* (Frankfurt am Main, 1992) explores the contrasting elements of "security" and "welfare" in German policing, while the major study of Greg Marquis examines the police forces across Canada: *Policing Canada's Century: A History of the Canadian Association of Chiefs of Police* (Toronto, 1993).

There has also been considerable work on what have been called the marginal groups at the fringe of traditional criminality. This includes women, children, and the mentally "disordered." The recent work of Lawrence Stone, *Uncertain Unions and Broken Lives* (Oxford, 1995) and Andrew T. Scull, *Most Solitary of Afflictions: Madness and Society in Britain 1700–1900* (New Haven, 1993) are at the cutting edge of research in this area. Examining criminality in a broader perspective, pioneering books for American society include Lawrence Friedman and Robert Percival, *The Roots of Justice, Crime and Punishment in Alameda County California, 1870–1910* (Chapel Hill, 1981) and the recent award-winning study of Allen Steinberg, *The Transformation of Criminal Justice: Philadelphia, 1800–1880* (Chapel Hill, 1989).

Finally, there are a number of works that discuss the subject of crime or of criminal justice from a larger perspective. One subject that has not been addressed in this volume is that of aboriginals and the criminal justice system. Written from a law and society viewpoint, there have been a number of major works in this area that have contributed significantly to the historiography of crime and criminal justice. These include, most notably, the essays collected by Kayleen M. Hazelhurst in *Legal Pluralism and the Colonial Legacy: Indigenous Experiences of Justice in Canada, Australia, and New Zealand* (Aldershot, 1995) and Sidney L. Harring, *Crow Dog's Case: American Indian Sovereignty, Tribal Law, and United States Law in the Nineteenth Century* (Cambridge, 1994). Another area not addressed in this volume is that of the broader colonial experience with regard to the interaction of diverse ethnic groups with state criminal justice systems in the "new world." This subject also stems from the law and society perspective and includes the work of anthropologists and criminologists. Recent examples include the case study of Paula J. Byrne, *Criminal Law and the Colonial Subject: New South Wales, 1810–1830* (Cambridge, 1993), the studies of Tina Loo and L. McLean (eds.), *Historical Perspectives on Law and Society in Canada* (Toronto, 1994), and the essays in Louis A. Knafla and Susan Binnie (eds.), *Law, Society, and the State: Essays in Modern Legal History* (Toronto, 1995).

In the end, readers should be aware of the fact that a high percentage of the work in the crime and criminal justice area is published in the academic journals. This work includes not only articles, but also historiographical surveys, book reviews, and book review essays. The most significant venues in the English language include the *American Journal of Legal History, Criminal Justice History: An International Annual, Criminal Law Forum, Crime and Justice: An Annual Review of Research,* the *International Journal of the Sociology of Law,* the *Journal of Social History,* the *Law and Society Review, Past and Present, Research in Law, Deviance and Social Control,* and *Social History/Histoire Sociale.*

Index

About the Editors and Contributors

Marcos Luiz Bretas is a research associate of the Contemporary History Foundation in Rio de Janeiro, Brazil. He has just completed his doctoral dissertation at the Open University on the policing of Rio de Janeiro at the beginning of the twentieth century. He has published several papers on the subject, as well as "A Queda do Imperio da Navalka e da Rasteira: A Republica e os Capoeiras," *Estudos Afro-Asiaticos* 20 (1991).

Clive Emsley is professor of history and co-director of the European Centre for the Study of Policing at the Open University, Milton Keynes, England. Among his publications are *Crime and Society in England 1750–1900* (1987) and *The English Police: A Political and Social History* (1991). He is currently working on a study of *gendarmes* and peasants in nineteenth-century Europe.

Stephen Garton is associate professor of history at the University of Sydney, Australia. He has published *Medicine and Madness: A Social History of Insanity in New South Wales 1880–1940* (1988) and *Out of Luck: Poor Australians and Social Welfare 1788–1988* (1990). He is currently working on the cultural history of crime in Australia.

Steven C. Hughes is associate professor of history at Loyola College of Maryland. He is the author of "The Theory and Practice of Ozio in Italian Policing: Bologna and Beyond" in *Criminal Justice History* 10 (1989) and

Crime, Disorder and the Risorgimento: The Politics of Policing in Bologna (1994). He is currently working on a study of the duel in nineteenth- and twentieth-century Italy.

Louis A. Knafla is professor of history at The University of Calgary, Alberta, Canada. He serves as Editor of *Criminal Justice History* and has published extensively on English and Canadian legal history. His most recent books are *Kent at Law 1602: Assizes and Sessions of the Peace* (1994) and (with Susan Binnie) *Law, Society, and the State: Essays in Modern Legal History* (1995).

René Lévy is Director of the Centre de Recherches Sociologiques sur le Droit et les Institutions Penales in Paris. His research crosses the frontiers between history, law, and sociology. His recent publications include a study of the French law of *Le Flagrant delit* and an annotated French-language edition (with Hartwig Zander) of Rusche and Kirchheimer, *Punishment and Social Structure* (1994).

Alf Lüdtke is a research associate of the Max-Planck-Institut fur Geschichte in Gottingen, Germany, and teaches at the University of Hanover. He is the author of *Police and State in Prussia, 1815–1850* (1989) and has edited *"Sicherheit" und "Wohlfahrt." Polizei Gesellschaft und Herrschaft im 19. und 20. Jahrhundert* (1992).

Eric H. Monkkonen is professor of history at the University of California, Los Angeles. He has published extensively on urban and social history in the United States. His most relevant works in the area of crime history are *Crime and Poverty in a Nineteenth-Century City: The "Dangerous Class" of Columbus, Ohio, 1860–1885* (1973), *Police in Urban America, 1860–1920* (1981), and *Delinquency and Disorderly Behavior* (1991).

Eva Österberg is professor of history at Lund University, Sweden. She has published widely on medieval and early modern Scandinavia, most notably (with Dag Lindstrom) *Crime and Social Control in Medieval and Early Modern Swedish Towns* (1988).

Jim Phillips is associate professor and associate dean in the Faculty of Law, University of Toronto, Ontario, Canada. He has co-edited (with Philip Girard) *Essays in the History of Canadian Law: Volume Three, Nova Scotia* (1990) and *Essays in the History of Canadian Law: Volume Five, Crime and Criminal Justice* (1994). He has published in British imperial and Canadian legal history and is currently at work on a study of crime and criminal justice in Nova Scotia.

Herbert Reinke is a historian and sociologist based at the University of Cologne and is currently seconded to work in the Archives of the STASI in Berlin. His research has focused on analyzing the judicial statutes of nineteenth-century Germany, and he has moved recently to the study of policing.

Xavier Rousseaux is Professor of History at the University of Saint Louis, Brussels, Belgium. He has published several articles on criminal justice history in Belgium and more recently has co-authored "Etats, justice pénale et histoire, bilan historigraphique et relecture," *Droit et Société* 20/21 (1992), and a major bibliography on criminality in Europe from 1250 to 1850 in *Criminal Justice History 14* (1993). He is currently working on state formation and criminal justice in northwest Europe from 1750 to 1850.

Paul Vanderwood is professor of history at San Diego State University. A specialist in Latin American and Mexican history, his most recent works include *Juarez* (1983), *Border Fury* (1988), and *Disorder and Progress: Bandits, Police, and Mexican Development* (1992).